WHAT YOUR FIFTH GRADER NEEDS TO KNOW

THE
CORE KNOWLEDGE™
SERIES

RESOURCE BOOKS FOR
GRADES ONE THROUGH SIX
BOOK V

DOUBLEDAY

New York   London   Toronto   Sydney   Auckland

THE·CORE·KNOWLEDGE
SERIES™

WHAT YOUR FIFTH GRADER NEEDS TO KNOW

FUNDAMENTALS OF A GOOD FIFTH-GRADE EDUCATION

Edited by

E. D. HIRSCH, JR.

This Book Is Dedicated to
Cleo, fifth grader-to-be in 2000.

All author's earnings from the sale of this book go to the nonprofit Core Knowledge Foundation, dedicated to the improvement of education for all children. Information about the activities and materials of the foundation are available from the Core Knowledge Foundation, 2012-B Morton Drive, Charlottesville, VA 22901.

PUBLISHED BY DOUBLEDAY

a division of Bantam Doubleday Dell Publishing Group, Inc.
1540 Broadway, New York, NY 10036

DOUBLEDAY and the portrayal of an anchor with a dolphin are trademarks of Doubleday, a division of Bantam Doubleday Dell Publishing Group, Inc.

Previously published material is acknowledged on p. 388.

Library of Congress Cataloging-in-Publication Data

What your 5th grader needs to know : fundamentals of a good fifth-
   grade education / edited by E.D. Hirsch, Jr.
      p.   cm.—(The Core knowledge series ; bk. 5)
   Includes index.
   1. Fifth grade (Education)—United States—Curricula.
   2. Curriculum planning—United States.   I. Hirsch, E. D. (Eric
Donald), 1928– . II. Series.
   LB1571 5th.W43   1993
   372.19'0973—dc20   92-30548
                                                                    CIP

ISBN 0-385-41119-7

10 9 8 7 6 5 4 3

Acknowledgments

This series has depended upon the help, advice, and encouragement of some two thousand people. Some of those singled out here know already the depth of my gratitude; others may be surprised to find themselves thanked publicly for help they gave quietly and freely for the sake of the enterprise alone. To helpers named and unnamed I am deeply grateful.

Project Manager: Tricia Emlet

Editors: Tricia Emlet (Text), Rae Grant (Art), Elaine Moran (Text)

Artists and Writers: Nancy Bryson (Physical Sciences), Jacques Chazaud (Illustration), Bernadine Connelly (World Civilization), Tricia Emlet (Geography), Leslie Evans (Illustration), Jonathan Fuqua (Illustration), Julie C. Grant (Illustration), Marie Hawthorne (Science Biographies), E. D. Hirsch, Jr. (Physical Sciences), John Hirsch (Mathematics), John Holdren (Learning About Literature, Stories, World and American Civilizations), Jennifer Howard (Speeches, Science Biographies), Blair Logwood Jones (Stories), Phillip Jones (Illustration), Bethanne H. Kelly (Stories, Sayings), Gail McIntosh (Illustration), Elaine Moran (Visual Arts), A. Brooke Russell (Geography, Life Sciences, Physical Sciences), Peter Ryan (Music), Lindley Shutz (Learning About Language, Speeches), Joel Smith (Illustration), Helen Storey (Sayings), Steven M. Sullivan (American Civilization), Alexandra Webber (Illustration)

Art and Photo Research: Rae Grant

Research and Editing Assistants: Raphael Alvarado (Art), Elaine Moran (Text), Martha Clay Sullivan (Text)

Permissions: Martha Clay Sullivan

Advisers on Multiculturalism: Minerva Allen, Frank de Varona, Mick Fedullo, Dorothy Fields, Elizabeth Fox-Genovese, Marcia Galli, Dan Garner, Henry Louis Gates, Cheryl Kulas, Joseph C. Miller, Gerry Raining Bird, Dorothy Small, Sharon Stewart-Peregoy, Sterling Stuckey, Marlene Walking Bear, Lucille Watahomigie, Ramona Wilson

Advisers on Elementary Education: Joseph Adelson, Isobel Beck, Paul Bell, Carl Bereiter, David Bjorklund, Constance Jones, Elizabeth LaFuze, J. P. Lutz, Jean Osborne, Sandra Scarr, Nancy Stein, Phyllis Wilkin

Advisers on Technical Subject Matters: Richard Anderson, Andrew Gleason, Eric Karell, Joseph Kett, Michael Lynch, Joseph C. Miller, Margaret Redd, Mark Rush, Ralph Smith, Nancy Summers, James Trefil, Nancy Wayne

Conferees, March 1990: Nola Bacci, Joan Baratz-Snowden, Thomasyne Beverley, Thomas Blackton, Angela Burkhalter, Monty Caldwell, Thomas M. Carroll, Laura Chapman, Carol Anne Collins, Lou Corsaro, Henry Cotton, Anne Coughlin, Arletta Dimberg, Debra P. Douglas, Patricia Edwards, Janet Elenbogen, Mick Fedullo, Michele Fomalont, Nancy Gercke, Mamon Gibson, Jean Haines, Barbara Hayes, Stephen Herzog, Helen Kelley, Brenda King, John King, Elizabeth LaFuze, Diana Lam, Nancy Lambert, Doris Langaster, Richard LaPointe, Lloyd Leverton, Madeleine Long, Allen Luster, Joseph McGeehan, Janet McLin, Gloria McPhee, Marcia Mallard, Judith Matz, William J. Moloney, John Morabito, Robert Morrill, Roberta Morse, Karen Nathan, Dawn Nichols, Valeta Paige, Mary Perrin, Joseph Piazza, Jeanne Price, Marilyn Rauth, Judith Raybern, Mary Reese, Richard Rice, Wallace Saval, John Saxon, Jan Schwab, Ted Sharp, Diana Smith, Richard Smith, Trevanian Smith, Carol Stevens, Nancy Summers, Michael Terry, Robert Todd, Elois Veltman, Sharon Walker, Mary Ann Ward, Penny Williams, Charles Wootten, Clarke Worthington, Jane York

The Three Oaks Elementary School: Constance Jones, Principal; Cecelia Cook, Assistant Principal

Teachers: Joanne Anderson, Linda Anderson, Nancy Annichiarico, Deborah Backes, Katherine Ann Bedingfield, Barbara Bittner, Michael Blue, Coral Boudin, Nancy Bulgerin, Jodene Cebak, Cheryl Chastain, Paula Clark, Betty Cook, Laura DeProfio, Holly DeSantis, Cindy Donmoyer, Lisa Eastridge, Amy Germer, Elizabeth Graves, Jennifer Gunder, Eileen Hafer, Helen Hallman, Donna Hernandez, Kathleen Holzborn, Robert Horner, Jenni Jones, Zoe Ann Klusacek, Annette Lopez, Barbara Lyon, Cindy Miller, Lelar Miller, Laura Morse, Karen Naylor, Joanne O'Neill, Jill Pearson, Linda Peck, Rebecca Poppe, Janet Posch, Judy Quest, Angie Richards, Angie Ryan, April Santarelli, Patricia Scott, Patricia Stapleton, Pamela Stewart, Jeanne Storm, Phillip Storm, Katherine Twomey, Karen Ward

Benefactors: the Dade County School District, the Exxon Education Foundation, the Lee County School District, the National Endowment for the Humanities, the Shutz Foundation

Morale Boosters: Polly Hirsch, Robert Payton, Rafe Sagalyn, Nancy Brown Wellin

Our grateful acknowledgment to these persons does not imply that we have taken their (sometimes conflicting) advice in every case, or that each of them endorses all aspects of this project. Responsibility for final decisions must rest with the editor alone. Suggestions for improvements are very welcome, and I wish to thank in advance those who send advice for revising and improving this series.

Contents

II. GEOGRAPHY, WORLD CIVILIZATION, AND AMERICAN CIVILIZATION

III. FINE ARTS

IV. MATHEMATICS

V. NATURAL SCIENCES

General Introduction

I. What Is Your Child Learning in School?

I recently received a letter from a parent of identical twins. She wrote to express her dismay that her children, who are in the same grade in the same school, are learning completely different things. How can this be? Because they are in different classrooms; because the teachers in these classrooms have only the vaguest guidelines to follow; in short, because the school, like most in the United States, lacks a definite, specific curriculum.

Many parents would be surprised if they were to examine the curriculum of their child's elementary school. I urge you to ask to see your school's curriculum. Does it say just what specific core of content each child at a particular grade level is expected to learn by the end of the year? Most curricula speak in vague terms of general skills, processes, and attitudes. This vagueness is no virtue. It places unreasonable demands upon teachers and often results in years of schooling marred by repetitions and gaps. Yet another unit on dinosaurs. *Charlotte's Web* for the third time. "You've never heard of the Bill of Rights?" "You've never been taught how to add two fractions with unlike denominators?"

When identical twins in two classrooms of the same school have few academic experiences in common, that is a sign of trouble. When teachers in that school do not know what children in other classrooms are learning on the same grade level, much less in earlier and later grades, they cannot reliably predict that children will come prepared with a shared core of knowledge and skills. The result of this curricular incoherence is that many schools fall far short of developing the full potential of our children.

To address this problem, I started the Core Knowledge Foundation in 1986. This book and its companion volumes in the Core Knowledge Series are designed to give parents, teachers—and through them, children—a carefully sequenced body of knowledge based upon the model curriculum guidelines developed by the Core Knowledge Foundation.

Core Knowledge is an attempt to define, in a coherent and sequential way, a body of widely used knowledge taken for granted by competent writers and speakers in the United States. Because this knowledge is taken for granted rather than being explained when it is used, it forms a necessary foundation for the higher-order reading, writing, and thinking skills that children need for academic and vocational success. The universal attainment of such knowledge should be a central aim of curricula in our elementary schools, just as it is currently the aim in all world-class educational systems.

For reasons explained in the next section, making sure that all young children in the United States possess a core of shared knowledge is a necessary step in developing a first-rate educational system.

II. Why Core Knowledge Is Needed

Learning builds on learning: children (and adults) gain new knowledge only by building on what they already know. It is essential to begin building solid foundations of knowledge in the early grades when children are most receptive because research has shown that, for the vast majority of children, academic deficiencies from the first six grades *permanently* impair the success of later learning. Poor performance of American students in middle and high school can be traced directly to shortcomings inherited from elementary schools that have not imparted to children the knowledge they need for further learning.

All of the highest-achieving and most egalitarian elementary school systems in the world (such as those in Sweden, France, and Japan) teach their children a specific core of knowledge in each of the first six grades, thus enabling all children to enter each new grade with a secure foundation for further learning. It is time American schools did so as well, for the following reasons:

(1) Commonly shared knowledge makes schooling more effective. We know that the one-on-one tutorial is the most effective form of schooling, in part because a parent or teacher can provide tailor-made instruction for the individual child. But in a nontutorial situation—in, for example, a typical classroom with twenty-five or more students—the instructor cannot effectively impart new knowledge to all the students unless each one shares the background knowledge that the lesson is being built upon. When all the students in a class *do* share that relevant background knowledge, a classroom can begin to approach the effectiveness of a tutorial. Even when some children in a class don't have elements of the knowledge they were supposed to acquire in previous grades, the existence of a specifically defined core makes it possible for the teacher or parent to identify and fill the gaps, thus giving all students a chance to fulfill their potentials in later grades.

(2) Commonly shared knowledge makes schooling more fair and democratic. When all the children who enter a grade can be assumed to share some of the same building blocks of knowledge, and when the teacher knows exactly what those building blocks are, then all the students are empowered to learn. In our current system, disadvantaged children too often suffer from unmerited low expectations that translate into watered-down curricula. But if we specify the core of knowledge that all children should share, then we can guarantee equal access to that knowledge, and compensate for the academic advantages some students are offered at home. In a Core Knowledge school, disadvantaged children, like *all* children, enjoy the benefits of important, challenging knowledge that will provide the foundation for successful later learning.

(3) Commonly shared knowledge helps create cooperation and solidarity in our schools and nation. Diversity is a hallmark and strength of our nation. American classrooms are usually made up of students from a variety of cultural backgrounds, and those different cultures should be honored and understood by all students. Education should create a *school-based* culture that is common and welcoming to all because it includes knowledge of many cultures, and gives all students, no matter what their background, a common foundation for understanding our cultural diversity.

In the next section I will describe the steps taken by the Core Knowledge Foundation to develop a model of the commonly shared knowledge our children need (which forms the basis for this series of books).

III. The Consensus Behind the Core Knowledge Sequence

The content in this and other volumes in the Core Knowledge Series is based on a document called the *Core Knowledge Sequence*, a grade-by-grade sequence of specific content guidelines in history, geography, mathematics, science, language arts, and the fine arts. The *Sequence* is not meant to outline the whole of the school curriculum; rather, it offers specific guidelines to knowledge that can reasonably be expected to make up about *half* of any school's curriculum, thus leaving ample room for local requirements and emphases. Teaching a common core of knowledge, such as that articulated in the *Core Knowledge Sequence,* is compatible with a variety of instructional methods and additional subject matter.

The *Core Knowledge Sequence* is the result of a long process of research and consensus-building undertaken by the nonprofit Core Knowledge Foundation. Here is how we achieved the consensus behind the *Core Knowledge Sequence.*

First we analyzed the many reports issued by state departments of education and by professional organizations—such as the National Council of Teachers of Mathematics and the American Association for the Advancement of Science—which recommend general outcomes for elementary and secondary education. We also tabulated the knowledge and skills through grade six specified in the successful educational systems of several other countries, including France, Japan, Sweden, and West Germany.

In addition, we formed an advisory board on multiculturalism that proposed a specific knowledge of diverse cultural traditions that American children should all share as part of their school-based common culture. We sent the resulting materials to three independent groups of teachers, scholars, and scientists around the country, asking them to create a master list of knowledge children should have by the end of grade six. About 150 teachers (including college professors, scientists, and administrators) were involved in this initial step.

These items were amalgamated into a master plan, and further groups of teachers and specialists were asked to agree on a grade-by-grade sequence of the items. That sequence was then sent to some one hundred educators and specialists who participated in a national conference that was called to hammer out a working agreement on core knowledge for the first six grades.

This important meeting took place in March 1990. The conferees were elementary school teachers, curriculum specialists, scientists, science writers, officers of national organizations, representatives of ethnic groups, district superintendents, and school principals from across the country. A total of twenty-four working groups decided on revisions in the sequence. The resulting provisional sequence was further fine-tuned during a year of implementation at a pioneering school, Three Oaks Elementary in Lee County, Florida. The result is the *Core Knowledge Sequence* that forms the basis for this series.

The *Core Knowledge Sequence* may be ordered from the Core Knowledge Foundation (please see the end of this introduction for the address).

IV. The Nature of This Series

The books in this series are designed to be useful tools for parents and teachers, both at home and in school. They are called "resources" to signal that they do not replace the regular local school curriculum, but rather serve as aids to help children gain some of the important knowledge they will need to make progress in school and be effective in society.

Each book in the Core Knowledge Series presents knowledge upon which later books will build. Our writers have tried their best to make the content interesting, clear, and challenging. We have *not* used discredited grade-level formulas regarding vocabulary and sentence length. Drafts of some materials have been revised on the basis of teachers' experiences with children.

Although we have made these books as accessible and useful as we can, parents and teachers should understand that they are not the only means by which the *Core Knowledge Sequence* can be imparted. The books represent a single version of the possibilities inherent in the *Core Knowledge Sequence,* and a first step in the Core Knowledge reform effort. We hope that publishers will be stimulated to offer educational videos, computer software, games, alternative books, and other imaginative vehicles based on the *Core Knowledge Sequence.*

V. What You Can Do to Help Improve American Education

The first step for parents and teachers who are committed to reform is to be skeptical about oversimplified slogans like "critical thinking" and "learning to learn." Such slogans are everywhere, and, unfortunately for our schools, their partial insights have been elevated to the level of universal truths. For example, "What students learn is not important; rather, we must teach students to learn *how* to learn." "The child, not the academic subject, is the true focus of education." "Do not impose knowledge on children before they are developmentally ready to receive it." "Do not bog children down in mere facts, but rather, teach critical-thinking skills."

Who has not heard these sentiments, so admirable and humane, and—up to a point—so true? But these positive sentiments in favor of skills and understanding have been turned into negative sentiments against the teaching of important knowledge. Those who have entered the teaching profession over the past forty years have been taught to scorn important knowledge as "mere facts," and to see the imparting of this knowledge as somehow injurious to children. Thus it has come about that many educators, armed with partially true slogans, have seemingly taken leave of common sense.

Many parents and teachers have come to the conclusion that elementary education must strike a better balance between the development of the whole child and the more limited but fundamental duty of the school to ensure that all children master a core of knowledge essential to their competence as learners in later grades. But these parents and teachers cannot act on their convictions without access to an agreed-upon, concrete sequence of knowledge. Our main motivation in developing the *Core Knowledge Sequence* and this book series has been to give parents and teachers something concrete to work with.

It has been encouraging to see how many teachers, since the first volume in this series was published, have responded to the Core Knowledge reform effort. A small but growing number of schools around the country—over fifty as of this writing, in diverse regions serving diverse populations—are working to integrate the *Core Knowledge Sequence* into their curricula.

Parents and teachers are urged to join in a grass-roots effort to strengthen our elementary schools. The place to start is in your own school and district. Insist that your school clearly state the core of *specific* knowledge that each child in a grade must learn. Whether your school's core corresponds to the Core Knowledge model is less important than the existence of *some* core—which, we hope, will be as solid, coherent, and challenging as the *Core Knowledge Sequence* has proven to be. Inform members of your community about the need for such a specific curriculum, and help make sure that the people who are elected or appointed to your local school board are independent-minded people who will insist that our children have the benefit of a solid, specific, world-class curriculum in each grade.

You are invited to become a member of the Core Knowledge Network by writing the Core Knowledge Foundation, 2012-B Morton Drive, Charlottesville, VA 22901.

Share the knowledge!

E. D. HIRSCH, JR.
Charlottesville, Virginia

How to Use This Book

FOR PARENTS AND TEACHERS

The book you are holding in your hands is an unusual one. It is a collection made for children, but it is not limited to the usual treasury of best-loved stories and poems. It offers in addition engaging accounts of language, literature, history, geography, science, fine arts, and math—the core academic subjects that our children need in this new age of global information. It also contains knowledge that may help them become fulfilled and productive people. But it is not a textbook or a workbook filled with exercises. It offers the academic core—the sort of knowledge that the best educational systems provide to children all over the world—written in a lively and absorbing manner that includes tips for making those knowledge domains come alive. But such a book must also leave much to you and to your child in the way of additional conversation and practice.

Each book in *The Core Knowledge Series* builds upon knowledge presented in previous books. We know from learning theory that we learn best by building upon what we already know. Hence, this fifth-grade book refers back to previous books. Moreover, the sections of the fifth-grade book also refer you to other sections of the same book. Because subjects and interests cut across disciplines, we encourage you to help your child see connections between art and math, history and literature, physical sciences and language just as we have tried to do. And you should also feel free, using the tables of contents or the indexes, to make your own connections among the books of the series.

We have tried to make this book attractive and interesting by using an interactive, storybook format. We address the child directly as reader, asking questions and suggesting projects that he or she might do. Advice to parents and teachers about teaching specific subject matter is provided in the introduction to each section. You can help your child read more actively both by conversing while you are reading and by bringing the subjects up at a later time when connections occur to you. You and your child can read the sections of this book in any order. You need not begin at the beginning and work your way through to the end. In fact, we suggest that you skip from section to section, and that you reread as much as your child likes.

To help your child use this book, you might think of it as a guidebook that tries to be as informative and suggestive as possible in a concise format. We encourage you to help your child find ways to explore further what she or he reads here. If possible, take your child to plays, museums, and concerts; help your child find related books (some are suggested here). In short, this guidebook recommends places to visit, and describes what is important in those places, but only you and your child can make the actual visit, travel the streets, and climb the steps.

Bon voyage!

I.

LANGUAGE ARTS

Introduction to Stories and Speeches

FOR PARENTS AND TEACHERS

In the fourth-grade volume of this series we began including excerpts and condensed versions of long novels. While some fourth-grade children are mostly interested in simple tales, others are ready for more complex prose. By the fifth grade, still more children will be eager to move on to longer prose pieces. In this book we have continued to excerpt or condense novels and plays so that all children can enjoy the engaging stories told in great works. When a child is ready and interested, he or she can read the full novels or plays that we have excerpted here. A parent or teacher can gauge the child's ability and desire to read full works, and steer her in that direction when the time comes.

As in our previous books, we have included great speeches in Book Five in the belief that these belong to our literary heritage as fully as stories do. While the ringing language of the speeches allows them to stand alone, presenting them in the context of the historical period and describing the personality of the speakers can help make these speeches come alive as their own kind of "story." We suggest that adults and children read these speeches along with the relevant episodes in the American Civilization section of this book.

Children recognize the power of story-telling every time they tell a story of their own. Encouraging them to narrate their own stories carries many benefits, including, of course, practicing their language skills. While children at the fifth-grade level are rarely read to by adults—and may not *want* you to read to them—you can still further their enthusiasm for reading through well-chosen questions. You might ask, "What is this story about?" "What do you think is going to happen next?" "Why did that character act as he did?" "What might have happened if . . . ?" You might also ask your child to retell a story in her own words. Don't be bothered when children change events or characters, thus making the story their own. That is in the best tradition of story-telling, and explains why today we have so many different versions of traditional stories.

You can combine story-reading with writing and drawing by encouraging children to write and illustrate their own stories. Some children may be interested in keeping a journal, either as an autobiography or as a way to collect their own stories. This is a fine way for children to enjoy the fun of story-telling and also develop their own writing skills. Other children may be more interested in cultivating "pen pals": learning writing skills and the art of story-telling by relating the tales of their daily lives to others.

Stories and Speeches

Coyote Goes to the Land of the Dead

In earlier books in this series, you read stories that Native American peoples have passed down from one generation to the next. Different Native American peoples tell different tales, though some of these tales have much in common. For example, many stories are about the actions of a central character known as a "trickster." Sometimes the trickster is a clever fellow who, though he may seem weak, gets the better of someone strong and powerful. (This might remind you of characters from other traditions: Anansi and Br'er Rabbit). In other tales, the trickster is a vain, foolish, laughable figure. Often, the trickster gets mixed up in series of events that explain how things came to be: for example, how we came to have day and night, or how men got fire, or why the bear has a short tail. And in some tales, the tables are turned and the trickster has tricks played on him.

You may recall reading stories about one trickster figure, Iktomi. Another trickster, popular in tales of American Indians of the Northwest and Southwest, is called Coyote. Some tales of Coyote make us laugh. Others, like the one we tell here, are more serious: in this case, Coyote's actions have consequences for everyone.

The following adaptation of "Coyote Goes to the Land of the Dead" draws on elements from stories told by the Nez Percé and Zuni peoples. Because the Native American literary tradition is an oral tradition, in which tales are passed on by being told aloud, if you come upon this story in another book, you will find a slightly different version, depending on the teller of the tale.

I t had been a bitter winter, filled with sickness and death. Coyote's wife fell ill, then died. Coyote wept.

Eagle tried to cheer him. "Spring will soon be here," he said. "Soon the ice on the river will break and the bears will fish again." But still Coyote wept. His lonely howls filled the night.

One day the Death Spirit came to Coyote and said, "You feel great pain because your wife is dead. I will take you where she has gone. Follow me. But listen: you must do exactly what I tell you."

"Of couse, of course, whatever you say," promised Coyote. "But it is very hard to see you." It was hard, because the Spirit was invisible in the daylight.

"I will carry something for you to follow, then," said the Spirit. "Give me something your wife loved." Coyote hated to give away anything that reminded him of his wife. Reluctantly he gave the Spirit a feather his wife had worn when she danced.

They set off. In the daytime Coyote could see the feather. At night, he could not see the feather but he could see the shimmering Death Spirit.

Soon they were in a vast plain. The wind blew swirls of snow. Then the Spirit stopped. "Now," it said, "do as I do." The Spirit pointed ahead and said, "What a fine group of strong-looking horses there."

Coyote saw nothing, but pointed and said, "Yes, what a fine group of strong-looking horses there."

They walked on for some time, until the Spirit said, "There, just ahead, is the longhouse."

"Yes," said Coyote, though he saw nothing, "there is the longhouse."

The spirit walked ahead, then bent down as if to lift a skin-covered door and crawl into a longhouse. Coyote did the same.

"Take a seat there, next to your wife," the Spirit ordered. Coyote sat, though he saw nothing around him but open plain.

"Now, your wife will serve us something warm," the Spirit said. Coyote looked around eagerly but could see nothing. He cupped his hands before his chest, as the Spirit did. Then both drank from their hands. Strangely, Coyote felt warmed.

"Now we must wait for nightfall," said the Spirit. Coyote slept. When he woke, he heard the sounds of drums. When he looked around, he saw shadowlike figures in the darkness, dancing. He recognized his old friends who had died in the hard winter and in years past. Then he saw his wife. He greeted her with joy, then they all talked and danced till morning. When the sun rose, the spirits disappeared.

By day, Coyote slept fitfully on the open ground in the bitter air. At night, he woke to find himself in the great longhouse surrounded by the spirits of his loved ones. Night after night they talked and danced.

Then the Death Spirit came to Coyote and said, "It is time for you to go." Coyote began to protest but the Spirit silenced him. "Listen: your wife may go with you. She may leave the Land of the Dead and return to the Land of the Living, but only if you do exactly as I say. Follow your wife for five days over five mountains. On the sixth day, when you have crossed all five mountains and see the fires of home, only then may you touch her. Do not touch her before then. If you do anything foolish, then the spirits of the dead will never again be able to return to the Land of the Living."

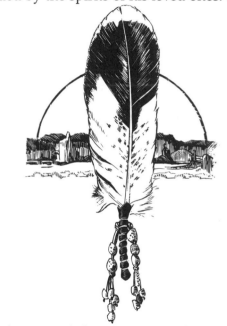

The Death Spirit tied the feather that had belonged to Coyote's wife to her hair so Coyote could follow her spirit in the daytime. In the morning Coyote set off, following the feather as it floated along. On the first day they crossed the first mountain. On the second day they crossed the second mountain. As they went on, Coyote no longer needed to watch the feather, for the farther they went, the more clearly he could see his wife.

On the fifth night they camped on the fifth mountain. Coyote sat and watched the glow of the fire on his wife's face and hair. He could see her well, so well. Then—who can say what drove Coyote to do this?—he jumped across the fire and gathered his wife into his arms. As he touched her, she vanished. He cried out as the feather dropped to the ground.

The Death Spirit appeared before Coyote and said sternly, "See what you have done. Because of you, no spirit will ever again return from the dead."

Coyote ran howling back over the five mountains till he came again to the open plain. Though he saw nothing but swirling dust and snow, he stopped and said, "What a fine group of strong-looking horses there." Then he went on and said, "There, just ahead, is the longhouse." Then he bent as though to lift a skin-covered door and crawled in on his knees. Then he cupped his hands and drank from them but felt nothing. He waited through the night to hear drums and see spirits dancing. But he heard only wind, and saw only darkness.

The next day, he began the long walk home.

You can read more stories of Coyote in these books: Keepers of Animals: Native American Stories and Wildlife Activities *by Michael Caduto and Joseph Bruchac (Fulcrum, 1991); and* Earth Sky, Earth Magic: North American Indian Tales *by Rosalind Kerven (Cambridge, 1991).*

The Adventures of Tom Sawyer
(retold with excerpts from the novel by Mark Twain)

Mark Twain, one of the most beloved and famous American writers, is the pen name of Samuel Clemens. Born in Missouri in 1835, he worked as a Mississippi riverboat pilot, a journalist, and finally, a novelist. His writings gained him a lasting reputation as one of the greatest American writers.

Some of Mark Twain's own childhood experiences can be seen in The Adventures of Tom Sawyer, *first published in 1876. As Twain wrote in an introductory note to the novel, "Most of the adventures recorded in this book really occurred. . . . Huck Finn is drawn from life; Tom Sawyer also, but not from an individual—he is a combination of the characteristics of three boys I knew. . . ."*

Tom Sawyer and Huck Finn (the central character in another great novel by Mark Twain, Adventures of Huckleberry Finn) *have become two of the most popular and memorable figures in American literature. In our selection from* The Adventures of Tom Sawyer *we begin with Tom in trouble—as he often is—but able, as usual, to figure a way out.*

Saturday morning was come, and all the summer world was bright and fresh, and brimming with life. There was a song in every heart. There was cheer in every face and a spring in every step.

Tom Sawyer appeared on the sidewalk with a bucket of whitewash and a long-handled brush. He surveyed the fence, and all gladness left him and a deep melancholy settled down upon his spirit. He had been caught sneaking in late last evening, and now Aunt Polly was determined to punish him by turning his Saturday into captivity at hard labor, whitewashing a fence. Thirty yards of board fence nine feet high. Sighing he dipped his brush and passed it along the topmost plank; repeated the operation; did it again; compared the insignificant whitewashed streak with the far-reaching continent of the unwhitewashed fence, and sat-down discouraged.

Soon the free boys would come tripping along on all sorts of delicious expeditions, and they would make a world of fun of him for having to work—the very thought of it burnt him like fire. At this dark and hopeless moment an inspiration burst upon him! He took up his brush and went tranquilly to work.

Ben Rogers hove in sight presently—the very boy, of all boys, whose ridicule he had been dreading. Ben gave a long, melodious whoop, followed by a deep-toned ding-dong-dong, for he was imitating a steamboat. Tom went on whitewashing—paid no attention to the steamboat. Ben stared a moment, then said:

"Hello, old chap, you got to work, hey?"

Tom wheeled and suddenly said: "Why, it's you, Ben! I warn't noticing."

"Say—*I'm* going in a-swimming, *I* am. Don't you wish you could? But of course you'd druther *work*—wouldn't you?"

Tom contemplated the boy a bit, and said: "What do you call work?"

"Why, ain't *that* work?"

Tom resumed his whitewashing, and answered carelessly: "Well, maybe it is and maybe it ain't. All I know, is, it suits Tom Sawyer."

"Oh come, now, you don't mean to let on that you *like* it?"

"Well, I don't see why I oughtn't to like it. Does a boy get a chance to whitewash a fence every day?"

That put the thing in a new light. Ben stopped nibbling his apple. Tom swept his brush daintily back and forth—stepped back to note the effect—added a touch here and there—Ben watching every move and getting more and more interested, more and more absorbed. Presently he said:

"Say, Tom, let *me* whitewash a while."

Tom considered, was about to consent; but he altered his mind. "No—no—I reckon it wouldn't hardly do, Ben. You see, Aunt Polly's awful particular about this fence. I reckon there ain't one boy in a thousand, maybe two thousand, that can do it the way it's got to be done."

"Oh come, now—lemme just try. Only just a little. I'll be careful. Now lemme try. Say—I'll give you the core of my apple."

"Well, here—No, Ben, now don't. I'm afeard—"

"I'll give you *all* of it!"

Tom gave up the brush with reluctance in his face, but alacrity in his heart. And while Ben worked and sweated in the sun, the retired artist sat on a barrel in the shade close by, dangled his legs, and munched his apple.

Boys happened along every little while; they came to jeer, but remained to whitewash. By the time Ben was tired out, Tom had traded the next chance to Billy Fisher for a kite. Johnny Miller bought in for a dead rat and a string to swing it with—and so on, hour after hour. By the middle of the afternoon, Tom was rolling in wealth. He had besides the things before mentioned, twelve marbles, part of a jew's harp, a piece of blue bottle glass to look through, a key that wouldn't unlock anything, a fragment of chalk, a tin soldier, a couple of tadpoles, six firecrackers, a kitten with only one eye, a brass doorknob, a dog collar—but no dog—the handle of a knife, four pieces of orange peel, and a dilapidated old window sash. If he hadn't run out of whitewash, he would have bankrupted every boy in the village.

Tom had discovered a great law of human action, without knowing it—namely, that in order to make a man or boy covet a thing, it is only necessary to make the thing difficult to attain.

Monday morning on his way to school, Tom came upon the juvenile pariah of the village, Huckleberry Finn, son of the town drunkard. Huckleberry was always dressed in the cast-off, ragged clothes of full-grown men. He came and went at his own free will. He slept on doorsteps or empty hogsheads; he did not have to go to school or to church or obey anybody; he could go fishing or swimming when he chose; he was always the first boy that went barefoot in the spring; he never had to wash; he could swear wonderfully. So while their mothers forbade them to keep company with this romantic outcast, every respectable boy envied and admired him.

"Hello, Huckleberry!"

"Hello, yourself, and see how you like it!"

"What's that you got?"

"Dead cat."

"Say—what is dead cats good for, Huck?"

"Good for? Cure warts with."

"How do you cure 'em with dead cats?"

"Why, you take your cat and go to the graveyard, long about midnight, where somebody that was wicked has been buried; and when it's midnight a devil will come, or maybe two or three; and when they're taking that feller away, you heave your cat after 'em and say, 'Devil follow corpse, cat follow devil, warts follow cat. *I'm* done with ye!'"

Tom and Huckleberry agreed to meet that night to try the wart cure, then off Tom went to school. As soon as he entered the little schoolhouse, the master called out sharply: "Thomas Sawyer! Come up here. Now, sir, why are you late again, as usual?"

Tom was about to take refuge in a lie, when he saw two long braids hanging down a back that he recognized by the electric sympathy of love as belonging to a lovely little blue-eyed creature, an angel in Tom's eyes, Becky Thatcher; and next to her was *the only vacant place* on the girls' side. He instantly said:

"I STOPPED TO TALK WITH HUCKLEBERRY FINN!"

"You—you did what?"

"Stopped to talk with Huckleberry Finn!"

"Thomas Sawyer, this is the most astounding confession I have ever listened to. Go and sit with the *girls!* And let this be a warning to you."

The titter that rippled around the room appeared to abash the boy, but in reality that result was caused rather more by his worshipful awe of his idol and the pleasure that lay in his high good fortune. He sat down upon the end of the pine bench and Becky Thatcher hitched herself away from him with a toss of her head. Tom placed a peach before her. She thrust it away. Tom gently put it back. She thrust it away again, but with less animosity. Tom patiently returned it to its place. Then she let it remain.

Tom took out his slate and scrawled something on it, hiding the words from the girl. She begged to see. Tom said, "Oh, it ain't anything."

"Yes it is."

"No it ain't. You don't want to see."

"Yes I do, indeed I do. Please let me." And she put her small hand on his and a little scuffle ensued, Tom pretending to resist in earnest but letting his hand slip by degrees till these words were revealed: *I love you.*

"Oh, you bad thing!" And she hit his hand a smart rap, but reddened and looked pleased, nevertheless.

Just at this juncture the boy felt a slow, fateful grip closing on his ear, and a steady lifting impulse. In that vise he was borne across the schoolhouse and deposited in his own seat, under a peppering of giggles from the whole school. Then the master stood over him during a few awful moments, and finally moved away to his throne without saying a word. But although Tom's ear tingled, his heart was jubilant.

When Tom and Huck accidentally witness a murder, they enter a series of adventures that you can enjoy reading about in The Adventures of Tom Sawyer.

Julius Caesar

(retold from the play by William Shakespeare)

Shakespeare (1564–1616) wrote many plays about great events and people in history. In Julius Caesar, *he dramatizes the last days and the murder of Julius Caesar, one of Rome's great leaders. Shakespeare portrays both the murder and the circumstances that led to it, and then follows the fates of the men who committed it. Here we retell the play in prose, but quote some of its famous passages in Shakespeare's original verse.*

It was mid-February, time for the Feast of the Lupercalia in honor of the god of fertility. Ancient Rome was in a holiday mood. Many citizens had gathered along the streets in order to see their leader, Julius Caesar, on his way to the festival games. Some of his well-wishers had been up early, decorating his statues with garlands in honor of Caesar's recent triumph over his enemy, Pompey.

But many citizens of Rome did not hold Caesar in such high regard, for they had known and respected Pompey. They resented Caesar's attempts to glorify himself, and they feared that they would lose the freedom they cherished as Roman citizens if he became too powerful.

Soon Caesar and his retinue came along. Caesar's wife Calpurnia and the young officer Mark Antony were beside him. Suddenly a voice from the crowd called to Caesar. It was a soothsayer, one who predicts the future. "Caesar," the soothsayer cried, "beware the ides of March." (The ides was the fifteenth day of the month.)

"He is a dreamer," said Caesar to his companions. "Let him pass."

When Caesar's procession had moved out of sight, two noble citizens who knew Caesar well, Brutus and Cassius, remained behind and began to talk. Both were worried about Caesar's growing power. Rome, as a republic, had a Senate that helped make the laws: would Caesar's growing power threaten this way of government and the freedom of Roman citizens?

As Brutus and Cassius talked, they could hear shouts and applause for Caesar in the distance. "What means this shouting?" Brutus asked Cassius. "I do fear the people choose Caesar for their King."

"Ay, do you fear it?" responded Cassius. "Then must I think you would not have it so."

"I would not, Cassius," said Brutus. "Yet I love him well."

Cassius became agitated and spoke to Brutus. "I know you for an honorable man, Brutus," he said. "I cannot tell what you and other men think, but for myself, I am not in awe of Caesar. I was born free as Caesar. So were you!" There was another cheer from the people, then Cassius continued. "Why, man, Caesar doth stand like a giant, and we little men walk under his huge legs. Men at some time are masters of their fates. The fault, dear Brutus, is not in our stars, but in ourselves, that we are underlings. In the names of all the gods, upon what meat doth this our Caesar feed that he is grown so great?"

Cassius's heated words seemed to trouble Brutus. He turned to Cassius and said, "For the present, say no more, I beg you!" Then he added, "Till we meet again, my noble friend, consider this: Brutus would rather be a slave than to call himself a son of Rome and live under a tyrant."

Now Caesar's procession returned. As they passed by, something about Cassius made Caesar uneasy, and he remarked to Antony, "Yond Cassius has a lean and hungry look. He thinks too much: such men are dangerous."

Brutus and Cassius stopped their friend Casca to ask the reason for all the shouting and applause they had heard. Casca said that Mark Antony had offered a crown to Caesar three times, and that each time Caesar had refused it, which caused the people to shout their approval for his show of humility. "But to my thinking," said Casca, "he would fain have had it." Cassius sensed that Casca too did not trust Caesar, and feared his growing power.

In the days that followed, Cassius secretly gathered a number of men who were willing to take violent steps to stop Caesar's growing power. Among the conspirators were Casca, Decius, Metellus Cimber, and other prominent men; but they still needed the support of Brutus to lend dignity to the plot, for Brutus was known throughout the city to be an honorable man. During this time, it is said that many strange signs foretold that something terrible was about to happen: fire filled the skies, lions walked the streets, an owl hooted in the public square at midday, and men walked abroad with fire at their fingertips.

One day it was rumored that the Senate was on the verge of crowning Caesar king. At last Brutus gave in. He would join the conspirators at the Senate the next morning, and there they would put Caesar to death.

On the night before the bloody deed was to be done, Brutus was troubled. His wife, Portia, approached him. "Brutus," she said, "yesternight at supper you suddenly rose and walked about, musing and sighing. And when I asked you what the matter was, you stared upon me with ungentle looks. Dear, my lord, tell me the cause of your grief."

"I am not well in health, and that is all," said Brutus.

But Portia knew that something greater troubled her husband. She knelt at his feet and said, "No, my Brutus. You have some sickness within your mind. I beg you, by all your vows of love, that you unfold to me why you are so worried."

Brutus helped his wife to her feet, saying, "Kneel not, gentle Portia. Wait a while and by and by, thy bosom shall know the secrets of my heart."

The next morning, a number of the conspirators went to Caesar's house to accompany him to the Senate. Before they arrived, Caesar was approached by his wife, Calpurnia. Three times during the night she had cried out in her sleep, "Help, ho! They murder Caesar!" She had dreamed that Caesar's statue poured forth blood like a fountain with many spouts. Now she pleaded with her husband to stay at home: "I never believed in omens," she said, "but now they frighten me. Alas, my lord, do not go forth today!"

But Caesar was determined to go. He turned to Calpurnia and said

Cowards die many times before their death;
The valiant never taste of death but once.
Of all the wonders that I yet have heard,
It seems to me most strange that men should fear,
Seeing that death, a necessary end,
Will come when it will come.

But Calpurnia insisted: "Call it my fear that keeps you in the house and not your own," she pleaded. She dropped to the floor: "Let me, upon my knee, prevail in this."

Moved by his wife's fear and sorrow, Caesar relented. "For you," he said, "I will stay at home."

But shortly thereafter, when Decius and the other conspirators arrived, Caesar changed his mind. Decius told Caesar that the Senate planned to offer him a crown

"Friends, Romans, countrymen . . ."

that day, and that they would mock him for staying home because of his wife's bad dream. So Caesar dressed and went with the conspirators. As they all entered the Senate House, Caesar saw the soothsayer again. "The ides of March are come," Caesar said to him.

"Ay, Caesar," said the soothsayer, "but not gone."

The senators stood as Caesar took his seat. Then Metellus Cimber drew near and knelt before him. Caesar bid him rise, for he knew that Metellus was about to ask that his brother, Publius Cimber, who had been banished from Rome, be allowed to return. Brutus and Cassius came forth to support Metellus's request, but Caesar would not be persuaded. "I am as constant as the northern star," he said. "I was constant Cimber should be banished, and constant do remain to keep him so." Other senators called upon Caesar to change his mind, but he spurned them all. Then Casca moved behind Caesar, and, saying, "Speak, hands, for me!" he struck him in the back with his dagger.

Suddenly the conspirators were upon Caesar, stabbing him from all sides. Despite their attacks, Caesar stood firm—until he saw Brutus raise his hand to strike too. "Et tu, Brute?" he said. "Even you? Then fall, Caesar!" And covering his face with his cloak, Caesar died.

The senators fled. The news of Caesar's death spread quickly, and the city was in an uproar. Brutus was anxious to restore order, so when Caesar's friend Mark Antony came to him, full of humility and willing to cooperate, he was relieved. Antony promised not to oppose the new government, and asked only that he be allowed to give a speech at Caesar's funeral. Brutus considered the request and agreed on the condition that Brutus himself speak first. In this way he could give good reason for the conspirators' bloody act, he felt, and prevent the crowd from sympathizing with Caesar. But Mark Antony had other plans: he was determined to avenge his friend's murder. He sent word to Caesar's nephew, Octavius, to attend the funeral, keep at a safe distance, and bide his time.

On the day of the funeral, Brutus ascended a pulpit in the Forum and addressed the people. "Romans, countrymen, and lovers!" he said. "Hear me for my cause, and believe me for mine honor. If there be here any dear friend of Caesar's, to him I say that Brutus's love to Caesar was no less than his. If then that friend demand why I rose against Caesar, this is my answer: not that I loved Caesar less, but that I loved Rome more. Had you rather Caesar were living, and die all slaves, than that Caesar were dead, to live all free men? As Caesar loved me, I weep for him; as he was valiant, I honor him; but as he was ambitious, I slew him. Who here is so vile that will not love his country? If any, speak; for him have I offended."

"None, Brutus, none," cried the people, who, though they once cheered Caesar, were now persuaded by Brutus that Caesar had become a threat to their freedom.

Now Mark Antony entered, dressed in mourning and helping carry Caesar's open coffin on a bier. Brutus announced that Antony had permission to give a eulogy. As Brutus departed, the crowd cheered him, some even shouting that he should be made the next Caesar. Antony entered the pulpit and spoke these words:

> Friends, Romans, countrymen, lend me your ears;
> I come to bury Caesar, not to praise him;
> The evil that men do lives after them,
> The good is oft interred with their bones,
> So let it be with Caesar. . . .

As the crowd listened, they began to think more kindly of Caesar. Antony went on:

> He was my friend, faithful and just to me:
> But Brutus says he was ambitious;
> And Brutus is an honorable man. . . .
> When that the poor have cried, Caesar hath wept:
> Ambition should be made of sterner stuff:
> Yet Brutus says he was ambitious;
> And Brutus is an honorable man.

The crowd began to get uneasy. How could this Brutus be so "honorable" if he had helped to kill a leader who, as Antony described him, was so just and kind? Antony continued:

> You all did see that on the Lupercal
> I thrice presented him a kingly crown,
> Which he did thrice refuse: was this ambition?
> Yet Brutus says he was ambitious;
> And, sure, he is an honorable man.

As Antony spoke some people began to blame Brutus and the others for their rash action. At length Antony seemed overcome with emotion. He called for the people to stand around the coffin, then he held up Caesar's torn, bloodstained cloak for all to see. He showed them where Cassius's dagger had run it through, and Casca's. As he showed them the rip made by Brutus's dagger, he said, "This was the most unkindest cut of all." Then he pulled the cloak aside to reveal Caesar's pitiful face. This was more than the people could stand, and they began to weep sorrowfully. Some called for mutiny; some were ready to burn the house of Brutus.

Then Antony, to win the people to his cause once and for all, began to read Caesar's will. It called for every Roman citizen to be given seventy-five drachmas. "Most noble Caesar!" they cried, "we'll revenge his death." Then the angry citizens rushed forth to burn the houses of the traitors who had killed Caesar.

Cassius, Brutus, and their followers were forced to flee from Rome. They assembled troops to fight against the army of Antony and Octavius. When they were prepared to do battle, they faced a decision: should they wait for Antony and Octavius to make the first move, or should they take the offense and attack them at Philippi? Cassius preferred to wait, but Brutus felt that the time was ripe for battle, for the enemy was growing stronger every day. "There is a tide in the affairs of men which taken at the flood leads on to fortune," he said. "On such a full sea are we now afloat, and we must take the current when it serves, or lose our ventures." Cassius agreed to Brutus's plan. The next morning they would seek the enemy at Philippi.

Brutus spent a troubled night. As he sat awake, reading, a strange sight suddenly rose before him. It was the ghost of Caesar himself! "Thou shalt see me at Philippi," warned the ghost; then it disappeared. Brutus ran to wake his servants, asking if they had seen or heard anything, but they could report nothing.

The next day the two armies prepared for battle. With their armies in position behind them, the opposing generals, Antony and Octavius on one side, and Brutus and Cassius on the other, met on the battlefield to exchange a challenge. Then the fighting began.

Brutus took charge of the right wing, and Cassius of the left. Brutus's soldiers fared well, but meanwhile, Cassius's men were struggling and Brutus and his men had moved too far away to help them. Cassius sent his friend and right-hand officer, Titinius, to communicate with Brutus. Titinius rode to the other part of the battlefield, where he was received with great shouts of victory by Brutus's men. But Cassius, barely able to discern his friend's progress through the haze, wrongly concluded that Titinius had been captured by the enemy. "O, coward that I am, to live so long, to see my best friend taken before my face!" he cried. Rather than suffer defeat and disgrace, Cassius, in the Roman way, ordered his servant to hold his sword, then thrust himself against the blade, saying, "Caesar, thou art revenged, even with the sword that killed thee!" When Brutus arrived, he looked upon Cassius's body in sorrow. "The last of all the Romans, fare thee well!" he lamented.

Brutus and the others continued to fight, but the armies of Antony and Octavius proved too strong for them. When Brutus knew at last that there was no hope of victory, he vowed to end his life as Cassius had done, rather than be captured. He asked each of his servants to hold his sword so that he might run upon it, but each refused and fled. Only loyal Strato remained to do as his master asked. Brutus ran upon his sword, and died.

When Antony found his enemy lying dead, he was moved with admiration. "This was the noblest Roman of them all," he said to Octavius. "All the conspirators save only he did what they did in envy of great Caesar; only he acted in common good to all. His life was gentle, and the elements so mixed in him that Nature might stand up and say to all the world, 'This was a man!'"

The victorious generals buried Brutus with great dignity. Then they set about the task of restoring order to the troubled city of Rome.

You can find retellings of more plays by Shakespeare in Tales from Shakespeare *by Charles Lamb (New American Library, 1986). An excellent condensed version of* Julius Caesar *that you can perform as a play is available from Steck-Vaughn publishers (1991).*

Adventures of Sherlock Holmes:
The Red-Headed League
(condensed from the story by Arthur Conan Doyle)

"The Red-Headed League" is one of many stories by Arthur Conan Doyle about a fictional detective named Sherlock Holmes, whose amazing powers of observation and deduction enabled him to solve crimes that remained mysteries to the police. This story, like Doyle's other stories about Holmes, is told in the voice of Holmes's friend and companion, Dr. James Watson. The time is around 1890; the place is London, England.

One day last fall I called upon my friend, Mr. Sherlock Holmes, in his lodgings at 221B Baker Street. I found him in conversation with a stout gentleman with fiery red hair. Holmes pulled me into the room and closed the door.

"You could not possibly have come at a better time, my dear Watson," he said cordially. "Mr. Wilson, this is Dr. Watson, who has been my partner in many of my most successful cases." The stout gentleman gave a little bob of greeting. "I know, my dear Watson," Holmes continued, "that you share my love of all that is outside the humdrum routine of life. You have shown your relish for it by writing down so many of my own adventures."

"Your cases have been of great interest to me," I observed.

"Now, Mr. Jabez Wilson here has been good enough to call upon me with a story which promises to be one of the most singular I have listened to for some time. Perhaps, Mr. Wilson, you would have the great kindness to recommence your narrative."

The portly client pulled a wrinkled newspaper from the inside pocket of his greatcoat. I took a good look at the man and endeavored, as Holmes might, to learn something about him from his appearance. Our visitor bore every mark of being a commonplace British tradesman. He wore baggy gray trousers, a black frock-coat, and a drab waistcoat. Look as I would, there was nothing remarkable save his blazing red head.

Sherlock Holmes smiled as he noticed my questioning glances. He said, "Beyond the obvious facts that he has done manual labor, that he has been in China, and that he has done much writing lately, I can deduce nothing else."

Mr. Wilson looked startled. "How did you know all that, Mr. Holmes? How did you know that I did manual labor? It's true, for I began as a ship's carpenter."

"Your hands, my dear sir. Your right hand is a size larger than your left. The muscles are more developed from hard work."

"Ah, of course. But the writing?"

"What else can be indicated by that right cuff so shiny for five inches, and the left one with the smooth patch near the elbow where you rest it upon the desk?"

"Well, but China?"

"The fish tattooed just above your right wrist could only have been done in China, where they stain the fishes' scales a delicate pink." Mr. Wilson laughed in surprise. Holmes asked, "But won't you let Watson read the advertisement you brought, Mr. Wilson?"

He gave me the paper and I read as follows:

To the Red-Headed League:

On the account of the bequest of the late Ezekiah Hopkins, there is now another vacancy open which entitles a member of the League to a salary of four pounds a week for purely nominal services. All red-headed men who are sound in body and mind are eligible. Apply in person to the offices of the League, 7 Pope's Court, Fleet Street.

"What on earth does it mean?" I asked.

"Well, as I have been telling Mr. Holmes," said Mr. Wilson, "I have a small pawn-broker's business at Coburg Square, near the City. I keep one assistant, who is willing to come for half wages so as to learn the business. His name is Vincent Spaulding, and I should not wish a smarter assistant; and I know he could better himself, but if he is satisfied, why should I put ideas into his head?"

"Why, indeed? You are fortunate to have such an employee."

"Oh, he has his faults, too," said Mr. Wilson. "Never was there such a fellow for photography. Always diving down into the cellar to develop his pictures. But on the whole he's a good worker, and we go about our business quietly. The first thing that put us out was this advertisement. Spaulding came into the office just eight weeks ago with this very paper in his hand, and he says: 'I wish to the Lord, Mr. Wilson, that I was a red-headed man.' 'Why is that?' I ask. 'Why,' says he, 'here's another vacancy on the League of the Red-Headed Men. It's worth quite a little fortune to any man who gets it.' 'Why, what is it then?' I asked. 'Have you never heard of the

League of the Red-Headed Men? Why, you yourself are eligible for one of the vacancies. As far as I can make out, the League was founded by a millionaire, Ezekiah Hopkins. He was himself red-headed, and he had a great sympathy for all red-headed men; so when he died he left instructions that the interest from his enormous fortune be applied to the providing of easy jobs to men whose hair is red. I hear it is splendid pay and very little to do; but it is no use applying if your hair is anything but real bright, blazing, fiery red.' Now, gentlemen, as you may see for yourselves, my hair is of a very rich tint, so it seemed to me I stood as good a chance as any man. So we shut the business up and started off for the address given.

"What a sight! From every direction tramped every man who had a shade of red in his hair. Orange red. Brick red. Irish setter red. When I saw the crowd, I would have given up, but Spaulding pushed me right up the steps and into the office. Behind a table sat a small man with a head even redder than mine. He managed to find some fault to disqualify each candidate that went before us, but when our turn came, he closed the door, looked me over, then suddenly plunged forward and shook my hand in congratulations. He explained that he was Mr. Duncan Ross, a member of the League himself. 'When shall you be able to begin your duties?' he asked. 'What would be the hours?' I asked. 'Ten to two.' Now a pawnbroker's business is mostly done of an evening, Mr. Holmes, so it would suit me very well to earn a little in the mornings. He told me that the job required that I stay in the office the entire time each day, and that I would forfeit my position if I left for any reason. The work was to copy out the Encyclopedia Britannica.

"I feared that the whole affair might be a hoax, but to my surprise and delight, everything was as right as possible the next morning. I found the table set out for me, and Mr. Duncan Ross there to see I got to work. He started me off upon the letter A, and then he left me. This went on day after day, and every Saturday the manager came in and put down four golden sovereigns for my week's work. Mr. Duncan Ross would appear from time to time to see that I was working. Eight weeks passed away like this, and I had filled a shelf with my writings, when suddenly the whole business came to an end. For this morning I went to work as usual and found this tacked to the door." He held up a card, which read: THE RED-HEADED LEAGUE IS DISSOLVED. OCTOBER 9, 1890.

"Well, Mr. Holmes, I was staggered. I went round to the landlord to ask what had become of Mr. Duncan Ross and the Red-Headed League, but he had heard of neither of them. The red-haired gentleman was known to him as Mr. Morris, who had rented the room temporarily and had since moved. But when I went to his new address, I found it was a manufactory of artificial kneecaps. Now I want to know who played this prank on me, and why."

"You were wise to come to me," said Holmes. "This assistant of yours, Vincent Spaulding—how did you find him?"

"He answered an advertisement. I picked him from among a dozen applicants because he was willing to work for half wages."

"What is he like?"

"Small, quick in his ways, no hair on his face (though he's not short of thirty), with a white scar on his forehead."

Holmes asked in excitement, "And are his ears pierced?"

"Yes, sir. He told me a gypsy had done it for him."

"That will do, Mr. Wilson. I hope I shall have this matter concluded in a day or two." When our visitor had left us, Holmes announced that he would like to be left alone for fifty minutes to smoke his pipe. "This is quite a three-pipe problem," he said. When the time was up, he invited me to accompany him to St. James Hall to hear a violin concert. On the way we took a walk through Saxe-Coburg Square, where we found Mr. Wilson's pawnshop. Holmes thumped vigorously on the pavement two or three times with his cane, then knocked upon the door. It was opened by a clean-shaven fellow of whom Holmes asked directions to the Strand.

"Third right, fourth left," answered the assistant promptly, closing the door.

"Smart fellow, that," said Holmes, "The fourth smartest man in London, in my judgment. I know something of him."

"Evidently he accounts for much in this mystery," I said. "I take it you asked your way in order that you might see him."

"Not him," said Holmes, "but the knees of his trousers." Holmes next led me around the corner to look at the row of businesses that lined the back of Saxe-Coburg Square. "Let me see," said Holmes. "There's the tobacconist, the newspaper shop, the City and Suburban Bank, and the carriage depot. And now, Doctor, we've done our work, so it's time we had some play."

My friend was an enthusiastic musician, being himself both a capable performer on the violin and a composer of merit. All the afternoon he sat listening to the concert in the most perfect happiness, a dreamy expression on his face. But as we emerged, he returned to the former subject. He had business to take care of regarding Coburg Square, he said. He feared a considerable crime was about to take place. I was to meet him in his quarters at Baker Street at ten, and to bring my revolver.

When I arrived at 221B Baker Street, I found Sherlock Holmes in the company of two men whom he introduced as Inspector Jones of Scotland Yard and Mr. Merryweather, a banker. Mr. Merryweather said that he hoped he had not given up his weekly card game to come on a wild goose chase. "I think you will find," said Sherlock Holmes, "that you play for a higher stake tonight than you have ever done yet. For you, Mr. Merryweather, the stake will be some 30,000 pounds; and for you, Mr. Jones, it will be the man upon whom you wish to lay your hands, John Clay, the murderer, thief, and forger."

"John Clay is a remarkable man, Mr. Merryweather," said Inspector Jones. "His grandfather was a royal duke, and he himself has been to Oxford. His brain is as cunning as his fingers. I've been on his track for years and have never set eyes on him yet."

"I hope I may introduce you to him tonight," said Holmes. The four of us drove to the same row of businesses we had seen earlier in the day, and when our cabs were dismissed, we followed Mr. Merryweather down a passage, into a side door, and down some steps through a number of locked doors and gates into a huge vault, piled all around with massive boxes. Holmes cautioned us to be quiet, then he got down on his knees and began examining the stones in the floor with his lantern and a magnifying glass. After a few seconds he sprang to his feet. "We have at least an hour to wait," he said, "for they can hardly take any steps until the pawnbroker is safely in bed." He then explained to me that we were in the cellar of Mr. Merryweather's bank, where a large amount of French gold was being stored temporarily. John Clay and his accomplice, Holmes believed, would appear shortly to attempt to steal it. He warned that we must be ready to shoot, if necessary, for they were daring men.

After we had waited for what seemed hours, my eyes suddenly caught a glint of light on the floor. It lengthened into a yellow line, then a gash seemed to open and a hand appeared. Suddenly there was a rending, tearing sound, and one of the broad stones turned over and left a gaping hole. Over the edge peeped a boyish face, then the man's two hands emerged to draw himself up and out. Next he hauled up a red-haired companion. Suddenly Sherlock Holmes sprung out and seized the first intruder by the collar. The second dived down the hole. "It's no use, John Clay," said Holmes blandly to the boyish-looking man. "You have no chance at all, and there are three men waiting for your companion at the door."

"I beg that you will not touch me with your filthy hands," remarked our prisoner as Jones put the handcuffs on his wrists to lead him away. "I have royal blood in my veins."

Later, Holmes explained what had happened. "You see, Watson," he said, "it was obvious from the beginning that the only possible object of this fantastic business of the Red-Headed League must be to get the pawnbroker out of his store every day. When I heard that the assistant came for half wages, I knew he had some strong, secret motive."

"But how could you guess what the motive was?"

"I thought of the assistant's fondness for photography, and his trick of vanishing into the cellar. He was doing something down there—something which took many hours a day for months on end. I could think of nothing save that he was running a tunnel to some other building. Our glimpse of him confirmed this, for the worn, stained knees of his pants spoke of hours of burrowing. You'll remember I tapped on the pavement with my cane and heard no hollow sound. I then knew the tunnel led in the other direction, behind the shop. I turned the corner, saw the location of the bank, and felt that I had solved my problem."

"You reasoned it out beautifully!" I exclaimed admiringly.

"It saved me from boredom," he answered, yawning.

The Adventures of Don Quixote
(retold with excerpts from the novel by Miguel de Cervantes)

The greatest work of the Renaissance in Spain was not in art or architecture but literature: the novel Don Quixote *(DON key-HOE-tay) by Miguel de Cervantes.*

Cervantes led an exciting and difficult life. In 1570, at the age of twenty-three, he joined the army and fought against the Turks. He was wounded in his left hand in a naval battle. Like the character he created, Don Quixote, Cervantes loved brave deeds. He fought in other battles in countries around the Mediterranean Sea. After a while, he got homesick for Spain, and decided to go back there. But on the way he was captured by pirates! They sold him into slavery in Algiers, in northern Africa. He spent five years as a slave before his family and a group of friendly monks raised enough money to buy his freedom.

Cervantes used some of the things that happened to him in Don Quixote. *(Don is a title of honor in Spanish, like "Sir" in English.) You can see the same love of glory and adventure in Don Quixote's character that Cervantes had in his own life.*

Today you might hear an idea or a person described as "quixotic" (kwik-SOT-ic). That means the idea or person is wildly idealistic and impractical. Sometimes it also suggests that a person, while unrealistic, dares to believe in dreams that would strike most people as impossible. You may also hear an expression that comes from one of the adventures you're about to read: to go "tilting at windmills" means to attempt, with great hope, an apparently hopeless task.

In a village in La Mancha, there once lived a lean, thin-faced, hardy old gentleman whose favorite pastime was to read books about knights in armor. He loved to read about their daring exploits, strange adventures, bold rescues of damsels in distress, and intense devotion to their ladies. In fact, he became so caught up in the subject of chivalry that he neglected every other interest and even sold many acres of good farmland so that he might buy all the books he could get on the subject. He would lie awake at night, absorbed in every detail of the fantastic adventures in his books. He would often engage in arguments with the village priest or the barber over who was the greatest knight of all time. Was it Amadis of Gaul or Palmerin of England? Or was it perhaps the Knight of the Sun?

As time went on, the old gentleman crammed his head so full of these stories and lost so much sleep from reading through the night that he lost his wits completely. He began to believe that all the fantastic and romantic tales he read about enchantments, challenges, battles, wounds, and wooings were true histories. At last he fell into the strangest fancy that any madman has ever had: he resolved to become himself a knight errant, to travel through the world with horse and armor in search of adventures.

First he got out some rust-eaten armor that had belonged to his ancestors, then cleaned and repaired it as best he could. Although the head-piece of the helmet was intact, unfortunately, the visor which protects the face was gone. Not to be discouraged by this deficiency, however, he fashioned another out of some pieces of stiff paper and strips of iron. In his eyes it was without a doubt the most splendid helmet ever fashioned.

Next he considered what glorious, high-sounding name he might give the horse who was to bear him on his quest. For though his horse was but a tired hack, practically skin and bones, to him it appeared as magnificent as Bucephalus, the horse of the great Alexander. After four days of inventing and rejecting various names, he at last settled on Rocinante (row-see-NON-tay), which he felt sounded suitably grand. And indeed, as *rocín* is Spanish for "hack," he had chosen a name appropriate to the grandest hack of all.

He then set about to choose a suitable name for himself. After eight days of hard consideration, he decided that he would be known as Don Quixote. Following the example of many knights he admired, he decided to proclaim the name of his native land as well, and so he called himself Don Quixote de la Mancha.

Now he needed to find a lady whom he might adore and serve, for a knight without a lady is like a body without a soul. It happened that in a neighboring village there lived a farm girl whom he had once admired from a distance. He decided that she would be the lady of his fancy, and that she should be known as Dulcinea del Toboso (dull-si-NAY-ah del toe-BOW-so), a name that to his ears sounded musical and anything but ordinary.

Now, with all these preparations made, Don Quixote was eager to sally forth: a world awaited, full of injustices to be made right, and great deeds to be performed. So, clad in his rusty armor, with his improvised helmet tied to his head, Don Quixote mounted Rocinante and started out through the back of the stable yard.

But then he had a terrible thought: he had never yet been dubbed a knight! He took comfort, however, in his memory of the many books of chivalry he had read, and determined that, like many of the heroes in those books, which he took for truth, he would simply have himself knighted by the first person who came along. So he rode on under a hot July sun, blissfully happy in his thoughts of how, in years to come, others would read of the brave exploits of Don Quixote de la Mancha and his faithful steed, Rocinante.

Now, almost the whole day had passed and still Don Quixote had encountered no wrong to set right, nor any adventure to test his valor. Neither had he eaten nor attended to any other bodily needs. His discouragement vanished, however, when, just at nightfall, he came upon a simple country inn with a stable beside it.

Everything that Don Quixote saw, or thought he saw, came out of the fantastic books he had read; so, when he neared the inn, he saw not a dingy hut but a gleaming castle with turrets thrusting to the sky, and, of course, a drawbridge and a moat and all the other things that go with such castles. He reined in Rocinante and awaited the blast of a trumpet to signal his arrival, for that is what always happened in the books he read. Just as he was getting impatient, a swineherd came along with a bunch of grunting hogs, which he called together by blowing upon his horn. With great satisfaction, Don Quixote took this to be the signal he awaited, and rode forth.

The innkeeper, in Don Quixote's eyes, was certainly the keeper of the castle. Don Quixote dismounted from Rocinante and told the innkeeper to take special care of his steed, which was surely the finest horse in the world. The innkeeper looked doubtfully at the bony hack, but decided to humor this person so strangely dressed in a bizarre assortment of ill-fitting armor.

As Don Quixote had not eaten all day, he requested some food. Unfortunately, he had tied on his helmet and could not undo the knots—and, as he refused to allow the helmet to be cut off, he wore it the rest of the night. The innkeeper had to hollow out a reed in order for Don Quixote to drink his wine. As for the food, which a country lass was kind enough to put into Don Quixote's mouth, it was an unappetizing meal of badly cooked fish and moldy bread. But Don Quixote remained firm in his belief that this was a brilliant castle, and the food a gourmet feast.

When the meal was over, Don Quixote dropped to his knees before the surprised innkeeper. "Never," he said, "shall I rise from here until you have consented to grant me the favor I ask, which will bring you great praise and benefit all mankind. I ask that you dub me a knight." The innkeeper obliged the Don by whacking him on the shoulder with the flat side of a sword, all the while mumbling some words from an account book in which he kept records of costs and charges for hay, grain, and the like.

The next day, Don Quixote set forth, joyous in having been quite officially made a knight. His destination was his own village for, following the innkeeper's advice, he planned to return home for some money and clean clothes (details which had been overlooked in all the books about knights and their adventures). And he planned to find a good man who could serve as his squire.

After he had gone but a little way, Don Quixote heard the groans of someone in distress. "Without a doubt," he exclaimed, "those are the cries of some unfortunate person in need of my assistance." He turned Rocinante into the woods where the cries were coming from. There he saw a boy, tied to a tree, his bare back being whipped by an angry farmer.

Don Quixote cried out, "It does no praise to you to strike someone who cannot defend himself. Now, you knave, take up your lance and prepare to defend yourself."

When the farmer saw before him this armed figure with a lance pointed at him, he feared for his life. He explained to Don Quixote that the boy he was whipping was a servant who watched over his sheep, and that the lad deserved to be punished because almost every day a sheep was missing from the flock. "And," said the farmer, "the boy here dares to claim that I punish him only because I am a miser and will not pay his wages. But I swear that he lies."

"You are the liar, you dog," shouted Don Quixote. "Now untie him or I will destroy you here and now!"

The farmer untied the boy. Don Quixote asked the boy how much his master owed him, and the boy said for seven months' work.

"But," said the farmer, "I don't have any money here. Let's go home, Andres, and I'll pay you there."

"With you!" cried the boy. "Never! I know how you'll pay me—with a terrible whipping."

"He would not dare to," said Don Quixote. "It is enough that I, Don Quixote de la Mancha, who brings justice where there is injustice, command him to pay you, and he will obey." That, of course, was how things always worked out in the books Don Quixote read. So Don Quixote commanded the farmer to pay, and the farmer swore he would. As soon as Don Quixote rode out of sight, the farmer turned to the boy and said, "Because I'm so fond of you I want to pay you even more than I owe"— and then proceeded to thrash the boy more severely than ever.

In the distance, Don Quixote was pleased with his first noble deed. "Ah, Dulcinea del Toboso," he said aloud, "your devoted servant, knighted only yesterday, has this day already put right the greatest wrong and stopped the greatest cruelty ever known." And he proceeded back to his village.

Upon returning, Don Quixote set about with all his powers of persuasion to convince a laborer of the village, whose name was Sancho Panza (SOHN-cho PON-za), to accompany him as his squire. At last, with the promise that Don Quixote would someday make him governor of his very own island, the country bumpkin agreed to leave his wife and children and follow the knight. The tall, lean knight sat upon bony Rocinante, while the plump Sancho Panza climbed astride his

Don Quixote and Sancho Panza

ass named Dapple, a leather wine bottle, and well-stocked saddlebags at his side. And so this unlikely pair set off in search of adventures.

As they crossed the plain of Montiel, they spied dozens of windmills. "Fortune has smiled on us," said Don Quixote to his squire. "Yonder stand more than thirty terrible giants. I will fight them and kill them all, and we shall make ourselves rich with the spoils."

"What giants?" asked Sancho Panza.

"Those giants there, with the long arms," said the knight.

"Be careful, sir," said the squire. "Those are not giants, but windmills, and what seem to be their arms are the sails which turn the millstone."

"If you are afraid of them, then go say your prayers," said Don Quixote. "But I shall engage them in battle." Immediately he spurred his horse forward, and, paying no attention to Sancho Panza's shouted warnings, he cried, "Do not run, you cowards, for a lone knight assails you!" Just then a slight wind caused the windmills to begin turning. "I fear you not, though you have more arms than the giant Briareus," cried the knight. "I ride forth in the name of the fair Dulcinea!" Covering himself with his shield, and thrusting forth his lance, he spurred Rocinante toward the nearest windmill. His lance pierced one of the whirling sails, which immediately wrenched it with such force that the horse was dragged along and the knight sent rolling across the ground. He lay without moving as Sancho Panza trotted to his side.

"Oh, Sir," said Sancho, "didn't I warn your worship to watch what you were doing when attacking those windmills?"

"I believe," replied the knight, "that some evil enchanter turned those giants into windmills to rob me of a glorious victory. But I shall prevail over him in the end."

"Oh, Sir," said Sancho, "didn't I warn your worship?"

"As God wills," said Sancho, helping the knight to his feet. They climbed upon Rocinante and Dapple once more, and continued on their way.

Just as Don Quixote desired, he and Sancho Panza encountered many dangerous and unusual adventures in the days that followed; for so often did the knight mistake shepherds, holy men, and peasant girls for miscreant knights, evil enchanters and ladies in distress that he was continually involved in ridiculous quarrels and brawls. No matter how frantically Sancho urged him to see things as they really were, Don Quixote paid no attention. Gradually his exploits became known all over the countryside, and there were few who had not heard of that flower of chivalry, Don Quixote de la Mancha.

Dr. Jekyll and Mr. Hyde
(adapted from *The Strange Case of Dr. Jekyll and Mr. Hyde* by Robert Louis Stevenson)

*This suspenseful tale of horror was written by the same man who wrote **Treasure Island**, which you can read in Book Four of this series. If you enjoy this story, you might also like another book by Stevenson,* Kidnapped.

All of London was talking about the murder of Sir Danvers Carew. A witness recognized the murderer as a certain Mr. Hyde. By the time the police arrived, however, this Hyde had long since fled. On the scene, the police found a walking stick, evidently the murder weapon, and in the dead man's pocket a business letter addressed to his lawyer, Mr. John G. Utterson.

The police brought this letter round to Mr. Utterson along with the walking stick, which they were taking in as evidence. When Utterson saw the stick, he was shaken. It was unquestionably the same walking stick that he had given many years ago to his old friend, Dr. Henry Jekyll.

Why, Utterson wondered, should his gift to Dr. Jekyll suddenly turn up as a murder weapon? And what was the relation between the murderer—the man a witness had recognized as Mr. Hyde—and a man of the same name who, Utterson recalled, was so strangely included in Jekyll's will? Utterson, who was not only Jekyll's friend but also his lawyer, knew the terms of Jekyll's will, which read that upon the death or "disappearance for longer than three months" of Dr. Jekyll, a certain Edward Hyde would inherit Jekyll's house and money.

As soon as the police left, Utterson went to see Jekyll. He wanted to ask his friend about the walking stick and about Hyde.

"Was the stick stolen from you?" asked the lawyer. "How awful that a murderer should use your property to commit his crime!"

Jekyll shook his head. "No, it was not stolen. Edward Hyde borrowed it from me some weeks ago. I had no idea he might use it for such a purpose."

Utterson was aghast. "Then he is the murderer!" His voice faltered. "My dear Jekyll, who is Edward Hyde?"

Dr. Jekyll's handsome face grew pale. "I do not care to discuss this with you," he said. "My friendship with Hyde is a very strange one."

"Come, come," said his friend. "You can trust me. Tell me something of this matter. Perhaps I can help."

"My good Utterson," said the doctor, "I believe and trust you, but the dilemma is not what you fancy. You're imagining blackmail, perhaps? I will tell you one thing: the moment I choose, I can be rid of Hyde."

Utterson could see that he would get no more on this subject from his friend. And for the sake of their friendship he promised to let the matter rest. But he felt there was more to learn, perhaps something dreadful. He determined to meet the mysterious Edward Hyde. "If he be Mr. Hyde," Utterson thought, "I shall be Mr. Seek."

Utterson waited several nights in the alley behind Jekyll's house. Late one evening, a small but powerfully built man appeared, carrying a key to that very house! Utterson stepped out and asked the man how he came to possess this key, and then demanded to see Dr. Jekyll at once. The man snarled that Jekyll was not at home and disappeared through the door with a savage, barely human laugh.

Surely such a creature would not know whether the respected doctor was at home or not. Utterson determined to ask Jekyll more about this dreadful person. He rounded the corner and rang the bell at the front of Jekyll's house, hoping to have his fears calmed. But Poole, the doctor's manservant, informed him that his master was not at home.

"What! Not home at this hour!" thought Mr. Utterson. "Something is indeed wrong."

The next morning Utterson called upon Jekyll again, and was led into his presence.

"Jekyll, you are my client and my friend. I must ask you if you have been insane enough to hide this fellow the police suspect of murder."

"Utterson, on my honor I tell you I will never set eyes on Edward Hyde again. He does not want or need my help. Indeed, he has removed himself from capture and says so right here."

The sinister Mr. Hyde.

Jekyll then produced a letter, which said much the same thing, and was signed "Edward Hyde."

"Did Hyde dictate the terms of your will?" asked Utterson. The doctor nodded. "I knew it!" said Utterson. "He meant to murder you, too. At least you can escape!"

Covering his face with his hands, Dr. Jekyll cried, "No, no, I cannot. But I have had a lesson. Oh, what a lesson I have had. . . ."

In the following weeks, Mr. Hyde made no reappearance, and so Utterson's fears diminished. With Hyde's influence out of the picture, Dr. Jekyll grew more social again. The doctor dined often with his friends.

But then, on two separate occasions when Jekyll had invited Utterson for a meal, the lawyer arrived at Jekyll's house only to discover the doctor was not at home. After this, Utterson received a mysterious note from his friend. It read: "I mean from now on to lead a life of extreme seclusion. You must not doubt my friendship if my door is closed to you; you must suffer me to go my own dark way. If I am the chief of sinners, I am also the chief of sufferers."

Utterson was soon to discover the sinister truth of this note. Late one evening, he was surprised to receive a visit from Jekyll's manservant, Poole, pale and breathless. "Mr. Utterson, please, will you come at once?" the servant cried. "There is something wrong. Some days ago Dr. Jekyll shut himself in his office, and now I think there's been foul play." Utterson did not hesitate; he followed Poole into the cold night. Jekyll's street was deserted. Inside, the terrified servants huddled around the hearth. Poole led Utterson downstairs to the doctor's office. At the door he called, "It's Mr. Utterson, sir, asking to see you," and beckoned the lawyer to listen.

A strangled voice answered from within, "Tell him I cannot see anyone." The servant and Utterson both knew that this was not Henry Jekyll's voice.

Poole shuddered and said, "I know Dr. Jekyll shut himself in there, sir. But he cannot be alone. I saw that creature Hyde digging wildly in these crates where the good doctor keeps his medicines. And someone's been crying out for medicine, but whatever I bring from the chemist is returned, with complaints." He produced a crumpled note, written in Jekyll's hand, to the apothecaries. Scrawled at the bottom, barely legible, was the note, "For God's sake, find me some of the old medicine!"

Poole said, "It looks like the doctor's handwriting, but—but—I'm very afraid that murder has been done."

"I fear you are right," replied Utterson. "We must break down the door. This will place us in peril, you know, Poole."

"Yes, sir, but we must get him free of that creature."

The two men called the footman, described what they were about to do, and told him to summon the authorities should anything go wrong.

"Jekyll, are you there? Open the door," called Utterson. "If you will not, we shall force it!"

"Utterson," cried a voice, "for God's sake, have mercy!"

"Ah, that's Hyde's voice!" cried Utterson. "Down with the door, Poole."

Poole swung an axe, and at the fifth blow, the door fell inward. They found Hyde lying on the carpet, dead. He was dressed in clothes far too large for him, the clothes of Henry Jekyll. A crushed vial clutched in his hand emitted a strong smell of poison. The men searched every corner of the building, but could find no trace of Dr. Jekyll. On top of the doctor's desk, however, they found a newly written version of his will, leaving his property not to Hyde, but to John Gabriel Utterson. With it was this letter:

My Dear Utterson,

When this falls into your hands, I shall have disappeared. But you have a right and the world has a need to hear my story.

From my earliest scientific experiments I was fascinated with the duality of life—I say that to mean that man is not one, but two creatures. One side of his nature is good, the other evil. What if, I thought, each side of man's nature could be housed in separate identities? Wouldn't this make life more bearable? The good identity could go his own way, walking steadfastly along the upward path. The unjust side might go equally steady downward, unburdened by the remorse of the good nature.

I had already begun to make experiments with certain substances that have the power to make the flesh change shape. For two good reasons, I will not tell you more about these substances. First, because I have learned what a burden such knowledge can be. Second, because, as my narrative will make clear, my discoveries were incomplete.

I hesitated before putting these substances to practice in separating the two sides of my nature. But soon the temptation of discovery overcame me, and I drank a potion much like the one you have just seen. The most racking pangs succeeded; a grinding in the bones, deadly nausea, and a horror of the spirit. Then these agonies subsided, and I felt something new. I felt younger, lighter, and reckless. I knew myself, at the first breath of this newness, to be purely wicked. I stretched out my hands, exulting in these sensations, and suddenly realized I had become shorter.

At that date, there was no mirror in my room, and so I stole through the corridors, a stranger in my own house, until I came upon a mirror and saw for the first time the appearance of Edward Hyde.

My theory as to Hyde's smaller body is that the evil side of my nature was less developed than the good side, which I had nurtured through the years in my medical profession. Even as good shone upon my face when I was Jekyll, evil shone upon my face when I was Hyde. All human beings, as we meet them, are commingled out of good and evil both; Edward Hyde, alone in the ranks of men, was pure evil.

I lingered but a moment at the mirror, knowing that I dare not be seen by any members of my household. I hurried back to my office, once more prepared and drank the potion, and once more suffered the pains of transformation, and came to myself with the character and appearance of Henry Jekyll.

The temptations of this metamorphosis were many, and I often succumbed to the potion. However, after Hyde committed an act of cruelty toward an innocent child, I gave up the elixir forever. Then two months before the murder of Sir Danvers, I awoke one morning with odd sensations. I was in my own room; its furnishings and proportions were familiar; yet I felt different. I was about to doze off when I saw my hand. You know the hand of Henry Jekyll to be of a good size and shape—firm, smooth, and clear. But the hand I saw on that morning was small and covered with thick dark hair. It was the hand of Edward Hyde.

Yes, I had gone to bed Henry Jekyll, and I had awakened as Edward Hyde. How could this have happened? At first, as I passed out of Hyde's body in only half an hour, I believed it to be an accident. But it happened again, and then again, and then a third time. The powers of Hyde seemed to grow as those of Jekyll weakened.

The love of life that Edward Hyde has is incredible. He fears the power I have over him, the power to kill the body we both inhabit. I am writing my story under the influence of the last of the old medicine. This will be the last time, short of a miracle, that I can think my own thoughts or see my own face (now how sadly altered!) in the mirror. I must not delay here too long, for the change may overtake me at any moment. I do not know at what hour I shall resume that hated identity. Will Hyde die upon the scaffold, the police having found him in Jekyll's abode? Or will he release himself at the last moment, through poison? I do not know; this is my true hour of death. Thus I bring to a close my confession and my life.

Henry Jekyll

The Iliad *and the* Odyssey

Homer's Epics

The greatest storyteller of ancient Greece was named Homer. We know very little about him. According to tradition, Homer was a blind poet who lived about three thousand years ago. At celebrations or religious festivals, he would tell poems of great heroes in battle, of gods and goddesses, of terrible monsters, and more. Homer told two of the greatest stories of all time, the *Iliad* (ILL-ee-ud) and the *Odyssey* (ODD-uh-see). The *Iliad* and the *Odyssey* are *epics*, long poems about great heroes and famous deeds.

Homer was an oral poet—that is, he spoke and sang his epic poems aloud, for writing was not very common in Greece thousands of years ago. Now, however, there are dozens and dozens of translations of the *Iliad* and *Odyssey*, into many languages, and in both poetry and prose.

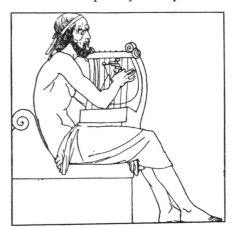

As you probably remember from some of the Greek myths you've read—like the story of Icarus and Daedalus, or the story of Demeter and Persephone—humans are not the only characters in these stories: there are also many gods and goddesses. The Greek gods, you recall, were in some respects like human beings. They needed food, drink, and sleep. They married and had children. They often quarreled, and could be very jealous and vindictive. But in other respects the gods were very different from humans. They were immortal: they never died. They could change themselves into various forms, and they could make themselves invisible. When they were not intervening in the affairs of humans on earth, most of them lived in splendid palaces high on top of Mount Olympus. These gods and goddesses are active in the *Iliad* and the *Odyssey*.

The Iliad

The Judgment of Paris: Background to the *Iliad*

The Iliad *tells the story of the Trojan War, the long war between the Greeks and the people of Troy, called "Trojans." (The name,* Iliad, *comes from another name for the city of Troy, Ilion.) Homer begins the* Iliad *after the Trojan War had been going on for nine years. Homer could assume that his Greek listeners were already familiar with the causes of the war, as told in the familiar story of the judgment of Paris, which, though not part of the* Iliad, *we provide here.*

Paris was one of the sons of Priam and Hecuba, king and queen of the high-walled city of Troy. Shortly before Paris was born, Hecuba dreamed that her next child would bring ruin upon his family and native city. So, when the baby was born, the king ordered a shepherd to take the infant to Mount Ida and leave it to die. Reluctantly, the shepherd took the baby and left him. When the shepherd returned a few days later, he found the baby alive and well. He took the baby to his home and raised the boy, whom he named Paris, as one of his own family.

Paris grew up strong, handsome, and athletically skilled. He did not know he was really King Priam's son. He was happy as a young shepherd, and he happily married a lovely nymph who was the daughter of a river god. But this happiness was not to last, for soon Paris would get involved in a quarrel among three goddesses.

The unhappy quarrel started in the middle of a happy occasion, the wedding feast of Thetis, a sea goddess, to a mortal king, named Peleus. Many gods and goddesses were at the feast, but one goddess was not invited: her name was Eris, the goddess of discord. She had caused so much quarreling among the residents of Mount Olympus that Zeus, king of the gods, had banished her forever from the palaces of the gods. But Eris had a plan for revenge. At the wedding feast of Thetis and Peleus, she threw a golden apple onto a table. On the apple were these words: "For the fairest."

At once all the goddesses began to claim the prize, each certain that she was the fairest. Soon the contest came down to three: Hera, queen of the gods; Athena, the goddess of wisdom; and Aphrodite, the goddess of love and beauty. Each vehemently claimed to be the fairest, and since no one could decide, Zeus was called on to choose one as the fairest of all.

Zeus knew this was an impossible task: no matter whom he chose, he would be faced with two angry goddesses. So Zeus gave the task of judging to Paris, the handsome young shepherd on Mount Ida. Each of the goddesses promised Paris something if he would choose her.

"Choose me," said Hera, "and I will grant you immense power and wealth."

Then Athena spoke: "If you award the apple to me, I will make you the wisest of men, and great in war." Then Aphrodite, with a subtle smile in her mild eyes, spoke gently, her sweet breath warming Paris's ear: "Ah, dear Paris, give the golden apple to me, and I will give you, to be your wife, the fairest woman in the world."

To Aphrodite Paris gave the golden apple.

Not even thinking of the wife he already had, Paris quickly made his judgment. To Aphrodite he gave the golden apple, and ever afterward Aphrodite was his friend, and a friend of Paris's homeland, Troy. But the goddesses not chosen, Hera and Athena, would afterward look with anger upon Troy.

Aphrodite would keep her promise to Paris: but first, she helped restore Paris to his place as a prince of Troy. Paris traveled from Mount Ida to take part in great athletic games being held at Troy. In the competitions he won all the first prizes, for Aphrodite had given him godlike strength and swiftness. Soon, people noticed how strikingly he resembled many of the sons and daughters of Priam and Hecuba. The shepherd who raised Paris, now an old man, was brought forth, and he told the story of how he had spared the infant's life. Now Priam and Hecuba welcomed their long-lost son with open arms, forgetting the prophecy that he would bring ruin upon Troy.

Paris was eager to voyage to Greece, for there dwelled the most beautiful woman in the world, Helen. Helen, however, was already married to a Greek king named Menelaus. But this was no obstacle to Paris, for he had Aphrodite on his side. In a great fleet splendidly outfitted, he set sail for Sparta, the home of Menelaus. When Paris arrived, Menelaus, little suspecting what Paris intended, received the Trojan prince with great hospitality. He held banquets in honor of Paris, and invited him to stay in Sparta as long as he wished.

Soon, Menelaus accepted an invitation to take part in a hunting expedition on a nearby island. He asked his beautiful queen, Helen, to see that Paris was treated graciously. When Menelaus left, Aphrodite made Helen fall in love with Paris, so he easily convinced her to leave her husband and go to Troy.

Paris carried off not only Helen but also much gold and many treasures belonging to Menelaus. When Paris and Helen arrived in Troy, they were welcomed by King Priam and Queen Hecuba with great rejoicing. But some in Troy strongly disapproved of what Paris had done. Prince Hector, another son of Priam, and one of the wisest advisers of his father, urged that Helen be returned to Menelaus. But Helen remained in Troy.

The carrying off of Helen was the cause of the Trojan War. It has been said of the beautiful Helen that hers was "the face that launched a thousand ships"—for all the Greek kings and their armies were called upon to join Menelaus and sail across the sea to attack Troy and restore Helen to his side.

The Greek kings were bound to Menelaus by a promise they had made long ago, even before Menelaus and Helen were married. At that time, *all* the Greek kings had wanted to marry Helen, so Helen's father prevented conflict by having them make a promise: "All of you must swear," he said, "that you will be good friends with the man whom my daughter will choose for her husband, and that, if anyone is wicked enough to steal her away from him, you will help him get her back." They had all promised, so now they responded to the call from the brother of Menelaus, Agamemnon, the wealthy and powerful king of Mycenae. Agamemnon called upon them to join forces against Troy, both to take back Helen and to gain great glory and riches for themselves.

The greatest of the Greek heroes was Achilles, the swift-footed warrior who fought like a god in battle. He brought with him to Troy his father's famous troops, the Myrmidons, who had never been beaten in battle. He also brought wedding gifts that had been given to his father, Peleus, by Zeus: two immortal horses and a suit of armor so strong and bright that it surpassed anything ever worn by mortal man. Achilles was accompanied by his dearest friend, another hero and warrior, named Patroclus.

Invoking the Muse

I n the Iliad, Homer established a tradition followed by later writers of epic poems. He begins by calling upon one of the nine Muses—the goddesses of poetry, song, and other arts—to inspire him and enable him to tell his tale.

Here are the opening lines of the Iliad (as translated from the Greek by a nineteenth-century American poet named William Cullen Bryant). This translation uses the Romans' name for Zeus (Jove), and refers to the family name of Agamemnon (Atrides, meaning "son of Atreus"). Homer does much in a few lines: he invokes (calls upon) the muse, then gives a kind of preview of coming attractions, including a glimpse of the many deaths in battle, as well as a terrible argument between Agamemnon and Achilles.

> O Goddess! Sing the wrath of Peleus' son,
> Achilles; sing the deadly wrath that brought
> Woes numberless upon the Greeks, and swept
> To Hades many a valiant soul, and gave
> Their limbs a prey to dogs and birds of air,—
> For so had Jove appointed,—from the time
> When the two chiefs, Atrides, king of men,
> And great Achilles, parted first as foes.

The Quarrel Between Agamemnon and Achilles

When the Greeks reached Troy, they found the Trojans ready for battle. The greatest of the heroes defending Troy was Hector. The Trojans, headed by Hector, came out from the city through the great gate in the high walls. They met the Greeks on the open plains between the walls of Troy and the beaches where the Greek ships had landed. They fought with swords, axes, bows and arrows, and sharp javelins. The ground ran red with the blood of many a hero whose groaning soul fled unwillingly to the realms of the dead.

The most feared of all the Greek warriors was Achilles. Clad in the shining armor that was a gift of Zeus, and hurtling forth in his chariot drawn by immortal horses, he struck terror into the hearts of Trojans, who, seeing him, would run back to their walled city.

Though the Trojans fought bravely, they were unable to keep up a steady fight in the open fields against the vast numbers of Greeks. Seeing that they must depend for safety on the high walls of their city, they withdrew inside those walls.

For nine years the Greeks besieged the city of Troy. Never could they break through the high walls. As years passed, the Greeks came to need food and clothes and supplies. So they left part of the army to watch over Troy, and sent part to attack other cities to get supplies and to take captives. After the raids, the spoils were divided among the

The ground ran red with the blood of many a hero.

chiefs, as was customary. For the Greek kings, honor and glory in battle were measured in part by the riches and captives they won.

In these raids, two maidens, named Chryseis and Briseis, were taken captive. They would soon become the cause of a bitter quarrel between Agamemnon and Achilles.

Chryseis was given to Agamemnon, while Briseis went to Achilles, who became very fond of the lovely maiden. The father of Chryseis, a priest named Chryses, came to beg Agamemnon to return his daughter. He wore his priestly garments, and brought many valuable gifts as ransom for his daughter. But Agamemnon scornfully refused his plea. "Away with you, old man," he barked. "As for your daughter, I will carry her back with me when I have taken Troy."

Now Chryses prayed to Apollo, the sun god, asking him to make Agamemnon return his daughter. Apollo answered these prayers. For nine days, from his fiery chariot in the sky he shot arrows that carried death, first to the dogs and mules, then to the men. Finally, when the funeral pyres of the dead were burning day and night, Achilles called the Greek chiefs together to consider what to do.

At the meeting, the Greeks' soothsayer—a wise man who could understand the ways of the gods—revealed the cause of the plague: "Apollo is angry because his priest has been dishonored by Agamemnon. Chryseis must be restored to her father, and we must offer a great sacrifice to the Archer God, if we are to appease him."

Furious, Agamemnon jumped up and growled, "You prophet from hell! Never have you spoken anything good for me. Now you say I must give up the maiden.

Then so be it—I would save our army, not destroy it. But hear me! Some other prize must be given to me, at once, for Agamemnon shall not be slighted!"

Achilles responded: "What prize is there to give? All the spoils have been divided. We cannot ask our men to return what has been given to them. So, be satisfied and let the girl go for now. When we have taken the strong city of Troy, we will make it up to you, three and four times over."

"Is that your game, then, Achilles?" snapped Agamemnon. "You are to keep your prize, and I am to lose mine? No! This council must award a suitable prize to me, or else I will seize yours, or that of Ajax or Odysseus."

At this, the wrath of Achilles flared. "You greedy dog!" he shouted at Agamemnon. "How can the Greeks be expected to fight bravely under you? I have no quarrel with the Trojans; they have done me no wrong. I have been fighting against them for your sake and your brother's. But you—you sit in your tent at ease, and then, when the spoils are divided, you take the lion's share. And now you would take the little that was given to me. I have no desire to stay here and be dishonored by you. I will take my men and go."

"Go, then," said Agamemnon. "Take your ships and your Myrmidons. But hear this: to make clear to all who is the stronger man, I will come to your tent, and take the fair-cheeked Briseis, your prize, for my own."

Achilles's hand gripped the hilt of his sword. Slowly he slid the sharp blade from its scabbard. "Now I will slay this villain where he sits," he thought. But then he stopped—for at that instant the goddess Athena seized him by his long yellow hair. When he turned, he saw the goddess, who was visible only to his eyes.

"Put back your sword, swift-footed Achilles," said Athena. "Hera, queen of the gods, and I love you and Agamemnon both. Now, show your anger, though not with a blade, but with words." So saying, she disappeared.

"When an immortal speaks," thought Achilles, "a man must obey." Then turning to Agamemnon, he lashed out with angry words: "Hear this solemn oath, you drunkard with the eyes of a dog and the heart of a deer! There will come a day when every Greek soldier will beg to have Achilles back.

"Put back your sword, swift-footed Achilles," said Athena.

But on that day, though a thousand perish at the hands of Hector alone, Achilles will not come to help. You will regret the dishonor you have heaped upon the bravest man in your army!"

So saying, Achilles, with his dear friend Patroclus, returned to his tent, where they were soon visited by messengers of Agamemnon, who led away the fair-cheeked Briseis. Now the Greeks would have to face the Trojans without their greatest warrior, who sat by the wine-dark sea, firm in his implacable wrath.

Hector and Andromache

At first the Greeks fought so fiercely that, even without Achilles, they pressed the Trojans hard, forcing them again behind the walls of Troy for safety. There, great Hector urged his people to offer prayers and make abundant sacrifices so that the gods would favor the Trojans in battle.

Before returning to battle, Hector made his way to his own house to see his wife, Andromache, and his son, yet a baby. Hector smiled when he saw his wife and child, but Andromache caught her husband by the hand and wept, saying, "O Hector, your courage will be your death. Have pity on your wife and child, and spare yourself. If I lose you, it would be better for me to die than to live. Stay here, lest you leave me a widow and your child an orphan."

"Your thoughts are mine, dear wife," Hector answered. "And yet, I would feel great shame before the Trojans if I were to shrink from battle. I have been raised always to be at the front of the fighting, and to win great glory for myself and my father. Still, I care most for you, and it grieves me to think that one day some Greek may carry you away captive, and say, 'See that slave woman there: she is the wife of Hector, bravest of the Trojans.'"

Then glorious Hector held out his arms to take his infant son. But the child shrank back with a cry, for he was frightened by his father's shining helmet, with its horsehair plumes on top that waved so awfully. With a laugh, Hector removed the helmet from his head and took his dear son in his arms and kissed him. Then he lifted his voice in prayer to Zeus: "O Father Zeus, grant that this child may be as I am, a great man in Troy. And some day let the people say of him, 'He is an even greater man than his father, for see how he comes home from the fighting, having killed his enemy, and brings with him the bloody spoils, to delight the heart of his mother.'"

"O Father Zeus, grant that this child may be as I am, a great man in Troy."

He handed the child back to Andromache, who was still weeping. Hector gently stroked his wife's hair and said, "Dear lady, do not be troubled. No man will kill me, unless it is my fate to die. And as for fate, no man, whether brave or cowardly, can escape it." Then Hector took up his helmet and left to prepare for battle.

The Combat Between Menelaus and Paris

There soon came a time when, at the bidding of Zeus, the combined forces of the Greeks, led by Agamemnon, marched across the plains to meet the massed troops of the Trojans, under the command of Hector.

The two armies advanced toward each other, the Trojans with shouts and clangs of arms, the Greeks silent and resolved. Suddenly, Paris rushed forward from the Trojan lines. Over his shoulders he wore a panther's skin; his weapons were a bow, a sword, and two sharp spears tipped with brass. Boldly, he challenged the Greeks to send their bravest warrior to fight him in single combat.

The challenge was speedily answered by Menelaus, who leaped from his chariot the moment he caught sight of Paris. At last he would have a chance to avenge himself upon the man who had so greatly wronged him by taking his wife!

When Paris saw who had come forth, he was seized with fear and ran back to the Trojan lines. There, he was rebuked by great Hector, who said, "Paris, you are good to look at, but you are worth nothing. You were brave enough to go across the sea and steal the fair Helen from her husband, but now, when he comes to fight you, you run away."

Paris answered, "You speak the truth, noble Hector. Now, let only Menelaus and me fight, man to man, and let him who conquers have the fair Helen and all her possessions. If he kills me, let him take her and depart; but if I kill him, then she shall stay here."

Hector announced these terms to the Greeks. Menelaus responded: "Greek and Trojan alike have suffered greatly for the sake of the wrong Paris has done me. Now, let this single combat decide: whomever fate ordains to perish, let him die. But let the rest be from this moment reconciled."

The Greeks and Trojans were happy at the prospect of a speedy end to the long war. And so the combat between the two heroes began. Paris hurled his javelin, but Menelaus warded off the blow with his strong shield. Then Menelaus, praying to Zeus to give him strength, cast his spear. It pierced the shield of Paris and might have made a fatal wound had not he bent sideways and so escaped the full force of the weapon. Instantly Menelaus rushed forward, sword in hand, and dealt a powerful blow to his enemy's head. The blade of the sword broke in pieces. Enraged, he rushed upon Paris and caught him by the helmet and began dragging him toward the army of the Greeks.

The end seemed at hand for Paris. But then Aphrodite, to whom Paris had awarded the golden apple, came to his aid. Standing invisible beside him, she broke the helmet strap from under his chin, thus releasing him from the powerful grasp of Menelaus. Then she cast a thick mist around the Trojan prince and transported him to his own house behind the walls of Troy.

With Paris nowhere to be found, the Greeks claimed victory, and demanded that the Trojans return Helen and her treasures. But on Mount Olympus, the gods argued among themselves whether the war should end here. Athena and Hera—who had been denied the golden apple by Paris—prevailed in their desire that the fighting continue, until such time as the high walls of Troy should tumble to the ground.

And so Athena flew down to earth and whispered a terrible thought into the ear of a Trojan soldier: "Imagine what great honor you will have, what a hero you will be, if you slay the son of Atreus. Let fly one of your sharp arrows and bring down Menelaus!" The soldier drew an arrow from his quiver, aimed, and let fly. The sharp point cut the air and would surely have killed Menelaus, had not Athena deflected it at the last moment, so that it caused only a flesh wound. Athena, after all, was friendly to the Greeks: she did not want to kill one of their heroes, only to rekindle the battle that would bring down Troy.

And so the truce was broken and the war began again. Many warriors showed themselves to be valiant men, but just as many groaning souls fled unwillingly to the realms of the dead, their bodies lying in pools of blood, to become the food of dogs and vultures.

The Arming of Achilles

As the fighting raged on, the tide began to turn against the Greeks. Their greatest heroes were all sorely wounded. Without Achilles, there was no one who could oppose the furious strength of Hector.

One night, Hector called his troops together and spoke: "Men of Troy, take your rest. Loose your horses from their chariots and give them food. Go, some of you, to the city, and fetch cattle, sheep, wine, and bread, that we may have plenty to eat and drink. For tomorrow we arm ourselves and drive these Greeks back to their ships! If the gods are willing, we will burn those ships with fire. We shall surely bring ruin upon these Greeks!" So Hector spoke, and the Trojans shouted with joy to hear such words.

While the Trojans made merry, the Greeks sat in worry and fear. And no one was more worried than Agamemnon. He called his chiefs together and spoke: "I acted as a fool the day that I sent my messengers to take the fair Briseis from Achilles. See how, when Achilles stands aside from battle, we Greeks are put to flight! As I did him wrong, so now will I make amends, and give him many, many times more than what I took from him. Now, three of you go and take my message to Achilles."

The messengers were graciously received by Achilles, who listened to their moving appeals. Then he made his answer. "Long ago," he said, "my mother, Thetis of the sea, said to me 'My son, you have two destinies, and you may choose only one. If you stay in this land and fight against Troy, then you may never go back to your own land, but will die in your youth. Only your name will live forever. But, if you will leave this land and go back to your home, then you shall live long, even to old age, but your name will be forgotten.' Once I thought that fame was a far better thing than life; but now that Agamemnon has shamed me before my people, and taken my fame from me, my mind is changed. So, find some other way to keep Hector and the Trojans from the Greek ships, for I will depart soon."

When the battle resumed the next day, Achilles remained in his tent. At first the Greeks did well, but then the Trojans came on more fiercely than before. Many a Greek hero fell, and the Trojans pressed closer to the ships.

Achilles was approached by that man he held dear above all others, his friend from childhood days, Patroclus. "Patroclus," asked Achilles, "why do you weep?"

"Do not be angry with me, great Achilles," said Patroclus. "The Greeks are in trouble, for all the bravest chiefs are wounded, and yet you sustain your wrath and will not help them. Now, listen: if you will not go forth to the battle, then let me go, and let your Myrmidons go with me. And let me put on your armor, for then the Trojans will think that you have come back to the battle."

So Patroclus spoke, not knowing that he asked for his own death. At first Achilles resisted, but when he saw the first of the Greek ships set afire, he bid Patroclus make haste. And so, clad in the shining armor of Achilles, gift of Zeus, Patroclus went forth, leading the Myrmidons. The Trojans saw the armor and, thinking that Achilles had returned to battle, they turned to flee. Over and over again Patroclus charged into the ranks of the Trojans, slaying many. Then Hector, aided by Apollo, realized, "This man is not Achilles, though he wears his armor."

Suddenly, Apollo struck Patroclus from behind, and he fell stunned to the ground. A Trojan soldier wounded him in the back with a spear. Then Hector arrived and thrust the mortal blow, driving his spear point in just above the hip. "Did you think, Patroclus," shouted Hector, "that you would take our city, and carry away our wives and daughters with your ships? This you will not do, for now the fowls of the air will eat your flesh."

"Mark you, Hector," gasped Patroclus with his dying breath, "death is very near to you, at the hands of the great Achilles."

When Achilles heard the news of the death of his dear friend, he threw himself upon the ground. "Cursed be the anger that sets men to strive with one another, as it made me strive with Agamemnon," he cried out. "As for my fate—what does it matter? Let it come when it may, as long as I may first have vengeance on Hector."

Then Zeus sent a messenger to Achilles, saying, "Rouse yourself, or surely Patroclus will be food for the dogs of Troy. You must hurry if you wish to save his body and give it proper funeral rites."

So Achilles, unarmed, went forth. Athena set about him a radiance that shone like a circle of fire. He shouted aloud, and his voice, trumpet-like, was terrible to hear, striking fear in the hearts of the Trojans, even frightening their horses, which startled and clashed chariots together. The awed Trojans retreated, and the Greeks took up the body of Patroclus, with Achilles, weeping, walking by its side.

Since the armor of Achilles had been captured by the Trojans, Achilles's mother, the sea goddess named Thetis, traveled swiftly to the forge of Hephaestus, the god who worked in gold and silver and iron. At her request, Hephaestus crafted strong and splendid armor, including a great shield upon which he inscribed images of war and peace, life and death, love and hate, work and play. It was as though the wide world were embraced within the rim of the huge, heavy shield.

When next the rosy-fingered Dawn arose, Thetis placed the great armor at the feet of her son. It dazzled the eyes of the Myrmidons, who dared not look directly at it. Only Achilles looked at it, and as he looked the wrath within him burned, and his eyes flared like the sun.

When he was fully armed, Achilles went to Agamemnon, and said, "Let our foolish quarrel end. Here I make an end of my anger. Make haste, and call the Greeks to battle!"

The Death of Hector

When he returned to battle, Achilles was like a wildfire that burns everything in its path, until the trees of the forest fall in flames, and the sides of the mountains are scorched black. In terror the Trojans ran like fawns to take refuge behind the high walls of the city—all except Hector, who waited to meet Achilles in mortal combat.

Hector's father and mother, old King Priam and Queen Hecuba, called out from atop the city walls, begging their son not to fight Achilles. But Hector refused, saying, "It is far better to meet in arms and see whether Zeus will give the victory to him or me."

Then Achilles approached, his armor blazing, and shaking over his shoulder a huge spear. Even brave Hector trembled at the sight, and he turned and ran. As when a hawk in the mountains swoops down upon a trembling dove, so Achilles in fury flew after Hector. Three times around the walls of Troy they ran. Then Athena appeared by the side of Hector, though in the form of one of his brothers. "My brother," she said to Hector, "we two will stand against Achilles." Encouraged by these words, Hector turned and faced Achilles, calling out: "Three times you have pursued me round these walls, but now I will stand and face you. Only let us agree: if Zeus gives me the victory today, I will give back your body to the Greeks; if you should be the victor, promise to do the same with me."

Achilles scowled. "Hector," he said, "lions do not make agreements with men, nor wolves with lambs." Then he threw his great spear, which Hector barely avoided. "You have missed!" cried Hector. "Now see whether my aim is true." And with all his strength he hurled his spear at Achilles. It struck full force upon the great shield, and bounced off. "Give me your spear, brother!" cried Hector—only to turn and find no one there. Then he knew his fate: "The gods have decreed my doom. But let me not die without a struggle. Let me do some great thing that men will remember in years to come."

So Hector drew his sword and charged at Achilles. Achilles ran at Hector, seeking the most vulnerable spot, not protected by strong armor. He found it where the neck meets the collarbone, and there he drove his spear deep through the soft part of the neck.

Dying, Hector gasped, "O Achilles, I entreat you, do not make my body food for dogs, but give it to my father and mother that they may duly bury it. They will reward you with silver and gold."

The gods, pitying Hector, kept his dead body from harm.

"No amount of gold will buy you back," said Achilles. "Now, cur, die!" To shame the dead Hector, Achilles stripped him of his armor, then bent down and cut holes in the space between the ankles and heels. Through these holes he drew cords of ox-hide, then fastened the cords to his chariot, and so dragged Hector's dead body back to the Greek ships. For the next few days, in his fury, Achilles caused the dead body to be dragged about the tomb of his fallen friend, Patroclus. Yet the gods took pity on Hector, and kept his dead body from harm.

It was, furthermore, the will of the gods that Hector's body should be returned to Troy. So the gods helped old Priam make his way safely to Achilles. When he entered Achilles's tent, Priam, great King Priam, threw himself at Achilles's feet and kissed his hands, saying, "Achilles, take pity; I kiss the hands of the man who has killed my children."

Achilles was moved, remembering his own father, and his fallen friend, Patroclus. He called upon two servants to wash and anoint the body of Hector. This done, he went out to the wagon full of treasures brought by Priam. He accepted the treasures but left one cloak to cover Hector's body, which he now lifted into the wagon.

When Achilles returned to his tent, Priam asked, "Let there be a truce for nine days between the Greeks and Trojans, that we may bury Hector with all due ceremony."

"It shall be as you ask," replied Achilles. Then he took the aged king by the hand, and led him to a place of rest. The next day Priam returned to Troy, and so began the splendid funeral for Hector, fallen son of the city whose high walls would soon fall.

Epilogue to the *Iliad*

Homer's *Iliad* ends with the funeral of Hector. Other accounts tell us of the fate of Achilles, and the end of the Trojan War.

The Fate of Achilles: After the funeral of Hector, fighting resumed. Achilles killed many Trojans, but he was himself slain by Paris. Paris was no match for Achilles in single combat, but he was a skilled archer. He shot Achilles in the one place he could be hurt, his heel. Except for his heel, Achilles was invulnerable. When Achilles was a baby, his mother had dipped him into the river Styx, the magical waters of which protected his body from injury. But in dipping him, Thetis had held the infant by his heel, so his heel was unprotected. Even today, we speak of a person's "Achilles' heel," meaning a person's one great weakness.

The Trojan Horse: Troy fell because of a clever plan on the part of the Greeks, devised by the wily Odysseus. The Greeks built an enormous, hollow horse out of wood. They left it outside the walls of the city, and then pretended to sail away, though they went no farther than a nearby island. Inside, however, were hidden some of the bravest Greek warriors.

When the Trojans saw the huge wooden horse, some were suspicious, but most thought it was an offering to the gods, so they hauled it within the walls of the city. That night, the Greek warriors crept out of the horse and opened the gates of the city to the other soldiers, who had returned under cover of darkness. The Greeks set fire to Troy, and conquered the great city at last.

The story of the fall of Troy is told in moving detail in an epic poem called *The Aeneid*, written by Virgil, a great Roman poet who lived in the first century B.C.

The Odyssey

Background to the *Odyssey*

Homer's *Odyssey* is an epic poem about the adventures of a Greek hero, Odysseus, as he made his difficult journey home after the Trojan War. You might also hear Odysseus sometimes referred to as Ulysses, which is the name given to him by the Romans, who were great admirers of Homer and the rest of Greek culture.

Odysseus was famous for his intelligence, ingenuity, and resourcefulness—fitting qualities for a hero favored most of all by Athena, goddess of wisdom. You can see his cleverness in the scheme he hatched to try to avoid going to fight at Troy in the first place.

According to some accounts, Odysseus was unwilling to go to Troy because he didn't want to leave behind his month-old son, Telemachus, and his loving wife,

Penelope. So, when a messenger from King Agamemnon arrived to call Odysseus to war, Odysseus pretended to be mad. He hitched a plow and took it down to the beach, where, instead of sowing seeds, he planted salt in the sand. The messenger was almost convinced that Odysseus was mad, but then, to test him, the messenger took the infant son, Telemachus, and placed him in the path of the plow. Odysseus quickly turned the plow away from his son, thus showing he was not mad. So he was obliged to respond to the summons from Agamemnon and join the other Greek kings and their armies in the campaign against Troy.

After the ten long years of the Trojan War, Odysseus looked forward to a speedy voyage home. But it was not to be: it took Odysseus another ten years before he reached his native island, Ithaca. Through the will of the gods, and sometimes through mistakes of his own or his crew, Odysseus wandered far and wide before returning home.

His wanderings took him to the island of Circe, a beautiful sorceress who turned men into swine; to Hades, the realm of the dead, where he spoke with the sad shade of Achilles; between Scylla, a six-headed monster, and Charybdis, a devouring whirlpool; and, past the Sirens, maidens who sang alluring songs that drew sailors to their deaths.

As Homer tells it, the *Odyssey* is not only the story of the wanderings of Odysseus, but also of the voyages of his son, Telemachus, who goes in search of Odysseus, and during his travels hears many tales of the adventures of his famous father.

Here we present one episode from the *Odyssey*, the story of Odysseus and the Cyclops, which reveals the great cleverness of the hero. You can read about Odysseus's other adventures in one of the fine versions of the *Odyssey* written for young readers, including:

The Children's Homer by Padraic Colum (Macmillan, 1982).

The Adventures of Ulysses by Bernard Evslin (Scholastic, 1989).

The Legend of Odysseus by Peter Connolly (Oxford, 1986).

The complete *Odyssey* is available in many accessible translations, including (in prose) those by W. H. D. Rouse and E. V. Rieu, and (in poetry) a vigorous rendering by Robert Fitzgerald.

Odysseus and the Cyclops

Sing in me, Muse, the story of the man resourceful beyond all others, the wanderer, who met with woes unnumbered, after raiding the ramparts of the strong city of Troy.

This was Odysseus, king of Ithaca, one of the Greek chieftains who fought at Troy. They fought for ten years until, after the fair Helen had been retrieved, the great city was at last destroyed, and Greek ships, filled with plunder, set sail for home.

When Troy had been taken, Odysseus set sail for the island of Ithaca in twelve ships with fifty good crewmen in each. Little did these mariners think that it would be ten years before any saw their home. Nor did they know that by their own recklessness, and despite the brave efforts of their king to save them, only one—Odysseus himself—would return.

Not long into their journey, a great storm fell upon the ships and carried them far to the south, past their island home. Late one evening, in a dense fog, the ships' keels grazed the shore of an island. Odysseus and his crew beached the ships, then slept through the night. When the rosy fingers of Dawn touched the sky, they woke and found fresh water, as well as numbers of wild goats, which made a fine feast for the hungry sailors.

Nearby was another island. Odysseus and his men could see wisps of smoke rising from it, and heard the bleating of flocks. "Friends and shipmates," announced Odysseus, "in my own ship, with my own crew, I will make the crossing to that island, and find out who lives there, and whether they be good people or lawless savages."

Odysseus thought to bring some food, as well as a big goatskin full of strong, sweet wine, a gift from a priest of Apollo. There never was a more precious wine: one measure of it could be mixed with twenty measures of water, and still it would remain wonderfully sweet and potent.

Upon reaching the island, Odysseus picked twelve of his bravest men. They set off and soon found a huge cave, apparently the home of some shepherd, since many rams and goats were walking about. The men looked inside and saw pens full of young sheep and goats, baskets full of cheeses, and milk pans stacked against the walls. "Let us take these cheeses," cried the men, "and open the pens and drive the goats and lambs aboard our ships, then head back out to sea."

Odysseus knew this was good advice. But he wanted to see what kind of man this shepherd might be. So the men built a fire, helped themselves to some cheese, and sat down to wait.

As evening neared, they were startled by a loud *crash*! It was the sound of a huge bundle of logs dropped into the cave from the shoulder of a great giant, one of those creatures called Cyclops. He was a brutish man, with only one large eye in the middle of his forehead, and one shaggy eyebrow above it.

Odysseus and his frightened men scrambled to the back of the cave. The Cyclops drove his flocks into the cave, then closed the entrance with a boulder so big that twenty wagons could not carry it. He milked the ewes and she-goats, setting aside half the milk to curdle for cheese, and half for his own supper. He threw some logs on the fire and stirred up a great flame, the glare from which revealed Odysseus and his men.

"Who are you?" said the giant, his voice a deep rumble. "Are you men of the sea—traders or pirates?"

Odysseus replied, "We are Greeks, sailing home from Troy, where we have been fighting for King Agamemnon, whose fame is known far and wide. We are homeward bound, but great gales have blown us off course. Now, as the gods love those who show hospitality to strangers, we ask you to be hospitable to us."

"The gods!" roared the Cyclops. "We Cyclops care not for the gods. We are greater and stronger than your Zeus with all his thunder. Now, tell me, puny one—where have you left your ship?"

Odysseus knew that, if he revealed the location of the ship, the Cyclops would crush it to splinters and leave them no hope of escaping. So with his quick and ready mind, he answered, "We have no ship, for our ship was driven upon the rocks and broken. My men and I are the only survivors."

The giant said nothing, but quickly grabbed two of the men, as a man might pick up two squirming puppies. He dashed them on the ground, then tore them limb from limb. Like a mountain lion gnawing and crunching a fresh kill, he devoured them entirely—flesh, bones, organs, everything—and washed it all down with great swallows of milk. And when he had filled himself with this awful food, he lay down among his sheep and slept.

Odysseus drew his sharp sword and rushed to the giant's side, preparing to stab him to the heart, when he stopped: "If I kill him," he thought, "then I condemn myself and my men as well, for we could never move that great boulder from the doorway." So, sad at heart, he waited, thinking.

When morning came, the giant awoke, milked his flocks, then seized two of the men and devoured them as before. He opened the cave and went forth with his flocks to the pastures, though before leaving he placed the great boulder over the entrance.

All day Odysseus thought of how he might save himself and his companions. He noticed a great pole in the cave, the trunk of an olive tree, which the giant planned to use as a walking staff. Odysseus cut off a six-foot section and sharpened one end, then turned the pointed end in the fire to harden it.

In the evening, the Cyclops returned, and once again seized two prisoners and feasted on them. Then Odysseus stepped forth, holding in his hands a bowl filled with wine from the wineskin he had brought, full of the powerful and tempting drink. "Drink, Cyclops," said Odysseus. "Wash down your scraps of flesh. I had meant to offer this to you as a gift if you would help us home."

The Cyclops greedily swallowed all that was in the bowl. "Give me more," he commanded, "and tell me your name. Then I will make you a gift as a proper host should."

Then wily Odysseus said, "My name is No-Man. Now, give me your gift."

"My gift," laughed the giant, "is that you shall be eaten last." Saying this, he toppled over in a drunken sleep. Drops of wine and bits of human flesh dribbled out of his mouth.

"Come, my brave friends," said Odysseus. They grabbed the sharpened stake and heated the point in the fire till it glowed red. Then, running at top speed, they thrust it into the giant's single eye, and leaned with full force, twisting and turning the stake as a man turns a drill. The burning wood hissed in the eye as a red-hot iron hisses when dipped in water.

The Cyclops roared and thrashed out. Odysseus and his men fell back in fear. Blood spurted as the Cyclops tore the hot stake from his eye. He roared so loudly that other Cyclops came running from their nearby caves to see what had happened. From outside they called out, "Polyphemos!"—for that was this giant's name—"Polyphemos, what's wrong? Why do you cry out? Is someone stealing your sheep or hurting you?"

The giant bellowed, "No-Man! No-Man has hurt me! No-Man!"

"Well," replied the other Cyclops, "if no man is hurting you, then it must be yourself or the gods, and we can do nothing about that." And they returned to their caves.

Groaning, the Cyclops groped till he grabbed the boulder blocking the entrance to the cave. He removed the boulder then sat down in the entrance, feeling around him to grab any of his prisoners that should try to escape. Odysseus could see that there was still no easy way out. So, he called upon all his wits to devise yet another plan.

He took strips of willow from the giant's bed. With these he tied together three rams, side by side, then bound a man under the belly of the middle ram. He did this for all six of his remaining men. Then he found the largest, woolliest ram and pulled himself tight under his belly, gripping the fleece as tightly as he could.

When morning came, the Cyclops, as was his habit, let his flocks out to graze. He stroked each ram but did not feel the men hiding beneath. When he felt the biggest ram, however, he stopped it and spoke: "What is this, my sweet creature? You never lag behind, but are always first out of the cave in the morning. What now keeps you back?" Odysseus remained as silent and still as possible. "Could it be," continued Cyclops, his huge fingers rubbing the ram's fleece, "that you are sad for your poor master's eye, which that villain No-Man has destroyed? I swear he will not get out alive! If only you could speak and tell me where he is—I would splatter his brains upon the ground!" Then, with a sigh, he let the ram proceed.

Once outside, Odysseus released his grip and ran to untie his companions. They rounded up as many of the giant's sheep as they could, then hurried back to their ship. Their worried companions welcomed them, but were saddened to see that six men were missing. "Quiet yourselves," said Odysseus, "I will explain. For now, row with all your might!"

When they were far from shore, Odysseus could not resist shouting back, "O Cyclops! You beast who feeds on men! How do you like what No-Man has done to you? May the gods punish you even more!"

The Cyclops heard Odysseus and was angered. He broke off a hilltop and heaved it in the direction from which he had heard Odysseus's voice. It struck just in front of the ship and caused a great wave, pushing the ship all the way back to the shore! "Row, men, row or die!" urged Odysseus. So they rowed, and when they were twice as far out as before, Odysseus again stood up and cupped his hands to shout. His men exclaimed, "Captain, stop! For the love of Zeus, don't make the brute angry! He'll smash us to bits!"

But Odysseus, enraged, cried out again: "Listen, Cyclops! If any man asks you who put out your eye, then tell them truthfully that it was I, Odysseus of Ithaca!"

The giant took up another huge rock and threw it. This time it struck just behind the ship and propelled the craft farther away. The blind giant dropped heavily upon the ground and sobbed. "So, my fate has come," he groaned. "Long ago, a wizard on this island predicted that I would lose my eye at the hands of Odysseus. But I always thought Odysseus would be some giant, powerful and armed—not a puny, scrawny thing."

Then the Cyclops rose and, turning his blind eye to the heavens, prayed to his father, Poseidon, god of the sea: "Hear me, father! Grant this one request: may Odysseus of Ithaca never reach home! Let him lose all his companions, and taste bitterness in days to come."

Poseidon, who rules the seas, heard this request and granted it. He turned his rage upon Odysseus, sending storms, shipwrecks, and disaster at every turn, forcing Odysseus to wander for ten years before returning home.

Chief Joseph's "I will fight no more forever"

In 1863, a group of Tsutpeli (Nez Percé) Indians refused to follow the agreement that some of their chiefs had signed with the United States Government. They wished to remain on the land where their people had lived for centuries; they did not want to move to a reservation and lose their homeland to the white settlers. Among those who resisted was the Wallowa band of Oregon.

In 1877 the army tried to force the Wallowa band onto the reservation. Although their leader, Chief Joseph, did not like war, he fought with his band against the U.S. troops. They fought well, but when his people began to die of hunger and cold, Chief Joseph decided to lead them to safety in Canada. Just thirty miles from the border, they were captured by U.S. troops and forced to surrender. This is the message that Chief Joseph sent to the U.S. troops.

Tell General Howard I know his heart. What he told me before, I have it in my heart. I am tired of fighting. Our chiefs are killed. Looking Glass is dead. Toohool-

hoozote is dead. The old men are all dead. It is the young men who say "yes" or "no." He who led the young men is dead. It is cold, and we have no blankets. The little children are freezing to death. My people, some of them, have run away to the hills, and have no blankets, no food. No one knows where they are—perhaps freezing to death. I want to have time to look for my children, and see how many of them I can find. Maybe I shall find them among the dead. Hear me, my chiefs! I am tired. My heart is sick and sad. From where the sun now stands I will fight no more forever.

Chief Joseph of the Nez Percé Indians.

Abraham Lincoln's Gettysburg Address

Our sixteenth president, Abraham Lincoln, was largely self-educated. The books he read, particularly the King James version of the Bible, gave him a sense of the power and beauty of the English language. In his great speeches, Lincoln used hard words, but they are no harder than the words he figured out on his own when he was a young child reading the Bible.

The speech you can read here in its entirety is Lincoln's most famous one. He gave it at the dedication of a cemetery during the Civil War, after a battle at Gettysburg, Pennsylvania. The story of this battle is told in the American Civilization section of this book.

Fourscore and seven years ago, our fathers brought forth upon this continent a new nation, conceived in liberty, and dedicated to the proposition that all men are created equal.

Now we are engaged in a great civil war, testing whether that nation, or any nation so conceived and so dedicated, can long endure. We are met on a great battlefield of that war. We have come to dedicate a portion of that field as a final resting place for those who here gave their lives that that nation might live. It is altogether fitting and proper that we should do this.

But in a larger sense we cannot dedicate—we cannot consecrate—we cannot hallow—this ground. The brave men, living and dead, who struggled here, have consecrated it far above our poor power to add or detract. The world will little note, nor long remember, what we say here, but it can never forget what they did here. It is for us, the living, rather to be dedicated here to the unfinished work which they

Lincoln addresses the crowd at Gettysburg.

who fought here have thus far so nobly advanced. It is rather for us to be here dedicated to the great task remaining before us—that from these honored dead we take increased devotion to that cause for which they gave the last full measure of devotion; that we here highly resolve that these dead shall not have died in vain; that this nation, under God, shall have a new birth of freedom, and that government of the people, by the people, for the people, shall not perish from the earth.

Introduction to Poetry

FOR PARENTS AND TEACHERS

In this book, we continue to offer a selection of poems, many of which use strong rhythm and rhyme as well as engaging narratives, on the premise that children delight in the music and fun of the spoken language. With this in mind, the best way to bring children into the spirit of poetry is to read it to them and encourage them to speak it aloud so they can experience the sounds of language directly.

Poetry is also a way for children to begin to experience the power of language to create vivid word pictures. We have included several selections that are notable for their marvelous imagery. With these poems, children can begin to enjoy the play between literal and figurative language.

A child's knowledge of poetry should come first from pleasure and only later from analysis. But certain basic concepts—like imagery and alliteration—can help parents and children, or students and teachers, talk about particular effects that enliven the poems they like best. Adults and children may want to read the Learning about Literature section of this book in conjunction with the poetry in this section and, when appropriate, discuss poetic effects.

A Few Poems for Fifth Grade

The Living World

Fog

by Carl Sandburg

The fog comes
on little cat feet.
It sits looking
over harbor and city
on silent haunches
and then moves on.

A Bird Came Down the Walk

by Emily Dickinson

A bird came down the walk:
He did not know I saw;
He bit an angle-worm in halves
And ate the fellow, raw.

And then he drank a dew
From a convenient grass,
And then hopped sideways to the wall
To let a beetle pass.

He glanced with rapid eyes
That hurried all abroad—
They looked like frightened beads, I thought;
He stirred his velvet head

Like one in danger; cautious,
I offered him a crumb,
And he unrolled his feathers
And rowed him softer home

Then oars divide the ocean,
Too silver for a seam,
Or butterflies, off banks of noon,
Leap, plashless, as they swim.

Trees

by Sergeant Joyce Kilmer

I think that I shall never see
A poem lovely as a tree.

A tree whose hungry mouth is prest
Against the earth's sweet flowing breast;

A tree that looks at God all day,
And lifts her leafy arms to pray;

A tree that may in Summer wear
A nest of robins in her hair;

Upon whose bosom snow has lain;
Who intimately lives with rain.

Poems are made by fools like me,
But only God can make a tree.

The Tiger
by William Blake

Tiger! Tiger! burning bright
In the forests of the night,
What immortal hand or eye
Could frame thy fearful symmetry?

In what distant deeps or skies
Burnt the fire of thine eyes?
On what wings dare he aspire?
What the hand dare seize the fire?

And what shoulder, and what art,
Could twist the sinews of thy heart?
And when thy heart began to beat,
What dread hand and what dread feet?

What the hammer? what the chain?
In what furnace was thy brain?
What the anvil? what dread grasp
Dare its deadly terrors clasp?

When the stars threw down their spears
And watered heaven with their tears,
Did he smile his work to see?
Did he who made the lamb make thee?

Tiger! Tiger! burning bright
In the forests of the night,
What immortal hand or eye,
Dare frame thy fearful symmetry?

A Wise Old Owl
by Edward Hersey Richards

A wise old owl sat on an oak,
The more he saw the less he spoke;
The less he spoke the more he heard;
Why aren't we like that wise old bird?

The Eagle
by Alfred, Lord Tennyson

He clasps the crag with crooked hands:
Close to the sun in lonely lands,
Ringed with the azure world, he stands.

The wrinkled sea beneath him crawls;
He watches from his mountain walls,
And like a thunderbolt he falls.

Humor

Casey at the Bat
by Ernest Lawrence Thayer

The outlook wasn't brilliant for the Mudville nine that day;
The score stood four to two with but one inning more to play.
And then when Cooney died at first and Barrows did the same,
A sickly silence fell upon the patrons of the game.

A straggling few got up to go in deep despair. The rest
Clung to the hope which springs eternal in the human breast;
They thought if only Casey could but get a whack at that—
We'd put up even money now with Casey at the bat.

But Flynn preceded Casey, as did also Jimmy Blake,
And the former was a lulu and the latter was a cake;
So upon that stricken multitude grim melancholy sat,
For there seemed but little chance of Casey's getting to the bat.

But Flynn let drive a single, to the wonderment of all,
And Blake, the much despised, tore the cover off the ball;
And when the dust had lifted, and the men saw what had occurred,
There was Jimmy safe at second and Flynn a-hugging third.

Then from five thousand throats and more there rose a lusty yell;
It rumbled through the valley, it rattled in the dell;
It knocked upon the mountain and recoiled upon the flat,
For Casey, mighty Casey, was advancing to the bat.

There was ease in Casey's manner as he stepped into his place;
There was pride in Casey's bearing and a smile on Casey's face.
And when, responding to the cheers, he lightly doffed his hat,
No stranger in the crowd would doubt 'twas Casey at the bat.

Ten thousand eyes were on him as he rubbed his hands with dirt;
Five thousand tongues applauded when he wiped them on his shirt.
Then while the writhing pitcher ground the ball into his hip,
Defiance gleamed in Casey's eye, a sneer curled Casey's lip.

And now the leather-covered sphere came hurtling through the air,
And Casey stood a-watching it in haughty grandeur there.
Close by the sturdy batsman the ball unheeded sped—
"That ain't my style," said Casey. "Strike one," the umpire said.

From the benches, black with people, there went up a muffled roar,
Like the beating of the storm waves on a stern and distant shore.
"Kill him! Kill the umpire!" shouted someone on the stand;
And it's likely they'd have killed him had not Casey raised his hand.

With a smile of Christian charity Casey's visage shone;
He stilled the rising tumult; he bade the game go on;
He signaled to the pitcher, and once more the spheroid flew;
But Casey still ignored it, and the umpire said, "Strike two."

"Fraud!" cried the maddened thousands, and echo answered, "Fraud!"
But one scornful look from Casey and the audience was awed.
They saw his face grow stern and cold, they saw his muscles strain,
And they knew that Casey wouldn't let that ball go by again.

The sneer is gone from Casey's lip, his teeth are clenched in hate;
He pounds with cruel violence his bat upon the plate.
And now the pitcher holds the ball, and now he lets it go,
And now the air is shattered by the force of Casey's blow.

Oh, somewhere in this favored land the sun is shining bright;
The band is playing somewhere, and somewhere hearts are light,
And somewhere men are laughing, and somewhere children shout;
But there is no joy in Mudville—mighty Casey has struck out.

Jabberwocky
by Lewis Carroll

If this poem seems odd to you, well, that's the way it struck Alice, too. You remember Alice from Alice in Wonderland, *don't you? To learn more about the Jabberwock, you can read* Through the Looking Glass *by Lewis Carroll. See the chapter called "Humpty Dumpty."*

'Twas brillig, and the slithy toves
    Did gyre and gimble in the wabe:
All mimsy were the borogoves
    And the mome raths outgrabe.

"Beware the Jabberwock, my son!
    The jaws that bite, the claws that catch!
Beware the Jubjub bird, and shun
    The frumious Bandersnatch!"

He took his vorpal sword in hand:
    Long time the manxome foe he sought—
So rested he by the Tumtum tree,
    And stood awhile in thought.

And, as in uffish thought he stood,
    The Jabberwock, with eyes of flame,
Came whiffling through the tulgey wood,
    And burbled as it came!

One, two! One, two! And through and through
    The vorpal blade went snicker-snack!
He left it dead, and with its head
    He went galumphing back.

"And hast thou slain the Jabberwock?
    Come to my arms, my beamish boy!
O frabjous day! Callooh! Callay!"
    He chortled in his joy.

'Twas brillig, and the slithy toves
    Did gyre and gimble in the wabe:
All mimsy were the borogoves,
    And the mome raths outgrabe.

American Themes

Battle Hymn of the Republic
by Julia Ward Howe

Julia Ward Howe, a reformer, writer, and lecturer, wrote this anthem at the height of the Civil War. It immediately became a popular marching song for the Union troops. But you can see from its title and final lines that Mrs. Howe meant it as a plea to end slavery, a plea "to make men free."

Mine eyes have seen the glory of the coming of the Lord:
He is trampling out the vintage where the grapes of wrath are stored;
He hath loosed the fateful lightning of His terrible swift sword:
      His truth is marching on.

I have seen Him in the watch-fires of a hundred circling camps:
They have builded Him an altar in the evening dews and damps;
I can read His righteous sentence by the dim and flaring lamps.
      His day is marching on.

He has sounded forth the trumpet that shall never call retreat;
He is sifting out the hearts of men before his judgment-seat;
Oh! be swift, my soul, to answer Him! be jubilant, my feet!
      Our God is marching on.

In the beauty of the lilies Christ was born across the sea,
With a glory in his bosom that transfigures you and me:
As He died to make men holy, let us die to make men free,
      While God is marching on.

Ballad of John Henry
by Useni Eugene Perkins

John Henry was born
With a hammer in his hand
And no one in Alabama
Could really understand

    Hold your hammer, John Henry
    Hold your hammer, John Henry

At five years of age
He was strong as an ox
Could work all day
And never once stop

> Lift your hammer, John Henry
> Lift your hammer, John Henry

When he reached the age of ten
He could out-hammer any man
And never went anyplace
Without his hammer in his hand

> Hit the steel, John Henry
> Hit the steel, John Henry

He yearned to work on the railroad
So he could hammer steel
Nothing else mattered to him
Cause he had a strong will

> Hammer away, John Henry
> Hammer away, John Henry

And when he got the chance
To show what he could do
There wasn't a man around
That could hammer so hard and true

> Don't give up, John Henry
> Don't give up, John Henry

But one day he was challenged
To out-hammer a machine
And though he did his best
He finally ran out of steam

> The machine done won, John Henry
> The machine done won, John Henry

And so John Henry died
Driving steel in the ground
But no one will deny
He was the best driver in town

> You'll always be remembered, John Henry
> You'll always be remembered, John Henry

O Captain! My Captain!
by Walt Whitman

(This poem was written shortly after the assassination of President Abraham Lincoln.)

O Captain! my Captain! our fearful trip is done,
The ship has weather'd every rack, the prize we sought is won,
The port is near, the bells I hear, the people all exulting,
While follow eyes the steady keel, the vessel grim and daring;
    But O heart! heart! heart!
        O the bleeding drops of red,
            Where on the deck my Captain lies,
                Fallen cold and dead.

O Captain! my Captain! rise up and hear the bells;
Rise up—for you the flag is flung—for you the bugle trills,
For you bouquets and ribbon'd wreaths—for you the shores a-crowding,
For you they call, the swaying mass, their eager faces turning:
    Here Captain! dear father!
        This arm beneath your head!
            It is some dream that on the deck,
                You've fallen cold and dead.

My Captain does not answer, his lips are pale and still,
My father does not feel my arm, he has no pulse nor will,
The ship is anchor'd safe and sound, its voyage closed and done,
From fearful trip the victor ship comes in with object won;
    Exult O shores, and ring O bells!
        But I with mournful tread,
            Walk the deck my Captain lies,
                Fallen cold and dead.

I Hear America Singing
by Walt Whitman

I hear America singing, the varied carols I hear,
Those of mechanics, each one singing his as it should be blithe
    and strong,
The carpenter singing his as he measures his plank or beam,
The mason singing his as he makes ready for work,
    or leaves off work,

The boatman singing what belongs to him in his boat,
    the deckhand singing on the steamboat deck,
The shoemaker singing as he sits on his bench,
    the hatter singing as he stands,
The wood-cutter's song, the ploughboy's on his way
    in the morning, or at noon intermission or at sundown,
The delicious singing of the mother, or of the young wife
    at work, or of the girl sewing or washing,
Each singing what belongs to him or her and to none else,
The day what belongs to the day—at night
    the party of young fellows, robust, friendly,
Singing with open mouths their strong melodious songs.

I, Too

by Langston Hughes

I, too, sing America.

I am the darker brother.
They send me to eat in the kitchen
When company comes,
But I laugh,
And eat well,
And grow strong.

Tomorrow,
I'll be at the table
When company comes.
Nobody'll dare
Say to me,
"Eat in the kitchen,"
Then.

Besides,
They'll see how beautiful I am
And be ashamed—

I, too, am America.

Feelings and Ideas

Narcissa
by Gwendolyn Brooks

Some of the girls are playing jacks.
Some are playing ball.
But small Narcissa is not playing
Anything at all.

Small Narcissa sits upon
A brick in her back yard
And looks at tiger-lilies,
And shakes her pigtails hard.

First she is an ancient queen
In pomp and purple veil.
Soon she is a singing wind.
And, next, a nightingale.

How fine to be Narcissa,
A-changing like all that!
While sitting still, as still, as still,
As anyone ever sat!

The Arrow and the Song
by Henry Wadsworth Longfellow

I shot an arrow into the air,
It fell to earth, I knew not where;
For, so swiftly it flew, the sight
Could not follow it in its flight.

I breathed a song into the air,
It fell to earth, I knew not where;
For who has sight so keen and strong
That it can follow the flight of song?

Long, long afterward, in an oak
I found the arrow, still unbroke;
And the song, from beginning to end,
I found again in the heart of a friend.

Incident

by Countee Cullen

Once riding in old Baltimore,
    Heart-filled, head-filled with glee,
I saw a Baltimorean
    Keep looking straight at me.

Now I was eight and very small,
    And he was no whit bigger,
And so I smiled, but he poked out
    His tongue, and called me, "Nigger."

I saw the whole of Baltimore
    From May until December;
Of all the things that happened there
    That's all that I remember.

Some Opposites

by Richard Wilbur

What is the opposite of *riot*?
It's *lots of people keeping quiet.*

The opposite of *doughnut*? Wait
A minute while I meditate.
This isn't easy. Ah, I've found it!
A cookie with a hole around it.

What is the opposite of *two*?
A lonely me, a lonely you.

The opposite of a *cloud* could be
A white reflection in the sea,
Or *a huge blueness in the air,*
Caused by a cloud's not being there.

The opposite of *opposite*?
That's much too difficult. I quit.

Introduction to Language and Literature

FOR PARENTS AND TEACHERS

Children delight in stories and in the sounds of language. It is important that this joy in the spoken and written word not be stifled by too heavy an emphasis on analysis. By fifth grade, however, children are ready to begin learning about the parts of prose and poetry in more depth. Such knowledge will enhance their enjoyment. In this book, we have included an introduction to several basic kinds of literature, and to figurative language. We suggest that these topics be read along with the appropriate selections in the Stories and Speeches section of this book and the Poetry section so that children early on learn the excitement of thinking with greater precision about different kinds of writing.

In Book Four of this series, children learned how to look up information about favorite topics or for homework by using a bibliography. They can continue to practice researching topics for essays, and may also learn how to revise and improve their writing throughout their fifth-grade year.

Experts say that our children already know more about the grammar of language than we can ever teach them. But standard spoken and written language does have special characteristics that need to be discussed with children. As with other parts of this book, the account of language conventions for fifth grade is a summary. It needs to be complemented by giving the child opportunities to read and write and to discuss reading and writing in connection with grammar and spelling.

In the classroom, grammar instruction is an essential part—but only a part—of an effective language arts program. In the fifth grade, children should continue to work on vocabulary and spelling. They should enjoy a rich diet of fiction and nonfiction, poetry, drama, and biography. They should regularly be involved in the writing process: inventing topics, discovering ideas in early drafts, and revising toward polished finished drafts—all with encouragement and guidance along the way. They should practice writing often and in many forms: stories, poetry, journal entries, formal reports, dialogues, and descriptions.

Writing often is one key to writing well. Another is not to discourage children by too severe an emphasis on correctness. Still, we do our children no service if we fail to give them some knowledge of the conventions they are expected to follow in most public discourses. Children will become good writers when they know both the magic and the rules and regulations of written language.

Learning About Language

Direct Objects

Every sentence needs a subject and a verb to be complete. "John ate" is a complete sentence. But as sentences get more complicated, they use more words in different ways. Sometimes a word may function as a direct object. For example, in the sentence "John ate *popcorn*," "popcorn" is the direct object of the verb "ate." A direct object is a noun or pronoun that the verb *does* something to. It is the object of the verb. It is called a direct object because the verb acts directly on it.

Jim threw the *ball* to first base.
During the Renaissance, Michelangelo painted the *ceiling*
  of the Sistine Chapel.
Harriet Tubman led many *slaves* to freedom.

To find a direct object in a sentence, first find the subject and the verb. Then ask yourself "Who?" or "What?" the verb is acting on. For the first sentence above, you could ask, "Jim threw what?" and the answer would be the direct object, "ball."

Indirect Objects

Sometimes, when a sentence has a direct object, it can also have an indirect object. The indirect object answers the question, "To whom?" or "To what?" An indirect object is the person or thing that receives the direct object from the subject.

Jim threw Tina the ball.

In the above sentence, "ball" is the direct object and "Tina," who received the ball, is the indirect object. "Tina" is the answer to the question, "Jim threw the ball to whom?" Here's another example. If you had lived in 1920, you might have awakened to the headline

THE NINETEENTH AMENDMENT GIVES WOMEN THE VOTE!

To find the indirect object in this sentence, remember to find the direct object of the verb first. You would ask "gives what?" and the answer would be "the vote." And then you would ask, "gives the vote to whom?" The answer would be "women." So "vote" is the direct object and "women" is the indirect object of the sentence. Do you see how we don't use the "to" with an indirect object, even though "to" may be understood? Notice the difference between

> John threw Tina the ball.
>
> and
>
> John threw the ball to Tina.

The meaning is the same in both sentences, but the first sentence uses "Tina" as an indirect object while the second sentence uses the phrase "to Tina." In the second sentence, "to Tina" is called a prepositional phrase that uses the preposition "to." So, in your search for indirect objects, be careful to distinguish between indirect objects and phrases with "to." Compare the following sentences:

> The Nineteenth Amendment gives women the vote!
>
> The Nineteenth Amendment gives the vote to women!

In the second sentence, "women" is the object of the preposition "to," not an indirect object.

Now You Try

Find the direct object and the indirect object in the following sentences.

> Magellan handed the sailor the spyglass and smiled.
>
> Sancho Panza handed Don Quixote a book.

Linking Verbs

Hurray for linking verbs!

Linking verbs do not have objects. They don't do anything like "throw" or "send" or "fix." Rather, they tell us something about the subject itself.

> John *feels* awful.
> The baby *smells* good after her bath.
> You *seem* sad.
> I *turned* eleven today.
> The food *tastes* nice.

Notice how these verbs point back to the subject rather than forward to an object. And that's why they're called linking verbs—because they link or join the subject with another word in the sentence that reflects back on the subject, as in "Cake tastes sweet."

Sometimes the very same verb can be used in one sentence as an action verb that takes an object, and in another sentence as a linking verb. Whether the verb is a linking verb or action verb depends on whether it does something or whether it points back to the subject.

Linking Verbs	Action Verbs
John *feels* awful.	John *feels* the cat's fur.
The baby *smells* nice after her bath.	The baby *smells* the flower.
I *turned* eleven today.	I *turned* the wheel.
The food *tastes* good.	He *tastes* the food.

Some verbs are always linking verbs and never take an object, for example, to *be*, to *seem*, to *become*. They always refer back to the subject; they never "push" or "throw" or in any way act upon things.

Can you find the subjects, the linking verbs, and the words that reflect back on the subject in these sentences?

The wind sounded eerie, like an old person crying.
"She is nice," Ms. Hernandez answered.
I feel so sleepy.

One way to test for a linking verb is to flip a sentence around. If you flip "The ice was cold" to "Cold was the ice," the sentence expresses the same thought. So you know that "was" is a linking verb that links the subject, "ice," to the word that reflects back on it, "cold." You can flip "The biscuits tasted sour" to "Sour tasted the biscuits." But could you flip "Jo tasted the biscuits" to "The biscuits tasted Jo"?

Personal Pronouns

There are several kinds of pronouns. The kind we use most often is the personal pronoun, the pronoun that can replace the name of a person or thing in a sentence:

When Louis Armstrong played *his* trumpet, *he* moved people's hearts with *his* music.

If you put Louis Armstrong's name in place of all the underlined words in the sentence above, you'll see how using personal pronouns makes our sentences shorter and less cumbersome.

When Louis Armstrong played Louis Armstrong's trumpet, Louis Armstrong moved people's hearts with Louis Armstrong's music.

When you make a sentence, how do you know which personal pronoun to use? Most people use the pronoun that fits without knowing its name or the rule for its use. They say, "Give *me* the book," not "Give *I* the book." But the rule for choosing personal pronouns is easy to learn and can help you make decisions about which pronoun to use when you aren't sure. The personal pronoun must agree with the noun it replaces in case, gender, and number. Let's see what that means.

Agreement in Case

Nominative and Objective Case

Think of the various pronouns you can use to refer to yourself: *I, me, my,* or *mine.* Which form of the pronoun you choose depends on how you use it in a sentence. As you know, a pronoun takes the place of a noun. The particular form a pronoun takes—that is, the *case* of a pronoun—must agree with the function of the noun that the pronoun replaces in a sentence. There are three cases: nominative, objective, and possessive. Let's look at the nominative and objective cases by considering the following sentence:

The teachers gave Carlos the award for academic excellence.

If you were to replace "The teachers" with a pronoun, what would you use? Here are the pronouns you could choose, each in a different case:

nominative case: *they*
objective case: *them*

What is the function of "The teachers" in the sentence? It is the subject. When the noun acts as the subject, you replace it with a pronoun in the nominative case:

They gave Carlos the award for academic excellence.

Now, what pronoun would you use to replace "Carlos" in that sentence? Here are your choices:

nominative case: *he*
objective case: *him*

What is the function of "Carlos" in the sentence? It is an indirect object. When the noun to be replaced is an object—either a direct object, an indirect object, or the object of a preposition—then the pronoun must be in the objective case:

They gave *him* the award for academic excellence.

Here are the personal pronouns in the nominative case:

I

we

you

> he, she, it
> they

Notice that any of the nominative pronouns will work as the subject of a sentence like the following:

> ——— danced to the music.

Here are the personal pronouns in the objective case:

> me
> us
> you
> him, her, it
> them

Notice that any of the objective pronouns will work as the object in a sentence like the following:

> He threw the ball at ———.

Often you will use the nominative and objective case correctly without thinking about it, although there's one practice to watch out for. Sometimes, when people speak casually, they use the objective case when they should use the nominative case. For example, you might hear someone say:

> My brother and me are going to the market.

What is the function of *me* in that sentence? It's part of the subject. What case—nominative or objective—should a pronoun acting as the subject be in? If you take away the other part of the subject—"my brother"—you'll see how odd it sounds to say

> *Me* am going to the market.

So, the correct form is

> My brother and *I* are going to the market.

Also, be on the lookout for the occasional mistake people make when they use a nominative pronoun as the object of a preposition, as in the following:

> Michiko is going with Daniel and *I* to the parade.

In that sentence, *I* is an object of the preposition *with*. So you need a pronoun in the objective case:

> Michiko is going with Daniel and *me* to the parade.

Possessive Case

Here are the personal pronouns you use when the noun is showing possession: *mine, ours, yours, his*, and *hers, its*. Reasonably enough, they are called "possessive pronouns."

Jane's story is as adventurous as _____.

Mine, ours, yours, his and *hers* will all fit in the blank.

But we can also change "Jane's story" to "her story." The possessives that come *before* a noun are a little different from those that stand by themselves. The ones that come before a noun are: *my, our, your, his, her*, and *its*.

_____ story is as adventurous as hers.

The "her" in "her story" is still called a possessive personal pronoun. But you see that it doesn't stand alone. It's a word that modifies the noun "story," just as an adjective would. Notice that you can use *mine, ours, yours*, and *hers* all by themselves, as in "This dog is mine" or "That dog is hers." But *my, our, your*, and *her* always come before the thing they possess, as in "my dog" or "her cap." *His* and *its* can be used all by themselves, or to modify a noun.

Agreement in Gender

Pronouns also need to agree in gender with the noun they replace whether female, male, or neither. If you were describing Napoleon's great defeat, you wouldn't say, "She lost at Waterloo." You would say, "*He* lost at Waterloo," because Napoleon is a man, and "he, him, and his" are the pronouns we use for nouns that are masculine. Do you know the pronouns we use for feminine nouns? Try this:

Queen Elizabeth I sent _____ (his, her) navy to a surprising victory against the Spanish Armada.

While people always have a gender, things often don't. "It" is the pronoun we use for things that we say are gender neutral, such as a heart, a painting, or a hammer. For instance, when describing the heart, we might say, "It is an amazing muscle!"

Agreement in Number

A noun and the pronoun that replaces it also need to agree in number, that is, the pronoun must be singular or plural like the noun it replaces. You should use singular pronouns when talking about one thing and plural pronouns when talking about more than one thing.

Here are the singular pronouns we use for one thing:

> I, me, my, mine
> you, your, yours
> he, him, his
> she, her, hers
> it, its

Here are the plural pronouns we use for more than one person or thing:

> we, us, our, ours
> you, your, yours
> they, them, their, theirs

See if you can figure out the personal pronouns to substitute for the italicized words in the following sentences:

> *The peasants* stormed the Bastille and released *the prisoners.*
> *John and I* loved the book about *the Sun King.*
> *Leonardo da Vinci* is often called "a Renaissance man."
> Give the book to *Merlin* so *Merlin* can find *the spell.*

Learning About Literature

Kinds of Literature: Tragedy and Comedy

Look at the masks pictured here. How would you describe the emotions they express?

These masks are often used as a symbol of the theater, associated with two different kinds of literature, tragedy and comedy.

People today use the words "tragedy" and "comedy" in general ways that go beyond kinds of literature. For example, a terrible hurricane or plane crash in which many people die might be called a tragedy. Or, people might refer to a television show that makes them laugh as a comedy.

This basic real-life difference between tragedy—something terribly sad or disastrous—and comedy—something funny—also applies most of the time when we are talking about tragedy and comedy as specific kinds of literature.

Comedies tell stories in which everything works out well for the main characters. Sure, the characters may face problems and difficulties along the way, but when the comedy is over, things work out fine. Comedies tend to be funny, but in different ways. In some comedies, we might like the characters and laugh with them through their troubles. In other comedies, we might laugh at silly characters whose actions show just how foolish people can sometimes be.

In literature, a tragedy tells a serious story of a central character—usually an important, heroic person—who meets with disaster because of some personal fault or because of events that cannot be helped. The great English playwright William Shakespeare wrote a tragedy about the life and death of the Roman ruler Julius Caesar, who achieved great power but was murdered by men he thought were his friends. (You can read a retelling of Shakespeare's play in the Stories and Speeches section of this book. You can also learn more about Shakespeare later in this section.) Other great tragedies by Shakespeare include *Romeo and Juliet*, *King Lear*, and *Hamlet*. These plays continue to be read, performed, and admired, even though in each play, after we get to know the main characters well, at the end we are made to feel very sad when we see them dead on the stage.

While it seems natural that people like comedy, since most comedies make us smile and laugh, why do people enjoy watching tragedies? Perhaps one reason people continue to be drawn to the painful stories of tragedies is that we all want to experience and understand tragic stories without having to live through one. A tragedy allows us to experience strong emotions vicariously, meaning through the experience of others ("vicarious" comes from the Latin word *vicarius*, which means "substitute").

In watching a tragic play, our emotions are strongly aroused: we can feel fear for the dangers that face the hero, or anger at his or her enemies, or frustration at not being able to change the course of events, or pity for the hero's sad fate. But when the play is over and we have lived through those strong emotions, we can go back to our own lives. We have a deeper understanding of what it means to be human, of the struggles and disappointments of life. But we also have a sense of relief that we can carry on, and perhaps a sense of determination to overcome the obstacles that defeated the tragic hero.

While many great tragedies end disastrously, they often provide glimpses of comedy along the way. Categories like "tragedy" and "comedy" can help you describe and understand literary works, but you'll find that literature, like life, often mixes joy and sorrow, laughter and tears.

Literal and Figurative Language

When you speak or write, you use language in different ways. Sometimes you use literal language; you say exactly what you mean. But sometimes you use figurative language, a more colorful and imaginative way of expressing yourself in which you don't say exactly what you mean. After a really tough game of basketball or soccer, you might say:

Literal: I'm exhausted.
or
Figurative: I'm dead.

True, the game might have worn you out and you might be lying flat on your back out of breath, but you're still alive! In saying, "I'm dead," you figuratively express just how very tired you feel.

Look at the use of the verb "floated" in the following sentences. Which use is literal and which is figurative?

The graceful ballerina floated across the stage.
The leaf floated on the water.

Have you ever heard someone say, "That's a figure of speech"? A figure of speech is an expression in figurative language, not meant to be taken literally. You probably know this old joke: "Why did the little boy throw the clock out the window? Because he wanted to see time fly." That's funny (or it was when you first heard it!) because someone takes a figure of speech literally. What does it really mean to say that "time flies"?

Scientists and mathematicians often use the literal meanings of words because they need to be clear and precise. Poets often use figurative language to stir our emotions or to help our imaginations see things in new ways. For example, an engineer working for the U.S. Navy would want to be very precise and literal in referring to specific kinds of ships and their functions. But the nineteenth-century American poet Emily Dickinson wrote about ships using figurative language in an imaginative way. These two lines compare a book to a frigate (a sailing ship) that can take us on imaginary voyages:

> There is no frigate like a book
> To take us lands away. . . .

Imagery

Writers often use figurative language to help us see things in our minds. We call the language writers use to create mental pictures and other imaginary sensations *imagery*. The American writer Ernest Hemingway uses imagery in the title of a story called "Hills Like White Elephants." Comparing hills to elephants is his way of trying to give us a clear mental picture of those hills in the distance.

An English writer of the 1800s, Christina Rossetti, uses images of animals in this poem:

> White sheep, white sheep,
> On a blue hill,
> When the wind stops
> You all stand still.

That might seem like a straightforward description, but you can see how imaginatively Christina Rossetti is using imagery when you know that the title of the poem is "Clouds"!

In a poem by William Blake called "The Tiger" (which you can read in this book), Blake uses images of fire to make the tiger seem fierce and menacing. Blake writes, "Tiger! Tiger! burning bright," and then asks, "In what distant deeps or skies / burnt the fire of thine eyes?"

Simile and Metaphor

When writers use imagery, they often put their images into special kinds of figurative language called simile (SIM-uh-lee) and metaphor (MET-uh-for). In fact, if you've ever said something like, "She's fast as lightning," or, "He's an angel," then you've used similes and metaphors yourself.

Similes and metaphors help us see things in unusual or imaginative ways by *comparing* one thing to another. Sometimes similes and metaphors bring together things you normally wouldn't think of comparing. For example, fog might not make you think of an animal, but see the surprising comparison Carl Sandburg makes in a poem called "Fog":

> The fog comes
> on little cat feet.
> It sits looking
> over harbor and city
> on silent haunches
> and then moves on.

A simile is a figure of speech that compares unlike things but makes the comparison obvious by including the word "like" or "as." (Simile comes from the Latin *similis*, meaning "like.") You've probably heard people use some common similes in everyday conversation: for example, "busy as a bee" or "sweet as honey" or "proud as a peacock." The great boxer Muhammad Ali described himself with some vivid similes: in the boxing ring, he said, he would "float like a butterfly, sting like a bee." A poem in this book called "Ballad of John Henry" uses a familiar simile to tell how strong the legendary John Henry was; see if you can find that simile in the poem.

Try making some similes of your own. We'll get you started with some examples. Then let your imagination carry you away!

> *As quiet as:*
> an empty classroom
> *As soft as:*
> an old blanket you've had since you were a baby
> *As hot as:*
> molten lava

Like a simile, a metaphor is a figure of speech that brings together unlike things. But a metaphor doesn't use "like" or "as," so the comparison is not so obvious. For example, in talking about someone who's really stubborn, you might say:

simile: He's stubborn as a mule.

or

metaphor: He's a mule.

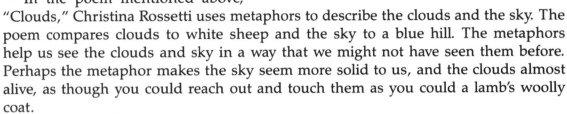

It's not important to dwell on the difference between metaphors and similes; they both make imaginative comparisons to help us understand and feel vividly.

In the poem mentioned above, "Clouds," Christina Rossetti uses metaphors to describe the clouds and the sky. The poem compares clouds to white sheep and the sky to a blue hill. The metaphors help us see the clouds and sky in a way that we might not have seen them before. Perhaps the metaphor makes the sky seem more solid to us, and the clouds almost alive, as though you could reach out and touch them as you could a lamb's woolly coat.

Here is a poem you may know by Langston Hughes, called "Dreams." It has two metaphors. Can you find them?

> Hold fast to dreams
> For if dreams die
> Life is a broken-winged bird
> That cannot fly.
>
> Hold fast to dreams
> For when dreams go
> Life is a barren field
> Frozen with snow.

If you close your eyes and let your imagination see the metaphors in Hughes's poem—the "broken-winged bird" and the "barren field"—then you can appreciate how powerful metaphors can be. Think how unexciting and flat it would be to say something literal like, "If you let go of your dreams, life will be very disappointing."

Sometimes a metaphor may be almost hidden in the words. For example, there's a metaphor lurking in the following sentence:

The snow blanketed the town.

Can you find the comparison in that sentence? Do you see how the snow is being compared to a blanket? Now find the metaphor in this sentence:

Darkness swallowed the explorers as they entered the cave.

Do you see how the figurative language creates an emotional effect different from a literal statement such as, "The explorers entered the dark cave"? When you use a metaphor to compare the darkness to a kind of hungry animal waiting to "swallow" the explorers, then you turn the cave into a place that most of us would rather not enter!

Keep your eyes and ears open for metaphors and similes. Use them when you talk and write and your words will spring to life.

 # Symbols

A symbol is something that stands for or suggests something else beyond itself. For example, you're probably familiar with certain symbols of our country. The bald eagle, the American flag, Uncle Sam: all of these are symbols for the United States of America. Another familiar symbol you may know is a heart. Especially

on Valentine's Day, what does a heart symbolize? In contrast, think of the skull and crossbones on a pirate's flag. What do they symbolize?

Advertisers often use symbols to express certain qualities they want associated with their products. One big oil and gas company uses the symbol of a tiger and says that filling your car with its brand of gasoline is like putting a tiger in your tank. What is this symbol trying to express?

Do you know the symbols of the major American political parties? An elephant is the symbol of the Republican Party. A donkey is the symbol of the Democrats. You might recall that at times during our history congressmen and senators have argued over whether America should go to war. Those favoring war are called "hawks"; those favoring peace are called "doves." Why are these symbols appropriate?

In works of literature, you will sometimes find symbols. Like the American flag or a Valentine heart, a literary symbol stands for or suggests something beyond itself, perhaps some emotion or idea. In a famous poem called "The Road Not Taken," Robert Frost uses two paths in a wood as symbols of the important choices we face in life. Here is the opening stanza of that poem.

> Two roads diverged in a yellow wood,
> And sorry I could not travel both
> And be one traveler, long I stood
> And looked down one as far as I could
> To where it bent in the undergrowth . . .

In a poem Dylan Thomas wrote to his father who was ill and dying, he uses night and light as symbols. Here is the first stanza of the poem (the first line is also the title).

Do not go gentle into that good night,
Old age should burn and rave at close of day;
Rage, rage, against the dying of the light.

In those lines, what do you think is the symbolic significance of "night" and "light"?

Sometimes the significance of a symbol is not so clear-cut. For example, what do you think the tree suggests in this poem by William Blake called "A Poison Tree"?

I was angry with my friend:
I told my wrath, my wrath did end.
I was angry with my foe:
I told it not, my wrath did grow.

And I water'd it in fears,
Night and morning with my tears;
And I sunned it with smiles,
And with soft, deceitful wiles.

And it grew both day and night,
Till it bore an apple bright;
And my foe beheld it shine,
And he knew that it was mine.

And into my garden stole
When the night had veiled the pole:
In the morning glad I see
My foe outstretched beneath the tree.

A symbol can mean different things to different readers, and not everything in a work of literature is a symbol. For example, let's say you're reading a poem about a bird: the bird may be a symbol, suggesting a quality like freedom. Or, the bird may simply be a bird. When you're reading stories and poems, you don't always need to search for symbols, but when you do notice them it's interesting to think about how they enrich what you're reading.

Personification

Imagine you're trying to sharpen a pencil but the lead keeps coming out broken. Frustrated, you exclaim, "This pencil sharpener refuses to work!"

Did the pencil sharpener actually *refuse*? Did it say, "I'm tired and I won't sharpen your pencil"? Of course not. But when you said that the pencil sharpener refused to work, you expressed yourself in an imaginative way and used a kind of figurative language known as personification.

To personify is to give an inanimate object or an animal the qualities of a person, a human. In a poem called "Trees" (which you can read in this book), the poet Joyce Kilmer personifies trees by giving them certain human qualities. Can you see the personification in the following lines?

> A tree that looks at God all day,
> And lifts her leafy arms to pray;
>
> A tree that may in Summer wear
> A nest of robins in her hair. . . .

Sounds in Poetry: Onomatopoeia and Alliteration

Onomatopoeia (ON-uh-mat-uh-PEA-uh) is a Greek word for a special effect that writers use. It might sound complicated, but if you've ever read a comic book you already understand it. When something explodes, you read, "BOOM!" Or when a superhero punches a villain, you read, "WHACK!" or "POW!"

BOOM

Onomatopoeia refers to words that sound like what they describe. If you drop a coin in a metal bowl, it goes "clink." If a car speeds by, it goes "varroom." "Clink" and "varroom" are examples of onomatopoeia.

varroom

clink

Try to think of what might produce these sounds:

buzz	clack	whoosh
boing	gurgle	hiss

Now think of some sounds that these actions might produce:

> bacon frying
> thunder in the distance
> windshield wipers going back and forth
> a car door closing
> fingernails scratching a blackboard
> dry leaves being crushed in a pile

Read the following lines aloud to appreciate how the nineteenth-century American poet Edgar Allan Poe uses onomatopoeia in "The Bells":

> Hear the sledges with the bells—
> Silver bells!
> What a world of merriment their melody foretells!
> How they tinkle, tinkle, tinkle,
> In the icy air of night!

Writers pay close attention to the way their words sound and sometimes use a technique called alliteration. Alliteration means starting several words in a row with the same first letter or the same sound. Here's an example from a poem called "The Eagle" (printed in this book):

> He clasps the crag with crooked hands.

Do you hear the repetition of the hard "c" sound? The hard sound might suggest something about the rough landscape where the eagle dwells.

Read aloud this line from Poe's "The Bells":

> What a world of merriment their melody foretells!

Do you hear two uses of alliteration in that line? Poe repeats both the "w" and the "m" sounds.

Read aloud the poem in this book called "Narcissa" by Gwendolyn Brooks. Do you hear the alliteration the poet uses?

It's fun to play with sounds of words. A little alliteration can provide a tickly, tingly treat for tired ears. Try it the next time you write!

Pen Names

If you wrote a book, you'd probably be proud and excited. You'd want your name in big bold letters right on the cover.

Some writers, however, choose not to put their own names on their books. Instead, they use a made-up name, called a pen name. Another word for pen name is pseudonym ("pseudo" comes from a Greek word meaning "false" and "nym" from a Greek word meaning "name").

Throughout history, writers have had a number of reasons for putting a pen name on something they worked hard to write. In eighteenth-century France, for example, François-Marie Arouet knew that his poetry could get him into trouble because it criticized and mocked some members of the French royalty and protested against some of the government's actions. To protect himself and his family, and to avoid being arrested by the king, Arouet used the pen name that he is still known by today: Voltaire.

A century later in England, Mary Ann Evans wrote serious novels that explored important social, economic, and political issues. Many novels written at this time, and especially those written by women, were full of romance and adventure. Only men wrote serious books—or so most people believed then. In order to have her ideas taken seriously, Mary Ann Evans published her novels under the pen name of a man: George Eliot.

During the 1800s pen names became fashionable. When Samuel Clemens began writing stories for American newspapers, he used a pen name that came from his experience piloting steamships down the Mississippi River. The Mississippi is shallow at some points, and since steamboats could travel only in fairly deep water, someone on the steamboat would occasionally throw out a rope with markers a fathom (six feet) apart to measure the depth of the water. If he called out, "Mark twain!" that meant the rope measured two fathoms— safe water, deep enough for the steamboat. You can read about Mark Twain's experiences as a young "cub" pilot in *Life on the Mississippi*, and you can read part of his beloved novel *The Adventures of Tom Sawyer* in this book.

Shakespeare

William Shakespeare is often called the finest poet and playwright in the English language, and one of the greatest writers in the world. Though he lived almost four hundred years ago, his plays are the most popular of all time and are still performed around the globe today. His poetry is quoted by writers in almost every language. People use phrases out of his plays as sayings even though they may not know where these phrases came from. Have you ever heard anyone say, "We cannot all be masters" or "The wheel is come full circle"? The phrase "All's well that ends well" is the title of one of Shakespeare's plays.

Shakespeare lived at the end of the great age called the Renaissance, which you can read about in the World Civilization and the Fine Arts sections of this book. His plays, written between 1592 and 1611, were popular in his own day, and have become even more popular since. Part of the greatness of his work is the richness of its characters: Shakespeare's plays are about all kinds of people: kings and queens, soldiers, merchants, servants, and beggars—and everyone in between. In his writing, Shakespeare seems to understand all kinds of

William Shakespeare

characters, both good and bad, heroic and selfish, brave and cruel. And he helps us to understand them as well. When you watch his plays, you feel that you are watching the world itself go by before your eyes.

Another reason for Shakespeare's greatness is the beauty and power of his poetry. People speak an almost magical language in his plays, and call up images before your eyes as they talk. Listen to the language a character called Caliban uses to tell you about his island, which is haunted by music.

> Be not afeard: the isle is full of noises,
> Sounds and sweet airs, that give delight, and hurt not.
> Sometimes a thousand twangling instruments
> Will hum about mine ears, and sometimes voices,
> That, if I then had waked after long sleep,
> Will make me sleep again.

Shakespeare loved to use unusual words like "twangling" to describe things. In fact, Shakespeare invented many new words, and many of the words he coined, or invented, we still use today. As far as we can tell, words like *gloomy, suspicious, countless, bumps, hurry, lonely, monumental,* and many others first appeared in Shakespeare's work! Shakespeare has had more effect on the English we speak today than any other writer in history. Many of his original phrases and words describe things so well that we use them as part of the way we talk, including expressions like "elbow room," "fair play," and even "catching a cold."

Coin Your Own Words

It's fun to make up words the way Shakespeare did. Sometimes it means combining two different words to get a word that's even closer to what you mean. "Twangling" for example, might be a combination of "twang," and "jangle"; it sounds just like the music Shakespeare is describing. Try making up your own new words from other words. You can just mix them together, or combine the beginnings, middles, and ends (prefixes, roots, and suffixes) of different words. Can someone else guess what your words mean?

Shakespeare wrote many different kinds of plays. His history plays tell stories from the history of England and ancient Rome. They're like our movies that tell stories of World War II or the Civil War. His comedies are funny and magical, and are usually about love and romance. People are often mistaken for other people, and because of this, funny things happen. His tragedies are about sad and terrible things and contain some of the greatest poetry ever written. His plays can make you want to laugh and cry at the same time. This mixture of funny and sad things makes his plays seem like life itself. We tell the story of a history play, *Julius Caesar,* in this book, and the story of the tragedy *Romeo and Juliet* in Book Six of this series.

Introduction to Sayings
FOR PARENTS AND TEACHERS

Every culture has phrases and proverbs that make no sense when carried over literally into another culture. For many children, this section may not be needed; they will have picked up these sayings by hearing them at home and among their friends. But the category of sayings in the *Core Knowledge Sequence* has been the one most singled out for gratitude by teachers who work with children from home cultures that are different from the standard culture of literate American English.

Sayings and Phrases

Birthday suit

When you were born (on your "birthday"), you weren't wearing any clothes. When someone is said to be wearing his or her "birthday suit," it means that the person is naked.

Anita's baby sister, Maria, took off all her clothes. Then she ran into their backyard and jumped into the small plastic wading pool.

"Maria," Anita laughed, "you're supposed to wear your *swimsuit* in the pool, not your birthday suit!"

Bite the hand that feeds you

An ill-tempered dog may bite his master, even though he depends on his master for food. When you do something to harm a person or thing that supports you, you are "biting the hand that feeds you."

Even though the bricklayer knew he was biting the hand that fed him, he decided to complain to his supervisor about his salary and long working hours.

Catch forty winks

To "catch forty winks" is to have a quick sleep.

"I'm too tired to do my homework," Liselle said to Henry. "I'm going to catch forty winks. Can you wake me up in fifteen minutes?"

Chip on your shoulder

When someone has a chip on his shoulder, it means that he is in a bad mood and would pick a fight eagerly.

When Sam drove through town, he yelled at every driver who moved too slowly, and honked at every car that took too long to go through a light. Finally, a truck driver pulled up next to him and asked, "You got a chip on your shoulder, buddy?"

Count your blessings

People use this saying to mean, "Be thankful for what you have."

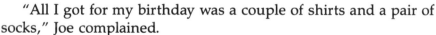

"All I got for my birthday was a couple of shirts and a pair of socks," Joe complained.

"At least some people remembered your birthday, Joe," Sima said. "You should count your blessings."

Eat crow

If you "eat crow," you are taking back something that you once said. It is usually a humbling experience, and is similar to "eating your words," or "eating humble pie."

The racing car driver bragged that his was the fastest, best-built car ever to run the Indianapolis 500. He said confidently that he was guaranteed to win the race. But he had to eat crow when his car got two flat tires and lost the race.

Eleventh hour

People use this phrase to mean "at the last possible moment."

The doctor arrived at the eleventh hour, right before Mrs. Bernstein gave birth to her baby.

Eureka!

Eureka is a Greek word that means, "I have found it!" It's well known as the expression of delight that the famous mathematician Archimedes used upon discovering how to find the volume of gold. (You can read the story of how he solved this mystery in Book One of this series.)

"Eureka!" Julio yelled, holding up his hand as he backed out of the bushes. "I finally found my key!"

Every cloud has a silver lining

This saying means that even bad things usually have a hidden good side.

"How's the pie you ordered?" Mrs. Wilson asked her husband.

"Awful. I can't eat it," he replied. "So I guess I won't be breaking my diet after all. Every cloud has a silver lining!"

Few and far between

When something is "few and far between," it means that it is rare or not easily available.

There used to be many Dall's porpoises in the Pacific Ocean, but excessive hunting and drift net fishing have made them few and far between. They may even become extinct.

The grass is always greener on the other side of the hill

This saying is usually used to console someone who feels that what others have is better than what he has—no matter what it is!

"I wish I was in the Wong family instead of this one!" Mabel said to her sister, Edie. "They take fun vacations, and they go out to restaurants all the time!"

"But you don't know how happy they really are, Edie. You never know what another family is really like. You just think the grass is always greener on the other side of the hill."

Great oaks from little acorns grow

Just as a small acorn can grow into a towering oak tree, a small undertaking can lead to great results.

Abraham Lincoln was born in a log cabin and read books by firelight. Even though his family was poor, he became one of the United States' greatest presidents. His life is true to the saying, "Great oaks from little acorns grow."

It's never too late to mend

This saying means that there is always time to improve yourself, or to change your ways.

Sally never studied, and she always got low marks on her report card. "I'm no good at school," she said.
"That's not true," her friend Ilana said. "Just start doing your homework. It's never too late to mend."

Kill two birds with one stone

When you do only *one* thing in order to accomplish *two* goals, you are "killing two birds with one stone."

"I'm going to do my homework while I ride the exercise bicycle. That way I'll kill two birds with one stone."

Lock, stock, and barrel

The lock, the stock, and the barrel were essential parts of a gun in earlier times. The phrase "lock, stock, and barrel" has come to mean "absolutely everything."

"What, the burglars took every jewel in the store?" Mrs. Mihm asked.
"They didn't just take every jewel," Mrs. Thorp sighed, "they took every watch, every piece of silver . . . they cleaned the store out, lock, stock, and barrel!"

Make a mountain out of a molehill

When someone makes a big deal out of something that is not very important, we often say they are "making a mountain out of a molehill."

"I can't believe you forgot to return your library book!" Damon wagged his finger at Yvonne.
"Look, it's only one day overdue and I'm returning it right now. Stop making a mountain out of a molehill!"

A miss is as good as a mile

This saying means that just missing by a little bit is no better than missing by a whole lot.

"Well, at least you only lost by one point," Camilla said to her brother, Sean, the quarterback on his school's team.

"I know you're trying to make me feel better, Camilla," Sean replied, "but we still lost. Like they say, a miss is as good as a mile."

 ## Out of the frying pan and into the fire

People use this expression to describe what happens when you go from a bad situation to an even worse one.

The explorer escaped the wild boar by leaping across a narrow canyon. When he reached the other side, though, he landed on the tail of a giant python and realized that he had jumped out of the frying pan and into the fire.

A penny saved is a penny earned

This saying means that when you save money instead of spending it, it is almost the same as earning money, because you'll have extra cash instead of an empty pocket.

"Grandma said I should put the money Aunt Donna gave me for my birthday into my bank," Kate told her father.

"That's just like your grandmother. She always says a penny saved is a penny earned," her father replied.

Read between the lines

When you "read between the lines," you go beyond the surface of what someone says or does so you can find out what they *really* mean.

"Clare keeps telling me she's too busy to go to school dances," Tanya said. "But when you read between the lines, you can tell she's afraid she won't have fun if she goes."

Sit on the fence

This expression means "not taking sides."

"So who do you think has a better chance at making the track team, Marco or me?" Leo asked George. Both Leo and Marco stared at George, waiting for a response.
"You're both pretty fast!" George said, trying not to hurt anyone's feelings.
"Don't sit on the fence," Leo said. "Make a decision!"

Steal his/her thunder

When another person does something extraordinary before you have the chance, that person is "stealing your thunder."

Sharon couldn't wait to show her mother the hip hop dance she had learned in school that day. When she got home, though, her sister Maya was already performing the dance for their mother.
"What's wrong?" her mother said, when she saw Sharon's look of disappointment.
"Oh, nothing, I guess. I feel like Maya just stole my thunder."

Take the bull by the horns

People use this phrase to mean "stop hesitating and take action."

Norma got to the end of the high diving board and froze. The water was so far down, and it looked as hard and shiny as glass. She was afraid to jump, and she was too scared to turn back and climb down.
"Come on, Norma," her brother called from below. "It's not as scary as it looks. Just take the bull by the horns and jump!"

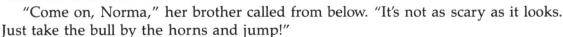

Till the cows come home

Cows come home to the barn from the fields at the end of a long day. So this expression has come to mean that something won't happen "for an extremely long time."

"Herman, you've been studying all day," Cora said. "When are you going to take a break?"
"No time soon. I'm going to get an 'A' on my test if I have to study till the cows come home!" he replied.

Time heals all wounds

When you scrape your elbow, you know that it will take a week or so to heal. But when people say "time heals all wounds," they are usually talking about feelings. And they mean that sometimes the only thing that can make you feel better after something bad happens is the passing of time.

When Shayna didn't invite Kara to the party, Kara thought she would never be able to forgive her.

"It's tough," Kara's mother said. "You feel hurt now, but you'll feel better after a while. Maybe then you can start being friends again. Time heals all wounds."

Vice versa

When people use this Latin term, they mean, "and exactly the same, but the other way round."

Martha comes to visit me once a year, and vice versa. That way we get to see each other twice a year.

A watched pot never boils

This saying means that when you are anxiously waiting for something to happen, it always seems to take longer.

Sara couldn't wait for the polish she had just put on her fingernails to dry. She blew on her nails and shook her hands in the air. "I can't do anything until this polish dries!" she moaned.

"Just relax," her friend said. "A watched pot never boils!"

Well begun is half done

This saying means that if you start something off well, it will be easier to finish.

Thomas cracked three eggs into the bowl without dropping any shell into the omelet mixture. "This sure is a good start!" he said to himself. "And if well begun is half done, then this is going to be one excellent omelet!"

What will be, will be

This saying means that some things are beyond our control.

"I'm so worried about the game tomorrow. We *have* to win!" Cleo said.

"Well, both baseball teams are good," Gordon said, "so it'll be a close game. But it doesn't pay to worry. What will be, will be."

When in Rome, do as the Romans do

This saying means that when you are in an unfamiliar situation or place, it's a good idea to follow the customs of the people around you. This can apply to visiting foreign countries, or simply to being in a situation where everyone but you seems to know how to act.

Marta, an exchange student from Brazil, looked worried. "Oh, please," she said to her friend Beth, "what do I do? I've never been to a pep rally before, and I don't know how to act."

"Don't worry. Just do what everyone else is doing, cheering. We have an expression here, 'When in Rome, do as the Romans do,' and that about covers it," said Beth.

Where there's a will, there's a way

People use this saying to mean that if you want something badly enough, you will figure out how to get it.

Helen Keller was blind, deaf, and mute, but wanted, more than anything, to be able to read. Everything was against her, but she worked and worked until, one day, she was finally able to read and write. She must certainly have believed that where there's a will, there's a way.

II.

GEOGRAPHY, WORLD CIVILIZATION, AND AMERICAN CIVILIZATION

Introduction to Geography

FOR PARENTS AND TEACHERS

The geography section of this book deepens the study of maps begun in Book Three, introducing globe quadrants, scale, climate zones, and time zones. It also details the many ways lakes are formed and discusses some of the world's great lakes.

One of the best activities for learning about maps is to make maps. Children can trace the maps in this book and then fill in the details for themselves. We also include a recipe for making a relief map out of newspaper and paste.

For schools or families with IBM or compatible computers, P. C. Globe offers GeoJigsaw, a set of on-screen jigsaw puzzles with geography themes. Each may be broken up into as few as 6 or as many as 294 pieces, depending on the age of the student ($39.95 suggested retail price). The same company makes several other games which involve geography.

Other resources: The National Geographic Society publishes the children's magazine *World*, which is unsurpassed for maps, articles, and photographs. The society also publishes many books about geography for children, as does Dover Publications. Their addresses are:

The National Geographic Society
1145 17th Street, N.W.
Washington, DC 20036-4688
(800) 638-4077

Dover Publications
31 East Second Street
Mineola, NY 11501
(516) 294-7000

Geography of the United States and the World

The Language of Geography

You may have noticed that just about every subject, from science to sports, has a language of its own. Geography does too. To understand a subject, it helps to learn the meanings of the words in its special language.

From reading the earlier books in this series, you already know some of the special words that help you understand maps and globes. In Book Four, you learned what the words "hemisphere," "latitude," and "longitude" mean. There are several other words you will need to learn in order to understand the language of geography. One is the word "parallel." You might remember this word from mathematics. It describes two lines that are equally distant at every point. In geography, a parallel is another way of saying a latitude line, parallel to the equator. Look at the following map. The

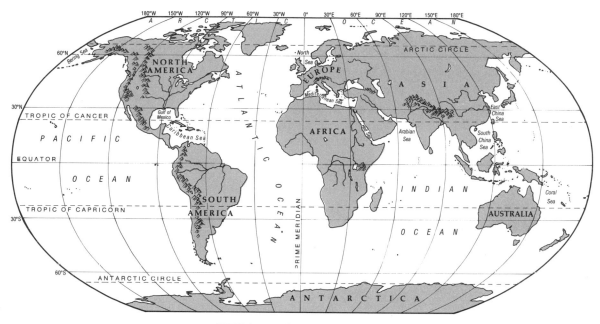

THE MAP OF THE WORLD

thirtieth parallel (north) is the line of latitude 30° north of the equator all around the globe. This line passes through Florida, northern Africa, the East China Sea, and other places that are equally distant from the equator.

Another important word for geographers is "meridian," from the Latin word meaning midday, or noon. We'll read more about the special meaning of this word when we get to the section about geography and time. For now, you should know that lines of longitude, which connect the North and South Poles, are called meridians. They cross the parallels, as you can see on your map or on a globe.

Hemispheres, parallels, and meridians are not actual features of the earth like mountains, rivers, deserts, or lakes. You cannot see them on a photograph of our earth taken from space; they are imaginary markings created by geographers to help them draw maps and make accurate globes. These markings, as well as others you will read about in this chapter, form grids, allowing geographers to divide the world into sections. Grids also make it easier to locate places on our earth.

The Prime Meridian

You may remember that the prime meridian, which is 0° longitude, passes through Greenwich, England. Here, the word "prime" means first or most important. The prime meridian is the most important meridian because all distance east or west is measured from this line.

The location of the prime meridian was agreed upon by geographers from around the world who met in 1884 in Washington, D.C. They could just as easily have chosen another meridian, but this one passed through the location of a famous observatory, where for centuries astronomers had studied the stars and prepared charts for navigators. Because many people were familiar with the location of Greenwich, it was chosen as the reference point for all other meridians.

Reference Points

If you want to tell a group of your friends how to get to a particular movie theater, it helps to give them directions from a place all of you know, such as Main Street, or your school. That way, everyone can understand the same set of directions.

In the same way, agreement on reference points is very important to geographers. Let's play a game that will show you why. You and five of your friends each pick a different continent that you will call "home base." Then choose a location (Greenland, for example), and give the compass directions (N, S, E, W, NW, NE, SW, SE) and distance (near or far) to Greenland from each home base. What happens? No two sets of directions or distances agree, though you are all talking about the same place—Greenland. That is because you all have a different home base, or reference point. This can be a problem for geographers, too, so they use agreed-upon reference points such as the equator and the prime meridian.

As the prime, or 0°, meridian continues on the other side of the two poles, it becomes the 180° meridian. This meridian is 180° both east *and* west of the prime meridian, because it is exactly halfway around the world from the prime meridian.

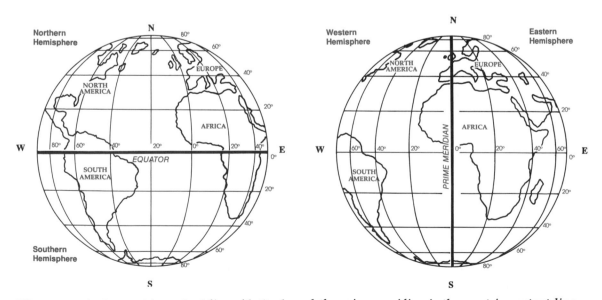

The equator is the most important line of latitude and the prime meridian is the most important line of longitude. They are the lines from which all other lines are measured.

Just as the equator divides the globe in half horizontally—into the Northern and Southern Hemispheres—the prime meridian and the 180° meridian divide the world in half vertically, into the Eastern and Western Hemispheres.

European geographers who first developed maps and globes as we know them today frequently used major cities or continents as reference points. The terms Near East and Far East, for example, described regions that were near to or far from the cities of London and Paris and the continent of Europe. (You may be familiar with the Near East if you've read the Geography section of Book Four. You can read more about the Far East in Book Six.) Similarly, the Eastern Hemisphere was described as the Old World, because it was familiar to European mapmakers and navigators, while the Western Hemisphere was described as the New World, because it was new and uncharted territory for them. Today, we still use some of the terms that describe distance and direction from European reference points.

Where on Earth Are You?

If you live in the United States, you live in the Western Hemisphere, which includes all parts of the world west of the prime meridian and east of the 180° meridian. Since a hemisphere is one half of the world, knowing which half you live in doesn't really pinpoint your exact location, does it? Let's take another step. You know that the world is also divided in half by the equator. The half above the equator is called the Northern Hemisphere, and the half below the equator is the Southern Hemisphere.

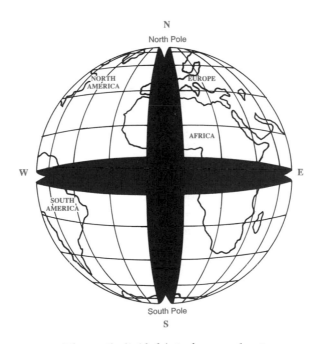

The earth divided into four quadrants.

If the world were a grapefruit and you cut it in half both vertically and horizontally, you would have four quarters of it to consider. Geographers call these quarters "quadrants," from a Latin word meaning fourth part. Can you see that the United States is in the northwestern quadrant of the world?

Map Scale

Locating your quadrant on the globe is helpful but it still doesn't show anyone exactly where you live. To do this, you'll need maps of the United States, your state, and your town.

Take a look at the three maps that follow. Notice how much more detail is included on each map. The U.S. map shows forty-eight of our fifty states, while the state map focuses on just one state. A U.S. map shows many more miles of the earth's surface than a state map, and a state map shows many more miles of surface than a town map. Each map is drawn to a different scale. Scale is the proportion between distance on the map and actual distance on the earth's surface. For instance, on one map a distance of one inch can represent one real mile; on another an inch can represent a hundred miles.

The scale of miles below each drawing tells you how many miles one inch represents. Compare the scales for the state and city maps. You'll see that on the city map one inch represents fewer miles, but gives you greater detail. With the scale of miles, you can measure distances between places on the map. How far is it from the Capitol to the stadium? From the Capitol to the fairgrounds?

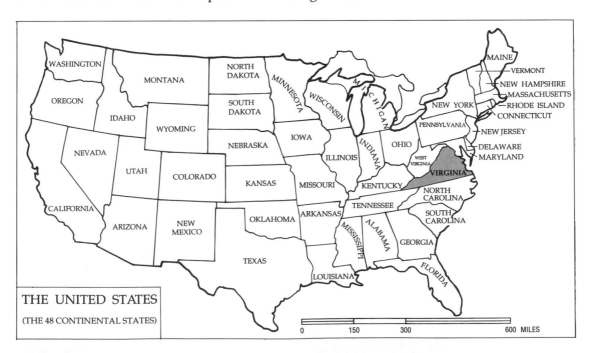

THE UNITED STATES

(THE 48 CONTINENTAL STATES)

0   150   300   600 MILES

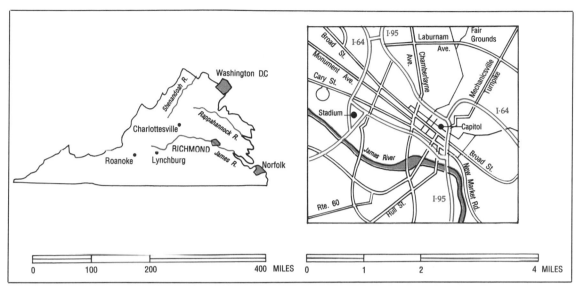

State map of Virginia.   *City map of Richmond, Virginia.*

Use an atlas of the United States and a map of your town to write directions to your home for a visitor from another town. You should be able to find the maps you need at your local library. First locate your town and your visitor's town in the U.S. atlas, and write down the set of roads that most directly connect them. Be sure to write your instructions as though traveling from your visitor's town to your own, and include compass directions and the number of miles to major turning points (for example, "Take Route 29 traveling north for twelve miles until you reach the intersection of Routes 29 and 33 . . ."). Once you've completed directions to the outskirts of your town, turn to your town map and use it to write directions to your street from the outskirts of town.

The Arctic Circle

Geographers divide the earth another way—in bands that are parallel to the equator. Those bands tell you a lot about the climate of those regions of the earth. The farther from the equator in either direction, the colder the climate tends to be.

Let's go back and look at the Northern Hemisphere again. Far to the north, at about 67°N latitude, there is an imaginary boundary called the Arctic Circle.

The lands and waters north of the Arctic Circle are called the Arctic Region. You can look at the lands inside the Arctic Circle in a new way on the map that follows—from a spot above the North Pole! You'll notice that these lands form a ring around a large body of water known as the Arctic Ocean. Much of this ocean remains frozen year after year in a thick pack of ice that floats on the surface. This is called the polar ice cap.

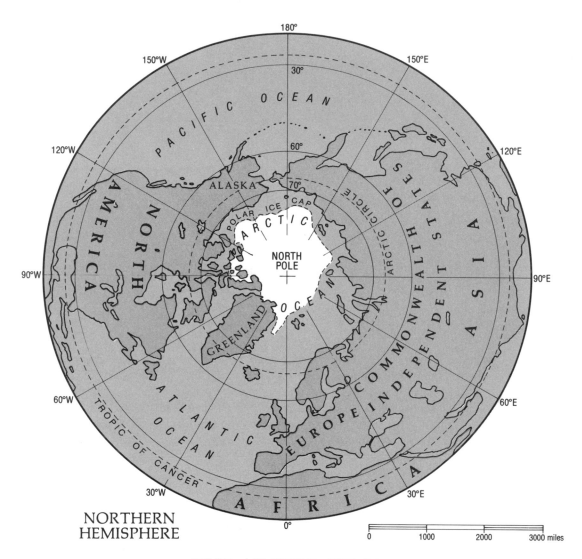

NORTHERN
HEMISPHERE

THE ARCTIC CIRCLE

The Antarctic Circle

On the other side of the world, in the Southern Hemisphere, there is another imaginary circle called the Antarctic Circle, located at about 67°S latitude. The prefix "anti-" means "opposite of" in Greek. The Antarctic is opposite the Arctic on a globe or map. Find the South Pole. See how it's surrounded by the continent of Antarctica? Use the scale of miles on the map to approximate how many miles it is from the southern tip of South America to the Antarctic Circle.

The Antarctic climate is even colder than that of the Arctic. Although mountains

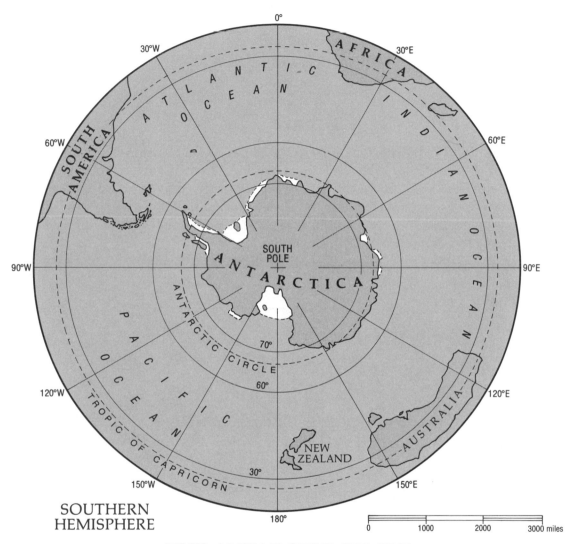

THE ANTARCTIC CIRCLE

do stick out along the coast and in central parts of the continent, most Antarctic lands are buried under a permanent ice cap big enough to cover the entire United States in a layer two miles thick! This southern polar ice cap contains over 75 percent of the world's fresh water.

The Tropics

Now let's find two more imaginary circles, the Tropic of Cancer and the Tropic of Capricorn. Both of these circles lie parallel to the equator at about 23° latitude: the

Tropic of Cancer to the north, and the Tropic of Capricorn to the south. Their names came down to us from ancient astronomers who named them for constellations called Cancer (which means crab in Latin) and Capricorn (which means goat horn).

These two circles mark the northern- and southernmost boundaries of the region known as the Tropics.

Climate Zones

The bands that lie between the imaginary circles we have been describing roughly mark climate zones that are called frigid (very cold), temperate (moderate; neither very hot nor very cold), and tropical (very hot) zones. Find these on your map.

The Greeks thought that climate remained constant along any line of latitude; so, for example, northern Greece and southern Italy would have the same climate. While this rule is often true, it is not true worldwide.

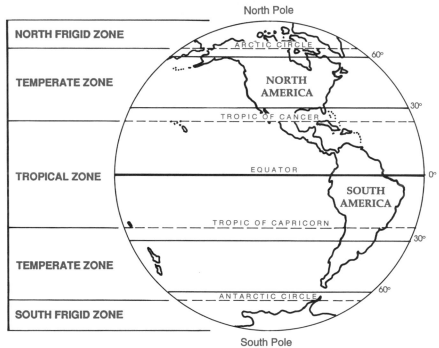

Simple Greek model of climate zones.

Geographers know now that the Greek model oversimplifies climate information. Let's take the Arctic or northern frigid zone as an example. Geographers today argue that the boundary line for the northern frigid zone should run through all locations with an average summer temperature of 50°F. That line doesn't neatly follow the Arctic Circle. Sometimes it dips south and sometimes rises north of the Arctic Circle, as you'll see on the map on the next page.

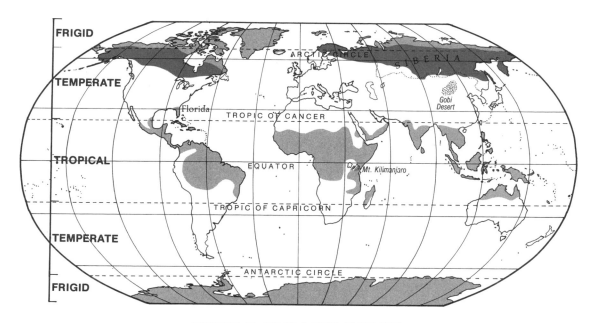

FRIGID

TEMPERATE

TROPICAL

TEMPERATE

FRIGID

WORLD CLIMATE ZONES

The tropical zones include lands ranging in climate from snowy Mount Kilimanjaro to dry desert to lush rainforest. Even the temperate zones contain lands as different as cold Siberia, hot, humid Florida, and the hot, dry Gobi Desert. Today geographers know that temperature and rainfall and other factors are at least as important to climate as latitude alone. While latitude plays a role, altitude (height above sea level) and distance from the sea are equally important in identifying climate zones.

Notice how much more complicated this more recent world climate map is than the simple map of latitude zones above. Because the original Greek model of latitude bands is simpler, modern geographers sometimes use them when discussing world climate zones in general.

On a photocopy of the map on page 96, draw or name two animals that live in each of the different regions. Some good sources of information on animals and their habitats are National Geographic's World *magazine, the National Wildlife Federation's* Ranger Rick *magazine, and the Young Naturalist Foundation's* Owl Magazine, *which you may find in your town or school library. An encyclopedia will also give a description of the animals found in different regions. Look under the names of each of the continents and find the sections for plant and animal life. Can you name any special adaptations of the animals you choose to include? In other words, is there anything that helps them live more easily in their particular climate? How do these animals get the three most important items for their survival—food, water, and shelter?*

Differences in climate have a tremendous effect on people, animals, and plants. Climate determines how much and what kind of housing and clothing we will need, how much food we can grow, even our customs. How might the lives of people who can live out-of-doors most of the year differ from those who must stay indoors during long, cold winters?

It's About Time

Suppose you want to call a friend who lives in Beijing (BAY-JING), China, on her birthday. When should you call her? Remember that China is halfway around the world from the United States. When it is noon in the United States, it is nighttime in China. If you call when it is noon where you live, your friend would already be fast asleep! To complicate matters further, China is a day ahead of the U.S. In other words, to reach your friend before bedtime in China on Monday, you would have to call her from the United States on Sunday in the afternoon or evening (or very, very early Monday morning if you live in the eastern United States). How could this be? It all has to do with the fact that we measure time by the spin of the earth around its axis—one rotation every twenty-four hours.

You read earlier that the prime meridian is the reference point from which distance east and west is measured. The prime meridian is also the reference point for measuring time. Using the prime meridian as the starting point, we divide the world into twenty-four hourly time zones, to match the twenty-four-hour cycle of the earth's rotation on its axis.

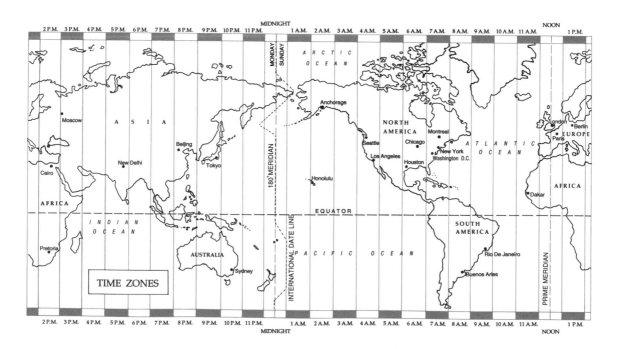

Find the 180° meridian on the Time Zones map. Do you remember reading about this line in Book Four of this series? It's halfway around the world from the prime meridian. Now look at the line that sometimes overlaps, sometimes zigzags back and forth across the 180° meridian: it's called the International Date Line. The International Date Line divides the twelfth time zone in half. The eastern half of this zone subtracts twelve hours from Greenwich time, while the western half adds twelve hours, so there is always a one-day difference between the eastern and western sides of the date line. If you cross the date line going east, today instantly becomes yesterday. If you cross it going west, today instantly becomes tomorrow. The reason the International Date Line zigzags rather than follows the 180° meridian exactly is to make timekeeping simpler for people who live nearby. You could keep moving from Monday to Tuesday and back again if you lived on the International Date Line.

The letters "A" and "M" in the term "A.M." stand for the Latin term ante meridiem. Remember reading earlier that the word "meridian" comes from a Latin word meaning midday, or noon? Meridiem *is that word. When the sun shines directly on any meridian, it is noon all along that meridian and in the time zone that contains that meridian. Ante means before in Latin, so the term* ante meridiem *means before noon. Can you guess what the abbreviation* P.M. *means? It stands for* post meridiem, *meaning after noon.*

Large Lakes of the World

Now that we've reviewed some of the features invented by geographers to chart our earth, let's look at natural features, beginning with the large lakes that lie scattered across the planet. The kind of map we will use to do this is called a physical map. Besides lakes and rivers, physical maps often show other natural features such as forests, mountains, grasslands, jungles, and deserts.

Lakes are bodies of water that collect in large dips or depressions in the land. These depressions are called basins. Lake basins are surrounded on all sides by land. They collect water from rainfall, melting snow and glaciers, rivers, streams, and brooks, as well as underground springs and groundwater.

Do you remember reading about river basins in Book Three of this series? A river basin is the land area drained by a river. Lake basins often occur in the wide, low parts of larger river basins.

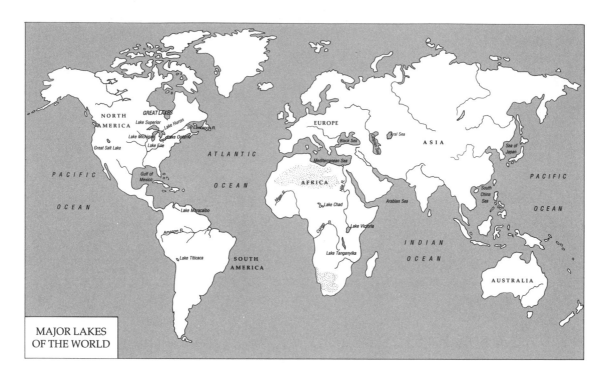

MAJOR LAKES
OF THE WORLD

How Lakes Form

Natural Dams

Lakes are formed in many different ways. Sometimes rocks and soil deposited by glaciers and landslides will block a river's flow and form a lake behind the natural dam. Sometimes the water of a river flows so fast it overruns the bends in the river-bed, leaving behind a lake the shape of a crescent moon or a horseshoe. This is known as an oxbow lake, because it is also the shape of an old-fashioned yoke that was used to harness oxen.

In places that receive a lot of rainfall, water overflows lake basins and runs out at the lowest point or outlet, forming a river either above or below ground. This water eventually leads to the ocean or sea, unless it passes through a desert area and dries up.

With time, this horseshoe bend in the Connecticut River may become cut off from the river body, forming an oxbow lake.

Salty Lakes and River Sources

In some desert climates, lakes lose water rapidly due to evaporation, and no outlets form. The minerals dissolved in the water begin to build up as more water evaporates, making very salty lakes that sometimes dry up completely. Perhaps you have heard of the Great Salt Lake in Utah. The Caspian and the Aral seas are even larger examples of salty lakes—so large they are called seas. The Caspian Sea is not just the largest saltwater lake in the world, it's also the largest inland body of water. It's about the size of the country of Japan. Can you find it on the map? The Aral Sea is not quite as salty as the Caspian. It is believed to have flowed into the Caspian Sea during glacial times.

Africa has some magnificent lakes. Find Lake Chad on the Major Lakes of the World map. This large, shallow body of fresh water seems to have no outlet. But, in fact, its waters sink under the ground and supply wells in a broad, low area spreading out hundreds of miles from the lake. Another African lake, Lake Victoria, is the primary source of the Nile, the longest river in the world. Find Lake Victoria on the map. In what direction does the Nile flow? Does its direction surprise you? Can you explain it? Into what major body of water does the Nile empty?

The Action of Waves

Near coastlines, lakes can be formed when bays are dammed off from the sea by the buildup of sand and silt at their mouths. Find Lake Maracaibo on the map. Lake Maracaibo, one of the largest lakes in South America, was formed this way. Eventually the land that formed the lake was washed away again by waves and currents, forming a narrow channel to the sea. Even though it is no longer surrounded on all sides by land, Maracaibo is still called a lake—perhaps because it was one for so long.

Faults in the Earth's Crust

Lake Titicaca in South America is the highest large lake in the world. It was formed when melting ice and snow filled a basin created by the folding of the Andes Mountains that caused cracks or faults in the earth's crust. Other lakes were also formed by faults caused by movements in the earth's crust. Lake Superior, in North America, and Lake Tanganyika, in east central Africa, were formed by the faulting of the earth's crust. Find Lake Superior on the Major Lakes of the World map. It is the

Lake Titicaca on the border of Peru and Bolivia. The reed boats in this picture are a common sight on the lake.

largest freshwater lake in the world. Find Lake Tanganyika on the map also. It is the deepest lake in Africa, and one of the longest.

The Action of Glaciers

Glaciers are responsible for scouring out the large basin that holds most of what are now called the Great Lakes. Find the Great Lakes—Superior, Huron, Michigan, Erie, and Ontario—on the map above. Where does the water from these lakes flow?

There are many smaller glacial lakes in the northern part of North America and in northern Europe.

There are several other ways that lakes can form in addition to the ones we just read about: extinct volcano craters can fill with water, groundwater can dissolve limestone to produce sinkholes, and man-made dams can interrupt the flow of rivers.

Have you ever read the book Paddle-to-the-Sea? *The story records the journey, from Lake Superior all the way to the Atlantic Ocean, of a small canoe carved by an Indian boy.*

You can find Paddle-to-the-Sea *in the library, listed under the title or under the author's name: Holling Clancy Holling. Perhaps after reading the book you'll want to make your own miniature boat or raft.*

Regions of the United States

You've learned that before the United States was formed there were thirteen original colonies and that when the United States was formed, these colonies became the first thirteen states.

We think of the thirteen original states as belonging to three regions: the New England states, the Mid-Atlantic states, and the Southern states.

As our country began to grow, newly formed states were added to these three regions. But as the country expanded all the way to the Pacific coast, new regions came into being: the Midwest, the Great Plains, the Southwest, the West, and the Pacific Northwest states were added, as you can see from the map above. States are grouped into regions according to similarities in their location, climate, landforms, economy, traditions, and history. Which two states are not included in any region? Why do you think this is so?

These names for regions are just convenient labels for different parts of the country. Their boundaries and even their names are not agreed on by everyone, but people will understand what you mean when you speak of these eight regions: New England, Mid-Atlantic, South, Midwest, Great Plains, Southwest, West, and Pacific Northwest.

REGIONS OF THE
CONTINENTAL UNITED STATES

Our Neighbor to the North: Canada

Several of the geographical features of our country are shared by Canada. Both countries are surrounded by great oceans which supply fish and other natural resources. Perhaps the most important geographical features we hold in common with Canada are the Great Lakes—freshwater treasures that were important for travel, fishing, and trade in the development of both countries.

But there are also geographical differences between the countries. The Rocky Mountains cover more territory in Canada, and the plains cover less. This gives the United States more farmland. The Canadian Shield, a broad, U-shaped region that curves around Hudson Bay and stretches from the Arctic Ocean to the Atlantic, also limits farmland in Canada. Long ago, ancient glaciers scrubbed this land clean of topsoil, making it unsuitable for farming. Find this area on the map of the United States and Canada. Notice that this region covers almost one half of Canada. Its two million square miles, though ill-suited for farming, are filled with beautiful rocky rounded hills and thousands of lakes and rivers.

If you look at the world climate map on page 97 you will see why there is another major physical difference between the United States and Canada. Since Canada is farther from the equator, it has colder weather. Note on the map the climate zones

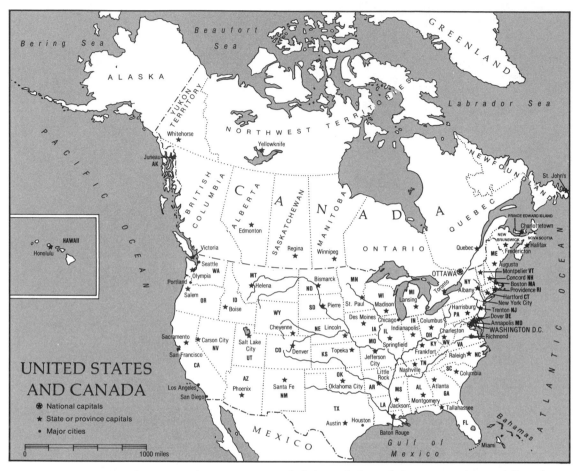

This map shows the fifty states of our country and their capitals and the ten provinces of Canada and their capitals. Can you find the Great Lakes?

labeled tundra and subarctic. Often the land in these zones is frozen the whole year. It's even hard to build a house or a road on such ground.

Canada has ten areas called provinces, comparable to our states. (Find them on the map). They are Newfoundland, Nova Scotia, New Brunswick, Prince Edward Island, Quebec, Ontario, Manitoba, Saskatchewan, Alberta, and British Columbia. In the vast northern regions, where few people live, Canada also has two regions called territories—the Yukon Territory and Northwest Territories.

Around the World Alone:
Learning About Geography the Hard Way

There's a person from southside Chicago who wants to make everyone as excited about geography and the world we live in as he is. He's Bill Pinkney, the "Southside Sailor," also known as "Captain Bill." Mr. Pinkney was the third American and the first African-American to sail around the world alone by way of the Cape of Good Hope (on the southern tip of Africa) and Cape Horn (on the southern tip of South America).

Along the way, Captain Bill videotaped parts of his journey and sent the images by satellite back to Chicago and other cities, so students like you could follow his travels. He also sent the students a monthly newsletter with updates on his travels aboard his boat, the **Commitment**. When Captain Bill, who is fifty-six, ended his twenty-seven-thousand-mile journey in Boston on June 9, 1992, thousands of children who had tracked his journey on maps welcomed him home.

In the library you may find magazine or newspaper articles about Captain Bill's journey. You can trace his route on a world map or globe.

You can also plan a round-the-world trip for yourself or others. Are the lands you will visit frigid, tropical, or temperate? What sort of clothing do you think you should bring? What kinds of adventures or weather might you encounter? (Remember reading about hurricanes, typhoons, and monsoons?)

Introduction to World Civilization
FOR PARENTS AND TEACHERS

The story of World Civilization in this book begins with a more detailed look at the great early civilizations of the Maya, Aztecs, and Incas that were introduced in Book One of this series. Book Five examines the clash between these civilizations and European explorers and conquerors, whose bold voyages often brought destruction to the native peoples in what was, for Europeans, a "New World." It describes the remarkable flowering of European culture during the Renaissance, and offers portraits of concurrent developments in other countries, including Africa, Japan, and Russia. It examines changes in ideas and attitudes that, from the Renaissance to the Enlightenment and beyond, led to the tremendous religious upheavals of the Reformation and Counter-Reformation, as well as the massive political and social shakeup of the French Revolution.

Here are a few resources for further reading arranged in the order these subjects are discussed in this chapter. The last two on the list are general resources:

The Aztecs *by Pamela Odijk (Silver Burdett, 1990).*
The Incas *by Pamela Odijk (Silver Burdett, 1989).*
In My Mother's House *by Ann Nolan Clark (Viking/Puffin, 1992). A historical look at the pueblo people of long ago.*
Exploration and Discovery *by A. Millard (EDC Publishing, 1979).*
Christopher Columbus: Admiral of the Ocean Sea *by Jim Haskins (Scholastic, 1991).*
The Cruelest Commerce *by Colin Palmer (National Geographic, 1992). An article on the slave trade.*
The Renaissance and the New World *by Giovanni Peter Caselli (Bedrich Books, 1985).*
One Day in Elizabethan England *by G. B. Kirtland (Harcourt Brace Jovanovich, 1962).*
Good Queen Bess *by Diane Stanley and Peter Vennema (Four Winds Press/Macmillan, 1990).*
Crusaders, Aztecs, Samurai *by A. Millard (EDC Publishing, 1978).*
Japan *by Carol Greene (Children's Press, 1983).*
Russia to the Revolution *by Susan Finney and Patricia Kindle (Good Apple, 1987).*
The Old Regime and the Revolution *edited by Trevor Cairns (Lerner, 1985).*
The True Story of Napoleon *by Anthony Corley (Children's Press, 1964).*
Atlas of World History *edited by Frances M. Chapham (Warwick, 1982).*
Calliope Magazine. *A magazine about world history for children. To subscribe, write Cobblestone Publishing, Inc., Peterborough, NH 03458 or call 1-800-821-0115. Two back issues that you can order, and which complement this section on world history, are:* Great Explorers to the East *(Sept./Oct. 1990) and* Great Explorers to the West *(Jan./Feb. 1992).*

World Civilization

INDIAN CIVILIZATIONS IN THE AMERICAS

The Maya, Aztecs, and Incas

Centuries before Europeans came to the New World, great civilizations had already arisen in Central and South America—the civilizations of the Maya, Aztecs, and Incas. The Maya, in Central America, were the earliest of the three, starting as far back as 500 B.C. The Aztecs developed their empire much later, and flourished in what is now central Mexico. The Incas thrived about the same time as the Aztecs, and lived in the Andes Mountains of South America. In this section you will learn about these great early civilizations, and about several smaller Native American cities in the lands that would become the United States, inhabited by peoples who were here long before the Europeans started their small settlements at Jamestown and St. Augustine.

The Maya

If you travel to Guatemala or parts of Mexico, you can still meet people who call themselves Maya and can speak the Mayan language. They are descendants of the ancient Maya who built and ruled dozens of highly civilized cities in Central America.

One of the most impressive Mayan cities was Tikal (teh-KAAL), whose ruins can still be seen in a jungle in Guatemala. Tikal had soaring temples and palaces decorated with colorful paintings and writing (called hieroglyphics). But not many people lived there. The city was used for special religious ceremonies and sacrifices.

If you were a Maya, your family's ancestors would be extremely important to you. Depending on who your ancestors were, you might spend your life as a laborer hauling rocks from the local quarries, or as a high-ranking soldier serving the em-

The Temple of the Giant Jaguar still stands at Tikal.

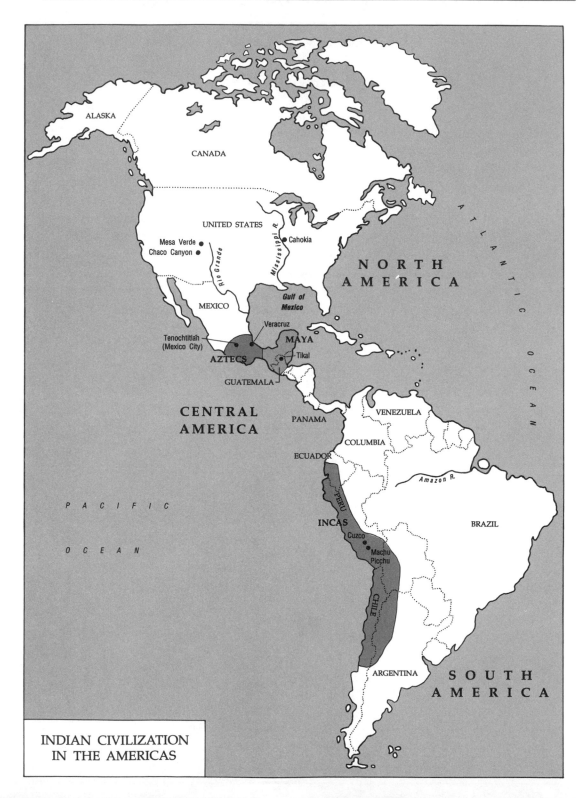

INDIAN CIVILIZATION
IN THE AMERICAS

peror. The Maya believed that the elite group who ruled them had descended from the gods. A family's line of descent was a common theme of Mayan art, including the many beautiful sculptures, paintings, and writings that decorated Mayan buildings.

Mayan Life and Learning

Most Maya were peasants. They lived outside the cities and worked as laborers or grew maize for the ruling lords. They visited the temples and palaces (at Tikal, for instance) on special occasions for religious ceremonies. Inside a Mayan city, on a normal day, you would find many crafts people and artisans, such as weavers, stonemasons, jewelry makers, and potters, working hard to please their lords and princes. At the royal court, musicians, poets, and storytellers also performed for their leaders.

We still don't know a lot about the Mayan religion. But we do know that the Maya believed in many gods who controlled the natural elements, such as the rain and the wind, the sun, the moon, and the stars. We also know that they believed they had to please the gods by shedding blood. In Mayan artwork, you can see both princes and slaves piercing themselves with thorns, or even drawing ropes through their tongues to feed their blood to the gods. The Maya believed that feed-

This figure carved by the Maya wears the fancy headdress of a rain god.

ing human blood to the gods was necessary in order to ensure that their crops grew and their children were born healthy.

The Maya were especially advanced in mathematics. Their knowledge of math was unequaled for many hundreds of years after their civilization had fallen. They discovered the concept of zero, and designed a calendar that is even more accurate than the 365-day calendar we use today.

Where Did They Go?

By A.D. 900, the Maya were no longer a flourishing people. Their soaring cities were ghost towns, to be inhabited later by new peoples. How did an entire civilization break down and abandon its cities? Archaeologists—the scientists who sort through the remains of ancient cultures—are still working like detectives to solve this ancient mystery. Some think that the cities collapsed because the lands were farmed so heavily that not enough corn could be grown to feed so many people. Others think that the peasants revolted against the ruling elite, leading to war and chaos. The Maya may have left the answer staring us right in the face. The code to Mayan hieroglyphics has been mostly solved, and these writings may explain the breakdown of a once-flourishing and highly advanced culture.

The Aztecs: The Eagle on the Cactus

The Aztecs were a great warrior nation that ruled a large empire in central Mexico from the late 1300s until 1519, when the explorer Hernando Cortés arrived on their shores from Spain. The Aztecs concentrated their power in the magnificent city of Tenochtitlán (tay-NOSH-tlee-TLAHN), much of which now lies under modern-day Mexico City.

This ancient map made by the Aztecs marks the location of Tenochtitlán with the legendary eagle on a cactus. Notice the warriors below the map and the hieroglyphs around its border.

The Aztecs began as a group of hunters and gatherers. According to Aztec legend, a god told these people to stop wandering when they found an eagle holding a snake in its mouth and sitting on a prickly-pear cactus, called a *tenochtli* (tay-NOSH-tlee). Aztec legend holds that around A.D. 1300, these people came across the eagle on the cactus. The cactus was on an island in the middle of a shallow lake, and the Aztecs chose to build their city right then and there, calling it Tenochtitlán. The island city grew to have nearly 150,000 inhabitants.

Tenochtitlán had carefully planned avenues that led out from a great temple. Other temples, shrines, and a royal court were the sites of study and training for the elite priests and warriors. Because the lake in which the city was situated was shallow, the Aztecs were able to build streets and create a maze of canals within their city: the main thoroughfares were built with a water lane for canoes and rafts and a dry lane for walking. Tenochtitlán amazed the first Spaniards to set eyes on it; as one of

Although this picture re-creates just part of Tenochtitlán, you can see how grand the Aztec city was. The large building at the left is the great temple, which is topped by the ruler's throne room.

them wrote, "Some of the soldiers among us who had been in many parts of the world, in Constantinople, and all over Italy and Rome, said that so large a market place and so full of people, and so well regulated and arranged, they had never beheld before."

The Aztecs gained their power by conquering neighboring tribes and demanding tribute from them. Tribute might consist of corn, cloth, gold, or even young men who would be later sacrificed to the Aztec gods. The fierceness with which the Aztecs exacted tribute made them many enemies. This would cost them dearly when the Spanish came.

At the height of its power, the Aztec empire stretched from the Pacific Ocean to the Gulf of Mexico. Its messengers and spies traveled in disguise to watch over warring neighbors. Its merchants covered great distances: it is said that one Aztec emperor living in Tenochtitlán ate fresh fish caught and delivered daily from what is now Veracruz on the Gulf of Mexico.

A Fierce Religion

In the Aztec culture, religion was not something separate from work or school. It touched every aspect of life. The Aztec emperor was considered a kind of god, and the high priests who advised him held great power over the people. These priests would read the sky and the stars to foretell future events. A comet might mean good fortune, for example, while any babies born on the day of an eclipse were considered doomed.

The Aztecs believed in a number of watchful gods who made it their business to bring good or evil upon the people. Their two most important gods were the god of the sun and war, and the god of rain. Many of their gods were depicted in the shapes of animals, such as jaguars or serpents. A warrior

The Aztecs believed that the appearance of comets and other celestial events could be interpreted to help them make decisions.

wearing a jaguar mask into battle would be asking the jaguar-god to help him win. The most distinguished warriors belonged to the knightly orders of the Jaguars and the Eagles. In battle they wore pelts or feathers to give them the fighting prowess of their namesakes.

One part of the Aztec religion is awful to think about: the practice of human sacrifice. The Aztecs believed that they had to offer their gods the gift of human blood. One function of the priests was to perform these sacrifices. The victims were prisoners of war and slaves. The method of sacrifice was particularly cruel: the priest would plunge a knife into the victim's chest and rip out the still-beating heart to give to the gods. The Aztecs sometimes practiced human sacrifice in horrifyingly large numbers, sacrificing thousands of victims at a time.

Two Worlds Meet

The year 1519 marks not only a fateful year for the Aztecs, but an irreversible encounter between two civilizations. It had been a terrible year for the Aztecs and their leader, Montezuma II (you may also see his name spelled "Moctezuma"). Crops had failed. Strange signs appeared in the sky. High priests squabbled among themselves. Montezuma, usually a firm leader, had been shaken by visions that a great disaster was to befall his people.

According to Aztec legend, a bearded, fair-skinned god named Quetzalcoatl (ketzal-co-AHT-el) had promised to come help his people if they needed him. That year the Aztecs felt they really needed his help. So when Montezuma's soldiers first reported seeing the bearded Spaniard Hernando Cortés, Montezuma sent messengers with gifts of jewelry, clothing, and food to welcome the god who would change their

Tenochtitlan.

This ancient Aztec drawing records the meeting of Hernando Cortés and Montezuma.

fortunes. And Cortés, at the urging of the enemies of the Aztecs, pretended to be the god Quetzalcoatl in order to trick Montezuma.

Despite their great numbers and well-honed skills as warriors, the Aztecs were at a great disadvantage when they first encountered the Spaniards. Unaware of civilizations so different from their own, they had no way to understand the strange beings marching toward their city. When the Spanish first arrived, the Aztecs described the Spanish ships as moving islands. The Aztecs could only compare the Spaniards' horses to gigantic deer or unearthly monsters.

Hernando Cortés sailed to the shores of Mexico seeking gold and hoping to convert the New World to Christianity. He arrived with only six hundred men, many of whom were afraid of being in the New World. Once they reached shore, they did not want to go on with the mission. Cortés, however, was so determined to go on that he burned the very ships they had sailed in to make sure that there was no turning back.

Cortés plotted with the various enemies of the Aztecs to bring about their downfall. One chief from the Yucatan area was so eager to seek revenge against the Aztecs that he gave Cortés a young slave girl, Malinche (mah-LEEN-chay), who was very smart and could speak a variety of languages. She quickly learned Spanish and became Cortés's translator and trusted spy.

Before long, Cortés and his men were led to Tenochtitlán. Montezuma, believing Quetzalcoatl had arrived, allowed Cortés and his men to enter the very heart of the city without resistance. Cortés, armed with horses, guns, and armor, took the shaken Montezuma hostage.

For a short time, it seemed possible that the Aztecs and Spaniards might avoid a bloody battle. The Spaniards would simply replace the Aztec priests and leaders as rulers. But the Aztecs did not want to become Christians. They worried that their gods would abandon them if they allowed them to be replaced by a Christian god. Cortés felt pressure from the enemy tribes who had helped him. And the Spaniards were becoming more greedy for gold. In this atmosphere of growing tension, the Spaniards fired upon a gathering of unarmed Aztecs. The Aztecs fought back, slaughtering all but a quarter of the Spanish troops. Cortés escaped only by chance.

Cortés soon returned to Tenochtitlán with new troops. He surrounded the city with cannons and cut off the Aztecs' supply of fresh water, holding the entire city hostage. The Aztecs fought back for eighty days—almost three months—but eventually too many of them died in battle or succumbed to diseases caught from the Spaniards. By August of 1521, the Aztec empire was lost forever.

The Incas

About the time that the Aztecs controlled most of Central America, the Incas ruled an even larger empire along the Pacific coast of South America. Unlike the Maya, the Incas had no system of writing. Still, they were able to administer the most highly organized ancient empire in the Western Hemisphere.

Through the high cliffs and deep valleys of the Andes Mountains, the Incas built more than fourteen thousand miles of curving roads. When necessary, they connected them with tunnels and rope bridges—all without the kinds of modern-day tools we take for granted. (What other ancient civilization have you learned about that built such extensive roads?)

The Incas lived in a land of mountains and oceans, cliffs and plains, lush vegetation and rocky sparseness. They used this varying landscape to their advantage. They fished the waters off the coast and raised llamas and alpacas for wool. They grew crops in the green valleys of the mountain ranges and in the steep fields that they terraced out of mountainsides. Did you know that the potato came from the Andes? The Incas developed a way to irrigate dry areas with canals, and farmed so successfully that extra food had to be stored in warehouses.

The Incas were skillful stonemasons. Many of their walls still exist because they built them so precisely. What is truly remarkable is that they built their walls without mortar! They shaped the stones so that they fit together perfectly. In many of their walls, the stones fit so tightly that even today a sharp knife cannot pass through the cracks.

Stones carried sacred meanings for the Incas. They believed that the gods created man out of stone, and that some of their ancestors and past leaders had been turned back into stone. Like the Aztecs, the Incas believed the ancestors of their rulers had

The ancient Inca city of Machu Picchu is high in the Andes north of Cuzco.

descended from the gods. They worshiped the sun, Inti, as their main god. When highborn leaders died, their bodies were preserved and then kept in their own palace homes. At harvest time these mummies were brought out, seated in places of honor, and offered food along with the rest of the dignitaries.

A Short-Lived Wonder

The Incas can trace their history back to A.D. 1200, but the real beginning of their dynasty starts in A.D. 1438 with the ruler Pachacuti Inca Yupanqui (PAH-cha-coo-tee IN-ca you-PANG-kee). Having the word "Inca" in his name meant that he was considered divine (a descendant of gods) by his people. Pachacuti Inca Yupanqui conquered the neighboring tribes both through battle and by dominating the trade routes through the mountains. In a short time, he turned a very small domain, based in the city of Cuzco (KOOZ-koh), into a huge empire that stretched one thousand miles from what is now Ecuador to the tip of Chile. That's about the distance from New York City to Miami, Florida.

Reports of the mighty Inca empire brought the Spanish conquistador Francisco Pizarro (pih-ZAHR-oh) to South America to conquer the Incas and convert them to Christianity. By the time of Pizarro's trip in 1532, the Spaniards were already governing Panama, which Pizarro used as a base to explore South America. He sailed from Panama to Peru in one ship with 180 men and 37 horses. Two ships with troops and ammunition later joined him in Peru. What allowed Pizarro to overpower the Incas, however, was not merely his soldiers, guns, and horses, but a civil war among the Incas, which Pizarro used to his advantage.

Two Inca princes, the brothers Atahuallpa (ah-ta-WHAL-pa) and Huascar (WHAH-scar), had battled over who should be the supreme ruler of the empire. Atahuallpa had kidnapped Huascar and was holding him prisoner. Just then Pizarro and his men approached the new leader's home and asked for a peaceful meeting. Believing that Pizarro would help him defeat Huascar and his allies once and for all, Atahuallpa, who had some thirty thousand men stationed nearby, agreed. He rode to the meeting on a golden litter, the soldiers who accompanied him unarmed.

Pizarro greeted him with brutal treachery: he slaughtered Atahuallpa's men and imprisoned Atahuallpa. From his prison cell, Atahuallpa sent an order that Huascar be murdered. The order was carried out, and Pizarro used it to turn the public against Atahuallpa. As soon as Pizarro knew that the Inca soldiers would not revolt because of his actions, he had Atahuallpa strangled. Within a short time, tens of thousands of Incas were killed not only by guns but by the foreign diseases they caught from the Spaniards. Their mighty empire had fallen.

SMALLER CITIES FARTHER NORTH

Cahokia, a Mound City

In the United States, you can find many man-made flat-topped hills called burial mounds—evidence of hundreds of ancient small cities stretching from the Pacific to the Atlantic Ocean. In some Indian cities in North America, burial mounds served as the city's central buildings just as pyramids did in the Mayan cities. The mounds were flattened on top to serve as platforms for public ceremonies, and the cities included roadways and other public buildings. The cities were often barricaded on the outskirts for protection against enemy tribes.

Around A.D. 600 in an area near what is now East St. Louis, Illinois, the Mississippi Indians started a settlement called Cahokia (kuh-HOE-key-uh). The settlement began at the site of the huge mounds the Indians shaped to serve as graves. By the time the city was at its most developed, between A.D. 1050–1250, there were over one hundred of these large mounds and about ten thousand people lived there. In Cahokia you can still see a famous mound, called the Monk's Mound, that is ninety feet tall. Its base is larger than the base of the Great Pyramid of Egypt.

Pueblo-Builders: The Anasazi

Do you think apartments are something you can find only in modern-day living? Not so. The Anasazi people, who settled in a dry desert with gigantic cliffs and rock formations, had the smart idea of living close together and using the overhanging cliffs to protect themselves from the elements. The Anasazi people lived at Mesa Verde (in present-day Colorado) from about A.D. 550 to A.D. 1300—more than 700

Anasazi ruins nestle in the cliff sides at Mesa Verde. These dwellings were so suitable for the landscape and climate that some present-day descendents of the Anasazi still build pueblos in a similar style. For example, see the picture on the Zuni pueblo on page 195.

years. No one is sure exactly why the Anasazi community at Mesa Verde disappeared after 1300. Perhaps a terrible drought killed the few crops that could be grown in the desert. Perhaps the area was invaded by other tribes.

From A.D. 950 to A.D. 1300, the Anasazi created another type of apartment-living in a city at Chaco Canyon (in present-day New Mexico). A fortresslike wall protected the entire city. The buildings had multiple stories and were ingeniously designed, with roofs of lower floors serving as balconies for upstairs rooms. Storerooms for corn and dried meat were tucked into the first floors. The people lived on the second floor. Rather than building stairs to enter their homes, they used one-story wooden ladders. That way, the Anasazi could keep attackers at bay by quickly pulling up the ladders.

EUROPEAN EXPLORATION AND THE CLASH OF CULTURES

The Muslim Control of Trade

Conquistadors like Cortés and Pizarro were part of a wave of Europeans who ventured from European shores to lands both near and far. Beginning in the fifteenth century, ship after ship sailed from Portugal and Spain, and later from the Netherlands and England, on voyages that would take them to the fabled East described by Marco Polo. They also sailed to continents that the Europeans called a "New

World," because before the 1400s most Europeans did not know that North and South America existed. For Cortés, Pizarro, and others, the voyages of exploration often turned into voyages of conquest. The Europeans didn't set out simply to find what was there. They set out to convert the people they met to Christianity. And they set out to grow rich, sometimes by trading with the people they met, sometimes by simply taking whatever they wanted.

Before the fifteenth century, Europeans had rarely sailed far from their own shores. They knew that China, Africa, and the Indies existed, because these lands were the sources of many goods that Europeans enjoyed, including silk, gold, and spices. But Europeans had not traveled to get these valuable goods for themselves. Instead, they relied on Muslim merchants, who brought spices and other riches from Asia, and dominated both the land and the sea routes to the East.

Muslims, you recall, are followers of the religion of Islam. In Books Three and Four of this series, you read how Islam was started in the seventh century by Mohammed. You learned that Arabs rapidly spread the new religion over many lands, from the Persian Gulf in the southeast to Spain in the west, and from the eastern coast of Africa into North Africa. As Arabs carried their religion far and wide, they forged bonds between many different peoples in many different regions bordering the Near East. Over time, as more and more people became Muslims, they all learned at least a little of the Arabic language as they studied the Islamic faith.

A common language helps make trade possible, for then people of different regions can communicate with each other as they go about buying and selling goods. For many years, adventurous Muslim merchants carried on most of the trade between eastern countries and Western Europe. By the thirteenth century, Muslim traders were regularly transporting spices from the islands now called Indonesia, gold from Africa, silk and porcelain from China, and grain from Egypt.

On their route from East to West, many merchants would pass through Baghdad (now the capital of Iraq), which is centrally located between the Tigris and Euphrates rivers. The remarkable wealth of the Muslim rulers in Baghdad made it possible to support the work of many artists and scholars. Baghdad flourished as a center of Islamic art and learning until it was raided by Mongol invaders in 1258.

Do you remember the Crusades? Beginning in the twelfth century, Christians fought wars called Crusades to try to take from the Muslims the region that Christians called the Holy Land. The Crusades brought Europeans into contact with the goods and luxuries of the East and spurred the European craving to have those same goods and luxuries at home.

Although Europeans had fought against Muslims in the Crusades, they later had to rely on Muslim traders to supply the goods and luxuries they wanted. The great success of Muslim traders was partly responsible for Europeans deciding to undertake explorations in the 1400s. They set out to find their own trade routes to the East, or to take over Muslim trade routes, in part because they wanted the riches of the East without having to pay the high prices demanded by the Muslim traders.

Early Portuguese Explorations

One small European country, Portugal, set out to find ways around the Muslim trade routes. In the process it went on to establish a vast trading empire. The Portuguese—like their Muslim rivals—were driven by a mixture of economic and religious motives. They wanted to grow wealthy from trade, but they also wanted to spread Christianity to other lands. In many cases, the economic struggle to control trade also became a holy war, pitting Christian against Muslim.

This mixture of economic and religious motives drove Prince Henry of Portugal. In the early 1400s, he fought in the North African area called Morocco against Muslims whom the Europeans called "Moors." Later, Prince Henry organized a number of voyages by Portuguese sailors to explore the western coast of Africa beyond Morocco, though Henry himself never went on any of these voyages. These ships often bore on their sails a large red cross.

Prince Henry is sometimes called "Prince Henry the Navigator" because for many years it was thought that he established a school in southern Portugal for the study of navigation and geography. Many historians now believe, however, that such a school never existed. In any case, it wasn't until shortly after Prince Henry's time that the Portuguese learned—from Muslim scholars—about the most significant advances in navigation, including improved instruments, accurate ocean maps, and celestial navigation (charting your course by reference to the position of the stars).

In Prince Henry's time, European sailors knew very little about the western coastline of Africa. It wasn't until 1434 that a Portuguese ship sailed for the first time past Cape Bojador (BAJ-uh-door) on the west coast of Africa. Before, sailors had feared that the sandy expanses of Cape Bojador might mark the "edge of the world," beyond which lay fire-breathing dragons and boiling seas. In the years ahead, Portuguese ships passed Cape Bojador many times and returned home with their cargo from Africa, mostly gold, ivory, and slaves. (You will learn more about the slave trade later in this section.) Portugal gained wealth from its trade with African kingdoms, but still the Portuguese were impatient to find a way around Africa to India.

In 1487, a Portuguese captain named Bartolomeu Dias set out with two ships and only a rough plan: to find out where the west coast of Africa led. Like most sailors of the time, Dias kept close to the shore, but then winds and currents drove him into unknown waters, out of sight of land. His ships were pounded by storms, and he lost many sailors and a ship along the way. He turned north and finally caught sight of land again. He had found the tip of Africa and sailed around it! Pressured by his weary sailors, he did not sail on to India but turned around to head home. He left a stone pillar to mark the tip of Africa, which he called the Cape of Torment. The Portuguese king renamed it the Cape of Good Hope because he was so happy his ships were that much closer to reaching the East.

Before reaching India, the Portuguese would find themselves challenged by another European country equally determined to gain wealth and make converts to

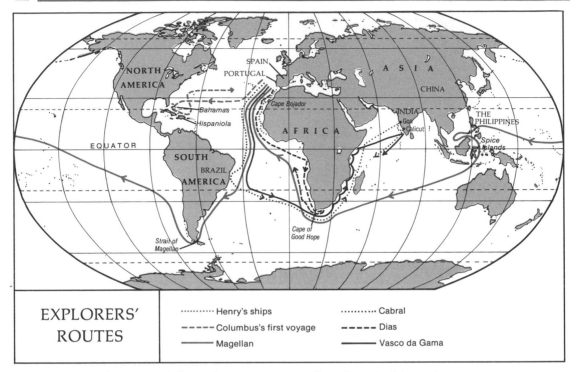

EXPLORERS' ROUTES

·········· Henry's ships   ·········· Cabral
- - - - - Columbus's first voyage   - - - - - Dias
———— Magellan   ———— Vasco da Gama

This map shows the routes of the explorers you are reading about in this section.

Christianity. That country was Spain, and one explorer who sailed under the Spanish flag is a figure you're familiar with—Christopher Columbus.

Columbus

"In fourteen-hundred-and-ninety-two, Columbus sailed the ocean blue." Unlike this simple rhyme, the story of Columbus is complex, and his place in history is perceived differently by different people.

You may be familiar with some of the details of Columbus's life. He was born in Genoa, a busy center of trade on the northwest coast of Italy. He was fascinated by the tales of Marco Polo's travels to China. His studies convinced him the world was round, and that he could reach the East by sailing west. Columbus was partly right: by sailing due west from Europe, he could reach Asia—only he would have to get across a huge unforeseen continent in between.

Columbus first took his ideas to King John of Portugal. But just as Columbus arrived, Dias returned with news of the sea route around Africa to India. With this knowledge of a route to the East, King John was not inclined to support Columbus's scheme to reach the East by sailing west.

Columbus then went to the court of Spain, where, after persistent appeals, he persuaded King Ferdinand and Queen Isabella to support his expedition. Ferdinand

Columbus presents his ideas to King Ferdinand and Queen Isabella.

and Isabella shared the mixture of economic and religious motives that drove Columbus. They wanted the great cargoes of gold and other goods Columbus promised to bring back. And they agreed with what may have been Columbus's strongest motivation, a fervent desire to spread Christianity wherever he went.

The rulers' desire to spread Christianity also extended to Spain itself. Though many Jews and Muslims had lived in Spain for a long time, Ferdinand and Isabella were determined to continue the centuries-old policy of Spain's Christian rulers to drive all non-Christians from the country. In 1492, shortly before Columbus sailed, they ordered all Jews in Spain to become Christian or leave the country, and they sent troops to expel all remaining Muslims who would not become Christian.

Columbus made four voyages. He began his first voyage in 1492 with three ships—two small ones, the Niña and the Pinta, and a larger ship, the Santa Maria. After two months of sailing west, the crew grew fearful. Columbus promised they would turn back if they did not sight land in three days. On the third day, October 12, 1492, Columbus landed at an island, which he called San Salvador (Spanish for "Holy Savior") in the Bahamas.

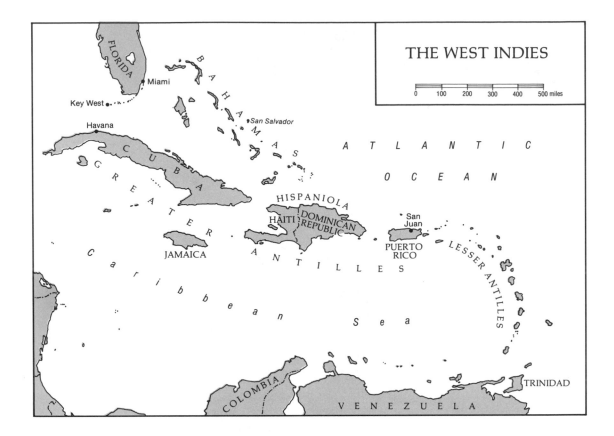

THE WEST INDIES

Columbus was convinced he was nearing India or China. He went from island to island looking for signs to confirm his belief. You've read in earlier books in this series that he called the native people living in the area "Indians" because he thought he had reached the islands south of China called the East Indies. Although he'd made an error, the name "Indies" stuck. The islands where Columbus first landed are today called the West Indies.

The West Indies: Miles of Isles

The islands of the West Indies stretch over 2,500 miles between North and South America. Some of these, like Cuba, are the tops of sunken mountains; others were created by volcanoes. They can be divided into three groups. The Bahamas, over seven hundred islands and reefs, are located in the Atlantic off the coast of Florida. The Greater Antilles include Cuba, Jamaica, and the island of Hispaniola (Haiti and the Dominican Republic). The Lesser Antilles include many small islands, like Trinidad, arcing to the southwest of the Greater Antilles.

The first people Columbus encountered were the Tainos (TIE-nos), one of the Arawak (ARE-a-wack) peoples in the region. The Tainos received Columbus with friendly greetings. Another native people, the Caribs (CA-reebs), proved more hostile: they were a fierce and warlike people who often raided the Tainos and other neighboring peoples.

When Columbus returned to Spain, he took six Tainos with him as "proof" that he had reached Asia. Queen Isabella honored Columbus with the title of "Admiral of the Ocean Sea." More than a thousand Spaniards accompanied Columbus on his next voyage. Columbus was placed in charge as governor, but he proved to be an ineffective and sometimes harsh leader, unable to keep peace and order among the many unruly adventurers who had come to the "New World" seeking their fortunes.

Columbus died in 1506, still believing that he had reached Asia, and unaware that he had stumbled upon lands previously unknown to Europeans. His encounter with what was, for Europeans, a "New World" opened the way for many more Europeans to come (including the Spanish conquerors you read about earlier, Cortés and Pizarro). His daring first voyage in three little ships across a great ocean altered the course of history.

Though Columbus did not "discover America," as people used to say, his voyage in 1492 marks the beginning of a complex story. It is a story of different peoples and cultures that would eventually, and sometimes painfully, come together to form different nations in the Americas.

The sense that Columbus defines a hugely important moment in history is one of the reasons why, in the United States, October 12 is set aside as Columbus Day. For many people, it has become a day of mixed emotions. They feel awed by the persistence and bravery of the "Admiral of the Ocean Sea" setting out for a voyage into the unknown that would change the course of history. Yet they also know that Columbus and European explorers who followed him came with mixed motives, that they sometimes acted viciously against native peoples, and that they (unknowingly) brought with them a host of diseases that wiped out great numbers of these peoples. They know that we have to go well beyond a simple rhyme about 1492 and the ocean blue to understand the complex significance of Columbus's first voyage as a decisive event in a story that is still going on.

Who Will Rule the Waves?

After Columbus's voyage in 1492, Spain and Portugal began competing to find and lay claim to new lands. This intense competition might have led to war. But there was one authority that both Spain and Portugal listened to—the leader of the Catholic Church, the pope.

The pope didn't want the two countries to go to war, but he did want both countries to continue their explorations, again for economic and religious reasons. Both Spain and Portugal gave large amounts of money to the church each year, so the richer these countries grew, the richer grew the church. The church also saw the new lands as fertile places to spread Christianity, and it often sent its priests as missionaries to convert the native peoples.

To keep peace between Spain and Portugal, the pope ruled that the two countries would share the seas and had them sign a treaty in 1494. This was the important Treaty of Tordesillas (tor-de-SEE-yas). The treaty drew a line of longitude from pole to pole, 370 leagues west of the Cape Verde islands (a league is about three miles). The treaty said that all land east of that line would belong to Portugal, including India and the African lands Portugal had claimed. The treaty went on to say that all land west of that line, including the lands Columbus had encountered, would belong to Spain.

The pope's treaty did not anticipate that other countries like England and the

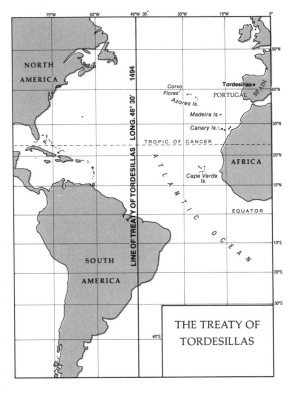

THE TREATY OF TORDESILLAS

Netherlands would soon begin their own explorations, which shows how thoroughly Portugal and Spain dominated the seas around Europe during the late 1400s. And the Treaty of Tordesillas failed to take account of something else: had anyone asked the peoples who lived in the Caribbean islands, or Africa, or India what *they* wanted? What does the very idea of dividing the world between Spain and Portugal suggest abut the Europeans' sense of themselves in relation to the rest of the world at this time?

> *S*ome missionaries were fascinated by the knowledge and cultures of the native peoples they wanted to convert. These missionaries were the Europeans most likely to write down and try to preserve native customs and languages. While many of these customs and languages have been lost, some of the missionaries' records have helped us know more about life in the Americas before Europeans arrived.

Da Gama and Cabral

With the treaty between Spain and Portugal in mind, the confident Portuguese continued to send expeditions to the south. Vasco da Gama, a Portuguese nobleman and businessman, knew he could grow rich by finding a route around Africa to India. He set out in 1497 with four ships and 170 men to find a way.

After finding and going around the Cape of Good Hope, Da Gama sailed up the eastern coast of Africa, an area entirely new to the Europeans. Da Gama was lucky when he landed in the port of Malindi, in what is now Kenya. There he met Ahmad ibn-Majid (ah-MAHD ih-bin-mah-JEED), an experienced Muslim sailor who joined the voyage and showed Da Gama the route to India.

The voyage was costly: more than half of Da Gama's sailors died of scurvy (a disease caused by the poor diet available for sailors at the time, especially a lack of vitamin C from fresh fruits and vegetables). Finally, in May of 1498, Da Gama arrived in the Indian city of Calicut, the place he had traveled so far to reach. (The colorful cotton cloth called "calico" is named after Calicut.)

By finding the sea route to India, Vasco da Gama brought back great wealth for the Portuguese, wealth that paid for even more exploration and conquests. After Da Gama's success, another Portuguese explorer and trader, Pedro Cabral (ca-BRAL), set out for India. On his way, he went far west of his planned course—so far that he crossed the Atlantic and unexpectedly landed on the coast of South America! He stayed there only ten days, but claimed the new land, which he called Brazil, for Portugal, because it lay east of the line established by the pope in the Treaty of Tordesillas. That's why today, while most people in South America speak Spanish, the language of Brazil is Portuguese.

When Cabral finally arrived in Calicut, the Muslim traders he met there greeted him with suspicion. What was this European doing in their territory? They realized that if Europeans could make it to India on their own, there would no longer be a need for the Muslims to bring their spices and cloth overland to Europe. And later they saw how the European desire to take over trade routes could turn into a kind of holy war: in one instance, Da Gama cruelly burned a Calicut ship crowded with Muslims returning from a pilgrimage to the Muslim holy city of Mecca. Cabral bombarded the city of Calicut, then sailed on to other Indian ports where he loaded his ships with spices and goods that he sold for great sums in Portugal.

The Portuguese ships had an advantage over most others sailing the seas: they were heavily armed with cannons. The Portuguese used this military advantage to take over many trade routes that had been controlled by Muslims. In other cases, the Portuguese allowed Muslims to continue trading but forced them to pay taxes to the Portuguese. Any Muslim ship sailing through the Indian Ocean, for example, had to have a permit and pay a tax, or risk being sunk by the Portuguese.

Magellan Goes Around the World

In 1519 (the same year Cortés encountered the Aztecs), a Portuguese seaman named Ferdinand Magellan set out on what would become the first journey around the world. Although Magellan was Portuguese, he had fallen out of favor with the Portu-

Magellan and his crew at the Strait of Magellan.

guese king, and his trip was financed by King Charles I of Spain. Magellan convinced the Spanish king that he would claim vast lands for Spain by sailing west from Europe and exploring the area allowed to Spain by the Treaty of Tordesillas.

Magellan's crew of five boats and 240 men sailed along the coast of Brazil, looking for what Magellan believed to be a strait (a narrow waterway) leading west to the Pacific Ocean. All of this was new territory for the Europeans: no one had yet sailed the length of South America. When Magellan did indeed reach a strait at the very tip of South America, he named it for himself, and we still call it the Strait of Magellan. Magellan also gave the Pacific Ocean the name we still use today.

Like Columbus, who set out to reach the east by sailing west, Magellan had hoped that by sailing west he would avoid having to go around Africa, and instead would reach the Moluccas (moh-LOO-cahs), or "Spice Islands," from the east. The name "Spice Islands" tells you what he was after: clove, nutmeg, cinnamon, and other spices desired by Europeans. But Magellan was killed in the Philippines during a fight with the native peoples there. His trip cost many other lives as well. Only 18 of the 240 sailors he'd set forth with returned home, and four out of his five ships were destroyed. One ship did survive, however, and in 1522, the first ship to sail around the world returned to Spain.

The Pacific Islands and the Ring of Fire

The Spice Islands, which were so sought after by European explorers, are in the island group south of the Philippines and southeast of Indochina and the Malay Peninsula. Look for them on the map. There are the islands that Columbus was trying to reach when he came upon the New World and that Magellan sailed around South America to find. The Portuguese were the first to claim the islands as a colony, but most were later taken over by the Dutch and became part of the Dutch East Indies.

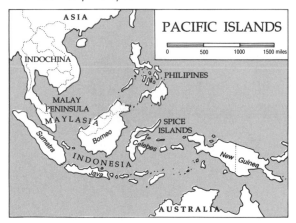

Today the Spice Islands are part of a country called the Republic of Indonesia. There are more than 13,000 islands and islets (small islands) in Indonesia, strung out from Sumatra to New Guinea. Most Indonesians live on the long, narrow island of Java. A large stretch of islands like these is called an archipelago (ar-keh-PEL-uh-go).

Dotting the entire rim of the Pacific Ocean, from Asia to North and South America, are many volcanoes. Some of these are quiet; others are ready to spew out lava in fiery eruptions. This circle of volcanoes around the Pacific is called the Ring of Fire. The same area is prone to frequent earthquakes as well.

The Ring of Fire passes through the Philippines. These islands—about 7,100 of them—were named for King Philip II of Spain (you'll read about him later in this section).

Zheng He

The Portuguese and Spanish weren't the only ones exploring the seas in the 1400s. Back in 1405, while the Portuguese still believed that sailing past Cape Bojador would mean burning in boiling seas, a Chinese navigator and explorer named Zheng He (JUNG HUH) sailed far and wide throughout the Indian Ocean. Zheng He introduced China to more than twenty nations, including those in east Africa and Arabia. One time he even brought an African giraffe back to China!

Zheng He was a favored member of the Chinese emperor's court. During his first voyage, he sailed with a huge fleet, including over 60 large ships, called junks, 255 smaller ships, and over 27,000 crew members. The Chinese junks were much larger and more advanced than the ships being built in Europe at the time. They held up to 500 people and had watertight compartments for storage and comfortable cabins for the crew. Rather than cloth sails, many had bamboo sails that folded neatly like window blinds.

Zheng He sailed a Chinese junk much like this one.

Unlike Europe, which was turning its face outward to new lands, China began to close its borders and turn away from the outside world. Chinese rulers were convinced their country and culture would only be harmed by contact with foreigners. So despite Zheng He's amazing travels to so many lands new to China, the emperor's court ordered him not to take any more trips abroad. China stopped exploring beyond its borders just when the Portuguese began to set out to find new lands.

The Dutch Head East

The Portuguese were the first Europeans to set out on voyages of trade and conquest, but other countries were not far behind. You've read about the voyages of Columbus, Cortés, and Pizarro for Spain. The Netherlands also sent many ships to sea. People from the Netherlands are called Dutch. If you look at the Netherlands on a map, you can see that much of the country is located on the coast; and, you can see why Amsterdam would become a very important port.

The flag of the Dutch East India Company.

Until the late 1500s, traders from the Netherlands had made their profits by transporting spices and cloth from Mediterranean ports back to Amsterdam. Then the Spanish king ordered that Dutch ships could no longer use

Dutch ships returning from their first expedition to the East Indies.

the trade routes along the Spanish and Portuguese coasts. What were the Dutch traders going to do?

Determined to keep their trade routes open, Dutch merchants set up the Dutch East India Company in 1602. Investors provided money to the Dutch East India Company to finance more trading voyages. The Dutch government provided its support and ordered the Dutch Navy to help as well. With navy ships to protect them—and fight the Spanish or Portuguese when necessary—Dutch trading ships managed to make many profitable journeys. Soon the Dutch East India Company controlled all trade between the Netherlands and the East Indies. Dutch trading ships traveled as far as Japan and the land that is now Vietnam. The East Indies, especially the port at Java, became an important trading area for the Dutch merchants. The Dutch became the leading suppliers to Europe of silk and indigo (a popular blue dye), as well as spices.

Look on the map of explorers' routes (page 120) at the water route from Amsterdam to Indonesia. Where do you think the halfway point is? It's at the Cape of Good Hope in South Africa. The Dutch founded Cape Town there as a supply station. It became important later as Europeans began to invade and settle parts of South Africa (which you'll read about in Book Six of this series). The people in South Africa who are today called Afrikaners descend from the early Dutch settlers, and their language, called Afrikaans, is a form of Dutch.

Where Are the English?

Although England was not a great sea power during the time of Magellan or Christopher Columbus, the English became aggressive traders and explorers (and even pirates) after 1600. In that year Queen Elizabeth I gave the English East India Company a charter establishing it as the only English company that could trade in the East Indies. The monopoly meant that English merchant ships would not fight among themselves over trade routes. As a result, the English East India Company grew very quickly. The English competed against the Dutch in Indonesia, and also began establishing trading posts in India, a country they would later take over entirely.

Because the Portuguese—and afterward the Dutch—controlled the southerly trade routes in the Indian Ocean, the English decided to try a northerly route to Asia. Since the English did not know the shape of the American continent, they searched in vain for a "northwest passage," a route that would allow them to sail above North America to Asia. Their search did not lead to stores of gold or a quick route to Asia, but they found out a great deal about North America when they landed at Newfoundland and other northern coasts. Just as the Spanish took the lead in exploring Central and South America, the English dominated exploration of the Atlantic coast of North America.

Europe's New World Colonies

Most European explorers sailed in search of gold, spices, and souls to convert to Christianity. But some Europeans were also interested in moving to the new lands and taking them over. These lands became colonies: regions under the control of faraway governments in distant lands.

When Cortés defeated the Aztecs and forced them to submit to Spanish rule, he colonized them; in later years, the Spanish created colonies in much of the rest of South America, as well as in the Caribbean islands that had been claimed by Columbus. When Cabral bumped into Brazil, he made it a Portuguese colony. The United States also started this way. As you know, when the English came to North America, they established thirteen colonies.

As Europeans colonized the Americas, the native civilizations began to disappear. Though most Europeans wrongly tended to see the Native Americans as "inferior" peoples who could be used as slaves, or as "heathens" to be converted to Christianity, they didn't want them to die out. Nevertheless, without knowing it, the Europeans brought a silent weapon. Whole villages were wiped out by diseases to which Europeans had built up some resistance, but the natives had not. The great killers were sicknesses such as smallpox, measles, and typhus.

Sugar, Plantations, and Slavery

The Portuguese began colonizing other lands as early as 1419, even before they sailed beyond Cape Bojador. They claimed islands in the Atlantic, such as Madeira (muh-DEAR-uh) and the Azores (A-zorz). These islands, along with the island of São Tomé (SOW toe-MAY), became sites for a new industry—the manufacturing of sugar. Portuguese citizens moved to these new lands, setting up homes and businesses, while still following the rule of the Portuguese king.

Growing sugarcane and turning it into the kind of sugar you might use to make cookies became a big business for the first time in the 1400s. By the early 1500s the Portuguese island colony of São Tomé was the largest single producer of sugar for Europeans to purchase. Harvesting and processing sugarcane was back-breaking work that required many men. The growing appetite for sugar and the money it would make had a tragic consequence: a demand for slaves to work the plantations.

At first, the Portuguese took Africans to work as slaves mostly to the island plantations or to Portugal and Spain. But then the European colonies across the Atlantic began to demand slave labor as well. The plantation system on São Tomé—where African slaves did the work while Europeans profited from their labor—became the model for plantations in the Americas and in the Caribbean. Let's look at how the awful practice of slavery spread, and why.

The Transatlantic Slave Trade

As you read earlier in this section, while the Portuguese were intent upon finding a way around Africa to India, the Spanish crossed the Atlantic and opened the way for European colonization of the Americas and the Caribbean. European settlers were quick to exploit the wealth of the New World, setting up gold and silver mines in the Andes Mountains, and plantations to grow sugar on the Caribbean islands.

At first, Europeans often forced the native peoples to work in the mines or on the plantations. When disease wiped out the native peoples, the Europeans looked to Africa for a new source of laborers. The demand for slave labor increased as more plantations were established: in South America and the West Indies, to grow sugar and coffee; and, in the English colonies that would become the southern United States, to grow rice, tobacco, and—much later—cotton.

By the mid-1600s, Spain had colonies in the West Indies and in Central and South America. The Dutch and Portuguese were in Brazil. The English and French were in North America and the West Indies. All of these European colonies imported Africans to work as slaves.

For the most part, European traders purchased as slaves those Africans who had been taken captive in wars between African states. A few powerful African rulers became very rich by selling prisoners of war into slavery. Part of the coast of West Africa became known as the "Slave Coast" because so many slaves were bought and sold there (you read about one kingdom on the Slave Coast, Benin, in Book Three). The Portuguese established a colony in Angola largely for the purpose of buying Africans to enslave them.

African traders would march groups of chained captives to the busy trading ports. There, European merchants would offer manufactured goods such as textiles, metalwares, and alcohol in exchange for people. In the late 1600s European traders also began offering guns in exchange for slaves. In the eighteenth century, some African states, like Ashanti and Dahomey, became wealthy when they used European guns to go to war against neighboring states for the specific purpose of taking captives to sell into slavery.

The European traders profited from a network of buying and selling known as "the triangular trade." It was called triangular because ships made three journeys that formed the sides of a triangle. Ships would leave Europe stocked with goods to exchange for slaves in Africa. From Africa, loaded with slaves, the ships would cross the Atlantic to the colonies in the Caribbean and the Americas. There, the traders would sell the slaves for goods like sugar, cotton, and tobacco—all of which were produced by slave labor. The traders would then return to Europe and sell those goods for their profit.

Africans sold into slavery had to suffer an agonizing voyage across the Atlantic called the Middle Passage. Enormous slave ships were built specifically for the purpose of making this terrible voyage. These ships carried from 150 to 600 slaves and could take more than ninety days to cross the Atlantic. The captains of these ships forced slaves to lie on their backs, crammed like sardines in a can, one person's head to the next one's feet. With red-hot irons, slave traders branded their captives like cattle, and shackled male slaves with heavy chains. So many slaves died during the Middle Passage—one out of every ten—that sharks followed the slave ships waiting to devour the corpses thrown overboard.

It is estimated that between 1520 and 1870, more than ten million African people were taken across the Atlantic to work as slaves, mostly after the mid-1600s. Most went to the Caribbean colonies and to Latin America. Beginning in 1619—when a Dutch ship left about twenty blacks at Jamestown, Virginia—the institution of slavery took hold in the English colonies that would become the United States. In the American Civilization section of this book, you can read about how arguments over slavery eventually pushed this nation into a bloody civil war, and about how slavery left a legacy of difficulties and injustices that Americans are still struggling to resolve.

East Africa: The Rise of the Swahili City-States

By the 1400s, when the Portuguese first arrived, Africa was a continent of diverse kingdoms, languages, and cultures. In earlier books in this series you read about the West African kingdoms of Benin, Songhai, Ghana, and Mali, as well as the southeastern African kingdom of Zimbabwe with its magnificently engineered stone walls

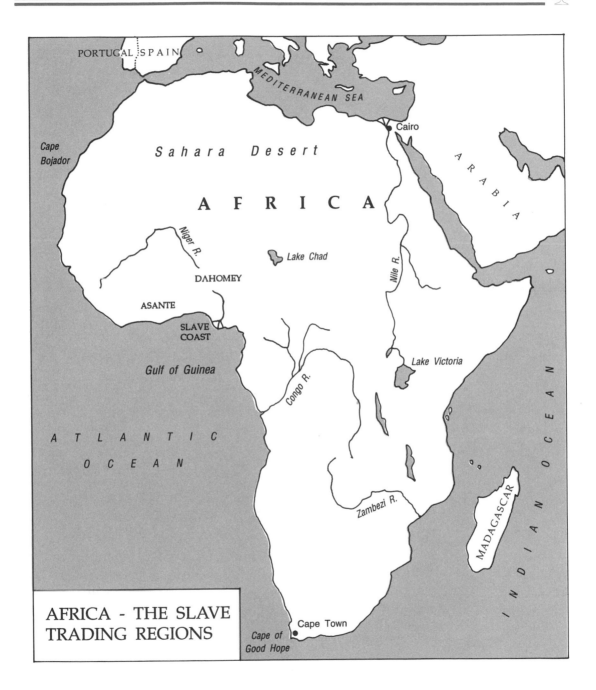

PORTUGAL SPAIN

MEDITERRANEAN SEA

Cairo

ARABIA

Cape
Bojador

S a h a r a   D e s e r t

A F R I C A

Niger R.

Lake Chad

DAHOMEY

Nile R.

ASANTE

SLAVE
COAST

Lake Victoria

Gulf of Guinea

Congo R.

A T L A N T I C

O C E A N

Zambezi R.

MADAGASCAR

I N D I A N   O C E A N

AFRICA - THE SLAVE
TRADING REGIONS

Cape Town

Cape of
Good Hope

surrounding the city. Now we will turn to the east African coast where a number of towns grew to be the thriving centers of trade that the Portuguese found when they arrived.

As early as A.D. 100, Greek and Roman ships made their way to the east African coast of the Indian Ocean. African towns began to flourish there as centers of trade when Arab traders learned how to use the seasonal winds known as monsoons. Every year between November and March the monsoon winds blow from Asia toward east Africa. Then, between April and October, the winds change direction and blow toward India and the Persian Gulf. Arab traders used these winds to set up a network of regular trade across the Indian Ocean. Towns like Mogadishu and Barawa grew to support them. In these towns, Arab traders loaded their ships with animal skins, gold, and especially ivory, much in demand in India and China. From India and China, the Arab traders brought back silk and cotton cloth, spices, and porcelain.

As the Arabs took up Islam in the seventh and eighth centuries, many Muslims settled in the east African trading towns and often married with the African peoples there. Some of the east Africans adopted Islam as their religion. They added a number of Arabic words to the Bantu language they spoke. They came to call themselves the Swahili, meaning "people of the coast," from the Arabic word *sahil,* meaning "coast." (The Swahili language is now the most widely spoken of the African languages among people in eastern Africa.)

The Swahili never united under a single king but lived in a number of separate towns under local rulers and with their own ways of life. About forty Swahili towns were located on the coast between Mogadishu in the north and Sofala (what is today Mozambique) in the south. Some were small towns while others grew to become wealthy city-states, including Mogadishu, Mombasa, Malindi, Zanzibar, and Kilwa.

Kilwa grew especially wealthy through trade in gold. The Muslim traveler Ibn Battuta (IHB-un bat-TOO-tah), whom you met in Book Four, described Kilwa as a "beautiful" and "elegantly built" city. A huge and splendid mosque was built in Kilwa during the mid-1400s.

In 1498, the city-state of Malindi welcomed Vasco da Gama, who, you recall, was lucky enough to find there a Muslim sailor to guide him to India. When Da Gama returned to Portugal with news of the wealthy Swahili city-states, the Portuguese decided they would seize them for their own. They sailed their heavily armed ships into the east African harbors and demanded that the African rulers become subjects of the Portuguese king and hand over many valuable goods as a tribute. Any town that resisted this arrogant demand was bombarded, looted, and burned. In 1505, Mombasa and Kilwa fell to the Portuguese. In the next decade, the Portuguese took control of most of the eastern coast of Africa, and stayed in control until some Swahili groups regained their towns in the late 1500s.

THE RENAISSANCE IN EUROPE

Islamic Civilization: A Long Tradition of Learning

Let's step back in time to the centuries just before the Europeans set out on their voyages of exploration and conquest. Do you remember the early middle ages, sometimes called the "Dark Ages," in Europe? These years (from the fall of Rome to about A.D. 1000) were called dark because, in a sense, the light of learning had grown dim: outside of isolated monasteries, not many people in Europe devoted much attention to literature, science, philosophy, or similar pursuits. During these same years, however, learning was alive and well in Islamic civilization, which produced many remarkable achievements.

When you do math, you use Arabic numerals. When you begin to study the kind of math called algebra, you will be learning about some of the principles explored by a ninth-century Muslim scholar who wrote a number of books on math, including one with the Arabic title, *al jabr*.

Muslim scholars translated many works by ancient Greek philosophers and scientists into Arabic: in doing this, they preserved the great insights and discoveries of classical civilization, and paved the way for insights and discoveries of their own. Muslim astronomers built on the work of the Greeks and, many years before Columbus sailed, came to the conclusion that the earth is round. Around A.D. 1,000, a remarkable Muslim thinker and writer named Ibn Sina (in Europe, he was called Avicenna) built on the work of the Greek philosopher Aristotle, and wrote about philosophy, astronomy, poetry, and more. Ibn Sina made especially important contributions to the knowledge of medicine and the treatment of disease at the time.

Before Christian forces took up arms to drive the Muslims out of Spain (a process completed during the reign of Ferdinand and Isabella), many Spanish cities thrived as centers of Islamic art and learning. One such city was Cordoba. In the tenth century, poets and musicians were supported by many wealthy Muslims who lived in gorgeous palaces throughout Cordoba. The city's seventy libraries contained many thousands of books—at a time when scribes had to copy out each book by hand! At the university in Cordoba, scholars from Baghdad met and exchanged ideas with scholars from western Europe.

In the 1100s and 1200s, at a university in Toledo, another thriving city in the Muslim part of Spain, Muslim scholars worked side by side with Jews and Christians to collect and translate Greek works into Arabic and also into Latin, the dominant language of learning in Europe at the time. Their work was partly responsible for a rebirth of interest in classical Greek and Roman learning in Europe beginning in the 1400s. Let's turn now to look at this exciting period.

A Rebirth of Learning

While the Portuguese and Spanish were exploring foreign lands in the 1400s, the Italians were exploring a world of new ideas and attitudes. For many years, these new ideas and attitudes spread from Italy throughout Europe. We call this period from about 1350 to 1600 the Renaissance: it was a time during which Europe moved from the Middle Ages toward our modern world, and produced great and lasting accomplishments in science, literature, and the arts.

The word "renaissance" comes from a Latin word meaning "rebirth." At first the Renaissance was a rebirth of ideas from ancient Greece and Rome. Inspired by the ideas and art of the ancients, the Italians began to place an emphasis on this world, focusing less on heaven and more on earth, on people here and now. While the Middle Ages had been an age of faith in God and heaven, the Renaissance was an age of humanity. As in the days of Greece and Rome, human beings were put at the center of thought. (You can see this new focus on humanity embodied in the statue of David by Michelangelo; see the Visual Arts section of this book.)

This new humanistic focus during the Renaissance grew out of changes that took place at the end of the Middle Ages. One important change was a great expansion of trade and commerce. You remember that for a long time in the Middle Ages, people lived on isolated manors. But then towns began to develop. In the towns, people bought and sold various goods: food, cloth, spices, jewels, tools, and more. A new class of merchants and shopkeepers, who made their living by buying and selling, began to grow. This middle class—between the laborers and the nobility—grew more wealthy and influential as more and more people wanted to buy the products they could provide. The growing middle class no longer relied on rich nobles to support or protect them. They began to support themselves and their own families, and to work for their own goals. They began to seek more education, and some devoted part of their wealth to the support of artists.

The growth of trade during the late Middle Ages especially benefited Italy, which was in an excellent position to grow rich from sea trade. Find Italy on a world map or globe. See how almost all of Italy is surrounded by the Mediterranean Sea? Italian merchants took advantage of Italy's many natural seaports by trading with countries along the Mediterranean Sea. Italian cities became the crossroads of trading routes between Europe and the East. Not only did these cities grow rich from trade, they also enjoyed the advantage of contact with a wide range of people and ideas from other cultures.

The Medici Family

Before the Renaissance, kings and other royalty were believed to have been chosen by God for the special responsibility of ruling. But during the Renaissance, people with no royal blood could rise to power on the basis of their wealth, their intelligence, and their accomplishments.

Wealthy men often emerged from the growing class of merchants. Italian merchants not only controlled Mediterranean trade routes, they also sold cloth, wool, leather, fruits, wine, and many other products. As wealth from trade grew, people needed to safeguard their riches, and banks began to develop in Italy. By the 1400s, one city, Florence, had become the banking center not just of Italy but of all Europe. One family controlled much of the banking system in Florence. This was the Medici family. One man, Cosimo de'Medici, made them the most influential family in Florence and the wealthiest family in Europe.

Cosimo knew that the Medici would be better able to keep their fortune if they had a say in how the city of Florence ran its affairs. He used his wealth and influence to make sure that the leaders of Florence were men whose policies would strengthen the Medici family's wealth and power. It marked a great change when people of intelligence and accomplishment like Cosimo, rather than people of royal descent, began to gain power over the political affairs of Italian cities.

City-States

In the early 1400s, Italy was not a united country. Instead, it was made up of five ruling cities: Florence, Naples, Venice, Milan, and the Papal States (which were run by the pope). We call them city-states because they controlled large amounts of surrounding land and because they operated almost like small countries. The Medici, who directed the affairs of Florence, were like the rulers of a small country.

The Italian city-states constantly competed with each other for power and glory. They competed in every way—through wars and by trying to outdo each other in the greatness of their scholars, in the grandeur of their buildings, and in the beauty of the art that adorned their cities.

Learning About This World

Before the Renaissance, learning and education were limited almost exclusively to churchmen and the nobility. Most formal education occurred in monasteries, and focused on religious studies. Control of education was one way the Catholic Church gained power over the political affairs of Europe. The aim of education in the Middle Ages was to train people to be useful to the church. Teachers were priests and monks, and everything they taught had to fit in with the policies of the church.

During the Renaissance, people still believed in God, but they began to value learning about all aspects of the world, not just learning that led to greater religious faith. As people like the Medici gained wealth, they realized that education was a key to political power. They made sure their children became educated, and that they studied not just religious topics but also classical learning: Greek and Latin writings on science, mathematics, philosophy, and the arts that had not been seriously studied since ancient times.

One reason this rebirth of classical learning took place was that, in the mid-1400s, the great city of Constantinople was attacked by the Turks, and many Greek scholars fled from Constantinople to Italy, where they taught a whole new range of classical writings to Italians hungry for knowledge. Italian leaders like Cosimo welcomed them to train a new generation of teachers for the children of the nobles and the new merchants.

Like many wealthy Florentines, Cosimo de'Medici wanted to plunge into the expanding world of ideas. His favorite leisure activity was visiting a monastery so that he could read the rare documents in its library and discuss them with the well-educated monks. He avidly collected books and manuscripts, and generously made them available to the people of Florence. He provided financial support for several scholars, one of whom translated the writings of the Greek thinker Plato.

Cosimo encouraged all Florentines to visit his "house of studies," nicknamed the Academy after Plato's school in ancient Greece. At Cosimo's Academy, not just scholars but Florentines from many walks of life—business, politics, medicine, mathematics, the arts, astronomy, philosophy—met to discuss Plato's ideas.

Such discussions sparked a hunger for knowledge and a new curiosity about the world. As new ideas and attitudes spread from Italy across Europe, the hunger for knowledge pushed people beyond "book learning" into direct observation of the world. People set about carefully observing the human body, the movements of the stars and planets, and other aspects of the physical world. They were not satisfied with old answers or religious explanations,

In order to make detailed drawings of human bodies, such as this one of chest and shoulder muscles, Leonardo da Vinci dissected human corpses and painstakingly observed the tissues.

Careful study and observation led to new knowledge during the Renaissance, but not all of this new knowledge was welcomed, especially by the Catholic Church. Do you remember learning about Copernicus and Galileo (in Books One and Two of this series)? Through his observations, Copernicus disproved the old belief that the earth was at the center of the universe, and showed that the earth and other planets actually revolve around the sun. But the Catholic Church declared that anyone who believed Copernicus was a heretic—a kind of religious outlaw. Later, the Italian scientist Galileo developed a telescope that helped provide proof for Copernicus's ideas. When Galileo published his findings, the church put Galileo on trial and threatened to torture him.

but believed that by studying the world carefully, they could understand the laws governing God's creation.

Art in Florence

Besides supporting the spread of education, wealthy Florentines spent money to make the city beautiful and magnificent. They hired artists to design monuments and buildings, and to create sculpture and paintings to grace their homes and public squares. They became personally acquainted with the outstanding artists of the day, and helped them in many ways. Cosimo de'Medici encouraged painters and sculptors to join other thinkers at his Academy. His grandson, Lorenzo, often brought artists to his house to live and work. Artists thus became an important part of the cultural life of the city.

The place of the artist in society began to change. In the Middle Ages, artists worked together in groups, and they rarely signed their names to an artwork. In the Renaissance, individual artists were well known and celebrated. Responding to public encouragement, artists like Leonardo da Vinci, Raphael, and Michelangelo strove for an individual style and greater recognition. Florence soon became a beehive of artistic activity, and other Italian cities followed its lead. (In the Visual Arts section of this book you can read more about the accomplishments of Renaissance artists.)

Lorenzo de' Medici.

The Renaissance Moves to Rome

In 1503 the Catholic Church had an unusual new pope, Julius II. Julius was very much like a soldier and led troops against neighboring areas to expand the Papal State. During one battle, he flew into a temper and beat his advisers on the shoulders with sticks because they would not take their horses into snow that rose to the horses' chests! Julius made sure the church regained its powerful influence in European politics.

Julius decided that works of art were one way to regain the church's influence and glory. He hired the most famous artists of the time, including Michelangelo, Raphael, and Leonardo da Vinci, to work on projects in Rome. Florence had been the center of the Renaissance since 1400, but, partly because Julius spent so much money on art and because he enlisted the most brilliant artists, Rome took over from Florence as the new cultural center of the Renaissance. (See the Visual Arts section of this book for the story of one of the most remarkable creations in Rome, the ceiling of the Sistine Chapel, painted by Michelangelo.)

The Printing Press and the Bible

Imagine a world without telephones, televisions, or computers. Well, you'd still have books, right? Now imagine a world without books! In the Middle Ages, very few people had books, which were rare and expensive because each and every book had to be copied by hand, page by page, line by line, by people called scribes. But around 1440 something happened that changed all this. Johannes Gutenberg invented the first printing press. Books could be made faster, cheaper, and in greater numbers. In less than 100 years, more than ten million books were printed and sold.

The first book Gutenberg printed was the Bible—two hundred copies. How do you think having the Bible and other books in their homes made a difference in the way people lived? One major change was that people wanted books printed in their own languages—English, German, French, Italian—rather than the Latin they heard at church and school. Another difference was that it took away some of the authority of the church. Before Gutenberg's press, most people could not read the Bible because it was in Latin. Once they could read the Bible themselves in their own language, many people began to have their own ideas on how the Bible should be understood.

One of those people was Martin Luther (for whom the great American leader Martin Luther King, Jr., was named). The preaching and writings of Martin Luther set off a sweeping change in religious ideas and institutions.

Gutenberg shows the wonder of printing. The box in the foreground is full of the movable type he inked to print a page.

Martin Luther and the Protestant Reformation

Martin Luther was born in the countryside of Germany in 1483. When he was twenty-one, he decided to join a monastery and became a friar. But, like many people of his time, Luther became very upset with the Catholic Church; it seemed more interested in making money than in saving souls and helping people. Some popes acted more like ruthless princes than spiritual leaders; without spiritual leadership from the pope, corrupt practices flourished in the church. During a pilgrimage to Rome in 1510, Luther saw priests living more like princes than monks. Luther knew that throughout Europe some priests made money by selling "indulgences": by paying a priest to pardon your sins, or by buying some little trinket, you would supposedly get to heaven despite your sins.

Luther believed in the Bible, but he did not believe that the church was carrying out its teachings. He felt that a person could get to heaven simply by reading the Bible and by having faith in God. This meant that a person did not have to be part of the church, and that the Catholic Church, the pope, and the priests had no real authority. During a time when the Catholic Church was more powerful than any single government or country, these were very risky beliefs for Luther to talk about.

In 1517, Luther wrote down what he felt needed to be changed in the church. He called his ideas the "95 Theses" and nailed them to a church door in Wittenberg, Germany, where he was a university professor. His ideas expressed what many people felt was wrong, but were afraid to say. With the help of the recently invented printing press, Luther's theses quickly spread across Germany and provoked notice in Rome. Luther was eventually condemned by both the pope and the emperor, but that didn't stop him. Luther abandoned the Catholic Church to begin a religion now known as Lutheranism.

At the same time voices of protest began to be heard in other parts of Europe. Out of these protests grew new churches that came to be called "Protestant," which means "protesting." This era in history, which happened at the same time as the later Renaissance, came to be called the Protestant Reformation. Europe, transformed by the inven-

Martin Luther nails his theses to the door of the Wittenberg church.

tion of the printing press and the ideas of people like Martin Luther, soon became split between the Catholics and the Protestants.

John Calvin

Along with Martin Luther, John Calvin is considered one of the foremost leaders of the Protestant Reformation. John Calvin was born in France in 1509 but fled to Switzerland when he converted to Protestantism. Calvin and his followers believed in predestination: the idea that God had chosen certain people to be saved. He rejected having priests and popes, which made kings and other established leaders very nervous. Calvinists often lived in strict communities and banned activities like dancing and theater-going. Eventually, Calvinism spread throughout parts of France, the Netherlands, Germany, and Scotland, and influenced the Puritans who settled in the Massachusetts Bay Colony.

The Counter-Reformation

The Protestants who left the Catholic Church were not the only ones who were upset with its corruption. Many bishops, priests, and nuns had long been trying to reform the church from within. Once the Reformation began, the church knew it could not wait any longer to make changes. A movement began inside the church, called the "Counter-Reformation" because its purpose was to counter, or work against, the effects of the Reformation. The Counter-Reformation was the church's attempt to renew itself, to examine what it really believed, and to reduce the growing popularity of Protestantism in Europe.

One of the leading figures of the Counter-Reformation was the man who came to be known as St. Ignatius of Loyola. At first, he was not an especially religious man. Born in Spain in 1491, he grew up loving adventure and became a soldier. In 1521, in a battle against France, a cannonball exploded, seriously wounding both his legs. It took a long time for his wounds to heal, and he suffered great pain. During this time, he began to study religion. He left behind his military life for a spiritual one, and became a Catholic priest.

While some corrupt church officials lived in luxury, Ignatius set a different example: he lived in poverty and devoted himself to study and self-discipline. He founded an order of priests called the Society of Jesus, whose members are known as Jesuits. Jesuits became missionaries around the world, as well as leaders in education.

Henry VIII

What was happening in England during the Renaissance and the Reformation? King Henry VIII was born in England in 1491, one year before Columbus's ships landed in America. He took the throne in 1509 and ruled England with an iron fist until his death in 1547—almost forty years! He was a complicated and arrogant ruler who beheaded not only his enemies, but two of his wives as well. He is remembered as the ruler who established England as a major European power. Before Henry's time, England had known strife and civil war. As king, Henry united the country under his own all-powerful rule.

Henry VIII.

King Henry VIII is also responsible for England's break from the Roman Catholic Church. Henry's reasons for breaking from Catholicism were more personal and political than religious. At first, in fact, Henry had even sided with the pope when Martin Luther nailed his "95 Theses" to the church door. But the break came when Henry decided he wanted to divorce his wife, Catherine of Aragon, because she had given birth to a daughter, but no sons—and Henry wanted a son to inherit the throne. When the pope refused to allow a divorce, Henry divorced Catherine anyway and married Anne Boleyn.

Then Henry took a bolder step with lasting consequences. He quickly established the Church of England, declaring himself its supreme head on earth. He seized the many monasteries and abbeys in England that belonged to the Catholic Church, and divided their lands among his followers. The new Church of England, in the spirit of the Reformation, soon translated the Bible into English and joined the Protestant movement growing throughout Europe.

Elizabeth I

Henry VIII married six times in his frantic effort to produce a male heir. Still, the next really important ruler of England was not a son of Henry's but a daughter, Elizabeth I. Elizabeth I took over the British throne only after the deaths of both her fifteen-year-old half-brother, Edward VI, and her half-sister, Mary Tudor. Mary, as queen, had tried violently and unsuccessfully to reconvert England to Catholicism (so violently that she was called "Bloody Mary").

Elizabeth I ruled England for forty-five years, and many consider her one of the most intelligent and able rulers of all time. As a Protestant, she officially led the Church of England, and used her power to appoint those loyal to her as bishops and church leaders. As queen, she was expected to marry and hand over the throne to her husband, but the redheaded queen remained unmarried all her life, despite the many ambitious suitors who lined up to ask for her hand.

Elizabeth filled her court with poets, playwrights, and musicians. She encouraged their talents but also made sure that their work glorified England—and the queen. The great English playwright William Shakespeare lived during the time of Queen Elizabeth. Shakespeare wrote plays about the history of England, and people crowded into his Globe Theater.

Elizabeth I knew the loyalty of her subjects was important, so she often traveled through England so her people would find her a familiar sight.

Mary, Queen of Scots

The greatest threat to Elizabeth's power came from her younger cousin, Mary, the queen of Scotland. Mary was a Catholic, but unlike Bloody Mary, she did not force her subjects to become Catholic. When she became queen, no one in Scotland knew her very well because she had been sent to France to school. When it was discovered that she played a part in the death of her husband, the Scots forced her to give up the throne and locked her in a castle.

Mary escaped and ended up in England. Elizabeth was not happy to see her. Mary was an anointed queen, which to many still meant that her right to be queen came directly from God. Her country had rejected her, and Elizabeth was afraid that Mary might join with other Catholic forces, such as France or Spain, to take over England. Again Mary was locked up, this time in England. Finally, when

Mary, Queen of Scots

a plot to overthrow the English throne was discovered, Elizabeth took the very risky step of ordering Mary to be executed.

Mary's execution sent shock waves throughout Europe—an anointed queen had been beheaded!

The Spanish Armada

Under Queen Elizabeth, the British Navy came to rule the seas. But first, it had to overcome the strong Spanish fleet.

Under King Philip II of Spain, Spanish ships were bringing in great riches from trade and plunder of the New World. (Remember the Philippines were named for this Philip?) Spain was a mighty sea power, dominating the Atlantic routes to the Americas. Elizabeth's response to this power had been to encourage her British ships to pirate the Spanish ships and claim their booty for England.

In the 1580s, Spain, which was Catholic, entered a war with the Netherlands, which was Protestant. Elizabeth decided to support the Dutch. King Philip II of Spain responded by assembling a huge fleet, complete with 130 ships and over 30,000 men. This fleet, known as the Spanish Armada, set sail for England. It seemed invincible, and many thought victory for the Spanish was certain.

The English fleet of 200 boats was manned by less experienced sailors, but the English boats were lighter and more agile than the Spanish. The British ships sailed into the heart of the massive Spanish fleet, breaking it up, and taking down ships at close range. The British set unmanned ships on fire and let the wind blow them toward the Spanish ships. The Spanish retreated, only to sail into a terrific storm that blew them onto the rocks of Ireland and Scotland. The defeat of the Spanish Armada marked the beginning of British dominance of the seas.

Leading the British fleet against the Armada was a pirate and sometime slave trader, a favorite of Queen Elizabeth's named Sir Francis Drake. Drake had been a feisty attacker of Spanish merchant ships. Following in Magellan's footsteps, he had sailed around the world, for which Elizabeth had made him a knight and later named him leader of the British Navy. Drake's voyages opened the seas to British exploration and led to the first British settlement in America.

FEUDAL JAPAN

Let's turn now to the other side of the globe. In 1492, as Columbus set out looking for a passageway to China, Japan was not a unified nation. Instead, it was a collection of feudal kingdoms, much like those in Europe during the Middle Ages. In fact, the period from about A.D. 1150 to A.D. 1600 is often called Japan's feudal period. It was similar in many ways to Europe's Middle Ages (which you can read about in Book Four of this series).

At the beginning of the 1500s there had already been a long line of emperors in Japan. The emperors were mainly religious and cultural leaders. The real political power was in the hands of clan leaders called *daimyos* (DIME-yos) and, later, *shoguns* (SHOW-guns). The daimyos were like European feudal lords; they controlled their lands and people through military might and fought each other to extend their lands and control. When very powerful daimyos extended their rule over several clans, they took the title of "shogun," which means "great general."

Because attack and defense were so important to this way of life, a special class of professional swordsmen and fighters arose—the samurai. Like medieval knights in Europe, the samurai began training for battle from a very early age. They followed a code called *bushido* (bush-EE-do), which required bravery, self-control, and loyalty to their daimyo.

In 1603, a powerful warrior named Tokugawa Ieyasu (ee-yeh-YA-soo) overcame all the daimyos and united the country

A samurai warrior. When the samurai went into battle, the hundreds of tiny wooden and leather plates that made up his armor clattered against each other, making an alarming sound.

under his rule. He called himself Shogun Ieyasu and his government the Tokugawa Shogunate. His family ruled Japan for the next 250 years. Shogun Ieyasu kept control over his kingdom by ruling over the daimyos' activities. Daimyos paid the shogun a percentage of every crop. They had to seek permission of Shogun Ieyasu before getting married, so that no two neighboring daimyos would strengthen their local empires through marriage. The daimyos even had to get approval from the shogun before renovating their own castles.

Japan's Many Religions

Japan was (and is) a land of various religions, including Buddhism, Confucianism, and Shintoism. Often a Japanese person would practice a combination of religions.

Buddhism originated in India in the middle of the sixth century B.C. from the teachings of a prince who gave up his riches to teach the poor and unhappy. His followers called him "the buddha," which means "the enlightened one." The beliefs of Buddhism are deeply moral. For example, Buddhists believe in "right speech," never lying or using bad language; in "right behavior," never doing anything one may later regret; and in "right effort," always working for the good and avoiding what is evil. For Buddhists, the goal of all these right paths is to be released from the sorrows and worries of life and reach nirvana, a state of enlightenment and release from suffering.

Confucianism started a little later than Buddhism in China, in the third century B.C. Its originator, Confucius, did not say much about God, but he did have much to say about how to behave. Confucius said you should always obey your parents. He said you should be kind to those who must obey you, and follow a version of the Golden Rule, which, as you remember, says "Do unto others as you would have them do unto you." He said you must always be polite and follow certain rules of behavior when you eat or speak or meet someone, and that you must act not only honorably but also courteously.

Shintoism began in Japan. Its followers

This giant bronze statue of Buddha at Kamakura, Japan, has survived tidal waves and earthquakes since it was cast in 1252.

worship nature spirits, called *kami* (KAH-mee), who live all around them—in rocks, trees, lakes, even in blades of grass. Shintoism is less a belief in gods than the practice of traditional rituals. Followers of Shintoism build many outdoor shrines and gardens to the kami. They also worship and honor their ancestors and great heroes. They believe that their emperor is a descendant from the sun goddess and so is himself divine.

The Land of the Rising Sun

Japan is the country farthest to the east in Asia. Since the sun rises in the east, Japan has long been called "the land of the rising sun." As you can see on the map, Japan is a small country made up of islands. There are four major islands and thousands of smaller ones, all of which, if combined, would cover an area about the size of

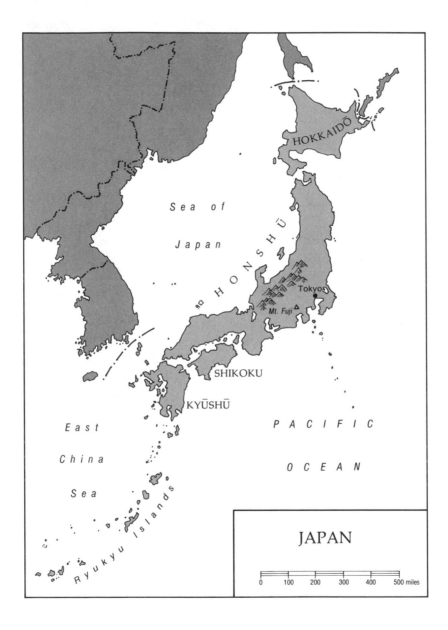

California. Japan's islands are actually the tops of a great mountain range. For this reason, much of Japan is covered with hills and rugged mountains.

Most of Japan's climate resembles that of the east coast of the United States, except during the monsoon seasons in summer and winter. In Japan, summer monsoons are winds that blow from the southeast, crossing a warm current of the Pacific Ocean and bringing heavy rains to southern and central Japan. Between the months of May and October, over forty inches of rain fall. These rains are crucial for growing rice and other crops.

Rice growing near a Japanese village.

Winter monsoons, starting in Siberia, blow cold air toward northwestern Japan. As these winds cross the Sea of Japan, they absorb some moisture, which they dump as snow on the northwestern mountains. Thus, the climate of Hokkaidō and the northwest coast of Honshū is cold and damp.

In late summer and early fall, destructive storms called typhoons strike the southeastern coasts of Japan. Typhoons are circular storms with winds of over seventy-five miles per hour. They form over the waters of the western Pacific and the Indian Oceans. In the United States, such storms, which sometimes strike the East Coast, are called hurricanes. (You can read about hurricanes in Book Four of this series.) Japan is also subject to the fury of tsunamis (soo-NAH-meez), or giant waves, caused when an earthquake on the ocean floor creates waves up to ten stories high.

During the thirteenth century, several typhoons protected Japan from invasion. The Mongol leader Kublai Khan decided to invade Japan, but his fleet was sunk several times by typhoons—the last of which the Japanese people named "Kamikaze" (kah-mih-KAH-zee), meaning "divine wind."

As an island country, Japan is naturally isolated, and the Japanese in the 1400s and 1500s wanted it to stay that way. They had little interest in the world beyond their islands. *Daimyos* did not send expeditions to faraway lands or even seek trade with outsiders. What little contact they had with Europeans was almost solely with Dutch traders, who for centuries were the only traders allowed to do business in Japan. While some shoguns briefly played with the idea of opening Japan to foreign influence, they worried that foreign ideas and religions would weaken their own control. Shogun Hirodata (hee-ro-DA-tah) formally shut down all contact with outsiders and even banned the Japanese from building oceangoing ships! The doors to the West stayed closed in Japan until 1854.

RUSSIA

Ivan the Great

In 1462, thirty years before Columbus first crossed the Atlantic Ocean, a Russian prince named Ivan III took the throne in Moscow. When he first became the grand prince, Russians were not thinking about the tremendous changes and discoveries happening in Europe. They were more worried about freeing themselves from the grip of the Mongols in the east and building their own nation. Ivan III, who came to be called Ivan the Great, did just that. In 1480, he broke Russia away from Mongol control and began to conquer huge nearby provinces, extending Russia's borders in every direction. Ivan also began to pinch control away from the many aristocratic princes throughout Russia, known as *boyars*.

By the end of Ivan's reign, Moscow had become the most important city in Russia. But even before Ivan's time, Moscow had been an important city. When Constantinople fell to the Turks in 1453, many leaders of the Eastern Orthodox Church had fled to Moscow, taking their religion, art, and culture with them. Under Ivan the Great, Moscow took over from Byzantium as the center of the Eastern Orthodox Church, and became the home of a grand royal court.

Ivan the Terrible

Ivan the Great's grandson, Ivan IV, furthered his grandfather's goals of uniting and expanding Russia by ruling with an iron fist. He arrested and murdered hundreds of landowners whom he suspected were traitors and killed church leaders who opposed him. This earned him the name of "Ivan the Terrible." In 1547, Ivan IV had himself crowned *czar*, the Russian word for Caesar, the great Roman leader. By taking this title, Ivan IV meant he was to be the all-powerful emperor of Russia.

Many people think that Ivan the Terrible was simply mad, especially since he suffered from moodiness and sudden tempers—during one tantrum he accidentally killed his own son. Mad or not, he managed to wrest control of huge tracts of land

GROWTH OF RUSSIA

Russia in 1462	Territory added by 1725 (at the death of Peter the Great)
Russia in 1505 (at the death of Ivan III)	Territory added by 1796 (at the death of Catherine the Great)
Territory added by 1584 (at the death of Ivan IV)	Present boundary of Commonwealth of Independent States

0   500   1000   1500 miles

from neighboring rulers and rid himself of any significant competition for power, a legacy that would pave the way for future all-powerful Russian czars.

During Ivan the Terrible's reign, Russians moved over the Ural Mountains into Siberia. What do you think of when you hear the name Siberia? Many people think it's a frozen land of ice and snow. But really Siberia is a vast land, with different climates and terrains varying from flat plains to wilderness plateaus and mountains. Russians farmed the fertile steppes of Siberia, which are treeless grasslands much like our own central plains or prairie.

Peter the Great Looks to the West

When Peter I, called Peter the Great, took control of Russia in 1682, he was determined to bring his country out of its isolation and make Russia into an international power. He visited other European countries in 1697, and decided that the best way to build his country was by adopting their ways. During his rule, Peter "westernized" Russia by forcing his country to adopt Western European practices of governmental administration and social customs. Russian government became more organized,

Peter the Great studying ship building in Holland.

nobles had to wear Western European clothes, and women, formerly excluded from social life, had to attend parties. Unfortunately, many of Peter's reforms, like heavier taxes and enforced labor, made life more miserable for tradespeople and peasants.

With the help of Western European advisers and ammunition, Peter built an army ready to take on even the highly advanced Swedish army that was pressing in on Moscow's border to the north. Russia fought the Swedes for over ten years, from 1709 to 1721, and in the end, pushed the Russian border all the way to the Baltic Sea. On newly won land near the Baltic, Peter had a new capital city built, which he named St. Petersburg after himself. Look at St. Petersburg on your map. Can you see why it was called Peter's "window on the West"?

Catherine the Great

Catherine the Great was actually a German princess who married into the Russian royal family. She took over the throne in 1762 at age thirty-three and proved to be a strong ruler. She separated the powers of church and state and seized the church's lands, much as Henry VIII had done in England. She kept up with the leading writers and thinkers of the day and tried to put their ideas into effect in Russia. She also created a new legal system and established schools and colleges. She even tried to create a government where people from all over Russia could be represented.

Just as Peter had reached into Swedish territory to get to the Baltic Sea, so Catherine put her army to work fighting the Turks to get Russian ships and trade routes to the Black Sea. Using both sea and land forces, Russia was victorious, and by 1774, Russia was building the port of Odessa on the Black Sea. The Black Sea, unlike the Baltic, is free of ice in winter. Why would having a warm-water port be important to the Russians?

Catherine's army also reached into Poland, extending Russian borders even closer to Western Europe. Under Catherine, more peasants were forced into serfdom than ever before, but Russia grew to become an international power. Catherine

Catherine the Great.

was an extravagant, egotistical leader who sought power for herself, but also progress for her people. Some people see her as a tyrant, and others see her as a very successful queen.

THE ENLIGHTENMENT

A New Way of Thinking

During the Middle Ages, the Catholic Church gave people in Europe answers to questions like, "How do the sun and moon move?"; "What happens to you after you die?"; and "Who should rule a country?" But during the Renaissance, as you've seen, people began to look for other answers. Some people began to lose confidence in the church. By the 1700s, more and more people were turning to science and their own experience and intelligence for guidance about the world and human affairs. This movement toward science and human reason became known even in its own day as "the Enlightenment," because people thought they were being enlightened by science and reason. They believed that, rather than waiting for some divine power to help them, they could apply human reason to understanding the world and improving it.

The Enlightenment did not just happen all of a sudden. Some trace it all the way back to the 1400s or even earlier. Some say it began in 1543 when Copernicus's book declared that the sun, not the earth, was the center of the solar system. Others say it started in 1610 when Galileo looked at the heavens with his telescope. But the Enlightenment was truly a gradual movement; there was no one moment when it was born. By the 1700s it was in full swing in many countries of Europe and in North America.

Early Enlightenment in France: René Descartes

In the 1600s, a French mathematician, René Descartes, tried a new approach to finding truth. He decided to start thinking from scratch without accepting any traditional idea from his parents or the church, and then to see how far he could get just by using the force of logic. By doubting everything, he felt he could carefully work matters out, and end up with ideas that he could prove to be true. Then knowledge would have a sound base. He began by doubting his own existence. But he decided he couldn't do that, because he couldn't doubt that he was doubting! So, his beginning point was the famous formula, *Cogito ergo sum*, which is Latin for "I think, therefore I am."

Other Enlightenment thinkers disagreed with Descartes. They thought you could not figure out the world just by thinking about it, but needed instead to build up knowledge and ideas from direct observations of the world. One such thinker was the Englishman Isaac Newton.

Isaac Newton

In 1687, Isaac Newton published a book that showed that the world and the heavens worked according to mathematical laws. Many of Newton's mathematical discoveries grew out of his observations about gravity. An old story says that Newton began thinking about gravity when, one day, he noticed an apple falling from a tree, and began to wonder why the apple fell down rather than sideways or up. Whether the story is true or not, it shows the Enlightenment spirit of investigating and analyzing the world.

Newton observed that the strength of gravity, the pull between two objects, depends on how much mass objects have. (You can find out about mass in the Physical Sciences section of this book.) He also observed that the pull of gravity increases when two objects come closer together and decreases when they move farther apart. These increases and decreases obey an exact mathematical law. From these observations of the world, Newton discovered that he could give a mathematical formula for the relationships between the distance, the mass, and the velocity of a planet in its relationship to the sun. A planet, Newton showed, had to follow a precise path and speed to avoid either falling into the sun or drifting off into space. The planets, Newton discovered, obeyed the exact formula for gravity!

After Newton's great discoveries, people began to view the universe as behaving according to precise mathematical laws. They began to see the universe not so much as the working out of God's plan, but more as an enormous, precise machine, like a large clock that ticked and tocked according to scientific rules. And, as Enlightenment thinkers saw it, it was man's responsibility to figure out those rules, and to make the universe run even more smoothly.

Enlightenment Thinkers Help Make the United States

John Locke, an Englishman, was an Enlightenment philosopher of the 1600s who believed that people should be given as much freedom as possible. He believed that every person had certain natural rights, including the rights to "life, liberty, and property." He said that government is based on a contract—an agreement—between the citizens and the rulers. The government should respect the rights of the citizens, and if it didn't, the citizens had the right to replace the government. These were radical ideas at the time, when rulers were insisting on their God-given right to rule, regardless of the will of the people.

In France, a great admirer of John Locke's works was Baron Charles de Montesquieu (MON-tes-cue). In 1748, he published a book entitled *The Spirit of Laws* in which he said that power in government should be divided into three separate groups: the legislative power, which could make laws; the executive power, which could put the laws into action; and the judicial power, which could judge whether the laws had been broken. Montesquieu insisted that the powers must remain separate to balance each other because if one power became too strong, it could lead to tyranny.

All this sounds familiar, doesn't it? As you've probably recognized by now, the ideas of Locke and Montesquieu played an important role in the formation of the United States government. One of our Founding Fathers, Thomas Jefferson, had read Locke and Montesquieu and had served as ambassador to France, where he was able to discuss ideas with other Enlightenment thinkers. Jefferson's admiration for Enlightenment ideas directly shaped the creation of the young American republic, because Jefferson used these ideas when he wrote the Declaration of Independence, which spells out some of the basic principles on which the United States is founded. It says that every citizen has a God-given right to "life, liberty and the pursuit of happiness," words that echo John Locke. (Why do you think Jefferson said "the pursuit of happiness" instead of what Locke said: "property"?) Later, Americans who wrote the Constitution followed Montesquieu's concept of separating and balancing the powers of government by dividing our government into three branches—legislative, judicial, and executive.

THE FRENCH REVOLUTION

The Sun King

From 1643 to 1715, France was ruled by a dazzling and extravagant monarch, Louis XIV. He called himself "the Sun King," and truly believed that, as the planets revolved around the sun, so the world circled about him. Under Louis, France was no longer a collection of provinces ruled by various barons, but a united nation-state ruled by a magnificent, all-powerful king. As Louis himself put it, "The state—I am the state."

Louis had an enormous palace built outside of Paris at Versailles (ver-SIGH). Versailles was full of dazzling mirrors, chandeliers, and works of art. Plays and concerts were held constantly. French aristocrats waited on Louis, and were considered lucky to be able to hold a candle while the king adjusted his wig.

Louis XIV built France into the most powerful European nation of the time. During his reign, France was considered the most elegant and advanced country in Europe. French linens, porcelain, and decorations were in demand from Moscow to Madrid. French became the international language, spoken among the upper classes throughout the world. French literature, music, and customs had great prestige in Europe and even in America.

But within a few decades, all this would change. Enlightenment ideas about natural rights and about the relations between the people and their rulers would give rise to the bloody events of the French Revolution.

The famed Hall of Mirrors at Versailles.

The Three Estates and the Old Regime

In France, everyone was part of one of three social classes, called "estates." The First Estate was the clergy (the church). The Second Estate was the nobility. And the Third Estate was everybody else. While the Third Estate was the biggest class by far—about 98 percent of the population—its members had almost no political power. This system of the Three Estates under the rule of a monarch came to be called the "Old Regime" in France—"old" because it would soon be replaced, violently, by something new.

By 1789, the unfairness of the Three Estates was all too obvious. The Third Estate had grown and included within it a middle class of prosperous merchants, traders, and business people. These *bourgeois* (boor-SHWA), as they are called in French, were grouped in the Third Estate with laborers and peasants. It was the *bourgeois* who first came to resent the Old Regime and demand that it be changed.

The Revolt of the Third Estate

After the reign of Louis XIV, wars and extravagance made France poor. Under the rule of Louis XVI (the great-great-grandson of Louis XIV), France finally fell into a serious financial crisis. The country had spent too much money in fighting various wars. Louis XVI's wife, the famous queen Marie Antoinette, liked to spend money. The queen and many bored courtiers dressed up in expensive costumes and played games in which they pretended they were milkmaids and shepherds. Marie Antoinette even went so far as to spend a fortune to build a tiny palace behind Versailles so she could live more "simply." A famous story says that when Marie was told that the people did not have enough bread to eat, she waved her hand and responded, "Let them eat cake." While the story is not true, many people believed it, and felt anger and hatred toward the queen, whom they saw as a symbol of the spoiled French nobility.

With France in financial trouble, Louis XVI decided for the first time to tax the nobles and clergy. The nobles were outraged and insisted that such taxes required a special meeting of representatives of the Three Estates. In May of 1789, the representatives came together in a meeting at Versailles that would have tremendous consequences for France and Europe. The nobles saw the meeting as a way to show their power and reject the proposed taxation. They planned to leave the meeting with more power in their own hands. They did not consider, however, what would be said by the group that far outnumbered them—the representatives of the Third Estate.

The First and Second Estates treated the representatives of the common people as inferiors, and even required them to enter the assembly room through a separate entrance. The representatives of the Third Estate soon saw that they were not going to be listened to at the meeting, and they became angry. Remember, this was 1789: the Enlightenment ideas of freedom and the natural rights of man were circulating through France. Exciting news from across the Atlantic told of developments in a new country, the United States, without any king or nobles at all. The Third Estate's representatives realized that, with the nobles and the clergy each receiving one third of the vote, the common people would always be outvoted even though they represented many more citizens. On June 17, members of the Third Estate left the palace and took over a nearby indoor tennis court. There, among speeches and shouting, the representatives of the people called themselves the National Assembly and took an oath that they would demand a more equal share of power.

Later the Assembly drafted the Declaration of the Rights of Man and Citizen, expressing the Enlightenment goal of equal rights for every citizen, as well as freedom of religion, and the right of a fair trial for everyone. The declaration was printed in the thousands and was read and talked about throughout France and Europe as a revolutionary view of man.

The Fall of the Bastille

When the Third Estate declared itself the National Assembly, Louis XVI responded in two ways. He seemed to support the Assembly by ordering the representatives from the First and Second Estates to join it. At the same time, he responded to the urgings of many nobles to send almost twenty thousand troops to Paris, near Versailles, to frighten the National Assembly.

The troops frightened no one. Mobs of hungry Parisians took to the streets. People began to collect arms for themselves. On July 14, 1789, a crowd of people was roaming the streets collecting weapons. They reached the Bastille, a fortress-like jail in Paris, and asked the commander in charge to give them weapons. He refused, and a riot broke out. The people stormed the Bastille, killing some soldiers and the commander in charge, and later killing the mayor of the city. In a bloody show of victory, the people stuck the heads of the commander and mayor on long poles and paraded them around the city.

The fall of the Bastille, long a symbol of royal oppression, is often considered the beginning of the French Revolution. Every year the French celebrate Bastille Day as a national holiday, much like July 4 in the United States, to commemorate their country's independence from the Old Regime and their quest for the ideals expressed in a phrase that became the motto of the revolution: "Liberty! Equality! Fraternity!"

Confusion and Terror

Many French nobles were frightened by the violence and left France. The people remained hungry, angry, and fearful that the king and nobles wanted to crush the Assembly. In October of 1789, over six thousand women who worked in the Paris marketplace, along with thousands of other revolutionaries, marched from Paris to Versailles. They broke into the palace and forced the king, the queen, and their

The women of Paris marching on Versailles.

young son to return to Paris with them. These people, hungry for bread, taunted their captives as "the baker, the baker's wife, and the baker's little boy." The king and queen were installed in a palace in Paris, where their actions could be kept in the public eye.

One night the royal family tried to escape and leave the country, but they were caught. They were brought back to Paris and greeted by jeering mobs. Soon afterward the king and queen's young son was removed from his parents, put in prison, and never heard from again.

The National Assembly met for two years. Many people, especially peasants and laborers, hoped the Assembly would make changes that would improve their lives. The Assembly drafted a bold new constitution that horrified the ruling classes in France and throughout Europe. The new constitution abolished the aristocracy, took away church lands, and gave peasants and laborers the same rights as nobles. But even with the new constitution, during these years most of the poor remained as poor as ever.

Other countries in Europe feared that the turmoil in France would spill over into their own lands. So France had to fight battles along its borders as well as cope with chaos inside the country. People felt that a strong hand was needed to restore order. The Assembly was replaced with a new radical government called the Commune, which punished those it considered traitors to its cause. It was a bloody time. Anyone thought to be a traitor was condemned to death, often without benefit of a trial. More than 1,600 people were executed, including the king. On January 21, 1793, Louis XVI was brought to the main square in Paris, and placed on the guillotine. Thousands cheered at his beheading. Nine months later his queen, Marie Antoinette, faced the same end.

D*uring the French Revolution a French doctor named Joseph-Ignace Guillotin invented a device that was intended to make executions by beheading more efficient. Replacing the ax-wielding, black-hooded executioner of former days, the guillotine got plenty of use during the chaos of the revolution. For a period of time it was set up in the main square of Paris so that crowds of people could witness the executions.*

Soon another government took power whose reign was so bloody it is known today as the "Reign of Terror." Leaders turned on each other, fighting over who would gain control. An especially famous leader named Danton, considered by many the ultimate French revolutionary, was guillotined by his former colleague Maximilien Robespierre. Only three months later, Robespierre and his followers were sent to the guillotine as well. The Reign of Terror lasted a year, from 1793 to 1794. Powerful courts were set up to "purge" the country of anyone judged an enemy to the revolution. Trials showed no respect for the rights supposedly guaranteed by the Declaration of the Rights of Man and Citizen. The Reign of Terror resulted in over forty thousand deaths: a revolution that began with high hopes for liberty and freedom had turned into a bloodbath.

France was in this dreadful state when a new leader arrived on the scene—Napoleon Bonaparte.

Napoleon

Napoleon Bonaparte was born on the Mediterranean island of Corsica in 1769. He attended military schools in France, and by age sixteen was an active member of the French Army. He fought in the wars against France's enemies during the revolution, and emerged as an outstanding leader. Winning campaigns against the British and the Italians, Napoleon made sure that news of his victories reached the right ears, and before long he was introduced to the key political leaders in Paris.

In 1799, with confusion still reigning, Napoleon seized control of the French government and became First Consul—a ruler, but not a king. His administration was one of action, which was a great relief to many citizens who had lived through the chaos and instability of the revolution. Napoleon promised peace and order, and soon achieved it by signing treaties with warring countries.

As First Consul, Napoleon renovated the French systems of law, education, and government. One of his most brilliant achievements was his reorganization of the

French legal system, creating "the Napoleonic Code," which covers everything from robbery to divorce. The laws were written in clear, specific language, so that they could be easily understood, and they ensured equal treatment for all citizens. They were farseeing enough that even today French law is based on the Napoleonic Code. (One of our states—Louisiana, named after King Louis XIV—once belonged to France and still bases some of its laws on the Napoleonic Code.)

Napoleon's desire for power was almost limitless. He admired Julius Caesar and other Roman emperors. In fact, in 1804 he announced that the revolution was over and had himself crowned Napoleon I, Emperor of the French. A country that had just fought one of the bloodiest revolutions in history to rid itself of monarchy now found itself with an emperor!

For his coronation ceremony, Napoleon and his wife, Josephine, wore long purple capes lined with ermine fur from Russia. To the ceremony Napoleon brought the pope from Rome, to show that the emperor of the French deserved the same respect as Charlemagne and the Holy Roman Emperors. But Napoleon placed the crown on his own head, to show that even the pope was not above him.

As time went on, although he still claimed to have democratic ideals, Napoleon became more of a tyrant. Still, the French overwhelmingly supported their emperor, mostly because of his continuing victories in battle. Napoleon wanted to win for himself the glory of earlier conquerors like Alexander and Caesar. His conquests brought great power and glory to himself and to France, and also had the effect of

Napoleon and his army retreating from Moscow.

spreading the Enlightenment ideals of the French Revolution throughout Europe by sweeping away old social systems and instituting the Napoleonic Code.

Napoleon is known as a brilliant soldier who won almost all the battles he fought. His forces conquered much of Europe. But then he made a mistake. He decided to conquer Russia by marching to Moscow. Look at a map with Paris and Moscow on it, and you can get an idea of what Napoleon was undertaking. In June of 1812 he took with him almost half a million soldiers. Three quarters of them never even made it to Moscow. The Russian Army never met the French with full force, but simply fought and then retreated, forcing Napoleon's soldiers to find new sources of food and march even farther away from their homeland. As the bitter Russian winter set in, many French soldiers died from starvation and exposure to the cold. When Napoleon finally arrived in Moscow, he found the city deserted. In November, he began a slow retreat from Moscow: men marched barefoot through wind and snow. Food supplies ran out. In the end, of the 450,000 men who had started out for Moscow, only about 40,000 returned.

Waterloo

Despite the devastating losses in his campaign against Russia, Napoleon was still unwilling to make peace with the other countries of Europe. He refused to admit that his army had been nearly destroyed. Soon, the Austrians, Prussians, Russians, and Swedes were marching on Paris. The French people did not want to fight. They had seen too many of their young men die. So they exiled Napoleon to the island of Elba, not far from his native Corsica.

Napoleon did not stay there long. He yearned for battle, and with the help of loyal troops and a few government officials, he sneaked back to France. In Paris he was welcomed by many who had recently urged his exile. He went straight to war. He took on the combined forces of many nations at Waterloo in Belgium, where he was thoroughly and permanently defeated. Perhaps you've heard the expression "to meet your Waterloo." It means to come face to face with a task or obstacle that defeats you completely, as Napoleon was defeated at Waterloo.

After this final defeat, Napoleon was exiled once again. This time he was sent to St. Helena, a tiny tropical island in the South Atlantic, where he was guarded night and day. There, the man who had changed Europe lived in isolation until his death in 1821.

> After the French Revolution and the conquests of Napoleon, Europe and the world would never be the same again. The ideas of liberty and equality spread, sparking movements for independence in many lands. At the same time, other leaders arose who, like Napoleon, wanted to build vast empires with little regard for liberty or equality. The story of these struggles and other changes that shaped our modern world lies ahead in Book Six of this series.

Introduction to American Civilization

FOR PARENTS AND TEACHERS

"Through the battle, through defeat, moving yet and never stopping": these words of the American poet Walt Whitman describe the part of America's story that we tell in this book. It is a story that includes the trial by fire of the Civil War, and the struggles to reconstruct the "house divided" by that war. It tells of our country's westward expansion, and the terrible cost of this growth to Native American civilizations. It examines both the progress and the problems that industrialization brought to America. It introduces reformers who worked for the rights of women, African-Americans, and the urban poor. And it shows our country taking on the complexities and compromises of becoming an international power, "moving yet and never stopping" into the twentieth century.

American Civilization

North and South

In the mid-1800s, America's population and industry were growing rapidly. But the country was also growing apart. Serious disagreements had developed between people in the North and South.

The North and the South had very different economies. The economy of the North was becoming industrial, based on factories that made such things as iron and steel and machinery and cloth. The South's economy was mostly agricultural. Most Southern farmers owned small farms and did not own slaves. But much of the most profitable crop, cotton, was grown on large plantations that relied on slave labor. In the mid-nineteenth century, slaves in the South did all of the hardest work, and about four-fifths of the skilled labor as well. A whole way of life developed in the South that depended upon slavery.

Many Southerners came to accept slavery as necessary. Even so, up to the 1830s there were many outspoken critics of slavery in the South. In earlier years, prominent leaders in Southern states, such as Thomas Jefferson of Virginia, had felt uneasy about slavery, and objected to it on moral grounds. Yet, despite their objections to slavery, they continued (like Jefferson) to own slaves—which indicates just how deeply whites in the South had come to rely upon slavery, and how much they would have to give up if it were ever abolished.

Slavery had existed in the North as well during colonial times. But as the Northern economy developed, it came to rely less on slave labor. In the North there were no plantations. People made their living as small farmers, shopkeepers, craftsmen,

A Southern cotton plantation.

The thriving Northern town of Brooklyn, New York.

merchants, and factory workers. Because they did not rely on slave labor, many Northerners were opposed to slavery. Some were opposed for selfish reasons: they saw slavery as a threat to the jobs of white workers. Others, however, considered slavery morally wrong, and saw it as a threat to the basic principles of American democracy.

For a variety of reasons, then, the South had come to rely upon slavery, and the North to oppose it. More than anything else, disagreements over slavery would drive the nation closer to war.

The Missouri Compromise

As more people moved west throughout the early nineteenth century, more territories became eligible to become new states. The original states were very interested in these new states: they wanted the new states to be on their side in the arguments between North and South. The North wanted the new states to vote for what the North wanted, while the South wanted the new states to vote for what the South wanted. Most of all, the South wanted new states to be slave states—states where it was legal to own slaves. The North wanted the new states to be free states, in

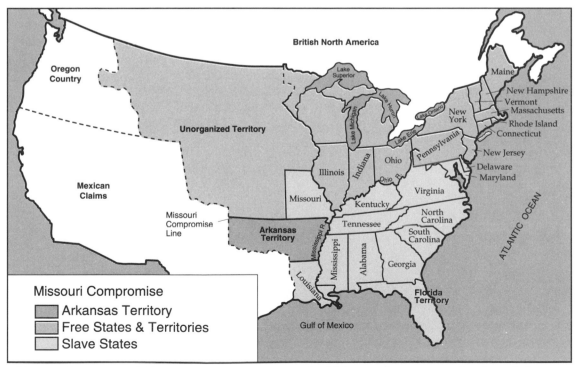

This map shows you which states were slave states and which were free states at the time of the Missouri Compromise. The orange line is the Mason-Dixon Line. If you're wondering why there's no West Virginia on this map, it's because West Virginia was formed later, during the Civil War.

which slavery would be forbidden. If either side gained a majority of senators and representatives in Congress, then it could pass laws against the wishes of the other side.

In 1819, the United States was evenly balanced between slave states and free states (eleven slave and eleven free). Then Missouri applied to become a new state—as a slave state. This triggered long angry debates in the Congress.

Finally, an agreement called the "Missouri Compromise" was reached in 1820. Missouri was admitted to the Union as a slave state, and to balance that, Maine was admitted as a free state. But this balancing act was only part of a larger agreement. Congress drew a line from east to west across the American territories. (This line included a boundary called the Mason-Dixon Line, which you can read about below). It was agreed that all lands north of the line (except Missouri) would be free, while settlers in all lands south of the line could own slaves.

But this was a dangerous agreement. Do you remember how the Constitution of the United States refers to "a more perfect *union*"? A union joins many parts into one whole—in this case, many states into one country. But the Missouri Compromise seemed to be saying that our one country was really two: one slave, one free.

The Mason-Dixon Line

Back when the United States was still a collection of colonies, there was an argument over the boundary between two colonies. From 1763 to 1767, two Englishmen, Charles Mason and Jeremiah Dixon, surveyed the boundary between Maryland and Pennsylvania. This boundary became known as the Mason-Dixon Line. Around the time of the arguments leading to the Missouri Compromise in 1820, people began to speak of the Mason-Dixon Line as it is sometimes referred to today: as an unofficial boundary between the North and the South.

Uncle Tom's Cabin

As you might recall from reading about Frederick Douglass in Book Four of this series, northern reformers called "abolitionists" worked to abolish slavery. They persuaded many people to oppose slavery. But even those who were unmoved by the writings and speeches of the abolitionists found themselves convinced by a novel called *Uncle Tom's Cabin*, published in 1852 by Harriet Beecher Stowe.

Over three hundred thousand copies of *Uncle Tom's Cabin* sold in one year, an amazing number of books for that time. The novel tells the story of Uncle Tom, a kind and religious slave. He saves the life of a white girl, but is later sold to a cruel master, Simon Legree. When Tom refuses to tell where two escaped slaves are hiding, Simon Legree whips him until he dies. Tom's fate filled Northern readers with anger and outrage, and even made some want to take up arms and force the South to end slavery.

How Some Slaves Resisted

Slaves responded to their bondage—their lack of freedom—in different ways. Some did their best to run away. Perhaps you remember the story of Harriet Tubman and the Underground Railroad that helped slaves escape to the North. Some slaves, instead of trying to escape, deliberately broke the tools they were given to work with. Some tried to poison their masters. Some, in despair, tried to kill themselves. Sometimes a group of slaves would revolt against their master.

Do you know the story called "The People Could Fly"? (See Book Three of this series.) This story, in which slaves rise from the ground and fly back to Africa, shows how slaves used their imaginations to keep up their hopes for freedom.

Some slaves worked and suffered quietly. Most slaves became Christians, and they often looked to heaven as a reward for their suffering on earth. Many slaves still held on to some of their African beliefs and customs. They made a new kind of music, songs called "spirituals," which brought together the old music of Africa and the newly learned Christian religion. These spirituals are moving and inspiring songs, often based on Bible stories about how the people of Israel were delivered from slavery in Egypt. Some of these spirituals, like "Swing Low Sweet Chariot" and "Go Down, Moses," are timeless, and beloved today. Here are some of the verses from "Go Down, Moses":

> Go down, Moses,
> Way down in Egypt land
> Tell old Pharaoh,
> To let my people go.
>
> When Israel was in Egypt land
> Let my people go
> Oppressed so hard they could not stand
> Let my people go.
>
> Go down, Moses,
> Way down in Egypt land
> Tell old Pharaoh,
> "Let my people go!"

To hear spirituals sung gloriously, try a recording called "Gospels, Spirituals, and Hymns" by Mahalia Jackson (Sony-Columbia Legacy).

To learn more about the experiences of African-Americans as slaves and their struggle for freedom, try these books:

Anthony Burns: The Defeat and Triumph of a Fugitive Slave by Virginia Hamilton (Knopf, 1988).

Many Thousands Gone: African Americans from Slavery to Freedom by Virginia Hamilton (Knopf, 1993).

To Be a Slave by Julius Lester (Scholastic, 1988).

"Wanted Dead or Alive": The True Story of Harriet Tubman by Ann McGovern (Scholastic, 1991).

Which Way Freedom by Joyce Hansen (Avon, 1992).

The Dred Scott Decision

A Supreme Court decision in 1857 pushed the North and South closer to war. This was the decision in the Dred Scott case.

Dred Scott was a slave who wanted his freedom. His owner had moved and had taken Scott from the slave state of Missouri to the free territory of Wisconsin. In Wisconsin, Scott got married, and two daughters were soon born. But then Scott's owner decided to move back to Missouri, and he took Scott and his family with him—as slaves. Dred Scott went to court to argue that he and his family were free because they had lived in free territory.

The Supreme Court examined Dred Scott's argument, but the Court didn't give Scott and his family their freedom. In fact, the Supreme Court, with a majority of justices from the South, used Dred Scott's case as an opportunity to take an extreme pro-slavery stand. The Chief Justice wrote down a racist opinion: all black people, he said, were "so far inferior" to whites "that they had no rights which the white man was bound to respect." For the Chief Justice—as for many people at the time— the idea that "all men are created equal" with "certain unalienable rights" did not apply to African-Americans.

The Court went even further and declared the Missouri Compromise unconstitutional, claiming that Congress had no right to exclude slavery from *any* territory.

Not long after the Supreme Court decision, Dred Scott and his wife were lucky enough to be freed by a later master. They got jobs in St. Louis. They died just before their country was about to erupt into war.

Dred Scott.

The Lincoln-Douglas Debates

When people want to be elected to Congress, they usually have to explain to the voters their beliefs about many important issues and ideas. In Illinois in 1858, one issue dominated the election for senator: slavery.

Senator Stephen A. Douglas was trying to get reelected. His opponent was Abraham—"Honest Abe"—Lincoln. Lincoln was a member of the recently formed Republican Party, which took a strong stand against slavery. In 1858 Lincoln made a speech in which he stated his belief that slavery was a great threat to the United States. Lincoln used a vivid passage from the Bible: "A house divided against itself cannot stand." He made clear what that meant for America: "I believe this government cannot endure permanently half *slave* and half *free.*"

Abraham Lincoln.

Lincoln challenged Stephen Douglas to a series of public debates on slavery. Douglas had argued that the people in the territories should be allowed to decide whether to own slaves—and this, said Lincoln, proved that Douglas was pro-slavery. In fact, the issue was not so clear-cut. But Lincoln wanted to insist that Douglas was too easy on slavery, and that it was necessary to take a moral stand against slavery. In the final debate, Lincoln spoke of "the eternal struggle between . . . two principles—right and wrong—throughout the world." He went on to condemn [the principle] . . . that says, "You toil and work and earn bread, and I'll eat it." No matter in what shape it comes, whether from the mouth of a king who seeks to bestride the people of his own nation and live by the fruit of their labor, or from one race of men as an apology for enslaving another race, it is the same tyrannical principle.

When the debates ended, Douglas was reelected to the Senate. But in a way, Lincoln was a winner: the tall lawyer from Illinois who had argued for the "ultimate extinction" of slavery gained national attention because of the debates, which put him on the road to the presidency of the United States.

To learn more about the life of Abraham Lincoln, try these books:

Abe Lincoln Grows Up *by Carl Sandburg (Harcourt, Brace, Jovanovich, 1940).*
Lincoln: A Photobiography *by Russell Freedman (Clarion, 1987).*
Meet Abraham Lincoln *By Barbara Cary (Random House, 1989).*

John Brown at Harpers Ferry

A year before the presidential elections of 1860, a violent event occurred that frightened Southern slaveholders. An abolitionist by the name of John Brown believed so strongly in the cause of freedom for blacks that he was willing to fight to gain it. In October of 1859, John Brown led a band of eighteen men, including five free African-Americans, to try to capture a large supply of weapons at Harpers Ferry, Virginia. His plan was to put guns in the hands of slaves and urge them to rebel against their owners.

John Brown's plan failed. At Harpers Ferry, he was met by local and federal troops. Brown was wounded, captured, and sentenced to be hanged. In the North, people made a hero of Brown: on the day of his death, church bells tolled and cannons were fired. Southerners were amazed and angered by the Northern sympathy for a man they believed to be a dangerous fanatic.

Many Southerners believed that the whole North was like John Brown: ready to use violence against the slaveholding South. More and more, Southerners began to argue that the only way to protect the South and its way of life, including slavery, was to secede (break away) from the rest of the United States.

The United States was clearly becoming "a house divided against itself."

The Argument over States' Rights

Do you remember how the Founding Fathers avoided dealing with slavery when they wrote the Constitution? Now it was coming back to haunt the country.

The Tenth Amendment to the Constitution says that "powers not . . . prohibited by [the Constitution] to the States, are reserved to the States." In other words, if the Constitution doesn't forbid the states to do something, then the states have the right to do as they choose (though the Supreme Court may also determine whether a state's actions are constitutional).

The Southern states claimed that slavery was a matter of states' rights. Southerners believed that, since the Constitution did not prohibit slavery, each state should have the right to decide whether to allow slavery, without the involvement of the federal government.

Turning the argument about slavery into a legal matter of states' rights distracted attention from the larger question of the morality of slavery: can a state have the "right" to do something that is morally wrong? The answer to this would have been a clear *No!* if the framers of our Constitution had resisted political pressures and explicitly prohibited slavery in the first place.

Lincoln Elected: Southern States Secede

Opposition to the spread of slavery was a central issue in the campaign of Abraham Lincoln for president. Thus, many Southerners considered it a disaster when Lincoln was narrowly elected president in 1860, without the support of a single Southern state. Even though Lincoln promised not to interfere with slavery in the states where it already existed, many Southern leaders didn't believe him. They called Lincoln a "friend of John Brown" and saw his election as proof that the North was the enemy of the Southern way of life.

Many Southerners no longer wanted to have anything to do with a government that they saw as an enemy. So they took the dangerous and dramatic step of leaving the Union. In December 1860, South Carolina became the first state to secede from the Union. By February 1861, six other states in the Deep South had seceded. When Lincoln officially took over as president in March 1861, five states in the upper South still had not seceded: Virginia, North Carolina, Kentucky, Tennessee, and Arkansas. Some people in these states were against slavery, but they didn't want to fight against their neighbors in the lower South to bring them back into the Union. Some Northerners agreed that the Southern states that had seceded should just be left alone. To fight them, they said, would just hurt the North.

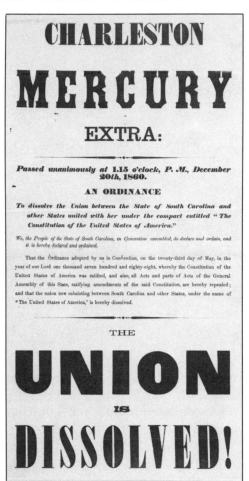

Here's how a Charleston newspaper reported South Carolina's secession.

Fort Sumter: The Civil War Begins

But the fighting, so long in coming, began in 1861, on an island off South Carolina, at Fort Sumter.

Southerners wanted the United States soldiers to get out of the South. Fort Sumter was one of the few forts with Union soldiers remaining in the South, and it was running out of supplies. Lincoln knew the South would probably resist any attempt from the North to send supplies to Fort Sumter. But he decided to send them anyway.

When the Southerners heard that supply ships were on the way, they decided to

Southern forces attack Fort Sumter.

consider this a hostile act. They began bombing Fort Sumter on the morning of April 12, 1861. The Civil War had begun.

Lincoln called for a Union Army to stop what Northerners saw as the South's "rebellious ways." The South, said Lincoln, had fired the first shots. Southerners claimed they had been forced into it. But the question of "who started it" really didn't matter. The causes of the Civil War, as you've seen, go way back, long before the firing on Fort Sumter.

Days after the firing on Fort Sumter, Virginia seceded from the Union, and three other Southern states quickly followed. Each side expected quick victory. They were horribly wrong.

Eager to Fight

When Fort Sumter fell, President Lincoln asked for seventy-five thousand volunteers to join the fight to save the Union. The Southern states—or, as they were called, the Confederate states—planned to bring together an army of about a hundred thousand men to defend the South. These might seem like large numbers, but before the Civil War was over, the Union would send over two million soldiers to fight against almost a million Confederate troops.

Though neither the North nor the South was ready to fight, both sides were eager to get started. Few Americans at this time had any firsthand experience of the horrors of war. When they clamored for the fighting to begin, they didn't think about bloodshed and death. Instead they thought of war as an exciting adventure, like stories they had read about famous battles and brave heroes. Each side expected the fighting to end quickly.

Some people in Washington, D.C., were so excited about the coming war that, on July 21, 1861, they packed picnic baskets and lined up, like spectators at a football game, to watch the first major battle. In what would later be called the First Battle of Bull Run, Union troops attacked Confederate troops by a creek called Bull Run, near Manassas, Virginia (about thirty

Confederate soldiers ready to fight.

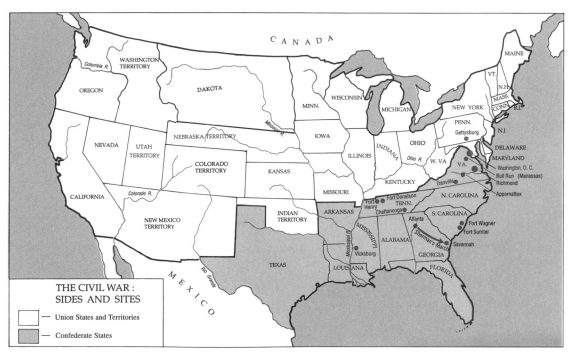

This map shows you which states belonged to the Union and which to the Confederacy. It also shows the cities and battles you'll read about in this section.

miles west of Washington, D.C.). At first it appeared that the Union soldiers were winning, but then the Confederate general Thomas J. Jackson arrived with reinforcements. His troops held their ground "like a stone wall," thus earning the general the nickname of "Stonewall" Jackson. The Confederate troops then turned the tables and attacked the Union soldiers, who retreated in panic, along with the frightened sightseers.

The Confederate Army won the battle. Confederates would continue to win most of the major battles from 1861 to the summer of 1863. Still, at Bull Run the Civil War had just begun. For the next four years, many soldiers would fall.

The Confederacy

Eleven states in total seceded from the Union: South Carolina, Florida, Georgia, Alabama, Mississippi, Louisiana, Texas, Virginia, Arkansas, North Carolina, and Tennessee. They formed the Confederate States of America. Their name was a reminder of the Articles of Confederation (which you read about in Book Four of this series). Back in the 1780s, you remember, just after the United States broke away from Britain, many Americans were suspicious of any strong central government. So they established a weak central government under the Articles of Confederation. Similarly, in 1861, many Southerners wanted the Confederacy to be no more than a loose collection of states, without much central government at all. The Confederate states adopted a constitution that contained strong rules in favor of slavery and states' rights.

The Confederate government established a capital at Richmond, Virginia, only a hundred miles from Washington, D.C. The Confederates chose Jefferson Davis to be their first president. Davis had been both a congressman and a senator. He had served as Secretary of War under Franklin Pierce, the fourteenth president of the United States. He had fought in the Mexican-American War. But despite these qualifications, he was not an effective leader. He was often ill. One member of the Confederate government called Davis "the most difficult man to get along with" he'd ever met. At the beginning of the war, most Southerners looked up to Jefferson Davis as a hero. But as the war went on, more and more Confederate leaders blamed Davis for the South's problems.

The Soldiers

Most of the people who fought in the Civil War had never been soldiers before. At this time, most Americans lived on farms, so most of the soldiers were farmers. They fought alongside workers and shopkeepers from the cities and small towns. About one out of every four Union soldiers was an immigrant (someone who was born in another country but then came to this country to live).

Men of all ages became soldiers. One was as old as eighty; one was as young as nine. Most soldiers were young men, but some were not yet men—they were boys. Usually, the boy soldiers didn't fight. Instead, they helped the adult soldiers by carrying food and water, taking care of the horses, and doing other chores.

Boy soldiers filled two other important roles, as buglers and drummers. Since there were no radios, loudspeakers, or walkie-talkies at this time, Civil War soldiers relied on the sound of the bugle or drums to tell them when to wake up, when to march, when to attack, and when to take cover. On a battlefield clouded with gunsmoke, a soldier could listen for the sound of drums to find out where to go and what to do.

A proud young soldier in the Union Army.

Sometimes boys had to take up weapons and fight with the men. Johnny Clem was eleven years old in 1861 when he became a drummer for the Union Army. When a shot from a Confederate cannon destroyed his drum, Johnny picked up a gun and fired back at the Confederate troops. From that day on he fought alongside the adults. He even became a sergeant—at the ripe old age of thirteen!

> For firsthand accounts of the experiences of boys in the Civil War, read The Boy's War *by Jim Murphy (Clarion, 1990).*

Robert E. Lee

The commander of the Confederate Army was General Robert E. Lee. A graduate of the military academy at West Point, Lee had served in the United States Army for more than thirty years. He had been a hero of the Mexican-American War. It was Lee who led the federal troops that put down John Brown's raid at Harpers Ferry in 1859.

When the Civil War broke out, Lee faced a painful decision. He felt strong loyalty to the Union he had served for so many years. A few days after the attack on Fort Sumter, Lee was asked to take command of all Union forces and lead the fight against the Confederacy. But Lee was a Southerner from Virginia. "With all my devotion to the Union, and the feeling of loyalty and duty of an American citizen," Lee said, "I

Robert E. Lee.

have not been able to make up my mind to raise my hand against my relatives, my children, my home." Lee resigned from the federal army and joined the Confederate Army.

By the spring of 1862 Robert E. Lee was President Davis's top military adviser. In battle after battle, Lee proved himself a master of planning and a strong leader. Soldiers who served under Lee liked and respected him. He set a good example for his men: he did not curse, smoke, or drink alcohol.

Yanks and Rebs, Blue and Gray

Soon after the war began, Northerners and Southerners started using nicknames to refer to each other. The Southerners called the Northerners "Yankees"—remember the song "Yankee Doodle"? Northerners referred to the war as a "rebellion," and so called the Southerners "Rebels." These nicknames were often shortened to "Yanks" and "Rebs," or sometimes turned up as "Billy Yank" and "Johnny Reb."

Today if you see pictures of Civil War soldiers, you might see Union soldiers dressed in dark blue and Confederate soldiers dressed in gray. Eventually, the Union Army settled on blue as its official color, and the Confederate Army chose gray, and that's how the two sides are remembered: the North in blue, the South in gray.

At first, however, soldiers tended to wear the uniform of the militia from their home state or city. These uniforms might be blue, gray, red, black, brown, or some other color. As the war dragged on, the South did not have enough uniforms for all its soldiers. Many Confederate soldiers wore the same clothes they had worn at home before the war. Other Rebels would take the uniforms from Yankees who had been killed or captured. These uniforms would then be dyed a light brown color that Southerners called "butternut."

Ulysses S. Grant

Ulysses S. Grant.

On the Union side, the first years of the war were very disappointing. Again and again Union troops failed in their efforts to achieve their goal: the capture of the Confederate capital at Richmond. Several times President Lincoln replaced the general in charge of Union troops in hopes of finding someone who could lead the army to victory. As the war went on, a few good officers began to prove themselves in battle; the most important of these was Ulysses S. Grant.

Like Robert E. Lee, Grant had attended West Point. Both men fought in the Mexican-American War. Otherwise, Grant and Lee had little in common. Grant was fifteen years younger than Lee. Unlike Lee, Grant sometimes drank too much alcohol. Grant was not an army officer when the Civil War began. Instead, he was working in his father's leather shop in Illinois.

As soon as he learned of the firing on Fort Sumter, Grant began organizing volunteers in his town. He entered the war as a colonel in charge of an Illinois regiment. (A regiment was a group of a thousand soldiers.) President Lincoln soon made Grant a general.

Grant led the Union to its first important victories of the war. In February 1862 his Union troops captured Fort Henry and Fort Donelson in Tennessee. When the Confederate commander at Fort Donelson realized his troops were outnumbered, he sent Grant a message to see if he would like to make a deal. Grant sent back a message saying, "No terms except an unconditional and immediate surrender can be accepted." After a three-day battle, the Confederates at Fort Donelson surrendered completely. News of the battle spread quickly. Northerners joked that Grant's initials—U.S.G.—stood for "Unconditional Surrender" Grant.

Grant's leadership and bravery impressed everyone, including President Lincoln. "I can't spare this man," Lincoln said, "he fights." Lincoln had finally found the general who could bring victory and end the war. In the spring of 1864, Lincoln placed Grant in charge of the entire Union Army.

The Emancipation Proclamation

If one issue more than any other divided North and South, it was slavery. Yet when the war began, President Lincoln insisted that the purpose of the war was not to end slavery. According to Lincoln, the North was fighting for one reason: to save the Union, to keep the United States *united.*

Lincoln wanted slavery to end, but first he wanted to bring the nation back together. He had to be careful about how he expressed his opposition to slavery because some states fighting on the Union side actually allowed slavery. These were the "border states": Delaware, Maryland, Kentucky, and Missouri. Lincoln was concerned that if he took too strong a stand against slavery, the border states would secede and join the Confederacy.

Northerners who opposed slavery urged President Lincoln to use his power to end slavery. At first the President refused to act, but in the spring of 1862 the Congress began to pass laws against slavery. Several months later President Lincoln became convinced that freeing the slaves in the South would help the Union win the war. So he issued what is called the Emancipation Proclamation. To "emancipate" means to set free; a "proclamation" is an official announcement. The Emancipation Proclamation announced that all slaves in areas controlled by the Confederacy would be free beginning January 1, 1863.

Of course, neither the Congress nor President Lincoln could force Southern slave owners to free their slaves right away. But news of the Emancipation Proclamation brought hope and joy to African-Americans. In the North, Frederick Douglass wrote, "We shout for joy that we live to recall this righteous moment."

African-American Troops in the Civil War

African-Americans had fought bravely in the Revolutionary War and the War of 1812. Yet when the Civil War began, neither the Union nor the Confederacy allowed African-Americans to serve as soldiers. Prejudice still gripped the minds of many whites in both the North and the South who thought blacks were not smart enough or brave enough to be good soldiers. But Northern blacks and those who had escaped from the South wanted a chance to fight against the Confederacy.

Even when they were denied the opportunity to be soldiers, African-Americans helped the Union cause in any way they could. Some helped the Union Army by

spying on Confederate troops. Harriet Tubman was one of many African-Americans who sneaked behind the battle lines to gather important information about Confederate armies.

In the North, many African-Americans believed that as free citizens they deserved an opportunity to fight for their country. At the same time, the Union Army needed more soldiers. Since there were not enough volunteers, the Union Army drafted thousands of white men, many of whom did not want to fight. Frederick Douglass called the Union foolish for not using black soldiers. This, said Douglass, was "no time to fight only with your white hand, and allow your black hand to remain tied."

More and more Northerners began to agree with Frederick Douglass. In the summer of 1862, the Union government passed laws to allow blacks to become soldiers. Many African-Americans rushed to volunteer. The Emancipation Proclamation also encouraged many blacks to escape the South and join the Union cause. By the end of the war, one out of ten Union soldiers, and one out of four sailors in the Union Navy, was African-American.

A Brave Black Regiment

The first Union Army regiment to be made up entirely of African-American troops was the 54th Massachusetts Volunteers. Their leader was Colonel Robert Gould Shaw, a young white officer who was the son of an abolitionist. Colonel Shaw believed in the ability of his black troops. The regiment's African-Americans also believed in themselves. One soldier wrote home, "We aim to be the finest regiment in the whole army! And we're going to do it!"

In July of 1863, the 54th went into action near Charleston, South Carolina, where the Civil War had started with the attack on Fort Sumter. If the Union Army could defeat the Confederates at Charleston and take back Fort Sumter, it would be an important victory. But first, the Union soldiers would have to drive the Confederates out of the forts that protected the city of Charleston.

In their first battle, the soldiers of the 54th defeated a Rebel charge. Days later, however, the 54th faced a much tougher test. They were ordered to attack Fort Wagner, a huge Confederate fortress with thick walls and many powerful guns. To prepare for the attack, gunboats of the Union Navy bombarded Fort Wagner. Colonel

Shaw's soldiers saw so many shells explode that it seemed very little of the fort would be left to attack. But they were mistaken. The bombing caused only minor damage. When the 54th charged the fort, Confederates inside opened fire.

Colonel Shaw and a black flag-bearer, Sergeant W. H. Carney, bravely climbed to the top of one of Fort Wagner's walls. Sergeant Carney fell wounded, but caught the flag before it touched the ground. Colonel Shaw shouted back to his troops, "Rally, 54th! Rally!" Then a Confederate bullet struck Colonel Shaw in the heart. His dead body toppled into the fort. Almost half the men of the 54th died in their brave attempt to take Fort Wagner. Though the fort remained in Confederate hands, the soldiers of the 54th Massachusetts proved that African-Americans were capable of great courage and sacrifice for their country.

Despite their bravery, black soldiers usually were not treated as well as white soldiers. For example, African-Americans received less pay. Many black soldiers became so angry about their "short pay" that they refused to accept any wages until the government agreed to pay them the same as white soldiers. Finally, in June of 1864, Congress passed a law requiring equal pay for all soldiers, regardless of color. Even then, blacks usually were not allowed to become officers. One African-American who did become an officer was Major Martin R. Delany, the highest-ranking black soldier in the Union Army.

The story of the Massachusetts 54th has been made into a powerful movie called Glory. *Also, try these books:*
The Storming of Fort Wagner: Black Valor in the Civil War *by Irving Werstein (Scholastic, 1970).*
Undying Glory: The Story of the Massachusetts 54th Regiment *by Clinton Cox (Scholastic, 1991).*

The Misery of War

When the Civil War began, many people thought only of heroism and adventure. But as the fighting dragged on, both soldiers and ordinary citizens learned that war brings with it hunger, illness, suffering, and death.

Soldiers were often hungry. The food each soldier received from the army was called his "rations." Soldiers rarely had fresh meat or vegetables: instead, they often ate cold salted pork or perhaps some beans. When their rations ran out, soldiers would search for whatever food they could find. If soldiers were on the march, or if supply wagons were blocked by enemy troops, soldiers might go several days without any food.

For a Union soldier on the battlefield, an important part of most meals was a biscuit called "hardtack." It was so hard to chew, soldiers had to soak it in water or coffee, or fry it in pork fat, before they could eat it. As bad as hardtack was, hungry Confederate soldiers might have gladly traded their rations for some of the Yankees' food. Instead of hardtack, Confederate soldiers ate hard black cakes of fried cornmeal called "pone."

Diseases spread quickly from soldier to soldier. Today you know you shouldn't eat or drink from a plate or cup used by someone who's sick. But at the time of the Civil War, most doctors didn't believe diseases were caused by germs. A Civil War soldier would see nothing wrong with sharing a cup with a sick man, or using a dirty bandage that had been used by another wounded soldier.

Often, half of all the troops would be too sick to fight. Most of the medicines we have today had not been invented at the time of the Civil War. If a soldier was sick or wounded, there was little that anyone could do. Even soldiers with only minor injuries or illnesses would sometimes suffer and die. Surgery was crude: a severely wounded arm or leg would more than likely be amputated. While many thousands of soldiers were killed in battle, twice as many died of disease. In fact, an illness we no longer consider serious, diarrhea (which can lead to dehydration), was the number-one cause of death during the war.

Gettysburg: A Turning Point in the War

When the summer of 1863 arrived, the Confederates still seemed to be winning most of the battles. But the Union's Army and Navy were attacking the Confederacy from all sides. The Union Navy bombarded cities and forts all along the Southern coastline. Thanks to Grant's leadership and Union gunboats, the Union controlled all of the Mississippi River except a single Confederate fort. That fort, at Vicksburg, Mississippi, was already surrounded by General Grant's Union troops.

Robert E. Lee knew that he must do something to draw the attention of Union forces away from the weary South. Most of the war had been fought on Southern soil. But if Lee's troops could capture some Northern cities, then General Grant might have to send his troops north, away from Vicksburg, to fight Lee's army. So, General Lee led seventy-five thousand troops northward from Virginia on a long march into Pennsylvania. Lee and his troops got a good head start before the Union generals realized Lee's tactics and prepared to chase after him.

On July 1, 1863, part of Lee's army headed toward the town of Gettysburg, an important crossroads in southern Pennsylvania. Just outside Gettysburg, the Confederates were surprised to find Union soldiers waiting for them. They fought all day long, until the Union soldiers took cover on top of some ridges south of the town.

General Lee then ordered all of his troops into battle at Gettysburg. Ready to fight against them were ninety thousand Union troops. For two days, Lee's troops and artillery attacked again and again. But the Union troops had the advantage of being positioned on hilltops, from which they could fire down at the Confederates. Each time the Confederates charged, cannonballs and bullets would rain down on them.

Finally, on the hot afternoon of July 3, the Union cannons held their fire. It was a trick, and the Confederates fell for it. The Confederates believed the Union cannons must have been destroyed in the fighting. General Lee ordered some fifteen thousand Confederate troops to make one massive attack, to be led by General George Edward Pickett. General Pickett rallied

The Battle of Gettysburg, which lasted three days, changed the tide of the war. Confederate forces, retreating in defeat, left over twenty thousand fellow soldiers behind—many dead, some wounded, and others captured.

his troops, calling out, "Up, men, and to your posts. Don't forget today that you are from old Virginia."

But many of the Confederate soldiers who took part in what is known as "Pickett's Charge" never made it back to Virginia. Pickett's men marched forward in orderly rows, as if they were in a parade. They made easy targets for the Union soldiers standing behind a stone wall with guns loaded. Pickett's Charge lasted only half an hour; nearly half of the Confederates who took part in it were killed. When Pickett and his surviving troops returned to the Confederate lines, General Lee asked Pickett to gather his division and prepare for a possible Union counterattack. "General Lee," replied Pickett, "I have no division."

The next day, July 4, 1863, Lee waited for the Union troops to attack his weary men in gray. The attack never came. That night, Lee began the long retreat back to Virginia. He did not know that earlier in the day, a thousand miles away, the Confederate fort at Vicksburg, Mississippi, had fallen to Union troops led by Ulysses S. Grant, thus putting the entire Mississippi River under Union control.

At the Battle of Gettysburg, each side suffered over twenty thousand men either killed, wounded, or missing. Still, the Union had defeated the mighty army of Robert E. Lee. It was a turning point in the war. Although there were many months of fighting ahead, the Union could now see the possibility of victory over a weakened Confederacy.

Lincoln's Gettysburg Address

To honor their soldiers who had fallen at Gettysburg, the governors of the Northern states decided to create a national cemetery there. The governors asked President Lincoln to come to Gettysburg to speak at the opening of the new national cemetery. Another man, Edward Everett, had also been asked to speak. Everett was a statesman and the most famous speaker in America. At the ceremony on November 19, 1863, Everett gave a speech that lasted two hours.

Then it was President Lincoln's turn. He spoke his words slowly and carefully, but it took the President only a little more than two minutes to deliver his speech. Lincoln's words were few but well chosen. His speech, which we call the Gettysburg Address, has become one of the most famous speeches in American history. In it, Lincoln echoed the Declaration of Independence and reminded his audience, and all Americans since, of the high ideals behind the founding of this country, "conceived in liberty, and dedicated to the proposition that all men are created equal." And he affirmed that those who died at Gettysburg did not die in vain, but so that "this nation, under God, shall have a new birth of freedom, and that government of the people, by the people, for the people, shall not perish from the earth."

(See the Language Arts section of this book for the complete Gettysburg Address.)

Sherman's March to the Sea

In the spring of 1864, the Confederates continued to hold back Union troops in Virginia. But elsewhere the Union was winning battle after battle. General William Tecumseh Sherman began to lead Union troops into the heart of the Confederacy. From May to the middle of July 1864, Sherman's army fought its way from Chattanooga, Tennessee, to the outskirts of Atlanta, Georgia, one of the South's largest cities. By the end of the summer, Confederate troops had to abandon Atlanta. Sherman's troops marched into Atlanta and forced all the citizens to leave. When Union troops left Atlanta two months later, soldiers started fires that burned down much of the city.

General Sherman told General Grant his plan was "to cut a swath to the sea, [and] divide the Confederacy in two." Sherman believed that only the horror of war would convince Southerners to give up their fight. He said he intended to "make old and young, rich and poor, feel the hard hand of war." On their march to the sea, Sherman's troops, spread out in a line sixty miles wide, destroyed houses, barns, and crops all the way from Atlanta to Savannah. Wherever Sherman's troops went, they left behind them starving Southerners—men, women, and children. Years after the Civil War ended, Sherman said, "War is hell"—words that accurately describe his march to the sea.

Richmond Falls

Encouraged by Sherman's capture of Atlanta, more and more Northerners became convinced that the Union would win the war. In the presidential election of November 1864, Northern voters showed their new faith by reelecting President Lincoln.

By the spring of 1865, the end of the war was near. Union troops controlled at least part of every state in the Confederacy. Lee's tired and hungry Confederate troops had spent the cold winter in damp trenches, waiting for Grant's Union troops to attack. Lee knew Grant would attack as soon as good spring weather arrived. So Lee decided to surprise the Union troops by attacking them first. At the end of March, the Confederates attacked, but there was little they could do against Grant's larger, better supplied army.

General Lee sent an urgent telegram to Jefferson Davis in the Confederate capital, Richmond. It was Sunday morning and a messenger delivered the telegram to the church Davis attended. Davis turned pale when he read the telegram. It said Richmond must be given up to the Yankees. Soon Davis and other Confederate officials boarded trains headed south to Danville, Virginia, where they hoped to set up a new capital. On their way out, Confederates set fire to much of Richmond so that the Yankees wouldn't be able to use the city.

On April 3, 1865, Union troops led by a group of black soldiers marched into Richmond, Virginia, where they were greeted by crowds of cheering African-Americans, many of them slaves. The capital of the Confederacy had fallen; the end of the war was in sight.

Surrender at Appomattox

Meanwhile, Lee's remaining troops were hurrying west across Virginia to escape the onrushing Union forces. Lee made it to a small town called Appomattox Court House, in the south central part of Virginia. There the war would come to an end for Lee and his weary soldiers. Grant sent a note to Lee: "The results of the last week must convince you of the hopelessness of further resistance," the note said. Grant called upon Lee to end the bloodshed by surrendering.

Lee sent back a note asking what terms Grant would offer for the Confederates' surrender. This time, Grant did not ask for unconditional surrender. Instead, he asked only that Lee's soldiers lay down their weapons and stop fighting until they could be exchanged for Union soldiers captured by the Confederates.

General Lee learned from his scouts that his troops had no way to escape. "Then there is nothing left for me to do but go and see General Grant," Lee said, adding, "and I would rather die a thousand deaths." On Sunday afternoon, April 9, 1865, Lee met with Grant and several of his officers in the front room of a house in the village of Appomattox Court House. When Grant arrived at the house, he and Lee shook hands. Grant tried to make Lee feel at ease by talking about the time they

After the surrender at Appomattox, Confederate soldiers roll up their flag. How do these men seem to feel?

fought together in the Mexican-American War. But Lee solemnly interrupted. "I suppose, General Grant," he said, "that the object of our present meeting is fully understood." Then the two generals got down to the business at hand: the surrender of Lee's troops.

Grant had fought long and hard to defeat the Confederates. But now that he had won, he was kind to them. Instead of taking prisoners, Grant agreed to let Lee's soldiers return to their homes. Grant insisted that the Confederates give up their guns and military supplies, but he said that the Confederate officers would be allowed to keep their horses and personal weapons.

This unexpected kindness pleased Lee, but he was worried about his soldiers who were not officers. Many soldiers of lower rank had brought their own horses to the war. "I should like to understand whether these men will be permitted to retain their horses?" Lee asked. Grant saw the concern in Lee's face and quickly understood. Grant promised "to let all the men who claim to own a horse or mule take the animals home with them to work their little farms." Lee thanked Grant for his generosity.

Finally, Lee mentioned that his troops had no food. Grant promptly ordered his officers to send beef, bread, coffee, and sugar to the hungry Confederates. For many of Lee's soldiers, it would be the first decent meal they had eaten in months.

Once the generals had reached complete agreement on the surrender, Lee rose to leave. He shook hands with Grant, bowed to the other Union officers, and left the room. Lee did not speak, except to call for his beloved horse, Traveller. A Confederate officer who was there said Lee seemed suddenly "older, grayer, more quiet and reserved . . . very tired."

As Lee rode away, Grant stood quietly on the porch and removed his hat to show his respect for Lee. Then the other Union officers did the same. Happy Union soldiers started to celebrate the surrender. They yelled and fired off cannons, but Grant ordered the soldiers to be quiet. Grant did not want the rebel soldiers to feel worse than they already did. "The war is over," Grant said. "The rebels are our countrymen again."

Back in the Confederate camp, a saddened General Lee told his troops about the surrender. Though they were tough soldiers who had fought bravely, many of them could not help but cry. Lee's last orders to his troops were simple: "Boys, I have done the best I could for you. Go home now, and if you make as good citizens as you have soldiers, you will do well, and I shall always be proud of you."

Lincoln Is Assassinated

Northerners rejoiced at the news of Lee's surrender. In Washington, D.C., crowds of people filled the streets outside the White House and cheered for President Lincoln. But the celebrations would soon end.

On April 14, 1865, only five days after Lee surrendered, President Lincoln and his wife were attending a play at Ford's Theater, not far from the White House. An actor named John Wilkes Booth was also at Ford's Theater that night. Booth was from Maryland, but he strongly supported slavery and the Confederacy. As Lincoln watched the play from a seat high above the stage, Booth sneaked up behind the President and shot him in the head. Then Booth jumped down onto the stage and shouted to the frightened audience, "*Sic semper tyrannis*"—Latin words meaning "Thus ever to tyrants." Booth ran from the theater and rode away on a fast horse. Lincoln was carried to a house across the street from the theater, where he died the next morning.

A week later, soldiers trapped Booth in a barn in northern Virginia. When Booth refused to give himself up, the barn was set on fire. Booth was shot and killed as he ran from the burning barn.

The joy Northerners had felt after Lee's surrender now turned to deep sadness. President Lincoln had guided the nation through its most difficult time. As Walt Whitman wrote in a poem called "O Captain! My Captain!" it was as though a brave captain had brought a ship through a terrible storm—but now, just as the sun had begun to shine, the captain lay dead.

Reconstruction: Repairing the "House Divided"

Before the Civil War, Lincoln had warned that "a house divided against itself cannot stand." When the nation was violently divided by the war, Lincoln wanted most of all to preserve the Union—to reconstruct the divided house. Even while the Civil War was going on, Lincoln began planning what is called "Reconstruction," the process of bringing the eleven Confederate states back into the Union.

Americans disagreed on how to go about reconstructing the country. President Lincoln wanted to make it easy for the Southern states to rejoin the Union. Before he died, he called upon all Americans to carry out the work of reconstruction "with malice toward none, with charity for all." Despite the President's plea, many Northerners held unfriendly feelings toward the South. They looked upon the Confederates as traitors who should be punished.

Within President Lincoln's political party, the Republican Party, there was a group that disagreed with Lincoln's desire to treat the Southern states gently. This group, called the Radical Republicans, wanted the federal government to force certain changes upon the South.

As the Radical Republicans saw it, since white Southerners had gone to war to

Part of what was involved in any plan for Reconstruction was the actual rebuilding of cities. This is Richmond, Virginia, in April 1865; it was destroyed by fires set by the retreating Confederate Army.

keep African-Americans in slavery, those same white Southerners couldn't be trusted to treat blacks fairly once the war ended. The Radicals said it wasn't enough to free the slaves; the federal government must now take an active role to guarantee the rights of freed African-Americans. Some Radicals wanted the government to take land away from white Southerners and give it to freed slaves. All Radicals insisted that blacks must have the right to vote.

As the Civil War was coming to an end, it appeared that the Radical Republicans and President Lincoln were headed for a long argument over how to proceed with Reconstruction. But then the President was assassinated. According to the U.S. Constitution, if a president dies in office, the vice president takes over. Now, all eyes turned to the man who had been Lincoln's vice president, Andrew Johnson. How would the new, seventeenth president handle the problem of Reconstruction?

Johnson's Plan for Reconstruction

Andrew Johnson—a native of North Carolina who had served as governor of Tennessee—was a Southerner at heart. He had even owned five slaves before the war. Johnson quickly announced a plan to grant amnesty to Southerners. To grant amnesty means to forgive or pardon: in this case, amnesty would give Southerners back their full rights as United States citizens. Most Southerners could qualify for amnesty simply by swearing to be loyal to the United States.

Johnson wanted to return control of the South to the state governments as soon as possible. While Johnson insisted that slavery must be abolished, he believed the states should decide what rights freed African-Americans would have. Under Johnson's plan, as soon as a Southern state amended its state constitution to abolish slavery and satisfy a few other requirements, then the people of that state could set up their own government with the same rights and powers as any other state in the Union.

Most white Southerners were happy with Johnson's plan. But the decisions made by the new Southern state governments angered blacks and Radical Republicans— with good reasons. Every former Confederate state continued to deny African-Americans the right to vote.

Black Codes

Many Southern states went even further to deny African-Americans their rights. Southern legislatures passed laws that came to be called Black Codes. These laws limited a black citizen's ability to own property and engage in certain trades and businesses. Some Black Codes gave whites the right to treat black workers almost like slaves. It was as though the clock had been set back to a time before the Civil War.

African-American Southerners felt angry and cheated. They had expected to be free citizens, but the Black Codes made them less than free. The Black Codes angered Radical Republicans in Congress. They saw many of the same Confederate leaders who lost the war now happily serving in state legislatures across the South, passing laws that denied blacks their basic rights. Radicals saw the Black Codes as proof that white Southerners could not be trusted, and that Johnson's plan for Reconstruction must be overturned.

In 1867 Congress passed a series of laws which forced ten of the eleven former Confederate states to start Reconstruction over again. President Johnson tried to veto these laws, but the Radicals in Congress had enough votes to override Johnson's veto. (You may recall learning about the veto in Book Four of this series.) The new laws required the ten states to allow all of their male citizens to vote, including blacks. Until these Southern states satisfied all of Congress's requirements, they would remain under the control of the federal army. Reconstruction was now proceeding as the Radicals wanted it to.

Scalawags and Carpetbaggers

Under the Radicals' Reconstruction plan, many former Confederate leaders were no longer allowed to hold public office. Federal military officials were working hard in the South to get blacks to register to vote. With fewer old Confederate leaders, and with more blacks voting, more Republicans were elected to the state legislatures. These changes in leadership led to the development of two stereotypes, "scalawags" and "carpetbaggers."

A scalawag is a rascal. In the South during Reconstruction, Southerners who cooperated with the new state governments were called scalawags by other Southerners who were disgusted with the new state governments and refused to have anything to do with them. Maybe some scalawags were rascals, but just as many were genuinely concerned about working to improve the South's future.

Southerners who disliked scalawags felt the same way, if not worse, about another group called carpetbaggers. Carpetbaggers were Northerners who came South to take part in Reconstruction. They were called carpetbaggers because they sometimes arrived with their belongings in a cheap suitcase made out of a fabric like carpet. Many Southerners were convinced that these carpetbags would soon be stuffed with whatever riches the greedy Northerners could get their hands on. True, some carpetbaggers came South to get rich quick. But others came to help rebuild the South and to work for civil rights.

The Freedmen's Bureau

For the millions of former slaves, freedom was a blessing, but a hard one. With no property of their own, how would they survive? Would there be schools for them? Who would protect their rights? Shortly before the end of the Civil War, the federal government made some effort to solve these problems by creating an agency that came to be known as the Freedmen's Bureau.

The Freedmen's Bureau tried to give African-Americans small plots of land from the vast areas the Union Army had seized during the war. During the war, General Sherman had distributed land and army mules to blacks who followed his "march to the sea." Ever since, word had spread across the South that the federal government intended to give every freed slave "forty acres and a mule." Congress did pass a bill giving the Freedmen's Bureau control of millions of acres of land for freed slaves, but President Johnson opposed the land giveaway and ordered the land returned to its former white owners. So, very few blacks ever received their "forty acres and a mule."

While the Freedmen's Bureau was not always successful, it did help to educate African-Americans by building freedmen's schools and colleges across the South.

The Impeachment of President Johnson

Do you remember the three branches of the American government? Then you might also remember how the Constitution set up a system known as "checks and balances" to give each of the three branches—executive, legislative, and judicial—the power to check (stop) the other branches, and so keep power balanced among the three branches.

One feature of this Constitutional system of checks and balances gives Congress the power to remove the president from office if he is found guilty of "treason, bribery, or other high crimes and misdemeanors." To begin the process of removing a president, a majority of the House of Representatives must vote to impeach the president. To impeach the president does not mean to remove him from office; it only means to formally charge him with "treason, bribery, or other high crimes and misdemeanors." Once impeached, the president must be given a trial, with the Senate serving as the jury and the Chief Justice of the Supreme Court presiding as judge. The president cannot be removed from office unless two thirds of the senators find the president guilty as charged.

In February of 1868, Andrew Johnson became the first and only president ever to be impeached. Radical Republicans led the move to impeach Johnson because of his repeated attempts to block their plans for Reconstruction. Since no president had ever been impeached before, no one knew exactly how the trial should be conducted. Senators argued about it, and the trial dragged on for more than two months. During the trial, Johnson promised the senators he would no longer stand in the way of their plans for Reconstruction. At the end of the trial, Johnson was found not guilty— but just barely. If only one more senator had voted against Johnson, he would have been removed from office.

Three Important Amendments: Thirteenth, Fourteenth, and Fifteenth

The Constitution, the highest law of our land, is not carved in stone—in other words, it can be changed. Changes to the Constitution are called amendments. Do you remember what we call the first ten amendments to the Constitution?

After the Civil War, the country adopted three new amendments to the Constitution. The amendments were intended to end the problems caused by slavery.

• The Thirteenth Amendment outlaws slavery.

• The Fourteenth Amendment has several parts. The first section says that all persons born in this country are automatically citizens of the United States and citizens of the states where they live. It says that no state may "deprive any person of life, liberty, or property, without due process of law." Due process of law

Following the ratification of the Fourteenth Amendment, polls were opened to black voters in seven Southern states.

usually requires the government to give every person a chance to defend his rights in court. The Fourteenth Amendment also says that no state may deny to any person "equal protection of the laws." In our own time, this "equal-protection" clause has continued to help achieve fairness for all citizens.

• The Fifteenth Amendment prevents the state and federal governments from denying or limiting a person's rights on account of race, color, or the fact that the person was once a slave.

If you were to propose one amendment to the Constitution, what would it be? Here's a research project you can undertake at your school or public library. Find out what has to be done to amend the Constitution. You'll see that it's a long process, and that most of the American people have to agree before any change can be made.

The End of Reconstruction

Reconstruction lasted about twelve years, from 1865 to 1877. During that period, most of the South continued to suffer from hunger and hard times. By the early 1870s, angry whites across the South were trying to overthrow their Republican state governments. Southern whites were fighting to regain control of their lives. Many Southerners claimed the Republican state governments were corrupt, and in some cases they were. But mostly white Southerners were fighting against the state governments because these whites did not want African-Americans to be their equals.

Some whites formed secret organizations to scare both blacks and those whites who were friendly to blacks. The worst of these secret organizations was called the Ku Klux Klan. Members of the Klan wore white hoods to hide their faces when they went on raids. Klansmen would burn black churches, schools, and houses, and even kill innocent black people.

In election after election in the early 1870s, whites found underhanded ways of denying African-Americans their right to vote. For example, some states imposed a poll tax, which required a payment before voting. Many blacks couldn't afford to pay, and so they couldn't vote.

By 1877 the federal government was no longer willing to come to the aid of African-Americans. By then most Northern voters were willing to let white Southerners govern themselves, even if it meant blacks would suffer. In the last decades of the 1800s, Southern whites took ever greater steps to deny African-Americans their basic rights. Not until the middle of this century would African-Americans begin to achieve the equality promised by the Thirteenth, Fourteenth, and Fifteenth Amendments.

Westward Expansion: At What Price?

As you may remember, in the 1830s and 1840s many Americans believed it was the "manifest destiny" of the United States to expand across the entire continent. History soon proved them right. Midway through the 1800s, the outer boundary of our country looked much as it does today. The United States claimed as its own a vast land stretching from the Atlantic Ocean in the east to the Pacific Ocean in the west.

In 1846 a treaty with Great Britain added to the United States the land that would become the states of Washington, Oregon, and Idaho. In 1848, as a result of victory in the Mexican War, the United States acquired territory that later became California, Nevada, Utah, and parts of Arizona, New Mexico, and Colorado. Finally, in 1853 the federal government bought from Mexico the land that now makes up the southern part of Arizona and New Mexico. With that purchase, the United States had come to include all of the land that it holds today, except for Alaska and Hawaii.

Even though in the mid-1800s the United States reached "from sea to shining sea," not very many United States *citizens* lived farther west than Kansas. The West

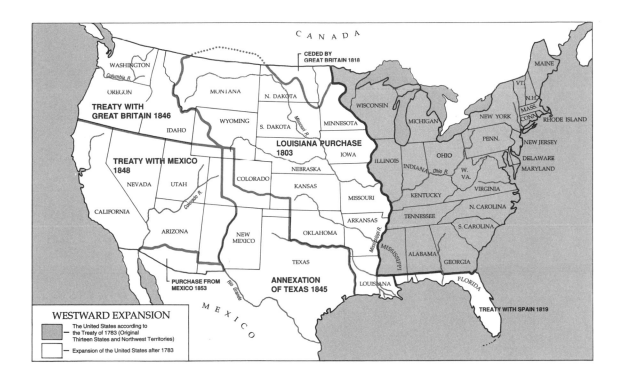

WESTWARD EXPANSION

The United States according to the Treaty of 1783 (Original Thirteen States and Northwest Territories)

Expansion of the United States after 1783

was home to many Native Americans, but most of these people were not considered United States citizens.

As you know, American Indians had lived on the North American continent for centuries before the first European explorers arrived. As European settlers took over lands east of the Mississippi River, they forced many Eastern Indians to move farther west. As white settlers kept pushing west to find new land and new opportunities, the Indians, with good reason, saw them as a threat to their way of life.

Struggles between the Indians and the settlers went on for most of the 1800s. By the end of the century, many thousands of white settlers had set up farms, cities, and towns across the West. But for Native Americans, the westward expansion of the United States proved to be a catastrophe.

Before we examine the westward expansion of the United States, let's look first at the way some American Indians lived before the arrival of the settlers. Keep in mind that the term "American Indian" does not describe only one group of people who share the same customs or speak the same language. Before the Europeans arrived in North America, between five hundred and one thousand different languages were spoken among Native Americans. You may recall reading in Book Three of this series about some of the major Indian tribes east of the Mississippi River: Cherokee, Seminole, Delaware, Susquehanna, Mohican, Massachuset, and Algonquin. The land west of the Mississippi was home to over one hundred major Indian tribes, each

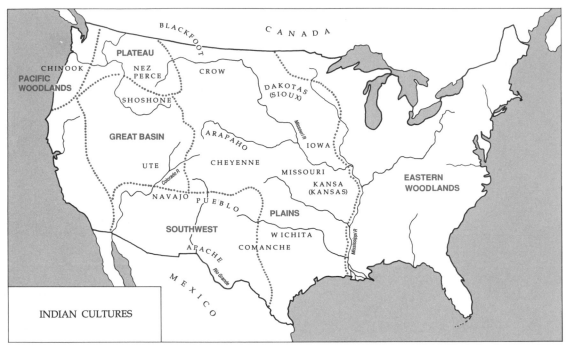

American Indian cultures of the Eastern Woodlands are shown in more detail in Book Three of this series.

with its own distinct customs and beliefs, though tribes that lived in the same region might share some ways of life.

Indians of the Southwest

In the desert that makes up the southwestern corner of this country, Indians had been living in highly organized towns and cities for centuries before the Europeans arrived. Spanish conquistadores found the Indians living in towns with "apartment buildings" up to six stories high. These buildings were made mostly of bricks of adobe, a mixture of clay, sand, and straw. The explorers called the Indians "Pueblos," the Spanish word for towns. The name "Pueblos" came to be used to describe a number of different tribes that shared some of the same customs. (You can read about some early pueblo-builders, the Anasazi, in the World Civilization section of this book.)

The Pueblo Indians were peaceful; they went to war only when they believed it was necessary to defend themselves. They were excellent farmers. Shortly before the Spanish arrived in the New World, more warlike Indians from the north came raiding Pueblo villages and stealing food. Some of the Pueblos called the raiders *Apaches de*

A pueblo built by the Zuni, one of the Pueblo tribes. Though many pueblos are ancient, pueblos are still built and inhabited today.

Nabahu, which meant "enemies of the cultivated fields." From that phrase came the names of two major tribes: the Apache and the Navajo.

The Apache people did not settle in towns. They were nomadic, roaming the mountains of the Southwest, hunting and gathering wild foods. They also made raids against other Indians and, later, against white settlers. The Apache became feared as some of the fiercest fighters in the West. Young Apache boys learned to be warriors by playing games with a bow and arrow. Because the desert was very dry, the Apache had to learn how to go long distances without water. In one game, an Apache boy would fill his mouth with water, and then run four miles—without swallowing a drop!

At first the Navajo (also called Diné) roamed like the Apache. But from the Pueblos the Navajo learned how to grow crops and raise sheep. Pueblos also taught the Navajo how to weave beautiful blankets. By the early 1800s, the Navajo were living in settlements across a large area in the present-day states of Arizona and New Mexico. The Navajo lived in dome-shaped houses called hogans, which had wooden frames covered with a mixture of brush, clay, and mud.

As an important part of their religion, the Navajo sang songs that told of their beginnings and of their prayers for the future. Here is part of a song called the "Night Chant," in which a Navajo prays to a mythical dark bird:

> With your headdress of dark cloud, come to us.
> With the dark thunder above you, come to us soaring.
> With the shapen cloud at your feet, come to us soaring.
> With the far darkness made of the dark cloud over your head,
>   come to us soaring.

Indians of the Pacific Northwest

In the Northwest, along the rocky shores of the Pacific Ocean, lived a number of Indian tribes with similar customs. They devoted much of their lives to fishing, hunting for seals, sea lions, and otters, and trading. Long before Europeans came to America, these Northwest Indians used the Columbia River and its tributaries as a trade route. Dugout canoes enabled them to transport goods back and forth. In this way Indians from the Pacific Coast could trade with Indians who lived hundreds of miles from the shore.

One Northwestern tribe was called the Chinook. Since they lived along the banks of the Columbia River, the Chinook became important traders. Although Indians of the Pacific Northwest spoke many different languages, when different tribes wanted to trade they often used a version of the Chinook language called "Chinook jargon." When white fur traders and sailors appeared on the scene, they too learned to use Chinook jargon. They also brought with them some French and English words that soon blended into the jargon.

Indians of the Pacific Northwest carved designs in tree trunks to make totem poles. Many included animals or even monsters to show the legendary beginnings of a family.

Indians of the Great Basin and the Plateau

East of the Sierra Nevada Mountains and west of the Rocky Mountains is a mostly barren area called the Great Basin. There you will find the Great Salt Lake, with water much too salty to drink. Few animals or plants can survive on the dry, rocky soil. But some Indians managed to live there. To survive, these Indians had to forage for long hours every day. If they were lucky, supper might include an antelope, a rabbit, a bird, a snake, or a rat. But more often the Indians of the Great Basin ate grasshoppers and other insects, pine nuts, and the seeds, roots, and leaves of over a hundred different plants. Two of the major tribes in the Great Basin were the Shoshone and the Ute, from whom the state of Utah gets its name. You may remember from Book One that Sacajawea, a Shoshone, guided Lewis and Clark on their expedition.

North of the Great Basin is high, mostly level land that extends into Canada, called the Plateau. Its climate is less dry than the Great Basin. Though more plants and animals can live there, it is not a good place to raise crops or livestock. The Plateau Indians lived by hunting, fishing, and gathering berries, nuts, seeds, and roots. Among the Plateau Indians were the Nez Percé, which in French means "pierced nose." French traders gave them that name because some of the Indians wore rings in their noses. They called themselves Tsutpeli, which means "people of the mountains." Since the Nez Percé lived near the upper part of the Columbia River, they were able to trade with Indians from the Pacific Coast. (In the Language Arts section of this book you can read a speech by Chief Joseph, a Nez Percé leader.)

The Great Plains Indians

From the Rocky Mountains in the west to the Mississippi River in the east, an enormous grassland called the Great Plains stretches across the middle of our country. Before the Europeans arrived, the Great Plains provided a giant pasture for large herds of wild bison, or buffalo, as they are better known. At one time, as many as sixty million buffalo roamed freely across the Great Plains.

Because buffalo were so plentiful, most Plains Indians hunted the buffalo for food. The Plains Indians found ways to use every part of the buffalo, even the parts they could not eat. From the bones and sinews of the buffalo, the Indians made tools and weapons. The hide of the buffalo provided both clothing and shelter. Most Plains Indians lived in cone-shaped tents made of buffalo hide. You may know the name of these tents: they were called tepees.

To kill the buffalo, Plains Indians used the lance and the bow and arrow. Guns were also used once they became available. Before the Spanish brought horses to America, the Indians hunted on foot, often guiding a stampeding herd over a cliff. But by the 1800s, the Plains Indians had mastered the art of hunting on horseback. Sometimes, Plains Indians on horseback would hunt buffalo by stampeding a herd over a cliff. Horses could run faster than buffalo, but both horse and rider had to be careful to keep from being trampled by a stampeding herd.

A buffalo on the Plains.

In the eastern part of the Great Plains, in addition to hunting buffalo, many of the tribes raised crops for part of the year. During the growing season, these Indians lived in houses called earth lodges. To build an earth lodge, an Indian dug a shallow hole, placed a frame of logs and twigs over the hole, and then covered the frame with soil. The names of some of these eastern Plains tribes later became the names of states: Kansas, Iowa, and Missouri. Another major tribal group was often called the Sioux, but they called themselves Dakotas or Lakotas, which meant "allies" or "the friendly ones."

Tribes of the western Great Plains did not farm. They were nomadic, moving often to keep up with wandering buffalo herds. Some of these Indian tribes became famous for their fighting skills. To the north lived tribes called the Blackfoot and the Crow. To the far south lived the Comanche and the Wichita. And in between were the Arapaho and the Cheyenne.

To learn more about the Indians of the Great Plains and the importance of the buffalo, you can read a wonderfully illustrated book called Buffalo Hunt *by Russell Freedman (Holiday House, 1988).*

"There's Gold in Them Thar Hills"

In the first half of the 1800s, white settlers made slow, unsteady progress in their efforts to move west. But in 1848 something happened to speed up the westward movement. In fact, it made thousands of people rush toward the West. On January 24, 1848, by a river in California, a man named James W. Marshall was building a sawmill for John A. Sutter. When Marshall looked down into the water that ran through the mill, he saw little flakes of dull yellow metal. It was gold!

News of this discovery spread quickly throughout the country,

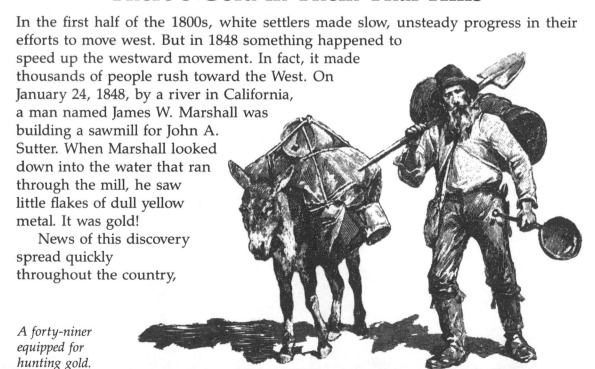

A forty-niner equipped for hunting gold.

and even across the sea. Soon thousands of Americans, as well as people from many other countries, headed to California in hopes of striking it rich. The Gold Rush had begun. By the time most of the miners reached California, the year was 1849, so they were called "forty-niners." (Do you know the song, "Clementine"? Clementine's father, you might remember, was "a miner, forty-niner.")

Most forty-niners prospected (looked for gold) by sifting soil in a pan or sieve. Some forty-niners found gold and became rich. Many more found only misery in crowded mining camps where gamblers tried to cheat miners out of their money, and shopkeepers charged high prices for food and everything else. Some disappointed forty-niners returned home, but others kept looking.

The Gold Rush created an urgent need for better ways to transport people and goods out West. Californians asked the federal government to build a decent road across the country and to speed up mail service. Construction of the road did not begin until 1857. But by 1858, stagecoaches loaded with passengers and mail were leaving twice a week from Tipton, Missouri, for the bumpy three-week trip to San Francisco.

The Pony Express

Three weeks was still too slow for some people who wanted their mail in a hurry. So in 1860 a company in Missouri started the Pony Express. Every ten miles, all the way to San Francisco, was a relay station. A Pony Express rider would grab a mailbag, leap on his horse, ride at full speed for ten miles, then quickly switch to a fresh horse for the next ten miles. After traveling seventy miles on seven different horses, the rider would take a rest and hand the mail to a new rider. The process was repeated over and over, day and night, until the mail arrived in San Francisco. The trip took a little more than ten days.

Within a year and a half after the Pony Express started, Westerners had a much faster way to receive and send messages. In October of 1861, a coast-to-coast telegraph line was completed. The telegraph used electricity to send coded messages across the country in seconds, not days. The Pony Express soon went out of business.

The Transcontinental Railroad

Settlers intent on moving west and those already out west wanted faster, more reliable ways to move people and goods. By the 1850s most Americans agreed that the country needed a railroad stretching across the continent. A transcontinental railroad was far too expensive a project for any private business to attempt without government help. So, in 1863, Congress passed a law to pay for a transcontinental railroad by giving private companies federal land and loaning them money.

Two companies would build the railroad. In 1863 workers for the Central Pacific Railroad started laying track in California and headed east. In 1864 the Union Pacific

Driving the golden spike that completed the first transcontinental railroad was quite a celebration.

Railroad started from Nebraska and headed west. Finally, on May 10, 1869, at Promontory Point, Utah, the Central Pacific track was linked to the Union Pacific with a golden spike. The nation had its first transcontinental railroad!

By the time the crews met at Promontory Point, other companies, with government help, had already begun to build as many as six other transcontinental railroad lines. Settlers would be able to move West faster and in ever greater numbers.

"Go West, Young Man"

At the end of the Civil War, many Americans looked to the West as the land of hope and new beginnings. In July of 1865, the editor of the New York Tribune, Horace Greeley, helped point the way. In an editorial, Greeley wrote, "Go West, young man, and grow up with the country." Because the New York Tribune was one of the country's most important newspapers, many people read Greeley's advice. The phrase "Go West, young man" became popular across the country.

Cowboys

In stories and movies, a cowboy is often a brave hero or a dangerous outlaw. But in the real West, cowboys usually lived less heroic lives, for the most part minding cattle and doing chores.

Cowboys became a familiar sight out West after the Civil War. When the war ended, Americans in the East had a shortage of beef. Meanwhile, down in southern Texas millions of beef cattle roamed free. Some businessmen decided to gather wild Texas cattle and sell them back East, but they faced one big problem: the railroad had not yet reached Texas. The cattle would have to walk to the nearest train depot in Missouri, some fifteen hundred miles away! The trip was called the Long Drive, because cowboys would ride alongside the cattle herd and drive (guide or coax) the cattle in the right direction.

Newspapers spread exaggerated reports about the money to be made in cattle ranching. Soon many people rushed into the cattle business, just as the forty-niners had rushed West to hunt for gold. Cattle ranches sprang up across the West, wherever there was enough grass for pasture. With the spread of cattle ranching, the cowboy became a familiar sight on the Western frontier.

This photo of a cowboy was taken in 1867, two years after the Civil War ended.

The Wild West

Ever since Lewis and Clark brought back reports of their 1804 expedition, Americans have enjoyed stories about the West. Because the West seemed much less civilized and much more dangerous than the East, people often called it the "Wild West."

Some stories about the West stretched the truth. If an event happened out West, the facts would likely change a bit each time the story passed from person to person. Sometimes newspaper writers would spice up stories to make more people want to buy the newspaper. By the time the report traveled back East, the story might have very little truth left in it. A sheriff who had arrested one drunk cattle thief might be transformed into a hero who had singlehandedly gunned down a dozen murderous outlaws. In this way, legends about heroes and villains grew and spread.

You may know some stories about famous Western outlaws. Some of the most feared outlaws were men who had served in the Civil War. During the war they had learned to kill without hesitation and to steal whatever was needed to survive. When the war was over, some desperate men continued to kill and rob as a way of life.

One of the most notorious Western outlaws was Jesse James. He fought in the Civil War with a group of Confederate raiders who behaved much like outlaws. After the war, Jesse and his brother Frank formed a gang to rob banks. Later they turned to robbing railroad trains, too. For twenty-five years, as Jesse and Frank James kept robbing banks and trains, legends about them spread. Then one morning in 1882, Jesse was at home in Missouri with two young members of his gang, Charles and Robert Ford. When Jesse stood on a chair to straighten a picture on the wall, Robert Ford shot and killed him. His brother Frank was captured and put on trial for his crimes, but he was found not guilty.

Another famous outlaw was Billy the Kid, whose real name was William Bonney. Before he reached his eighteenth birthday, Billy may have killed as many as twelve men. He and his gang stole cattle and killed anyone who tried to stop them. For a time it seemed no one could stop Billy the Kid. Then Billy's friend Pat Garrett became a sheriff. At the end of 1880, Garrett trapped Billy's gang and forced Billy to surrender. Before he could be hanged for murder, Billy killed two jail guards and escaped, but not for long. Within a couple of months, Garrett tracked Billy to his hideout. Garrett fired a shot into a dark bedroom, and at the age of twenty-one, Billy the Kid was dead.

Based on colorful stories they had heard or read, some people admired Billy for his daring acts. But Billy's hometown newspaper wanted everyone to know that Billy was no hero. Shortly after Billy died the editor of the town newspaper wrote, "Despite the glamour of romance thrown about his dare-devil life by sensational writers, the fact is, he was a low-down vulgar cut-throat, with probably not one redeeming quality."

Just as the West produced legendary outlaws, some men became famous for enforcing the law. One of the most famous marshals was Wild Bill Hickok, whose real name was James Butler Hickok. As a young boy, he became an excellent marksman. During the Civil War, Hickok was a scout and a spy for the Union. After the war, he was asked to serve as marshal in the rough towns of Kansas, where cowboys gathered at the end of their cattle drives. As marshal of Abilene, Kansas, Hickok wore his blond hair down to his shoulders. He also wore fancy clothes, expensive high-heeled boots, and a pair of ivory-handled pistols around his waist. He killed a number of men, and some people said not all of the killing was necessary to uphold the law. One man who knew Wild Bill Hickok called him "the most fearless and perhaps the most dangerous man . . . on the frontier."

American Indians Are Removed to Reservations

Back in 1840 the United States Government had promised American Indians they would be allowed to live freely on Western lands. The land west of Missouri and

Iowa would remain a "Permanent Indian Frontier," closed to whites except for trading purposes. At the time this promise was made, most Americans thought of the Great Plains as a wasteland. As far as the government was concerned, the Indians were welcome to live on such useless land. But, as we have seen, the Gold Rush, cattle ranching, and the spread of railroads showed that the West was far from useless. When Indians resisted attempts by settlers to take their land, the federal government came to the aid of the settlers. The government broke its promise; the "Permanent Indian Frontier" turned out to be only temporary.

The United States Government began pressuring Indian tribes to give up land to make way for settlers. To persuade them to give up land, the government made a new promise. If a tribe would agree to stay within a smaller area, the government promised the tribe could live there forever, free from the threat of more settlers. A tribe would be limited to an area set aside, or reserved, for them. Each of these areas was called a reservation.

Reservations tended to be much smaller than the areas the tribes had once lived in. Sometimes Indians were forced to move to reservations far away from their home-lands. Some Indians who had been farmers were forced to accept dry, rocky lands not suited for farming. Indians who had once roamed over vast stretches of the Great Plains hunting for buffalo might be forced to stay on small reservations where the hunting was poor.

Though the government promised Indians they could stay on a reservation for-ever, the government sometimes broke its promise. If the government decided the land was needed by settlers or other Indians, the government might force a tribe to leave its reservation and move to another.

A federal agency called the Bureau of Indian Affairs administered government policies toward Indians. Agents of the bureau were supposed to help Indians adjust to life on the reservation. The bureau also had responsibility for protecting the rights of Indians under their various treaties with the government. Sometimes the bureau did help Indians and guard their rights. But many bureau officials had no knowledge or experience of Indian life, and more than a few officials were corrupt.

The Indian Wars

Some Indians decided to fight to keep their lands and their way of life. Shortly before the Civil War began in the East, events in the West touched off a series of wars that pitted Indians against settlers and the United States Army.

In 1859 thousands of miners looking for gold in Colorado forced Cheyenne and Arapaho Indians to leave their homes. Federal officials tried to force the Indians to accept a smaller reservation away from the miners. Angry Indians took to the war-path and fought for over three years. Then the weary Indians tried to make peace. Led by Chief Black Kettle of the Cheyenne, the Indians offered their surrender at a federal army outpost.

Red Cloud (seated, second from the left) and other chiefs of the Sioux Indian Nation in a picture taken in 1870.

The Indians thought the war was over, but a band of white volunteers led by Colonel J. M. Chivington attacked them at a place called Sand Creek. Black Kettle waved an American flag and a white flag as a sign of peace. But Chivington's men brutally killed all the Indians except a few who escaped. Even babies and children were killed. When the Cheyenne and Arapaho signed a peace treaty the following year, the federal government apologized for "the gross and wanton outrage" of the Sand Creek Massacre.

To the north, another war broke out when Sioux Indians led by Chief Red Cloud vowed to block a road that the government wanted to build. The Sioux opposed the road because it would pass through their favored hunting grounds. Federal troops manned a series of forts in an effort to put down the uprising. For two years the Sioux attacked the forts and the white people who tried to travel through their lands. In the most famous battle, Indians ambushed and killed eighty federal soldiers.

General William Tecumseh Sherman called for revenge against the Sioux, "even to their extermination, men, women, and children." But many Easterners, horrified by reports of the earlier Sand Creek Massacre, wanted to try peace instead. In the spring of 1868, the government signed a peace treaty ending the Sioux War of 1865–68, sometimes called "Red Cloud's War."

The Buffalo Disappear

The most serious threat to the Plains Indians was not the United States Army. Indians suffered much more from the rapid disappearance of the buffalo. It wasn't disease or any other natural cause that led to the dwindling of the once great herds, but the careless, greedy actions of white settlers, hunters, and businessmen.

To feed their workers, railroad companies hired teams of hunters to shoot buffalo by the thousands. Many hunters simply shot buffalo for sport. Then a leather company back East began using buffalo hides in its manufactured goods. Even more hunters headed West to shoot buffalo and sell their valuable hides. Millions of buffalo were killed each year. By 1883 only about two hundred buffalo remained in the entire West. Only through the efforts of some conservationists was the buffalo saved from total extinction.

The Sioux War of 1875–76: Little Big Horn

In 1874 gold was discovered in the Black Hills, located on the Sioux reservation. Once again miners moved into the area. The government tried in vain to persuade the Sioux to sell the valuable land, or at least rent it to the miners. The Sioux considered the Black Hills sacred ground and were ready to fight for it. By the spring of 1876, large numbers of Sioux, Cheyenne, and Arapaho warriors joined in a war against the United States Army.

Two of the Indian leaders were Sitting Bull and Crazy Horse, both proud warriors determined to defeat the white men. For a time, it seemed they could do it.

Among the federal troops was a brash young officer, Colonel George Armstrong Custer. In June of 1876 Custer led a small band of soldiers along a stream called Little Big Horn. Custer was under orders not to attack until a larger group of federal troops arrived. But he was confident that even a small unit of United States Cavalry could defeat any number of Indians. Ignoring his orders, Custer tried to make a surprise attack against a camp where Sitting Bull and Crazy Horse were staying.

As it turned out, the Indians surprised Custer. A force of 2,500 Indian warriors quickly surrounded Custer's 265 federal troops. Within a few hours, Custer and all his men lay dead. The Battle of Little Big Horn became famous as "Custer's Last Stand."

Despite their victory at Little Big Horn, the Indians did not win the war. Months after Custer fell, most of the Indians were forced to surrender. Sitting Bull and a small group of followers refused to surrender and escaped north to Canada. Starvation later forced Sitting Bull's group to return.

For an interesting account of Custer's Last Stand as it might have been witnessed from the perspective of one of the Indians in the battle, try Red Hawk's Account of Custer's Last Battle *by Paul Goble (University of Nebraska Press, 1992). Also of interest:*
The Battle of Little Bighorn *by Charles Willas (Silver Burdett, 1990).*
Custer and Crazy Horse *by Jim Razzi (Scholastic, 1989).*

The Ghost Dance

As the 1800s drew to a close, American Indians were losing the struggle for the West. They longed for the return of their lands and the old ways of life. They expressed their longing in a practice started by a Paiute Indian named Wovoka. He told Indians to dance a sacred dance, called the Ghost Dance. If Indians kept dancing, the white men would be swept away, dead Indians would return to life, and herds of buffalo would again wander the plains. Belief in the power of the Ghost Dance spread across the northern Plains. The feverish dancing alarmed white settlers.

Among the Sioux, Ghost Dancers began wearing guns when they danced. The Sioux were angry because the government had failed to send food it had promised. Fearing a new uprising, in late 1890 the federal government sent troops to stop the dancing. The troops began by ordering the arrest of the Sioux's chief, Sitting Bull. He did not put up a fight, but another Indian shot one of the arresting officers. That officer in turn shot and killed Sitting Bull.

Two weeks later, at a place called Wounded Knee, a group of Sioux under Chief Big Foot prepared to surrender peacefully to federal troops. Soldiers surrounded the Indian camp and ordered the warriors to give up their weapons. Women and children became frightened when soldiers searched the tepees for guns. A medicine man began to dance and chant. "You have nothing to fear," he assured the Indians: "The Ghost Dance has turned your shirts to iron. No bullet can harm you." One Indian held a gun over his head and screamed. Soldiers grabbed the gun, but a shot from another rifle rang out. The soldiers opened fire. Powerful cannons fired exploding shells into the camp. The frenzied cries of the Ghost Dance came to a sad end as Indian men, women, and children were left lying in the bloodstained snow.

Attempts to Assimilate the Indians

Many white Americans felt compassion for the Indians and wanted to help them. But even those who cared about the plight of Native Americans rarely respected Indian ways. For most well-meaning Americans, helping the Indians meant assimilating them, absorbing them into the general culture—in other words, helping them become more like white Americans.

Schools were started to assimilate young Indians. In 1879 the Carlisle Indian School opened in Carlisle, Pennsylvania. Young Indians from the Western reservations were sent to the Carlisle School for mechanical and agricultural training, as well as lessons in good citizenship. While many Indians understood the need for education, they distrusted the new schools, which often taught them to reject the ways of their own people. At the Carlisle School, students were forbidden to wear tribal clothes, speak tribal language, or practice tribal customs. The school's philosophy was bluntly expressed by its founder, who said, "Kill the Indian and save the man."

Splitting Up the Reservations

Traditionally an Indian tribe believed its lands belonged to the members of the tribe together. A single Indian did not own a piece of the land; he shared the land with all members of his tribe. In contrast to this idea of shared ownership of the land, Europeans brought to this country a system of private ownership, in which each piece of land could be owned by an individual person.

In the 1880s many white Americans believed that private ownership of land would help the Indians toward progress—another case of believing that the way to help the Indians was to make them more like white Americans. Senator Henry Dawes said that Indians "have got as far as they can go, because they own their land in common." According to Senator Dawes, the Indians could never be fully civilized as long as they owned their land in common. Among the Indians, Dawes reasoned, "There is no selfishness, which is at the bottom of civilization."

Most Indians would have been puzzled by this belief that "selfishness . . . is at the bottom of civilization." What do you think he meant? The U.S. Congress apparently understood Dawes, for in 1887 Congress passed a law called the Dawes Severalty Act (also known as the General Allotment Act). Under this law, tribal lands would be divided. The head of each Indian household would own 160 acres. Once every family had its "allotment," any leftover land could be sold to settlers.

Opponents of the law said that it would simply allow whites to take over more Indian land. They were right. Once an individual Indian owned land, he could also sell it. Since most Indians were poor, they sold their land to white people for money. Once the money was gone, however, the Indians were left with little to live on. So the allotment system eventually caused Indians to lose most of their remaining lands. Not until 1934 did Congress pass a law to stop the breakup of the reservations.

An Age of Industry and Invention

The period from the Civil War to the beginning of the twentieth century was an age of industry and invention in America. Between 1860 and 1900, a government agency called the United States Patent Office issued patents for more than a half million different inventions. A patent is a special right granted to an inventor who can show that his invention is both new and useful. Once a patent is granted, no one may use, make, or sell the invention without the inventor's permission. An inventor who holds a patent may become rich if enough people are willing to pay for the privilege of using the invention.

Perhaps no one embodied the spirit of invention more than Thomas Edison. Edison invented over one thousand devices and processes. He is most famous for three of his inventions: the phonograph, motion pictures (movies), and the electric lamp. Actually, Edison was not the first to invent the electric lamp. But he did what inventors often do: he solved problems and improved upon the ideas of others.

The Brooklyn Bridge, built in 1883, came to stand for American industry and know-how.

Before Edison, no one had invented a system that would make electric light affordable. Edison and his team of researchers developed a better electric lamp and a system for generating electricity cheaply. Thanks to Edison, cities soon replaced their relatively dim gaslights with bright electric streetlights.

Sometimes accidents lead to a new invention. Such was the case in the invention of the telephone by Alexander Graham Bell. Bell was working on a new type of telegraph. One day while Bell was experimenting, his machine accidentally made a familiar sound. It was the sound of human speech! With the help of an electrical engineer named Thomas Watson, Bell developed his chance discovery into the first working telephone. On March 10, 1876, Bell spoke the first sentence ever transmitted by telephone: "Mr. Watson, come here; I want you."

Industrialists, Capitalists, and Monopolies

In the decades after the Civil War, the United States became an increasingly industrialized nation. Many Americans went from working on farms to working in factories. The new industries brought both progress and problems to America. On one hand, the country grew wealthy. On the other hand, the wealth was not enjoyed by all. In this land dedicated to the proposition that "all men are created equal," the growth of America as an industrial power produced disturbing social inequalities, including a widening gap between the rich and the poor.

The basic gap was between those who worked in the factories and those who owned the industries. The owners were called "capitalists": "capital" means money,

George Washington Carver: Botanist, Chemist, Inventor

An important African-American scientist and inventor, George Washington Carver, was born into slavery during the Civil War. Though the Civil War ended slavery, most blacks of Carver's time received little or no schooling. Yet through sheer determination, Carver managed to earn an advanced college degree in botany, the study of plants. Because he believed education is "the key to unlock the golden door of freedom," Carver went to Alabama to teach botany and modern farming techniques to other African-Americans.

Carver found that the soil in Alabama and other parts of the South had been ruined by years of growing only cotton. Cotton takes nutrients from the soil without giving anything back. Carver told Southern farmers that in addition to cotton they must grow plants such as peanuts and sweet potatoes, which restore nutrients to the soil. Many farmers took Carver's advice, and it worked.

Farmers soon produced more peanuts and sweet potatoes than people were willing to buy. So Carver went to work in the laboratory, where he developed hundreds of products that could be made from the peanut and the sweet potato, including plastics, dyes, medicines, flour, powdered milk, and fertilizer. At lunchtime, you might enjoy one of Carver's most successful inventions—a food called peanut butter.

and capitalists were those who put their money into the development of businesses and industries, in the hope of making more money—profits—from what they produced and sold.

Many businesses and industries required a great deal of capital; for example, almost no one on his own could afford to start a railroad, which would require a lot of money to pay for locomotives, tracks, and more. In such cases, several capitalists would combine their money to form a corporation. Each person who invested money would own a share of the corporation, and would receive a share of the profits.

One tremendously rich American capitalist was Andrew Carnegie, who owned many factories that made steel. The steel industry in America was booming because of the growth of railroads, which required thousands of miles of steel track. After the Civil War, Andrew Carnegie saw that there would be a great need for steel, so he invested in the iron and steel industry that was developing in Pittsburgh, Pennsylvania.

Carnegie's success in the steel business shows the way some industrialists and capitalists built powerful monopolies. "Monopoly" comes from the Greek words for "one" and "sell": a monopoly is the one group that has the means to produce or sell all of something. If you had a monopoly on, for example, televisions, you would be very very rich! A monopoly has the power to control prices in an industry and can drive other companies out of the business. That's what Carnegie did in the steel industry. He built modern steel mills to produce steel faster. To ensure a steady supply of cheap raw materials, Carnegie's company acquired control of iron ore mines and coal mines. Carnegie's company even bought the railroads and shipping companies it used to transport iron and coal from the mines to the mills. Because Carnegie controlled everything needed to make steel, his company could sell steel at low prices that other companies could not match. Carnegie soon drove other steel companies out of business. Eventually, Carnegie controlled most of the steel business in this country.

Through similar methods, capitalists in other businesses created huge monopolies, which came to be called trusts. John D. Rockefeller's Standard Oil trust took over most of the country's oil industry by controlling the processing plants, called "refineries." John Pierpont Morgan gained a monopoly over the country's system of banks. By 1900 a small group of powerful trusts dominated America's most important industries, including copper, sugar, rubber, leather, farm machinery, and telephones. Carnegie, Rockefeller, Morgan, and some other capitalists became fabulously wealthy.

Some capitalists were also philanthropists, which means that they devoted part of their enormous wealth to helping others. Some helped the public by donating to charity, or by paying to build libraries, museums, and colleges.

Working in the Industrial Age

As machinery changed America's industries, it also changed the lives of the people who worked in factories. Machines took over many of the jobs once performed by human hands. Workers were needed only to tend the machines and do whatever work the machines could not do. To keep the factory machines running, men, women, and children worked from ten to twelve hours a day, six days a week. Despite the millions of dollars in profits a factory owner might enjoy, factory workers usually received very low pay. In the cramped, stuffy factories, work was hard, boring, and often dangerous. The powerful machines usually had no safety devices to protect workers from injury.

In an effort to improve working conditions, many workers joined together in organizations called labor unions. Through their labor unions, workers demanded better pay and better conditions. If the demands were not met, workers might go on strike, meaning they would stop working. If a large group of workers went on strike, they could disrupt or even shut down an entire company. Then, perhaps, the owners might be forced to listen to the workers.

Sometimes the corporations would respond to strikes by granting some of the workers' demands. But often the owners responded with force and violence. For example, in 1892, at one of Carnegie's steel mills in Homestead, Pennsylvania, workers went on strike because their already low pay had been cut by almost 20 percent. Rather than meet the workers' demands, the company locked them out of the factory and hired new workers. Then the company called in its own private army to battle the workers. In a violent exchange, three of the guards the company hired were killed; ten workers lost their lives. The union's demands were never met.

More Immigrants Arrive in the Land of Opportunity

Despite the growing troubles between workers and capitalists, the rapid growth of American industry made this country even more attractive to poor immigrants seeking a better life. Others were attracted by a vision of a vast land rich in natural resources. Many people in countries around the world looked upon the United States as "the land of opportunity" that seemed to offer the promise of prosperity for all.

In the years between 1850 and 1930, thirty-five million people immigrated to the United States—the greatest movement of people in the history of the world! Before the Civil War, most immigrants came from Great Britain, Germany, and other countries of Northern and Western Europe. After the Civil War, more and more immi-

Many immigrants endured crowded conditions on ships to come to "the land of opportunity."

grants arrived from countries of Southern and Eastern Europe, including Italy, Poland, Hungary, and Russia.

Eager for work, immigrants made important contributions to the building of America. Both Alexander Graham Bell and Andrew Carnegie were immigrants from Scotland. Immigrant workers from China and Ireland did much of the grueling work needed to build the transcontinental railroads. On arriving in this country, some immigrants pushed West to find opportunities, while others stayed in Eastern cities where they could remain close to other immigrants from their old country. In these cities, neighborhoods with names like Little Italy or Chinatown developed, where immigrants, struggling to survive, often crowded into run-down tenements. But in these neighborhoods, newcomers could also receive help and comfort from fellow countrymen who had settled in America before them.

Reformers and Reform Movements

In the decades after the Civil War, Americans could be proud of many of our country's accomplishments. The United States had developed into a powerful industrial nation. Thanks to our Constitution, Americans generally enjoyed greater civil liberties than any other people on earth. Free public education, which was only a dream in most parts of the world, was a reality in America.

As you've seen, however, Americans faced a number of difficult problems in changing from a mainly agricultural country, relying in the South on slavery, to an industrial country with big cities and lots of factories. With the cities and factories came hard conditions for workers and the poor. Before the Civil War, reformers like Dorothea Dix and Horace Mann worked to improve conditions in America. Later, toward the end of the nineteenth century, new reformers came forth to meet new problems besetting the urban poor, as well as African-Americans, women, and farmers.

Farmers and the Rise of Populism

After the Civil War many American farmers found themselves in a difficult bind. The opening of new farmland and the use of modern farm machinery made it possible for American farmers to grow more crops than they could sell at an acceptable price. So, while the cost of operating a farm went up, because of the cost of machinery, the prices farmers received for their crops went down.

The farmers banded together to gain more power and a bigger voice. In 1892, farmers formed the People's Party to challenge the Democratic and Republican parties. Followers of the party were called Populists, from the Latin word for people. The Populists didn't like what they saw happening to America. They saw a country moving away from Thomas Jefferson's vision of a land of independent farmers, and toward domination by big corporations and industries.

In the presidential election of 1896, a Democrat named William Jennings Bryan favored many of the Populists' ideas. Bryan was a fiery speaker with many admirers and followers. But the candidate supported by big business, the Republican William McKinley, won the election. Bryan's defeat marked the end of the Populists as an important national party. But some of the Populists' demands for reform lived on in the other parties, and today some American politicians who favor small business and workers are still called "populists."

Jane Addams and Hull House

In many of America's cities, poor people crowded into filthy slums. There were few government programs to help them. Jane Addams of Cedarville, Illinois, was not poor and she was not from a big city, but she was determined to help those less fortunate than herself. She could not stop thinking, as she once wrote, about "the old question eternally suggested by the inequalities of the human lot."

Like many young women from well-off families in the late 1800s, Jane Addams made a tour of Europe, accompanied by her friend Ellen Gates Starr. But Jane Addams and her companion did not visit museums and cathedrals; instead, they went to factories and slums. In London, they were inspired by the example of reformers who lived among the poor in what was called a settlement house.

In 1889, Jane Addams opened the doors of Hull House, a settlement house in a poor part of Chicago, Illinois. It became a kind of community center, providing food and shelter, medical services, and opportunities for people in the neighborhood to enjoy music and art. Hull House provided child care so that mothers could go to work. There were toys and games for the youngest children, and lessons in art, dance, and acting for older children. The hungry could always get a good, hot meal, and the unemployed could get help in finding a job.

"The Settlement," Addams wrote, "is an experimental effort to aid in the solution of the social and industrial problems which are engendered by the modern conditions of life in a great city." Addams's "experiment" went against generally ac-

Jane Addams with some of the children who came to celebrate the fortieth birthday of Hull House.

cepted beliefs of the time, including the idea that life was a matter of "survival of the fittest"—the idea that, in society, only the strongest get ahead, and if others suffer—well, that's too bad, and there's nothing to do about it. In contrast, Jane Addams wrote that "it is natural to feed the hungry and care for the sick. It is certainly natural to give pleasure to the young, [and] comfort the aged."

Addams also opposed another common belief of the time, the widespread feelings of suspicion and prejudice against the many thousands of newly arrived immigrants. Americans who were themselves the children or grandchildren of immigrants looked upon new immigrants as "foreigners" with dangerous, "un-American" ways. But Jane Addams and her co-workers at Hull House helped new immigrants make the difficult transition to life in urban America. Addams saw how prejudice against immigrants could cause the children, especially those who came from poor backgrounds, to feel ashamed and want to deny their heritage and customs. In response, she encouraged them not to deny their past but to draw strength from it. She pointed to Abraham Lincoln, who never denied his humble origins, as an example of, in her words, the "marvelous power to retain and utilize past experiences."

Hull House became famous, and reformers in many other American cities established settlement houses. Jane Addams described her experiences in an interesting book called *Twenty Years at Hull House*.

"How the Other Half Lives"

As this country approached the twentieth century, Americans were reading more stories in newspapers and magazines about corrupt practices in business and government, and about the suffering of poor people in big cities. These true stories were

This is a photograph by Jacob Riis from How the Other Half Lives. *It shows some of the many homeless boys he saw on the streets of New York.*

written by journalists who came to be called "muckrakers." They wrote about the muck—the unpleasant, dirty side—of American life, in order to urge the public to clean up the corruption and stop the suffering.

One of the first muckrakers was Jacob Riis, an immigrant from Denmark who settled in New York City. As a newspaper reporter, Riis witnessed life in New York's crowded, filthy slums. In 1890, Riis wrote a book entitled *How the Other Half Lives*, which described actual New York slums with names like Murderer's Alley and Misery Row. Through his words, Riis took readers into the slums: "Be a little careful, please! The hall is dark and you might stumble. . . . Here is a door. Listen! That short, hacking cough, that tiny helpless wail—what do they mean?"

Riis's vivid words were backed up by striking photographs. The pictures and photographs that we take for granted in modern newspapers and magazines first began to appear in the 1890s. When readers could actually see the crowded slums and suffering people that Riis described, many were angered and joined Riis in his demand for reforms, including better housing, better living conditions, and decent schools for the poor.

Reform for African-Americans: Washington and Du Bois

After the Civil War, African-Americans were no longer slaves, but they were still denied an equal opportunity to take part in American life. As you've read, blacks often did not have a chance to go to school. Booker T. Washington believed that education was the key to a better life for African-Americans. In 1881 Washington helped establish the Tuskegee Normal and Industrial Institute in Alabama. Under Washington's leadership, Tuskegee Institute grew to become an important center for black education. It prepared blacks to become teachers and skilled tradesmen. After Washington invited George Washington Carver to join the faculty, Tuskegee Institute also taught modern farming techniques.

Washington told blacks that, before they could expect to win social and political equality, they must first raise their eco-

W. E. B. Du Bois.

nomic status. In a speech he gave in Atlanta in 1895, Washington asked blacks to be patient, work hard, and not to fight for their rights. He said, "The wisest among my race understand that the agitation of questions of social equality is the extremest folly."

But another prominent African-American reformer, W. E. B. Du Bois (do-BOYS), strongly disagreed with Washington. While Booker T. Washington asked for quiet patience on the part of African-Americans, Du Bois urged them to insist loudly upon the equal rights promised in the Fourteenth Amendment. Du Bois said, "We claim for ourselves every single right that belongs to a free-born American, political, civil and social; and until we get these rights we will never cease to protest and assail the ears of America."

In 1905 Du Bois and other well-educated blacks met at Niagara Falls, Canada, to form a civil rights group called the Niagara Movement. In 1909 members of the Niagara Movement joined with white reformers to create the National Association for the Advancement of Colored People, better known by its initials, NAACP. As the first editor of the NAACP publication called *The Crisis,* Du Bois promised to "set forth those facts and arguments which show the danger of race prejudice." Throughout the twentieth century, the NAACP has been a leading organization in the fight for racial equality.

Ida B. Wells Fights Lynching

During the Reconstruction years, African-Americans in the South had gained a few rights and privileges, but in the late 1800s, many white Southerners increasingly ignored the civil rights of black Americans. Some whites attempted to turn back the clock to the time of slavery by imposing Jim Crow laws, by joining groups like the Ku Klux Klan, or by taking part in the especially cruel practice known as lynching.

Lynching is what happens when a mob takes the law into its own hands and punishes or even kills someone who has been accused of some wrongdoing, without ever giving the accused person a legal trial. In late nineteenth-century America, racial prejudice often fueled the mob violence that would lead to lynching. In the South, the victims of lynching were most often African-American men.

A brave African-American reformer

Ida B. Wells

and writer named Ida B. Wells made it her mission to help this country overcome racism and especially to stop lynching. Wells was born in 1862 in the state that has had the most recorded lynchings, Mississippi. When she grew up, she taught school, and then in 1891 she helped start a newspaper in Memphis called *Free Speech.* She wrote articles that condemned white people for lynching black men. She published evidence showing that when a white mob lynched a black man, it was rarely a genuine punishment for a crime. It was, instead, a way of spreading terror among blacks and of trying to assert white supremacy.

The only thing lynch mobs really asserted was their own savagery. They would sometimes hang their victims, but often torture and disfigure them, or kill them in especially painful ways, such as by burning them to death. It may seem hard to believe, but some lynchings actually became like parties for white Southerners. Newspapers would announce when and where the lynchings would take place, and families, including children, would gather to watch. In 1892, there were reports of 161 African-Americans killed by lynching, a figure that doesn't even include lynchings that went unreported.

Ida B. Wells's newspaper articles made white readers so angry that once, when she was away giving lectures in Philadelphia and New York, a mob burned down her newspaper office, and she was threatened with death if she returned. She decided to move North, where she bravely carried on her campaign against the horror of lynching. She continued to write and give lectures, and she worked with Jane Addams to stop the city of Chicago from establishing segregated public schools.

Women Struggle for Equal Rights

In the 1800s women had few rights. Women could not vote, and most states had laws limiting a woman's right to own property. Most colleges were closed to women, as were most professions. In Book Four of this series you read about the 1848 meeting at Seneca Falls, New York, in which Lucretia Mott, Elizabeth Cady Stanton, and other courageous women and men demanded equality for women.

In the years following Seneca Falls, Stanton joined forces with another determined advocate for women's rights, Susan B. Anthony. Together Stanton and Anthony helped found the National Woman Suffrage Association. ("Suffrage" means the right to vote.) Throughout the late 1800s, Stanton and Anthony gave speeches and organized petitions to gather support for a constitutional amendment to give women the right to vote.

In 1872 Anthony was arrested for breaking the law by casting a vote in the presidential election. At her trial, she told the displeased judge that her purpose was "to educate all women to do precisely as I have done, rebel against your man-made, unjust, unconstitutional forms of law."

The women's suffrage movement was strongly opposed by many politicians, church groups, and a fair number of women themselves. But the demand for women's

Susan B. Anthony.

rights grew stronger as America entered the twentieth century. Finally, in 1920 the Nineteenth Amendment was added to the Constitution. It says: "The right of citizens of the United States to vote shall not be denied or abridged by the United States or by any State on account of sex."

H*ere are some books you can read to learn more about the women's suffrage movement:* The First Women Who Spoke Out *by Nancy Smiler Levinson (Dillon, 1983).* The Story of the Nineteenth Amendment *by R. Conrad Stein (Childrens Press, 1982).* Women Win the Vote *by Betsy Covington Smith (Silver Burdett, 1989).*

Theodore Roosevelt:
Trust-Buster and Conservationist

The twenty-sixth president of the United States, Theodore Roosevelt—popularly known as "Teddy"—was also an active reformer. He set out to reform the practices of American businesses that joined together in large monopolies called trusts. Powerful businessmen who joined together in a big trust would sometimes do things that were unfair. Sometimes they would put unfair pressure on smaller businesses: for example, John D. Rockefeller's huge Standard Oil Trust often forced small oil companies to join the trust or go out of business. Sometimes trusts would agree to keep

Before he became president, Teddy Roosevelt served as a colonel during the Spanish-American War. His popularity as a national hero helped in his election to the vice presidency, and, later, to the presidency.

prices high: the beef trust, for example, made sure that Americans paid high prices for beef.

Teddy Roosevelt became known as a "trust-buster." In one famous case, he ordered government lawyers to break up the Northern Securities Company, a huge railroad trust largely controlled by J. P. Morgan. Roosevelt's action shocked businessmen, who were not used to being told what to do by the government.

Roosevelt was not against big business, but he was in favor of giving government the power to make sure that big businesses acted fairly. He said, "We do not wish to destroy corporations, but we do wish to make them subserve the public good." Under Roosevelt, the government became more active in passing laws that businesses had to follow. Thanks to Roosevelt, for example, you can be pretty sure that it's safe today to eat a hamburger: but, before the government passed the Meat Inspection Act of 1906, you never knew what you might bite into. (The disgusting practices of meat packers are described in a powerful book you can read called *The Jungle*, written in 1906 by Upton Sinclair.)

Roosevelt was also a sportsman who loved the outdoors. As president he took strong steps to stop Americans from destroying too much of our country's wilderness for industrial purposes such as logging or mining. At Roosevelt's urging, the government began a program of conservation, which called for more efficient use of natural resources and the protection of our forests. By doubling the number of national parks, Roosevelt did much to create the system of parks we still have today.

The Cuban War for Independence and the Spanish-American War

Around the turn of the century, the United States became involved in the affairs of three lands that were still colonies of Spain: Cuba, Puerto Rico, and the Philippines. Many people in these lands, like the American patriots of 1776, longed for their independence.

Cuba was the most important colony Spain still possessed in the Western Hemisphere. But most of Cuba's sugar and tobacco went to the United States, not Spain. In fact, many Americans wanted Cuba to belong to the United States. During the 1800s the United States Government tried several times to buy Cuba from Spain. (Remember, we acquired much of the land west of the Mississippi River by buying it from France in the Louisiana Purchase.) Although Spain refused to sell Cuba, the United States and Spain remained friends.

Until the end of the 1800s, the United States Government did not oppose Spanish rule over Cuba. Yet, in 1898 the United States entered a war against Spain. To understand why, we need to look back at what led up to the war.

Cuba Fights for Independence

Three years after the American Civil War, Cubans began a long struggle for their independence. Remember how the American Revolutionary War started in the little town of Concord, Massachusetts, with "the shot heard round the world"? In a similar way, the Cuban war for independence began when shots were fired in a small town named Yara. The *Grito de Yara* ("cry of Yara") soon spread through the countryside, and many Cubans rallied to fight the Spanish.

The *insurrectos*, as the revolutionary fighters were called in Spanish, faced huge problems. The Spanish soldiers had more training and better weapons. And, just as in the American Revolution not all Americans supported independence from Britain, so in Cuba the richest and most powerful citizens, who were mostly of Spanish origin, wanted Cuba to remain under Spanish rule. The militia of these citizens, the *voluntarios*, outnumbered the official Spanish troops when the war began.

After ten years of fighting, though independence had not been gained, a peace agreement ended the first stage of the Cuban war. Still, many Cubans vowed to continue the struggle against Spain. The most defiant revolutionaries became exiles, forced to leave Cuba, their home country.

One leader of the Cuban exiles was José Martí, a lawyer, journalist, novelist, and poet. He had grown up in Havana, the capital of Cuba. At sixteen Martí was sent to prison for supporting the war for independence. When he was eighteen, the government ordered him to leave Cuba. Martí eventually settled in New York City, where he published articles and gave powerful speeches to promote Cuban independence.

In 1892 Martí started the Cuban Revolutionary Party and was elected its first president. Then, along with other exiles, Martí began to put together a plan to win Cuba's independence once and for all.

On New Year's Day 1895, Martí and his followers were ready to launch their secret plan. Three ships would carry Martí, a force of a thousand soldiers, and a large shipment of weapons and ammunition from points in Florida and Costa Rica to Cuba. Revolutionary troops already in Cuba were to begin fighting as soon as the ships arrived. But the plan failed when the United States Government found out about it. Our government did not want to anger Spain by letting revolutionaries sail from our country to Cuba. The United States Navy seized one of the ships and refused to allow the other two ships to leave port.

It seemed that the new war for Cuban independence was over before it started. Yet the Cuban patriots were more determined than ever. The battle cry sounded again, and war broke out across Cuba. Sadly, Martí did not live to see an independent Cuba. He died in battle on May 17, 1895.

"Yellow Journalism" Urges War

By the end of 1895 it was clear the Cuban patriots were winning their war for independence from Spain. Spain brought in more and more soldiers, but the *insurrectos* kept fighting. News of the fighting in Cuba reached Americans through the newspapers. Each newspaper tried to outdo the others to attract more readers. Some newspaper publishers were willing to stretch the truth, or even make up wild stories, if it would help them sell more newspapers. "Yellow journalism" is the name people gave to reporting that showed more concern for excitement than for truth.

The war in Cuba became front-page news for American newspapers practicing yellow journalism. Newspapers printed exaggerated accounts that stressed the cruelty of the Spanish. Editorials urged America to join the war for Cuban independence. Largely because of these newspaper reports, many Americans wanted the United States Government to go to war against Spain.

"Remember the *Maine!*"

Even though more and more Americans favored the Cuban revolutionaries, the United States Government kept supporting Spanish rule in Cuba. But an unexpected event would soon change our government's position.

By the beginning of 1898 the fighting in Cuba had reached the capital city of Havana. It seemed only a matter of time before Spain would surrender. In fact, many people in Spain were urging their government to give Cuba its independence. Meanwhile, the United States Navy sent a battleship named the *Maine* to Havana harbor. Its mission was not to attack; the *Maine* was sent to help American citizens in Cuba who were caught in the fighting.

On February 15, 1898, an explosion on board the *Maine* sank the ship and killed 260 Americans. Today studies say an accident aboard ship may have caused the explosion. But in 1898 many American yellow newspapers blamed Spain. Newspaper headlines stirred up American anger with the cry, "Remember the *Maine!*" Many Americans echoed their demands for war against Spain to free Cuba and to avenge the deaths of the *Maine's* crew.

On April 25, 1898, Congress declared war on Spain. The United States had an immediate advantage over Spain: our navy. The American Navy was larger and had more modern equipment than the Spanish Navy. When war was declared, U.S. Navy ships had orders to attack Spanish ships wherever they found them. As a result, the first battle occurred far from Cuba.

Before the war, the American Navy already had some ships stationed in the western Pacific Ocean. On May 1, 1898, an American squadron under Commodore George Dewey sailed into Manila Bay in the Philippines, a colony of Spain. There they encountered ships of the Spanish Navy. Spanish guns fired on the American ships, but Dewey's squadron quickly sank or disabled all of the Spanish ships.

Commodore Dewey helped an exile from the Philippines, Emilio Aguinaldo, return to the Philippines with his rebel followers. Aguinaldo declared the Philippines independent from Spain on June 12, 1898, which is now celebrated as Independence Day in the Philippines.

Back in Cuba, the Spanish Navy found itself trapped. When the war started, most of the Spanish warships headed for cover in the harbor of Santiago. The American Navy quickly set up a blockade closing off the harbor. Then eighteen thousand American troops, many of them recent volunteers, landed on the Cuban coast. On July 1, 1898, Americans attacked Spanish outposts near Santiago.

One of the Americans who fought that day was Theodore Roosevelt (who would soon become our twenty-sixth president). His regiment of volunteers, called the Rough Riders, led a successful charge up San Juan Hill. One of the soldiers, American Lieutenant John J. Pershing (who would later become an important general), wrote that "white regiments, black regiments . . . fought shoulder to shoulder, unmindful of race or color . . . and mindful only of their duty as Americans." The fighting was fierce and bloody. Many soldiers on both sides were killed or wounded. But by the night of July 1, the Americans had taken control of the hills overlooking Santiago.

On July 3, American guns destroyed nearly all of the ships of the Spanish fleet as they tried to escape. By August 12, 1898, the Spanish-American War was over.

The United States Becomes a World Power

The peace treaty that ended the Spanish-American War gave the United States an overseas empire in many ways similar to the empire of Great Britain, except that the United States called its newly acquired lands territories instead of colonies. In the treaty, Spain gave up its claim to Cuba, and gave the United States control of Puerto Rico and Guam (one of the Mariana Islands in the Pacific). Both Puerto Rico and Guam are still territories of the United States. Spain also agreed to sell the Philippines to the United States for twenty million dollars.

Not all Americans wanted an empire. Many believed it was against the principles in our Declaration of Independence. After all, our country began when people in the thirteen colonies fought to free themselves from the British Empire. Opposition to the new, imperial America was so strong that when the peace treaty with Spain went before Congress for approval, it passed by only one vote.

After their long struggles, the patriots of Cuba and the Philippines still didn't enjoy full independence. Although Cuba was not a United States territory, American troops occupied and controlled Cuba for two years after the peace treaty was signed. In 1901 the United States forced Cubans to include in their new constitution a law that gave the United States the right to make sure Cubans had "a government adequate for the protection of life, property, and individual liberty." On several occasions in the early twentieth century, the United States would use this law to justify sending troops to protect American business interests in Cuba.

In the Philippines, patriots felt betrayed by the Americans. Americans had helped Filipinos (citizens of the Philippines) declare their independence from Spain, so Filipinos saw it as a mean trick when the United States decided to make the Philippines an American territory. Rather than accept the United States as their new master, Filipinos fought for more than two years after the Spanish-American War ended. Finally, the rebels surrendered soon after the Americans captured their leader, Aguinaldo, in 1901. The Philippines would not gain complete independence until 1946.

Impressed by America's easy victory over Spain, the world began to see the United States as a powerful nation. In the next book of this series, you can read about the important role our country played in the history of the twentieth century.

III.
FINE ARTS

Introduction to the Fine Arts

FOR PARENTS AND TEACHERS

In the Fine Arts section of this book, we elaborate on the material presented in previous volumes of the series. Discussion of harmony, melody, rhythm, and musical instruments continues in the Music section, and in Visual Arts, we introduce children to significant works from the Renaissance and describe the technical innovations that took place in painting, sculpture, and architecture at that time.

In the Music section, we introduce the 4 chord (or subdominant), and learn songs that use this chord along with the 1 and 5 chords we have already learned. Thus, by the end of grade five, the student will have learned the three major chords that occur in a major key. These chords are the harmonic basis of many of the songs students will hear throughout their lives. One goal in this section is to get students to recognize these chords in relation to each other when they hear them. (Repeating songs and chord progressions over and over will help train children's ears in this skill, which will add greatly to their enjoyment of almost any piece of music.)

We also talk about melody shapes, and how to listen for them. There are brief biographical portraits of Mozart and Beethoven, John Philip Sousa and Scott Joplin, as well as further description of the various musical instruments, their distinct sounds, and their place in the orchestra or band.

The discussion of music should be complemented by having the child play, sing, and listen to songs, and, when possible, follow along with printed music and tapes of orchestral instruments. It will help the child's learning and enjoyment if the parent or teacher plays the piano, guitar, or other instrument, but we have tried to write this section in such a way that parents and teachers who are not musically trained can also learn along with the student.

Resources for music include the following books: *Meet the Orchestra* by Ann Hayes (Harcourt Brace Jovanovich, 1991) and *The Orchestra* by Mark Rubin (Groundwood Books, 1986). An accompanying tape can also be purchased. We recommend that a child use both the book and the tape so that he can become familiar with both the appearance and the sounds of orchestral instruments.

In the Visual Arts section, we explore the changes in attitude that occurred between the Middle Ages and the Renaissance, and how those changes inspired a virtual revolution in European arts. We also introduce African, Muslim, and Japanese arts from approximately the same period.

The following sources may be helpful for your ongoing exploration.

Art for Children by Ernest Raboff (Harper & Row, 1988).
Da Vinci by Mike Venezia (Children's Press, 1989). Part of a series called Getting to Know the World's Greatest Artists.
Rembrandt by Mike Venezia (Children's Press, 1988). Part of a series called Getting to Know the World's Greatest Artists.
Great Painters by Piero Ventura (Putnam, 1984).
Michelangelo's World by Piero Ventura (Putnam, 1988).

To obtain a wide variety of large art prints, contact Shorewood Art Prints in writing at 27 Glen Road, Sandy Hook, CT 06482.

Music

How Melody Works with Chords

As we learned in Book Four of this series, songs can have chords that change as the melody goes along. You can make a chord by building a triple-decker sandwich of notes. In the key of C major, we can make the 1 or C major chord by sounding the 1, 3, and 5 notes, like this:

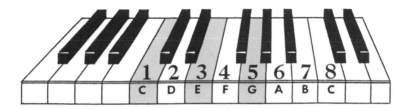

And we can make the 5 or G major chord by sounding the 5, 7, and 9 (or 2) notes like this:

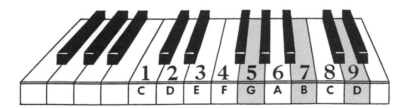

The 1 and 5 chords, called the tonic and dominant chords, are the most important chords, and many songs can be played with them.

Now let's learn about a third important chord, the 4 chord. How do you make the 4 chord? You simply go to the 4 note and make your triple decker sandwich, like this:

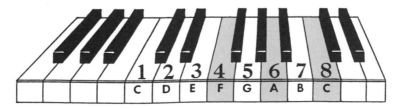

Because the 4 chord is just below the 5, or dominant chord, it is called the *sub*dominant chord, meaning *below* the dominant. In C major, the 4 chord is the F major chord. Now you have the three most important chords in the major scale: the 1 chord, the 5 chord, and the 4 chord.

If you have a keyboard, try playing the three chords in this order: 1, 4, 5 (C, F, G). Now play them again adding a 1 (C) chord at the end. Doesn't adding that chord make you feel like you just returned home after a trip? Play it again: C, F, G, C. Try them in another order: C, G, F, C. You'll find that in order to feel as though you've arrived "back home," you'll want to end on the 1 or C chord, just as lots of songs do.

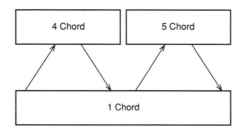

So, one way you might think of melody is that singing a melody can be like going on a walk and visiting different neighborhoods of sound.

Many other songs begin their walk at "home" (the 1 chord) and go to 4. The melody runs home to 1 again, goes to 5, and then ends back "home" on 1. Such a journey is called a chord progression.

Here's one familiar song that takes this journey. See if you can follow the walk through the chords. (As we sing and play songs in this section, try to hear what each chord sounds like. After a while, you may begin to identify the chords. Musicians can tell which chords are playing in the background just by hearing them.)

On Top of Old Smokey

C   F
On top of Old Smokey

              C
All covered with snow,

            G
I lost my true lover

            C
For courtin' too slow.

One familiar song about America uses this chord progression twice every verse:

This Land Is Your Land©

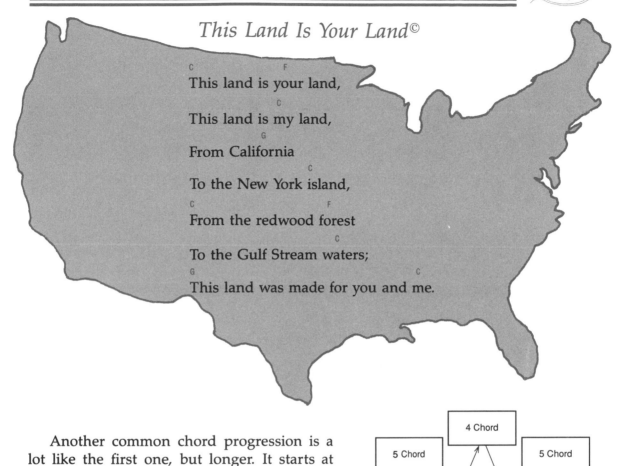

C   F
This land is your land,

      C
This land is my land,

      G
From California

         C
To the New York island,

C   F
From the redwood forest

           C
To the Gulf Stream waters;

G   C
This land was made for you and me.

Another common chord progression is a lot like the first one, but longer. It starts at home, then adds a visit to the 5 chord before going on the journey we told you about. You can picture it like this:

Red River Valley

C
From this valley they say you are leaving.

                           G
I will miss your bright eyes and sweet smile.

         C   F
For they say you are taking the sunshine,

         C   G   C
That has brightened our pathway awhile.

Chorus

C

Come and sit by my side if you love me.

G

Do not hasten to bid me adieu

C   F

But remember the Red River Valley

C   G   C

And the girl that has loved you so true.

"When the Saints Go Marching In" and "She'll be Comin' Round the Mountain" work this way, too.

Our three chords can be used in almost any order, in addition to the two progressions we have shown you here. Songs usually begin and end at home on the 1 chord, however, no matter what else happens. (The blues, an original form of African-American music that contributed to both jazz and rock-and-roll music, uses a variation of our three major chords which we will tell you about in Book Six of this series.)

The Shapes of Melodies

Melodies have shapes that you can picture. They go up and down in different ways as they go along. The shape to "Row Row Row Your Boat," for example, is a very simple one. It gradually goes up during the first half of the song and then goes down during the second half. Like this:

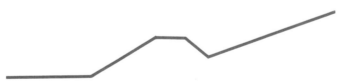

Row, row, row your boat gently down the stream,

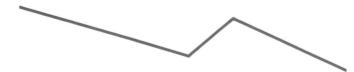

Merrily, merrily, merrily, merrily, life is but a dream.

Often you will find that the shapes of melodies are balanced in this way. Part of a melody will go one way, and then the other part will go the other way. That is something that makes a song feel right. Shapes often repeat in different parts of a song as well. The beginning of "Clementine" repeats the same shape a little higher up:

In a cavern in a canyon . . .

See how the line stays flat and then drops down both times? "Clementine" uses the same kind of shape, only upside down, to begin the second half of the melody:

Dwelt a miner . . .

A composer will try to make the shapes of a melody fit what the song is about. Some shapes are very dramatic, and go up and down quickly. You can almost see an eagle swooping down and soaring up high when you hear "The Star-Spangled Banner":

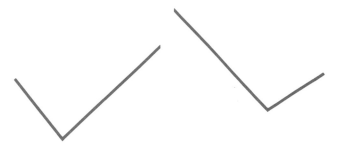

O-oh say, can you see? By the dawn's early light?

Other shapes are much gentler, and travel only to notes that are nearby:

This land is your land, this land is my land

See if you can picture the shapes of some of your favorite melodies. Why do you think they are that way?

Rhythm

Now let's have some fun with rhythm. As you read in Book Three, most basic songs are written in 4/4 time. This means that there are four beats to each measure, so we count: 1 2 3 4/ 1 2 3 4. Often the first and third beats in each measure get accented the most: 1 2 3 4/ 1 2 3 4. A fun 4/4 rhythm to say, which sounds like the drums on some popular records, goes: *Boonk*-a tik-a, *boonk*-a tik-a.

She'll be	com-in' round the	mountain when she	co-o-omes,	etc.
Boonk-a	tik-a Boonk-a	tik-a	boonk-a tik-a,	etc.

This gives a very steady rhythm. But notes and beats can also have different lengths—you can hold notes for a longer or shorter amount of time. So there are different note symbols to show how long or how short notes last. The most common note is the quarter note, which looks like this: ♩. There are four quarter notes to every measure in 4/4 time—one quarter note equals one beat.

Eighth notes are only half as long as quarter notes, so eight of them fit in a measure. Two eighth notes equals one beat. They look like this: ♪. If you have two eighth notes together, you often connect them, like this: ♫ .

Now let's have fun making rhythms with quarter notes and eighth notes. Here is a rhythm of just quarter notes, with an accent on the first beat.

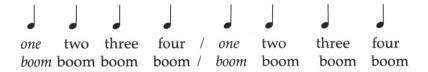

one	two	three	four	/	*one*	two	three	four
boom	boom	boom	boom	/	*boom*	boom	boom	boom

Now try these rhythms, which use both eighth and quarter notes:

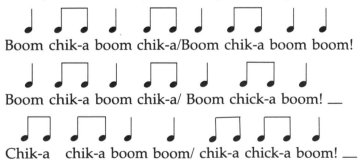

Boom chik-a boom chik-a/Boom chik-a boom boom!

Boom chik-a boom chik-a/ Boom chick-a boom! —

Chik-a   chik-a boom boom/ chik-a chick-a boom! —

Repeat them one after the other. Doesn't that sound neat? You see how many rhythms you can get just from these simple variations? By varying the length and loudness of our beats, we can get an infinite variety of rhythms. You can also add rests—places where you don't say anything—at different times.

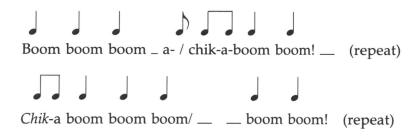

Boom boom boom _ a- / chik-a-boom boom! __ (repeat)

Chik-a boom boom boom/ __ __ boom boom! (repeat)

Mozart

One of the greatest composers of classical music was Wolfgang Amadeus Mozart (whom you read about in Book One). Mozart was born in Austria in 1756, and he lived there at about the time our country was founded. Mozart loved music from the very start. When he was just four years old, he learned to play the harpsichord! By the time he was five, he was already composing music. He was so gifted that when he and his sister, Nannerl, were still children, they played for many of the kings and queens of Europe.

Mozart had a head start on other musicians because his father was a famous violin teacher. When Mozart's father realized that his young son had a very

Wolfgang Amadeus Mozart.

special gift, he devoted most of his time to teaching him about music. It wasn't too long before Mozart was teaching his father about music!

While he became famous as a child prodigy, we remember Mozart today because of the wonderful music he composed. He wrote many kinds of music, including operas, which are like plays in which the characters sing instead of talk. One of his most famous operas is called *The Magic Flute.* In it, the music seems to cast a magical spell, just as the title says.

Mozart was also famous for his symphonies—long, grand pieces of music played by a large orchestra. Mozart influenced the way later symphonies were written, and many composers who followed him learned from what he wrote. Two of his most famous symphonies are the last two he wrote, and you can listen to them many times and still hear new, wonderful things in them. One is very dark, like a thunderstorm: the Symphony in G Minor (No. 40). The other is very grand and glorious: the *Jupiter* Symphony (No. 41).

Mozart's favorite instrument was probably the piano. The piano had just been invented at that time, and Mozart helped to make it popular. It is said that he could sit down at the piano and improvise music on the spot that would delight everyone who listened. A story goes that once, when a nobleman was dying, he was asked if he had a final wish, and he replied: "To hear Mozart improvise on the piano."

Some of Mozart's loveliest works are his piano concertos, in which the piano is accompanied by the orchestra, like a singer being accompanied by a band. Two of the most famous are the Piano Concerto No. 20 in D Minor, and the Piano Concerto No. 21 in C Major.

Other favorite works you might like are a piece called *Eine Kleine Nachtmusik*, which means "A Little Night Music"; the piano sonatas (especially the Sonata in C sometimes called "The Beginner's Sonata"); and the string quartets (especially the *Hunt* quartet). Many of Mozart's melodies are built using the three chords we have told you about: the 1, 4, and 5 chords. They often repeat their melodic shapes in different places. And the second half of a melody will balance the first half, as you've also read. Try to recognize these things when you listen to the music of Mozart.

Mozart became ill and died very young, but he still had managed to compose many wonderful pieces of music. Mozart's last work was his *Requiem*, music written for a funeral ceremony. Some people think Mozart was really writing it for his own funeral. Even though Mozart's life was often very sad, his music was filled with joy.

NOTE TO PARENTS AND TEACHERS: *Children love Ingmar Bergman's jovial movie of* The Magic Flute *with its funny characters and songs. You can use the movie's extravagant costumes, movable scenery, and backstage scenes added by Bergman to talk about staging an opera or play.*

Beethoven

Ludwig van Beethoven, a composer born in Germany, learned a great deal from hearing Mozart's music. But Beethoven developed his own style of music and wrote nine symphonies and a violin concerto that are among the world's greatest. Beethoven's Third Symphony, also known as the *Eroica*, makes you feel heroic and grand.

His Fifth Symphony, one of the most famous symphonies ever written, begins with a melody like a knock on the door that promises to bring something either very wonderful or terrible into your life. Listen to this melody, just three short notes and then a longer lower one, as it is repeated over and over again in different ways throughout the opening movement. Like much of Beethoven's music, this symphony tells us of triumph over struggle. The rhythm of three short notes and a long one became the Morse code signal for V, or Victory, so American soldiers and our allies in World War II used this symphony as a message proclaiming victory.

Beethoven's Sixth Symphony is like a long walk through woods and fields in the country. If you listen closely, you can hear birds calling, a storm coming up, and many other things. The Ninth Symphony has the "Ode to Joy," a song of hope and delight that is often performed today during the winter holidays.

People also love Beethoven's violin concerto, and his music for the piano. He was very popular and successful in his own day. But just when he was becoming a famous composer, he realized that he was going deaf! Could you imagine anything worse happening to a musician? He struggled against his fate, and after he became deaf he wrote some of his greatest music.

Ludwig van Beethoven.

John Philip Sousa

John Philip Sousa.

When you hear a band play during a parade on the Fourth of July, you will almost certainly hear the rousing music of one of America's most famous composers, John Philip Sousa. Sousa was born in 1854, before the Civil War, in Washington, D.C. Many of his pieces have a strong rhythm you can march to. That is why they are known as marches, and Sousa was often called the March King. When he was only thirteen, he played in the United States Marine Corps Band. He later became its leader and made it one of the finest bands in the world. He toured Europe with his own band, and was even decorated by the king of England. One writer at the time wrote, "There is probably no other composer in the world with a popularity equal to Sousa's."

He wrote many other kinds of music, but stirring marches like "Stars and Stripes Forever" and "Semper Fidelis" are the music that made him great. The next time you hear a band on the Fourth of July, think of John Philip Sousa. "I consider myself a truly American composer," he said. His music has become part of the tradition of our country, and is famous throughout the world.

Scott Joplin

Scott Joplin.

The great Scott Joplin was one of the first African-American composers to be recognized for his music. He was born in Texas in 1868, just after the Civil War, and brought up in a musical family. His father was a railroad worker who had been a slave. Against his father's wishes, Joplin left home and traveled to St. Louis to become a musician. There he heard the black pianists who were beginning to play ragtime music, and took it up himself. Joplin became the most famous composer of ragtime music. He led an orchestra at the great Chicago World's Fair in 1893. His "Maple Leaf Rag" became an immediate sensation around the country, and it is still one of his most popular pieces. Another piece, "The Entertainer," became popular all over again several years ago when it was used as the theme of the movie *The Sting*.

When you listen to Scott Joplin's ragtime, hear how the "ragged," uneven melodies fit in with the rhythmic, steady beat in interesting ways. Ragtime was very popular in its day, and was often used as dance music. It later contributed to the development of jazz, one of America's greatest forms of music.

The Orchestra

A symphony orchestra is made up of four main kinds of instruments: strings, woodwinds, brass, and percussion. The instruments in the orchestra are grouped into different families by the sounds they make and the way they make them.

Strings: The main family of instruments that make up the orchestra are the strings: violins, violas, cellos, and basses. You make sound on these instruments by drawing a bow across the strings, causing the strings to vibrate. You can also pluck the strings, which gives you a short sound, rather like a harp. The biggest stringed instrument, the bass, plays the lowest notes in the string family.

The different strings are grouped separately in their own sections. Listen for the high sound of the violins and the low sound of the cellos and basses when you hear a symphony by Mozart or Beethoven. (There are stringed instruments, like the guitar, that are not played with a bow, and are not usually played in a symphony orchestra.)

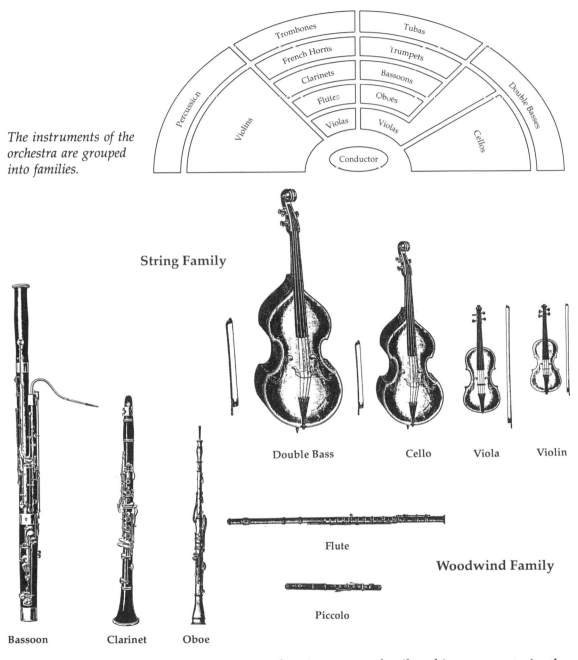

The instruments of the orchestra are grouped into families.

String Family

Double Bass Cello Viola Violin

Bassoon Clarinet Oboe

Flute

Piccolo

Woodwind Family

Woodwinds: The woodwinds are another important family of instruments in the symphony. You play a woodwind by blowing into the instrument to make air move through it. Some woodwinds, like the clarinet and the oboe, have a reed in the mouthpiece. Others, like the flute (one of the oldest of the wind instruments), are sounded by blowing air over a hole. You make different notes by opening and closing holes that run along the body of the instrument.

Trumpet

French Horn

Tuba

Trombone

Brass Family

Brass: Brass instruments are made of brass, and they have a bright, shiny sound. They include trumpets, horns, trombones, and tubas. You find brass instruments in symphony orchestras, and also in bands. Brass instruments are the heart of the marching bands you see in parades, community bands, and large jazz bands called Big Bands. Listen for them in the marches of John Philip Sousa or when you watch a marching band.

Like their cousins the woodwinds, brass instruments use your breath to make their sounds. Most brass instruments, such as trumpets and tubas, have valves that you open and close to make different notes. The trombone has a slide that you can make longer and shorter to produce different notes, so it has a very distinctive sliding sound. "Seventy-six Trombones," from *The Music Man* by Meredith Willson, is a song about brass bands and their instruments.

Percussion: Percussion instruments are instruments that you hit, such as drums. They are important in marching bands, where they help to keep the beat. You'll also find percussion instruments, like kettledrums, bells, and triangles, in an orchestra.

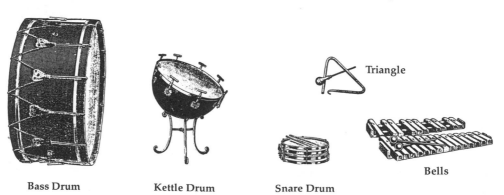

Triangle

Bells

Bass Drum

Kettle Drum

Snare Drum

Percussion Family

Try These

Here are some of the compositions we mentioned in this section and others that you might enjoy.

Mozart: The Magic Flute
   The Beginner's Sonata
   Hunt *Quartet*
   Eine Kleine Nachtmusik
Stravinsky: Rite of Spring

Beethoven: Third Symphony
    Fifth Symphony
    Sixth Symphony
    Violin Concerto in D
Gustav Holst: The Planets

Keyboards

Instruments that have a keyboard, such as pipe organs and harpsichords, are grouped together as keyboards. The piano is the most popular of the keyboards, and many composers, including Mozart, Beethoven, and Scott Joplin, played and composed for the piano.

New electronic keyboards called synthesizers make keyboards even more versatile. With the flip of a switch, you can make synthesizers sound like strings, woodwinds, brass, or even percussion instruments! Synthesizers can also make various electronic, sirenlike sounds. If synthesizers were around in Mozart's time, imagine what he might have done with them!

Visual Arts

From Gothic to Renaissance

In Book Four of this series, you read about the Gothic style of architecture, which spread across Western Europe in the Middle Ages. You met Abbot Suger (SUE-zhay), who thought of God as acting on the human spirit with the warmth and energy of fire. You can see how the high, pointed spires of Cologne Cathedral and the stonework tracery of the windows help give the feeling of leaping flames and of striving for the sky above. The people of the Middle Ages also thought of the space inside the cathedral as being a refuge like heaven itself, almost like a little heaven on earth. Their devotion to God not only inspired Gothic art, but also led later peoples to call the Middle Ages the "Age of Faith."

Now we will learn about a new period in European art, which corresponds to the period covered in the World Civilization section of this book (from about A.D. 1350 to 1600). That period, which in Western Europe followed the Middle Ages, is called the Renaissance. Much the same way that a new spring season brings flowers of every color and shape,

The cathedral at Cologne, Germany.

the Renaissance—which comes from a Latin word meaning "rebirth"—brought a blossoming of ideas in the arts and sciences to Europe. The people of the Renaissance created a new art style very different from the earlier Gothic style of the Middle Ages.

Harmony in the Human Form

The people of the Renaissance believed that all aspects of life were interrelated and in harmony, so they thought that by studying music, for example, they could also learn truths about geometry and the human body. Or by knowing mathematical laws,

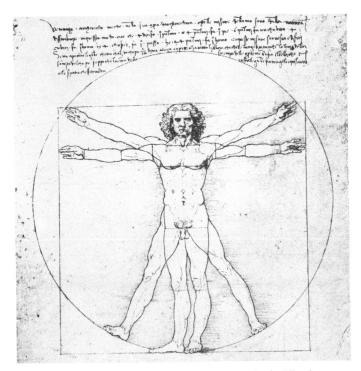

Diagram of human proportions by Leonardo da Vinci.

they would also know about the laws governing the movements of the heavens and about the best proportions for buildings. Renaissance artists took inspiration from the ancient Greeks and Romans because those peoples had already discovered much about the relationships among such laws. (You can read about ancient Greece in Book Two and about ancient Rome in Book Three of this series.) For example, one Italian artist, Leonardo da Vinci, was inspired by the writings of a Roman architect, Vitruvius, to create this drawing showing how the laws governing the proportions of the human form relate to the laws governing geometric forms.

Vitruvius wrote that if a perfectly proportioned man lay on his back with his hands and feet stretched out, his navel would be at the center of a circle while his fingers and toes would touch the edge, and that if he kept his legs together and stretched his arms out horizontally his toes and fingers would touch the edge of a square. This is exactly what Leonardo drew. Look at Leonardo's drawing and see how the man's fingers and toes touch the outlines of the circle and square.

This drawing had another meaning, too. The people of the Renaissance often thought of the circle in paintings as a symbol of the whole universe, and the square as a symbol of the earth. So Leonardo's drawing reminded them that the laws ruling the human body are related to the laws ruling geometry, and both kinds of laws are part of the rational harmony of all heaven and earth.

A City Proud of Its Architecture

It is not surprising that Leonardo da Vinci was impressed by the writings of an architect. The people of the city of Florence, where he lived for a time, were very proud of their city, and had a long tradition of creating grand buildings to grace it. The architects who designed these buildings got much attention. One of these architects, Filippo Brunelleschi (broo-nuh-LES-kee), became a hero when he designed this dome for the Cathedral of Florence in 1420.

Brunelleschi's dome, Florence Cathedral.

The Cathedral of Florence was first designed and begun around 1295, more than eighty years before Brunelleschi was born. The original design included plans for an enormous, eight-sided dome to cover the end of the church. This dome was to be bigger than any built in Western Europe for the last thousand years! At the time, the planners had no idea how to build such a dome so that it would not fall down from its own weight. They did not get around to working on this problem for almost eighty years, because they were busy building the church itself.

By the time Brunelleschi was born, however, the church was almost finished, and the city began to think about how to put up the dome. All the time Brunelleschi was growing up, architects, city planners, and even politicians and businessmen argued about the best way to build the dome, but no one gave a satisfactory answer. As a young man, Brunelleschi followed the debates and began dreaming of his own design. Finally, when businessmen in the wool industry gave money to build the dome, the city leaders knew a solution had to be found. They held a contest to find a design for the cathedral dome. The young Brunelleschi entered the competition, which was so fierce that he was afraid someone would steal his idea. He need not have worried, though—his design sketches convinced the judges to choose him as the architect!

Brunelleschi's Revolutionary Design

Brunelleschi's design for the dome of Florence Cathedral was a wonder in its time. Look at the picture of the dome. It may seem as though the dome is a single shell of bricks, but Brunelleschi's plans called for it to be made of two thin shells instead of one thick shell, which was the standard. The inner, circular shell supported the outer, eight-sided shell as both were being built and after construction was finished. This kept the dome from caving in from its own weight. No one had ever thought of a solution like this one!

To strengthen the dome even more, Brunelleschi added the strong, curved col-

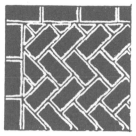

Herringbone pattern.

umns (called ribs) going from the walls of the cathedral up to the lantern at the top of the dome. See how the ribs are placed at the edges of the dome. The ribs connected the two shells and helped support them. Brunelleschi also taught the bricklayers how to lay bricks the way the Romans had, in a "herringbone" pattern like the one in this drawing, because that way the bricks themselves supported each other. And, in order to help the workmen reach the great height of the dome, he designed a new kind of wooden platform, or scaffold, for them to stand on. He even invented new hoists to lift heavy building materials up to the scaffold where the workmen needed them. You can see that in order to make sure his design went into place, Brunelleschi had to be an inventor and an engineer as well as an architect.

Building Styles Take a New Direction

Brunelleschi's ideas led to a building that looks very different from a Gothic cathedral. Look back at the picture of the Gothic cathedral of Cologne and then at the picture of the dome of Florence Cathedral. What most people notice about the Gothic cathedral is the feeling that the spires are rushing up into the sky. Brunelleschi's dome also soars high into the sky, but the curve of the dome helps slow down the movement of our eyes so that we notice its roundness as much as its height.

The Gothic cathedral is so big, with so many decorations and sculptures on the building, that many people feel there is no end to what can be seen. Brunelleschi's dome is also very big, but the dome looks simple and massive because there are few decorations. Many people feel that their eyes can rest for a long time looking at the dome.

Finally, it is hard to see what supports the spires of the Gothic cathedral because the columns are covered by decorations, and the flying buttresses are on the sides of the building. On Brunelleschi's dome the supporting ribs are easy to see because they stick out from the roof and are a different color. See how the white ribs seem to section off the dome into equal-sized, geometrical segments?

The people of Florence preferred their dome to Gothic architecture because Brunelleschi's work seemed to stand for much that was important to them. The dome looked geometrical and simple, and people could see what supported it. This reminded them of their belief that the laws of creation were rational and supported the harmony of the universe.

Brunelleschi studied for a very long time, and with great inventiveness overcame many difficulties to build the dome. This reminded the people of their belief that humans can understand the laws of creation and share in them. Finally, even though the dome did not look exactly like the architecture of the Greeks and Romans, its simple geometric form recalled Roman styles of architecture. All these things were so impressive that Brunelleschi's designs set a new direction in styles of architecture for the Renaissance, and inspired many grand public buildings, including St. Peter's Cathedral in Rome and our own U.S. Capitol.

A Sculptor Inspired by Greek Statues

About seventy-five years after Brunelleschi's dome was finished, a young Florentine sculptor named Michelangelo (my-kel-AN-je-lo) began creating works of art that amazed the Italian people. As a young man only thirteen years old, Michelangelo's artwork was already so impressive that he went to study at a special school for sculptors. There he met the leader of Florence, Lorenzo de Medici. Lorenzo liked Michelangelo's work so much that he invited the young artist to live with the Medici family. By day Michelangelo learned Greek and Roman forms of sculpture, while by night he listened to Lorenzo's educated guests talk about the ideas of the ancient Greek philosopher Plato.

These studies made a powerful impression on Michelangelo. For the rest of his life, he would believe strongly in the Greek idea that the human body is noble because the soul (the divine part of humans) lives in it. This led him to study the human body very carefully. He learned all he could by looking at living models, then decided he also needed to know what shaped the body from the inside out. In order to learn this with his own eyes, he cut apart human corpses to study the bones and tissues that make up the human body. All these studies helped him carve statues and paint figures that look amazingly lifelike.

A Sensational Work of Art

After Lorenzo died, Florence was troubled for many years by war and by the problem of who was to be the next leader. The city had just begun to solve some of its difficulties when Michelangelo was asked to carve a large statue for Florence Cathedral—the same cathedral topped by Brunelleschi's famous dome. Michelangelo was proud to be asked to make a statue for the cathedral because only the best artists were allowed to create art for it. He hoped to create a work that would remind people that even in times of trouble, Florence was still as great as it was in Brunelleschi's time.

Michelangelo faced a hard job. The city leaders gave him a stone to use that other artists had refused to carve. The trouble was that, years before, another artist had worked on the stone and made a mistake that no one knew how to correct. But Michelangelo was certain a wonderful figure lay hidden in the marble, waiting for a sculptor to set it free from the surrounding stone. For three years, from 1501 to 1504, he worked with intense dedication, carving a heroic figure. Finally, Michelangelo and his assistants rolled the huge statue out to the city square late at night and covered it with a cloth. In the morning, people who were passing the square stopped to stare and wonder what lay beneath the cloth. When the statue was finally uncovered, it caused a sensation!

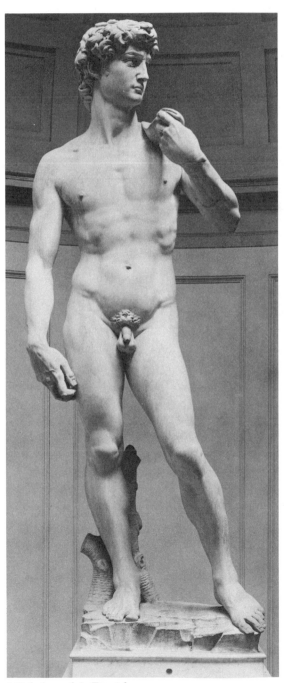

Michelangelo's David.

A Boy-Hero

The statue Michelangelo carved was a figure from the Bible named David. The Bible tells that the Israelites were being attacked by an enemy people. When the two armies met, a giant warrior named Goliath from the attacking army came out and challenged any soldier in the Israelite army to fight him to the death. If Goliath won the challenge, the Israelites would lose the whole battle. If the Israelite soldier won, the attacking army would go home.

The Israelites were terror-stricken because Goliath looked so big and strong they thought no Israelite could beat him. No one wanted to accept Goliath's challenge. Then David stepped forward to say that he would challenge Goliath. David was a shepherd. He was very young and had never fought a battle before, but he was not afraid. The Israelites wanted David to wear armor, swords, and spears for protection, but David went out to meet Goliath armed with only the slingshot and stones he always used to protect his sheep.

When Goliath saw David, he was amazed that an unarmed boy had come out to fight. He was sure he would win, and he laughed and cursed David for believing victory was possible. But David ran toward Goliath, and as he ran he loaded his slingshot with a stone and hurled the stone at the giant. The stone hit Goliath in the forehead and stuck there, killing him at once. The Israelites won the day because of one boy's bravery.

The story of David was a popular one

in Michelangelo's time. Florentines liked it because they had often faced enormous difficulties and overcome them bravely, just as David had. Many artists had already made statues of David, but all these statues had shown figures that looked like smiling, pretty, peaceful boys. Michelangelo's *David* is nothing like that, so the people of Florence knew they were looking at a sculpture that spoke differently to them. The people of Florence saw a David who stared into the distance with the muscles of his forehead tensed, as though looking at something that troubled him. He had the body of a strong, muscular young man who might stand a chance against a big enemy. Finally, although Michelangelo did not carve David in the act of slinging a stone at Goliath, many people felt that the figure was about to move. This is because Michelangelo carved David to stand the way he had seen many Greek statues stand.

Look closely at the photograph of the *David*. Notice that one leg is straight and

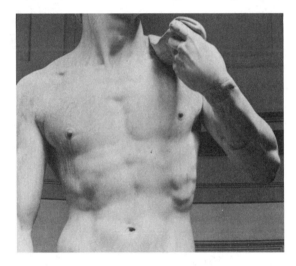

the other bent. Now stand up and shift most of your weight onto one leg so that it is straight and the other one is bent. Pay attention to what your chest and shoulders do when you stand like this. Most people notice that the shoulder of the side that bears weight usually drops slightly, while the other shoulder rises slightly. How did Michelangelo arrange David's shoulders and torso (the trunk of the body between the hips and the shoulders)?

When you are standing in this position, you may notice that even though you are standing still, your body does not feel entirely at rest: your weight-bearing side may feel more tense and your torso may feel a little twisted or strained. Michelangelo helped us see this clearly in several ways. For example, he emphasized the body's tension by making David's neck muscles stand out as though they are tense, and he helped us see the twisting of the chest area by making the line of the ribs go on a diagonal rather than a straight horizontal line. Like the Greeks, Michelangelo realized that showing the tension and twisting of a body in this position makes a statue look more interesting and lifelike by helping it look both at rest and ready to move at the same time. For the same reason, many other painters and sculptors of the Renaissance also showed human figures standing this way.

A Heroic Statue

Michelangelo wanted to create a statue that reminded people that Florence was a special city, and the *David* did just that. It was so big—fourteen feet tall, more than twice as tall as a fully grown man—that people could not overlook it. This huge sculpture showed the Florentines that, like David, they were strong and full of energy. Its expression and the position of its body reminded them that they were ready and able to face difficult challenges. And the majestic form of the statue reminded them that part of Florence's greatness came from its strong belief in the nobility of humans.

The Florentines were so awed by what they saw that they decided they didn't want the statue to go in a niche of the cathedral, where it would be hard to see. Instead, they decided to place it outside in the main city square, next to the door of their most important government building, so that everyone who passed would be reminded of what the city stood for. Even today many people feel that the *David* is the work that best expresses the spirit of the Renaissance.

Paintings Like Windows

This painting, by another famous Renaissance artist named Raphael (RAF-eye-el), was made the year Michelangelo finished the *David*. It is called *The Marriage of the Virgin* and shows Jesus' mother, Mary, accepting a wedding ring from Joseph. Like other painters of the Renaissance, Raphael dressed his biblical subjects like wealthy Florentines of his day and showed them in a public square of a Renaissance city.

Raphael's picture shows clearly how the work of artists like Michelangelo affected Renaissance paintings. Just like the statue of David, the figures in *The Marriage of the Virgin* seem lifelike and look as though they could move at any moment. One of the ways Raphael accomplishes this feat is by using some of Michelangelo's techniques. Look at the way Joseph stands. Notice that he stands as Michelangelo's *David* does. Raphael's ability to create lifelike figures led to his popularity as a portrait painter and as a painter of madonnas (artworks showing Mary with the baby Jesus).

We can also see how the Florentines' pride in architects like Brunelleschi affected Renaissance paintings. Look at the building in this painting. It has a dome similar to Brunelleschi's. Brunelleschi and others made architecture such a big part of Florentine life that many painters began to include parts of buildings or cities in their artworks.

Raphael's Marriage of the Virgin.

Brunelleschi also affected Renaissance painting by developing a way of drawing that painters like Raphael began to use. In order to plan buildings, Brunelleschi needed a way to draw them so that when he examined his drawing, it would appear as though he were standing on the ground looking at the finished work. Brunelleschi examined some Greek and Roman paintings, and he talked with friends who studied mathematics and the way the eye sees. After much thought, he developed a way of drawing called vanishing point perspective. At first, architects made the most use of Brunelleschi's system, but once his theory was written down, painters learned it and began using it too. By the time Raphael was painting, many artists used vanishing point perspective in their works to make paintings look like windows opening onto a real scene.

Vanishing Point Perspective

One of the things that Brunelleschi noticed in his studies is that when you look at a group of objects in real life, things in front seem to cover up all or part of things in back. Raphael has painted the group of people in *The Marriage of the Virgin* in this way. For example, look at the man who stands on one foot, at the bottom, right-hand corner of the painting. We see all of this man, but his body seems to cover up part of Joseph's arm, so we feel as though Joseph is farther away from us than the man standing on one foot. Even though the canvas is flat, this helps us feel as though we could "walk into" the painting. We say that the painting has depth.

Brunelleschi also noticed that things look bigger to us when they are close up than when they are far away. Close one eye and look at a window across the room. Hold up your thumb close to your eye and compare it to the size of the window. Now move your thumb far from your eye and compare it to the window. Notice that when your thumb is close to you, it seems big compared with the window. When you move your thumb farther from you, it seems to be smaller than it was.

Raphael used this idea in *The Marriage of the Virgin* by drawing some people bigger and some smaller to give us the feeling that some are close to us and some are far away. Notice that there are three groups of people. Mary, Joseph, and the people at the wedding are in the part of the painting called the foreground. The second set of figures is halfway between the wedding party and the building. These figures are in the middle ground. The last figures are walking under

the arches of the building in the background. Because all these figures are people, we know they are around the same size. But the figures in the foreground look many times larger than those in the middle ground and background. This gives the painting depth because it gives us the feeling that the people in the wedding are closest to us, while the people in the building are far away.

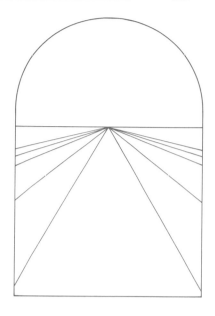

Another thing Brunelleschi noticed is that if a person stands between two parallel lines that stretch way into the distance, the lines look as though they get closer and closer together until they seem to come together at a point on the horizon. The lines then seem to "vanish" at this point, so it is called the vanishing point. You can test this yourself by standing at the bottom of a tall skyscraper and looking at how the sides of the skyscraper seem to be closer together at the top than they are at the bottom of the building. Or stand on a long, straight sidewalk and compare how the lines that form the edges of the sidewalk look close to you and far away from you. Raphael painted the lines of the pavement on diagonals so that they all seem to come together at the same point on the horizon—the open door of the building in the background. This helps make us feel as though the door of the building is far away from us.

A Renaissance Man

One of the highest compliments you can give a person is to call him a "Renaissance man." It means that he has an especially wide range of skills and a brilliant mind. Some people believe that this phrase best describes another famous artist from the Renaissance whose drawing you saw earlier, Leonardo da Vinci (lee-owe-NAHR-doh dah VIN-chee).

Leonardo was born in the small Italian town of Vinci in 1452. He kept the name of his town for his own last name when his father took him to Florence as a teenager to study art. Leonardo became one of Florence's most famous painters and was especially well known for his portraits (paintings that show a person). If you have read Book One of this series, you will already know about one of his amazing portraits called the *Mona Lisa*. Ever since the *Mona Lisa* was painted, people have wondered about her mysterious smile.

But Leonardo also became famous in his time because he was able to do so many other things as brilliantly as he painted. He was an architect, a musician, a sculptor, a botanist, an engineer, an inventor, and a mathematician. Like Michelangelo, he dissected corpses to study the human body, and his scientific drawings of what he

Da Vinci's The Last Supper.

saw were so accurate that they have been used to teach human anatomy. Some of his mechanical inventions were hundreds of years ahead of their time, like his designs for a flying machine and a submarine! However, if you ever plan to study the original notes Leonardo left about his inventions, bring a mirror. Leonardo was left-handed and often wrote from right to left so that all the letters were reversed. To decipher his writing, you must read its reflection in a mirror!

Sometimes Leonardo's habit of experimenting with everything, including the paints he used, led to unfortunate results. This artwork, called *The Last Supper*, looks faded because his experiment with paint had an unexpected effect. Leonardo wanted to make a paint that would dry very fast on plaster, so he experimented with a new mixture when he painted the mural. But Leonardo did not realize that his "new" paint would easily absorb moisture from the wall. Soon the paint got damp and began to crumble, and today we can barely see the bright colors and details that first made *The Last Supper* famous.

Leonardo's Faded Mural

Once painters understood how to use perspective, they began experimenting with it to create certain effects, like directing the viewer's attention to important parts of a painting. This is what Leonardo da Vinci has done in the painting of *The Last Supper*.

Raphael used the lines in the pavement of *The Marriage of the Virgin* to create the effect of vanishing point perspective. There is no pavement in *The Last Supper*, so

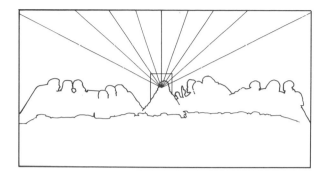

Leonardo used the lines of the ceiling to create this effect. Find these lines in the painting. If you kept drawing the lines down to the horizon, where would they meet? They would come together in the center of the painting, behind the head of Jesus.

Now look for the open door in the wall behind Jesus. The door is set off from the two windows because it has a half-arch above it. See how the lines of the door create an outline that looks almost like a small frame around the figure of Jesus. Together, the lines of perspective and the open doorway lead our eyes to the center of the painting so that we pay special attention to Jesus.

Why would this be important? The mural shows us one of the most crucial times in the life of Jesus, the last meal he ate with his followers. Christians believe that at this meal, Jesus said, "One of you will betray me." The followers' faces and bodies show that they have heard astonishing and awful news. They exhibit such emotion that it would be easy to pay more attention to them than to Jesus—but Leonardo has used many techniques, including perspective, to make sure that we know it is actually Jesus who is the center of attention. We say that the figure of Jesus is the focus of the painting.

The Sistine Chapel

You have learned in the World Civilization section of this book that Pope Julius II became an important patron of the arts. One of the big projects Julius decided to undertake was to adorn the ceiling of a famous building in Rome—the Sistine Chapel—with paintings of scenes from the Bible. Julius had seen Michelangelo's sculptures and decided that this was the artist he wanted to paint the ceiling. Michelangelo did not particularly like painting and already had a job he liked, carving statues for Julius, but Julius insisted that the ceiling should come first. The two men often argued hotly about whether Michelangelo should do the painting and how it should be done, but in the end Michelangelo could not refuse the pope.

Even though he finally agreed to paint the Sistine Chapel, Michelangelo desperately wanted to get back to his sculptures. In order to finish the mural so that he could continue carving, he worked so long and for so many hours at a time—night and day for seven years, lying on a scaffold inches away from the ceiling—that for a short time he overstrained his eyes and lost his sight! Though he would have preferred to be working on stone, Michelangelo was a perfectionist and believed that these important scenes from the Bible should be as well done as possible.

The Creation of Adam

One of the stories from the Old Testament of the Bible tells how the first man was created. This story says that God molded the body of the first man from the clay of the earth and then gave the body life. Because the body of this man was formed from the earth, he is called Adam, from a Hebrew word meaning ground or earth.

This detail from the Sistine Chapel is called *The Creation of Adam* and shows the moment when God is about to give life to the body of Adam. Because Adam's body has just been made from the earth, Michelangelo shows his body lying on the ground. Adam's torso is propped up on one elbow and one leg is bent, as though he is trying to push himself up from the ground. But even though Adam has a large and strong-looking body, the way most of it is pressed against the earth shows that Adam doesn't yet have the strength to stand. The hand that he stretches out is bent and limp, and Adam seems to rest his forearm on his knee, as though he does not have the energy to hold his arm out.

On the right, Michelangelo has painted a God whose hair, beard, and clothing swirl as though the wind created by God's movement pushes them away. By painting God this way, Michelangelo helps us feel as though God is rushing through the heavens toward Adam. We get a feeling that God has energy and power: the figure of God is so muscular and strong that we feel he must be full of life. Michelangelo has painted God's right hand so that it stretches firmly in a direct line from the torso to the tip of the finger. This helps show that God's power is flowing with much energy directly toward Adam. It looks as though all it will take to make Adam rise is for God's finger to brush Adam's waiting hand.

Michelangelo's paintings in the Sistine Chapel had a tremendous effect on Renaissance painters. After many other painters of the Renaissance saw the Sistine Ceiling, they were so impressed by figures like the ones you see in this detail that they followed Michelangelo's lead and began to paint people with strong bodies that seemed to move with great energy.

Michelangelo has done much to make sure we notice God's hand reaching out to Adam's. Michelangelo knew that when we look at a roughly square space, our eyes tend to look toward its center. Look at the meeting of the two hands in *The Creation of Adam*. Notice that it takes place roughly in the center of the painting, right where our eyes naturally tend to go. Now notice the way Michelangelo has painted light and dark spaces in this painting. The bodies of Adam and God seem to be surrounded by dark areas, but their hands seem to float in the light, empty space that runs down the center of the painting. We tend to pay attention to the hands because they seem to be the only objects to look at in this large, light area of the painting. By placing the hands in the center of the painting and by leaving lots of light and space around them, Michelangelo has made the hands of God and Adam the focus of this painting. This encourages us to think about what will happen when the hands meet—the drama of Adam receiving life.

Brighter, Light-Filled Colors

The artists from Italy taught other European artists about using vanishing point perspective. But Italian artists also learned a great deal from others, particularly Flemish painters (from the areas we now know as Belgium, the Netherlands, and Luxembourg). One Flemish artist named Jan van Eyck (JAN van-IKE) became a painter around the same time Brunelleschi was working as an artist in Florence. This painting by Van Eyck, called *Giovanni Arnolfini and His Bride,* shows the marriage of a wealthy Dutch merchant. There are many details in the painting that people of the time would recognize as symbols with special meanings related to Christianity and marriage—the single candle in the candelabra meant the couple hoped the spirit of Jesus was with them, the dog meant that the couple promised to be faithful to one another, and the fruit on the windowpane and table meant that the couple hoped to have children.

When Jan and his brother, Hubert, began painting, it was common for artists to use paints called tempera, which had egg yolk as one of the ingredients. Artists liked tempera because it dried quickly and made very bright colors. But it had some disadvantages—artists could only use one layer of paint to make a color and they could not make very tiny details with it. Jan and his brother started using paint that had oil as a major ingredient because they thought oil paints could create effects that tempera could not. They practiced very hard until they could layer shades to make colors that glowed and could represent the tiniest details.

The Van Eycks created a revolution in painting by learning new ways to use oil paints. From this time on, painters were able to create the effect of light glowing on furniture or on people's skins. They

Van Eyck's Giovanni Arnolfini and His Bride.

were able to show silk or velvet so that viewers could almost feel the material by looking at the painting. They were able to capture everything from the individual hairs on a person's head to the small decorations on a ring.

This photograph is in black and white, so you cannot see the full effect of oil paints in its colors. But you can still see some of the tiny details that make Van Eyck's work famous, like the fur on the merchant's robe, the individual flowers on the rug, and the little bits of lace on the bride's veil. You can also see how Van Eyck was able to create the look of light coming in from windows, shining on the couple's face and making shadows in the painting.

An Unusual Use for a Painting

During the time when Van Eyck was painting, Flemish portraits usually showed figures that were long, thin, and very still, and faces that showed little emotion. Jan van Eyck continued that tradition by showing the merchant and his bride this way.

However, portraits at that time mostly showed only the chest and head of the person. Instead, Van Eyck showed the whole bodies of the bride and the groom, and

he showed them inside their bedroom. Why did he do this? During this time, the Catholic Church did not always make couples have a priest at a wedding. Sometimes this practice later led to arguments about whether a couple had married legally. Many believe that Van Eyck painted this portrait in order to show that he was a witness at the wedding because he wrote the words, "Jan van Eyck was here," above the mirror painted on the back wall. If you look closely at this detail of the reflecting mirror, you will see that van Eyck painted it to reflect the backs of the wedding couple, as well as the figures of two others who were there. Perhaps one of these witnesses is Van Eyck himself!

Flemish Light

When European artists shared with each other their new knowledge of how to use oil paints and perspective, many began to create paintings on canvas that astonished viewers by how true to life the colors, lights, skin tones, shading, and depth seemed. These elements seemed to work together to show viewers the feelings and moods of the people in the paintings. And Flemish artists, more than any others, continued to create some of the most expressive portraits of their time.

One Dutch artist, Rembrandt van Rijn (REM-brant van RYN), lived about two hundred years after Van Eyck painted *Giovanni Arnolfini and His Bride.* Rembrant was interested in studying one person over a long period of time in order to see how a human face changes with age. Because he knew that he would always carry his own face and

Self-portrait by Rembrandt.

body with him wherever he went, he often studied himself in mirrors and painted self-portraits. Rembrandt's desire to study his face and paint it closely from real life shows how much the Renaissance idea of painting from real life had spread all over Europe by this time and had influenced artists outside Italy. This self-portrait shows Rembrandt as a middle-aged man.

Look back at the painting by Van Eyck and compare it to Rembrandt's self-portrait. The painting by Van Eyck shows many fine details—for example, the tiny flowers in the rug. Although Rembrandt does not show the tiniest individual details of his face, he does use lighter and darker paints to create the effect of faint shadows on the face. This helps the face look fuller and rounder. It also gives us a feeling that we can see the small dips, bumps, and wrinkles—the texture—of Rembrandt's skin. As a result, many people feel that this picture shows a face that looks full of life.

A Classic Work

Even after the Renaissance, some painters continued to be interested in the art and architecture of the ancient Greeks and Romans and used figures and architecture from these classical cultures in their works. This painting—called the *Oath of the Horatii*—by the French artist Jacques-Louis David (zhahk-loo-EE dah-VEED), is one example. In this work, David has painted Roman columns and arches, and people dressed in the Roman style. This scene shows three brothers holding out their hands as they swear to their father they will use his swords to fight the enemy. See how David has painted light falling from behind the brothers so that we pay attention to the father's upraised hand and face, and to the swords that he is handing to his sons. Notice that David has used parts of architecture to frame figures in the painting, just as Leonardo did in *The Last Supper*.

David's Oath of the Horatii.

If you have read the World Civilization section of this book, you may have learned that in the late 1700s the people of France were rebelling against their king—a time we call the French Revolution. Many people during the French Revolution thought that art should be used to get the people ready to fight. They liked this painting because even though the people in it are dressed as Romans, it reminded French people that they should be ready to fight and even die for their beliefs if necessary.

Moorish Architecture in Europe

At the end of the Middle Ages, the Muslim people who had conquered much of Spain had developed their own style of architecture, which was very different from both the Gothic and the Renaissance styles. On a hill that stands over the town of Granada in Spain, one Muslim leader began building a palace for his court that became known as the Alhambra (ahl-AHM-bra). By the late 1300s, just before Brunelleschi was born, the Alhambra was fully finished. It was made up of buildings for the royal family and their advisers, a great bath, and mosques set up around open areas or courtyards. The style of the Alhambra is called "Moorish" because Europeans often called the Muslims "Moors." The Moorish style spread throughout lands in Africa, the Middle East, and India that were ruled by Muslim peoples.

This photograph shows one of the Alhambra's courtyards. It is called the Lion Court because the fountain in its center is ringed by a group of lion statues. Many of the Alhambra's courtyards, like the Lion Court, have fountains or pools so that people in nearby rooms can enjoy the sound of water gently running and bubbling.

When the Muslims first took over Spain, they found many Roman buildings. Like the Italian people of the Renaissance, the Muslims in Spain were impressed by some of the Roman ways of building. They started using arches and columns as the Romans had, but in time they changed the designs to look very different from the Roman features they came from. Notice the columns with arches behind the fountain. If you have read Book Three of this series, you learned that Romans often used round arches and columns in their architecture both to please the eye and to support the walls and roof. Notice that the arches in the Lion Court are not half-circles, as Roman arches tended to be. They look more

The Lion Court at the Alhambra.

like horseshoe shapes that have been stretched. In addition, some of the arches have points on the top—they almost look as though they reach up in the shape of tiny, dancing flames.

Now look closely at the columns in the Lion Court. Roman columns are often very thick, and look as though they could support heavy weights. Unlike Roman columns, the columns at the Lion Court are thin, and sometimes the architect has even used two columns together to help add support. Finally, look at the area of the wall these columns support. Romans sometimes used mosaics and statues as decorations, but they left their walls looking very solid. Do the walls in the Lion Court look solid? The Muslim artists smoothed the walls with wet plaster (a mixture of lime, sand, and water that hardens when it dries) and made many swirling designs in the plaster before it hardened. Some of the designs include verses from the Koran, while others include poetry. These swirling designs give the wall a lacy, delicate look rather than a solid one.

The Taj Mahal

Among the many buildings that the Alhambra influenced is one in India even more famous than the Alhambra—the Taj Mahal. It was named for Mumtaz Mahal, the favorite wife of the Muslim emperor Shah Jahan. The shah married Mumtaz Mahal because he loved her, which may not seem unusual to you, but in those days princes often married for political or economic reasons rather than for love. Shah Jahan and Mumtaz Mahal were constant companions for nineteen years. Sadly, however, Mumtaz died shortly after Shah Jahan became emperor of India.

To honor the memory of the wife he loved so dearly, Shah Jahan ordered his architects to build a great tomb. It took twenty thousand workers around twenty-two years to carry out the plan. Completed about 1650, the Taj Mahal—with its onion-shaped domes, its pure white marble, and its peaceful gardens—is considered to be one of the most beautiful buildings ever built.

Look at the Taj Mahal. The slender towers, called minarets, are found in many Muslim religious buildings. Perched high in the minaret, a special caller five times a day beckons people to prayer.

Do any features of the Taj Mahal remind you of the Alhambra? By the time the Taj Mahal was built, some of the features that made the Alhambra famous—the pointed arches, the swirling designs on the walls, and decorative pools of water—had spread from Spain to many other Muslim-ruled countries.

The Taj Mahal.

Ife metal casting.

Faces of Kings

At about the same time that the Muslims were building Moorish architecture in Spain, a group of people in Nigeria, Africa, called the Ife (EE-fay), were developing a style of sculpture that was different from many of their African neighbors' works. African peoples often preferred to show figures that did not look true to life, but the Ife often made human faces very lifelike. This photograph shows a head made by an Ife artist. It was made by pouring hot, molten brass into a mold shaped in the form of a human head. This kind of sculpture is called a metal casting, and Ife artists created many like it from about 1100–1400.

The Ife often made sculptures like this one to honor kings and other special people who died. Two or three years after the person was buried, the body was dug up and a ceremony was held to show the spirit of the dead man that the living still remembered and respected him. The sculpture was an important part of the ceremony—it reminded the living of the dead person, and went with the body when it was buried for the second time.

Like the artists of the Renaissance, the Ife artists were interested in making sculptures that looked like living people. Some were even made with holes around the mouth and head so that false wigs and beards and sometimes crowns could be attached to the sculptures to make them look even more like a real person. Often the artist made lines running over the face of the bust. These lines do two things: they show the person's scarification patterns (scars made on purpose to create a kind of decoration on the skin), and they help us focus on the gentle curves of the face.

Gardens of Stone

Think of being by yourself on a summer day watching clouds as they move slowly across the blue sky. As you gaze at them, you become "lost in the clouds," and forget your everyday concerns. This kind of experience is called contemplation. Many people value contemplation because it brings them a feeling of relaxed attention, or moments of joy, inspiration, or wisdom.

The garden in this picture was built for contemplation. Its simplicity is part of its secret. Just as you might see many different forms when you watch clouds, those who gaze at this arrangement of stones may see many different things. People have described the rocks as a mother lion and her cubs crossing a body of water, as mountains rising out of the mists, or as islands floating in a sea. Others just admire the arrangement and texture of the weathered stones.

Nearby is a porch where people can sit and gaze at the stones, but the design of the garden encourages you to walk around it and see many different things. This is because, although the garden is made up of fifteen stones arranged in raked gravel, you can see only fourteen stones at any one time from the edge of the garden. You must keep walking in order to see all the stones.

This garden was built in Japan during the 1400s as part of a Zen Buddhist monastery called Ryōan-ji (ree-OW-ahn-jee). During the 1200s to 1400s, Japanese Zen Buddhists taught that contemplation was the best way to gain the wisdom of the Buddha. They believed that contemplation could take place anywhere, anytime, but that living a simple life in harmony with nature was a very good way to start.

Long before Zen Buddhists began teaching in Japan, Japanese people already had a tradition of revering nature. According to the ancient religion of Shinto, unusual stones and trees were thought to be places where *kami,* or divine energy, was found. Such stones and trees were marked with a sacred rope and honored as shrines. People sometimes put gravel around a Shinto shrine because they believed the sound of feet crunching over the stones calmed the mind and prepared people to approach the shrine with respect. Can you see how Shinto traditions affected the design of

The garden at Ryōan-ji.

Ryōan-ji garden? (You can read more about Shinto and feudal Japan in the World Civilization section of this book.)

The beliefs of Shintoism influenced the Japanese people to enjoy gardens where stones, plants, and water were arranged in beautiful but natural-looking ways. Gardens in Japan took many forms, but large, parklike gardens were once considered the best because people strolling in them felt they were in a different and better world. When Zen Buddhists began teaching around 1200, they gave people a new way to think about gardens. Zen priests showed that a well-designed garden could remind people of the importance of nature even when the garden was small, or contained only the barest essentials of a landscape, as the "dry garden" of Ryōan-ji does.

Gardens continue to be an important part of Japanese life and art. Many Japanese build small, simple gardens where they live or work, so that they can contemplate nature often.

IV.
MATHEMATICS

Introduction to Fifth-Grade Mathematics

FOR PARENTS AND TEACHERS

The math sections in *The Core Knowledge Series* are designed as detailed *summaries* of the math that should be mastered in each grade. We hope you will supplement them with continual opportunities for practice. Like the learning of music, the learning of math requires practice: not mindless repetitive practice, but thoughtful and varied practice that approaches problems from a variety of angles and encourages children to use intuition and develop a facility at quickly estimating correct results.

The difference between the typical math curriculum in the United States and those used by countries such as Japan and France, which have more successful math programs, becomes dramatic in the fifth grade. While our students usually spend most of the fifth-grade year on basic arithmetic, Japanese and French students have moved on to the kind of mathematics presented in this chapter. Countries that successfully teach mathematics at the elementary level believe that students must become fluent in and comfortable with more sophisticated mathematics at an earlier age. By mastering the concepts outlined in this chapter through daily practice, our students—all of them—can achieve similar success.

This chapter assumes that students have learned the techniques for adding, subtracting, and multiplying whole numbers; that they are ready to master arithmetic that will form the basis of algebra, and to pursue their studies in geometry. Work at the fifth-grade level includes long division with a quotient rounded to a certain decimal place. It also includes multiplication and division of decimals; addition and subtraction of fractions with different denominators; percents and the relationships between percents, decimals, and fractions; work with equations in simple ways; and some introductory work with functions. In geometry, students learn to measure angles, find the circumference of a circle, find the area of triangles and parallelograms, and perform some constructions. We detail working with both metric and customary units of measurement but recommend practicing metric measures whenever possible, since working with them can help develop an understanding of place value.

Math is potentially great fun, and improving math skills yields a sense of accomplishment and heightened self-esteem. Students who master this chapter will have taken great strides toward speaking the universal language of mathematics. They will be well prepared for math in the sixth grade and beyond.

Fifth-Grade Mathematics

Whole Numbers

Properties of Addition

The names for some of the rules about addition that you have been using are called properties of addition because they are always true about the operation of addition.

1. *The Commutative Property of Addition*
   Addends can be added in any order without changing the sum.

   $$5 + 3 = 8 \quad \text{and} \quad 3 + 5 = 8, \quad \text{so} \quad 5 + 3 = 3 + 5$$

2. *The Associative Property of Addition*
   Addends can be grouped in any way without changing the sum.

   $$(2 + 6) + 3 = 11 \quad \text{and} \quad 2 + (6 + 3) = 11, \quad \text{so} \quad (2 + 6) + 3 = 2 + (6 + 3)$$

Practice writing equations to show what each of these properties of addition means.

Variables

A letter can stand for a number. A letter that stands for a number is called a variable. For example, instead of writing $6 + \underline{\quad} = 8$, we can write $6 + a = 8$. In this equation, $a = 2$. We can also write $a + 4 = 10$. In the second equation, $a = 6$. We call a letter like "a" a *vari*able because it can stand for different numbers. To *vary* means to change.

Finding what number the variable in an equation stands for is called solving the equation.

Opposite Operations, Equations

Remember that addition and subtraction are opposite operations. That is why you can write a related subtraction fact from an addition fact, or a related addition fact from a subtraction fact.

$$8 + 7 = 15$$

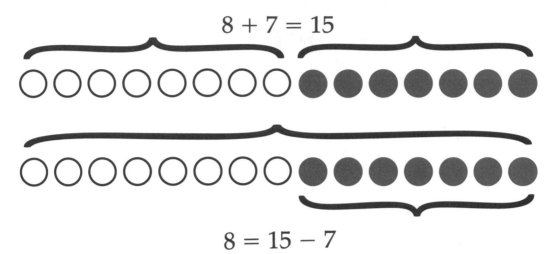

$$8 = 15 - 7$$

$8 + 7 = 15$ and $8 = 15 - 7$ are two different ways of writing the same problem. You can use addition and subtraction as opposite operations to solve equations.

To solve the equation $\quad$ n + 43 = 74 $\quad$ or $\quad$ 43 + n = 74
rewrite it as a subtraction $\quad$ n $\quad$ = 74 − 43
problem. Subtract 43 from 74. $\quad$ n = 31

You can check the solution n = 31 by putting 31 into the original equation, in place of n.

$$31 + 43 \stackrel{?}{=} 74$$
$$74 = 74 \ \checkmark$$

To solve the equation $\quad$ a − 6 = 8
rewrite it as an addition $\quad$ a $\quad$ = 8 + 6
problem. Add 6 to 8. $\quad$ a = 14

Properties of Multiplication

Like addition, multiplication is commutative and associative.

1. *The Commutative Property of Multiplication*
   Factors can be multiplied in any order without changing the product.

   $$8 \times 6 = 48 \quad \text{and} \quad 6 \times 8 = 48, \quad \text{so} \quad 8 \times 6 = 6 \times 8$$

2. *The Associative Property of Multiplication*
   Factors can be grouped in any way without changing the product.

   $$(4 \times 5) \times 2 = 40 \quad \text{and} \quad 4 \times (5 \times 2) = 40, \quad \text{so} \quad (4 \times 5) \times 2 = 4 \times (5 \times 2)$$

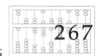
There is another property of multiplication which also involves addition, called the distributive property.

3. *The Distributive Property of Multiplication*
    When a sum is multiplied by a number, for example $5 \times (3 + 7)$,

    (1) you can multiply each addend by the number, and then add the products:
    $$(5 \times 3) + (5 \times 7) = 15 + 35 = 50$$

    (2) or you can add, then multiply: $5 \times (3 + 7) = 5 \times 10 = 50$

    You get the same result either way. So the distributive property tells us that:
    $$5 \times (3 + 7) = (5 \times 3) + (5 \times 7)$$

Learn the names of these three properties and be able to write equations showing what each one means.

Also practice using the distributive property to write the answers to problems in two different ways. For example, you could find what $(12 \times 6) + (13 \times 6)$ equals in two ways:

$(12 \times 6) + (13 \times 6) = 72 + 78 = 150$

$(12 \times 6) + (13 \times 6) = (12 + 13) \times 6 = 25 \times 6 = 150$

You could also find what $26 \times (6 + 9)$ equals in two ways using the distributive property.

$26 \times (6 + 9) = 26 \times 15 = 390$

$26 \times (6 + 9) = (26 \times 6) + (26 \times 9) = 156 + 234 = 390$

Multiplication and Division as Opposite Operations

Multiplication and division are opposite operations. $6 \times 4 = 24$ and $6 = 24 \div 4$ are two different ways of writing the same problem.

You can use multiplication and division as opposite operations to solve equations.

To solve the equation rewrite it as a division problem. Divide 192 by 12.

$a \times 12 = 192$ or $12 \times a = 192$

$a \quad = 192 \div 12$

$a = 16$

Check: $16 \times 12 = 192$?

$192 = 192$ ✔

To solve the equation $\qquad$ $n \div 13 = 12$
rewrite it as a multiplication $\qquad$ $n \qquad = 12 \times 13$
problem. Multiply 12 by 13. $\qquad$ $n = 156$

Billions

After millions, the next period is billions.

10 hundred millions = 1 billion

Billions				Millions				Thousands				Ones		
hundreds	tens	ones	,	hundreds	tens	ones	,	hundreds	tens	ones	,	hundreds	tens	ones
1	5	1	,	8	7	4	,	0	0	0	,	0	0	0

Over the course of one year, the U.S. Government spent $151,874,000,000 more than it received. You read 151,874,000,000: "one hundred fifty-one billion, eight hundred seventy-four million." Learn to read and write numbers in the billions. In digits, twenty billion, four hundred million is written 20,400,000,000. In words, 1,157,000,000 is written one billion, one hundred fifty-seven million.

A billion is a very large number. Counting one number a second, it would take you more than *thirty years* to count to one billion.

Learn to identify the place and value of underlined digits in numbers in the billions. In 31,45<u>7</u>,018,000, the underlined 3 is in the ten billions' place. Its value is 30,000,000,000. The underlined 7 is in the millions' place. Its value is 7,000,000.

Rounding

Remember that to round a number to a certain place, you look at the digit to the right of that place. If the digit to the right is 5 or greater, you round up. If the digit to the right is 4 or less, you round down.

Sometimes rounding a number to a certain place involves changing digits to the left of that place. Round 49,857 to the nearest thousand. 49,857 is between which two thousands? It is between 49 thousand and 50 thousand. The digit to the right of the thousands' place is 8. So you round 49,857 up to 50,000.

A good way to practice rounding (especially in problems like the last one) is to write a double inequality first, showing which two round numbers the number is between.

Round 2,947,024 to the nearest hundred thousand.

Write: $2,900,000 < 2,947,024 < 3,000,000$

2,947,024 to the nearest hundred thousand is 2,900,000.

Multiplying Large Factors

You multiply by a number in the thousands using the same methods you have already learned.

```
            5 6 2 7
          × 4 3 3 8
          4 5 0 1 6  —      8 × 5627
        1 6 8 8 1 0  —     30 × 5627
      1 6 8 8 1 0 0  —    300 × 5627
    2 2 5 0 8 0 0 0  — 4000 × 5627
    2 4,4 0 9,9 2 6
```

Notice that before you multiply by a digit in the thousands' place, you first write **3** zeros in the product. Using these same methods, you can multiply numbers that have even more digits than those in the example.

Sets

A set is a collection of things. The things in a set are called its members. You list the members of a set inside braces like these: { }. For example, here is the set of the first five odd numbers: {1, 3, 5, 7, 9}. Practice listing sets inside braces. For example, list the set of the even numbers between 21 and 29: {22, 24, 26, 28}. List the set of the different letters that are used to write the word Mississippi: {m, i, s, p}.

Decimals—Addition, Subtraction, and Multiplication

Decimal Place Value

ones	.	tenths	hundredths	thousandths	ten-thousandths
0	.	5	6	7	2

Five thousand, six hundred seventy-two ten-thousandths

The places to the right of the decimal point are called decimal places. When a number has four decimal places, you read the decimal places in ten-thousandths. 0.5672 is read: "five thousand, six hundred seventy-two ten-thousandths."

People often read decimals in a shorter way. You can read 0.5672 as "point five six seven two." You can read 18.289 as "eighteen and two hundred eighty-nine thousandths" or "eighteen point two eight nine."

Learn to give the value of each digit in a decimal in digits or in words. In 0.6728 the value of the 6 is 0.6 or six tenths; the value of the seven is 0.07 or seven hundredths; the value of the 2 is 0.002 or two thousandths; the value of the 8 is 0.0008 or eight ten-thousandths.

Decimals on a Number Line

You can show decimals that come between other decimals on a number line or by completing a pattern of numbers.

Here is a number line which shows nine numbers with two decimal places between 2.3 and 2.4.

2.3   2.31   2.32   2.33   2.34   2.35   2.36   2.37   2.38   2.39   2.4

Complete the pattern:

4.73, 4.731, 4.732, _____, _____, _____, _____, _____, _____, _____, 4.74

With this pattern in mind, think about how many numbers with three decimal places you can write between 2.33 and 2.34. Could you write other decimals between those decimals?

Estimating Decimal Sums and Differences

You can use the same methods to check decimal sums and differences that you have learned for checking whole number sums and differences. You can also make a quick check to see if a decimal sum or difference is about right by estimating. To estimate a decimal sum or difference, round each number to its greatest place value, then add or subtract.

To estimate	Round to greatest place value.		To estimate	Round to greatest place value.
9.607 $\longrightarrow$	10		95.27 $\longrightarrow$	100
3.23 $\longrightarrow$	3		$-$ 82.96 $\longrightarrow$	$-$ 80
$+$ 18.76	$+$ 20			20
	33			

One of the things your estimate tells you is whether you have put the decimal point in the right place.

We often estimate sums and differences by rounding all the numbers to the same place value. Suppose you wanted to know about what the difference of 95.27 and 82.96 was in whole numbers. You would round each number to the nearest whole number, then subtract.

Round to the nearest whole number.

$$
\begin{array}{r}
9\,5.2\,7 \longrightarrow \quad 9\,5 \\
-\ 8\,2.9\,6 \longrightarrow -\ 8\,3 \\
\hline
1\,2
\end{array}
$$

Notice that this estimate of 12 is much closer to the actual difference (12.31) than the estimate you got by rounding each number to its greatest place value.

Multiplying Decimals

Multiplying with different units can help you learn how to multiply a decimal and a whole number. If a small package of cookies costs 69¢, how much do 9 packages cost?

You can multiply 69¢ by 9; or you can write 69¢ with a dollar sign and a decimal point and multiply.

$$
\begin{array}{r}
6\,9\ ¢ \\
\times\ 9 \\
\hline
6\,2\,1\ ¢
\end{array}
\qquad
\begin{array}{r}
\$\ 0.6\,9\ \text{—two decimal places} \\
\times\ 9 \\
\hline
\$\ 6.2\,1\ \text{—two decimal places}
\end{array}
$$

621¢ = $6.21. You get the same product either way you multiply.

Notice that there are the same number of decimal places in the product ($6.21) as in the decimal factor ($0.69). Whenever you multiply a decimal by a whole number, the product will have the same number of decimal places as the decimal factor.

Here is another example. Multiply, then place the decimal point in the product.

$$
\begin{array}{r}
7.6\,3\ \text{—two decimal places} \\
\times\ 1\,2 \\
\hline
1\,5\,2\,6 \\
7\,6\,3\,0 \\
\hline
9\,1.5\,6\ \text{—two decimal places}
\end{array}
$$

Multiplying Decimals by 10, 100, 1000

When you multiply any decimal number by 10, you move its decimal point one place to the right. You make the place value of each digit ten times as large.

$$10 \times 2.345 = 23.45 \qquad\qquad 0.026 \times 10 = 0.26$$

Notice that when you are multiplying a whole number by 10, moving the decimal point one place to the right is the same as adding one zero.

$$10 \times 6.0 = 60. \qquad\qquad 10 \times 6 = 60$$

When you multiply a number by 100, you move its decimal point two places to the right. You make the place value of each digit 100 times as large.

$$100 \times 2.345 = 234.5 \qquad\qquad 0.026 \times 100 = 2.6$$

When you multiply a number by 1000, you move its decimal point three places to the right. You make the place value of each digit 1000 times as large.

$$1000 \times 2.345 = 2345 \qquad\qquad 0.026 \times 1000 = 26$$

Practice multiplying many decimal numbers by 10, 100, and 1000, observing how the decimal point moves in each problem.

Also practice doing problems like these, in which you must think what the multiplication has been.

$$\underline{\quad} \times 43.82 = 438.2$$
$$\underline{\quad} \times 0.008 = 8$$
$$100 \times \underline{\quad\quad} = 32.56$$

Estimating Decimal Products

You can estimate the product of a decimal and a whole number, or a decimal and a decimal, by rounding each factor to its greatest place value and multiplying. You can use this estimate to see if you have put the decimal point in the right place in the product.

Estimate to check: Round and multiply.

```
    7.6 3  ───────────────►      8
 ×    1 2  ───────────────►   × 1 0
    1 5 2 6                     8 0  ✔
    7 6 3 0
    9 1.5 6
```

80 is close to 91.56, so you know you have put the decimal point in the right place. The product is *not* 9.156 or 915.6.

Multiplying a Decimal by a Decimal

When you multiply a decimal by a decimal, the product has the same number of decimal places as the number of decimal places in the factors added together. Here are two examples. Multiply without worrying about the place values. Then place the decimal point in the product.

```
    4 9.6 — 1 decimal place          3.8 6 7 — 3 decimal places
  ×   3.8 — +1 decimal place        ×   8.2 — +1 decimal place
    3 9 6 8                           7 7 3 4
  1 4 8 8 0                         3 0 9 3 6 0
  1 8 8.4 8 — 2 decimal places      3 1.7 0 9 4 — 4 decimal places
```

Estimate to make sure the decimal point is in the right place.

50 × 4 = 200   4 × 8 = 32
188.48 is close to 200. ✔   31.7094 is close to 32. ✔

Sometimes when you multiply two decimals you need to add zeros to the product so that it has the right place value.

```
      0.0 3 — 2 decimal places
    × 0.0 2 — 2 decimal places
    0.0 0 0 6 — 4 decimal places
```

There should be four decimal places in the product, so you write three zeros to the left of the 6, and then the decimal point.

Checking Decimal Products

You can check decimal products by changing the order of the factors. Remember that multiplication is commutative.

```
      To check:                    Multiply.
          4 9.6                          3.8
        ×   3.8                      × 4 9.6
          3 9 6 8                        2 2 8
        1 4 8 8 0                       3 4 2 0
        1 8 8.4 8                     1 5 2 0 0
                                      1 8 8.4 8 ✔
```

Checking in this way lets you know if you have gotten the digits right, while checking by estimation lets you know if you have gotten the place values right. It can be useful to check a problem in both ways.

Practice multiplying decimals by whole numbers and decimals by decimals. Check each product by estimation or by changing the order of the factors.

Division
Writing a Division Problem in Three Ways

Remember that you can write a division problem in three ways. 28 divided by 7 can be written:

$$28 \div 7 \qquad 7\overline{)2\,8} \qquad \frac{28}{7}$$

All three ways mean the same thing.

Divisibility

We say that a number is divisible by another number if it can be divided by that number without leaving a remainder. For example, 30 is divisible by 2, because $30 \div 2 = 15$. 30 is not divisible by 7, because $30 \div 7$ equals 4 with a remainder of 2.

Rules for Divisibility

To find out if one number is divisible by another, you can always divide and see if the quotient has a remainder or not. There are also rules which can tell you *without dividing* whether a number is divisible by certain numbers.

Rules for divisibility:
                   A whole number is divisible

1. By 2, if it is an even number.
2. By 5, if it has a 0 or 5 in the ones' place.
3. By 10, if it has a 0 in the ones' place.
4. By 3, if the sum of its digits is divisible by 3.
5. By 9, if the sum of its digits is divisible by 9.

Examples:

32	Divisible by 2?	32 is an even number,	yes
265	Divisible by 5?	There's a 5 in the ones' place,	yes
242	Divisible by 10?	There's a 2 in the ones' place,	no
242	Divisible by 3?	The sum of the digits $(2+4+2)$ is 8, and 8 is not divisible by 3,	no
189	Divisible by 9?	The sum of the digits $(1+8+9)$ is 18; 18 is divisible by 9,	yes

Practice using these rules for divisibility to decide quickly whether a number is divisible by 2, 5, 10, 3, or 9.

Short Division

When the divisor is a one-digit number, you can use a shorter form of division, known as short division. Divide, multiply, and subtract in your head. Write the remainder, if there is one, in front of the next place, and continue dividing. For example, to divide 6258 by 8, you go through the following steps:

1. Divide the 62 hundreds.
Think: 8 into 62 goes 7 times.
62 − 56 = 6. Write the
6 hundreds next to the 5 tens.

$$7$$
$$8 \overline{)6\ 2_65\ 8}$$

2. Divide the 65 tens.
8 into 65 goes 8 times.
65 − 64 = 1. Write the one
tens next to the eight ones.

$$7\ 8$$
$$8 \overline{)6\ 2_65_18}$$

3. Divide the 18 ones.

$$7\ 8\ 2\quad R2$$
$$8 \overline{)6\ 2_65_18}$$

Practice using short division to do division problems with one-digit divisors.

Two-Digit Divisors

If you read Book Four of this series, you learned how to divide by a two-digit divisor. Now you can practice dividing larger numbers by two-digit divisors. Before you begin to divide, always figure out first how many digits the quotient will have.
Find the quotient of 227,180 divided by 74.

First think $74 \overline{)2}$—no, not enough hundred thousands to divide. $74 \overline{)2\ 2}$—no, not enough ten thousands to divide. $74 \overline{)2\ 2\ 7}$—yes, there are enough thousands to divide. The first digit of the quotient goes in the thousands' place. The quotient will have four digits.

1. Divide 227 thousands.

$$3$$
$$74 \overline{)2\ 2\ 7,1\ 9\ 4}$$
$$\underline{-2\ 2\ 2}$$
$$5\ 1$$

51 < 74
The remainder is less
than the divisor, so ✔

2. Bring down the 1 hundreds. You cannot divide 51 hundreds by 74. Write 0 in the hundreds' place.

$$3\ 0$$
$$74 \overline{)2\ 2\ 7,1\ 9\ 4}$$
$$\underline{-2\ 2\ 2}$$
$$5\ 1$$

3. Bring down the 9 tens.
   Divide 519 tens.

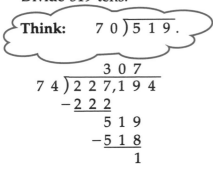

Think: 7 0)5 1 9 .

```
              3 0 7
   7 4 )2 2 7,1 9 4
      -2 2 2
          5 1 9
         -5 1 8
              1
```

1 < 74 ✔

4. Bring down the 4 ones. You cannot divide 14 ones by 74. Write 0 in the ones' place.

```
                 3 0 7 0 R14
      7 4 )2 2 7,1 9 4
         -2 2 2
             5 1 9
            -5 1 8
                 1 4
```

14 < 74 ✔

At each step in the division, check to make sure the remainder is less than the divisor. If it is not, you need to increase the quotient. You were dividing by 74 in the last problem so 73 is the greatest remainder you could have had. Why?

Check each division problem by multiplying the divisor and the quotient, and adding the remainder.

```
Check:          3 0 7 0
                  × 7 4
              1 2 2 8 0
            2 1 4 9 0 0
            2 2 7,1 8 0
        +         1 4
            2 2 7,1 9 4 ✔
```

You can write your answer in the same form as the check; as a multiplication and an addition, followed by an inequality.

$$227,194 = (74 \times 3070) + 14 \qquad 14 < 74$$

You can also do a quick mental check of your answer by estimating the quotient.
To estimate the quotient of $74)\overline{2 2 7,1 9 4}$, round the divisor (74) to the greatest place value. Then round the dividend to a number that makes it easy to divide.
You can divide 210,000 by 70 easily.

```
             3,0 0 0
   7 0 )2 1 0,0 0 0
```

$74)\overline{2 2 7,1 9 4}$ is about 3000.

Three-Digit Divisors

Practice doing long division problems with three-digit divisors. (1) First figure out how many digits the quotient will have; (2) then round the divisor to the nearest hundred to estimate each digit of the quotient.

1. Divide 163,220 by 321.

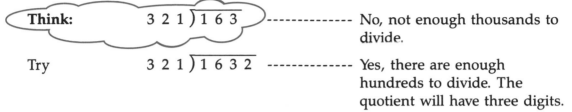

Think: 3 2 1) 1 6 3   ------------- No, not enough thousands to divide.

Try   3 2 1) 1 6 3 2   ------------- Yes, there are enough hundreds to divide. The quotient will have three digits.

2. Divide 1630 hundreds.

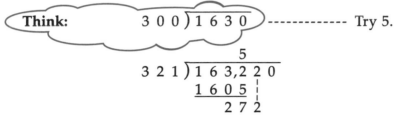

Think: 3 0 0) 1 6 3 0   ------------- Try 5.

```
            5
 3 2 1 ) 1 6 3,2 2 0
         1 6 0 5
             2 7 2
```

You cannot divide 272 tens by 321. Write 0 in the tens' place and divide 2720 ones.

Think: 3 0 0) 2 7 2 0   ------------- Try 9.

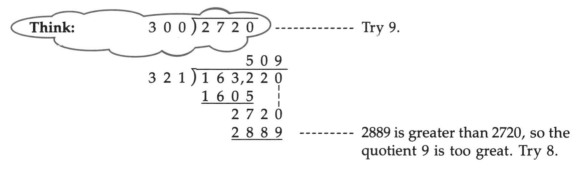

```
            5 0 9
 3 2 1 ) 1 6 3,2 2 0
         1 6 0 5
             2 7 2 0
             2 8 8 9     -------- 2889 is greater than 2720, so the
                                  quotient 9 is too great. Try 8.
```

```
            5 0 8
 3 2 1 ) 1 6 3,2 2 0
         1 6 0 5
             2 7 2 0
             2 5 6 8
               1 5 2
```

152 < 321

Check:
$$
\begin{array}{r}
5\ 0\ 8 \\
\times\ 3\ 2\ 1 \\
\hline
5\ 0\ 8 \\
1\ 0\ 1\ 6\ 0 \\
+\ 1\ 5\ 2\ 4\ 0\ 0 \\
\hline
1\ 6\ 3\ 0\ 6\ 8 \\
+\ \ \ \ \ \ \ \ \ \ 1\ 5\ 2 \\
\hline
1\ 6\ 3{,}2\ 2\ 0 \quad ✔
\end{array}
$$

In this problem, because $300\,\overline{)2720}$ is just barely 9, and you rounded 321 *down* to 300, you might have guessed that 9 was too large a quotient. When making your estimated quotients, always think about whether you rounded the divisor up or down. The more you do long division, the better you will get at estimating quotients.

Decimal Division

Dividing Decimals by Whole Numbers

You divide decimals by whole numbers the same way you divide whole numbers by whole numbers. You put the decimal point in the quotient above the decimal point in the dividend.

$$
\begin{array}{r}
3.1\ 4 \\
6\,\overline{)1\ 8↑8\ 4} \\
-1\ 8 \\
\hline
8 \\
-6 \\
\hline
2\ 4 \\
-2\ 4 \\
\hline
0
\end{array}
$$

You can estimate the quotient by rounding the dividend to a number that is easy to divide.

$$
\begin{array}{r}
3 \\
6\,\overline{)1\ 8}
\end{array}
$$
✔
The quotient is about 3, which is close to 3.14. So you know that you have put the decimal point in the right place.

Sometimes you need to put zeros in the quotient, so that it has the right place value.

$$
\begin{array}{r}
0.0\ 3 \\
3\ 2\,\overline{)0.9\ 6} \\
-9\ 6 \\
\hline
0
\end{array}
$$

You can't divide 9 tenths by 32 (32 $\overline{)0.9}$ —no); you *can* divide 96 hundredths by 32 (32 $\overline{)0.9\,6}$). Write a zero in the tenths' place to show that the quotient is 3 *hundredths*.

Writing Zeros in the Dividend

When you divide a decimal, you do not usually write a remainder. You continue to divide, adding zeros after the last place of the decimal.

Divide 505.8 by 12. Since 505.8 = 505.80 = 505.800, you can add as many zeros after the last place of the dividend as you need in order to complete the division.

1. Divide 50 tens, 25 ones, and 18 tenths.

```
          4 2.1
1 2 ) 5 0 5.8
    - 4 8
        2 5
      - 2 4
          1 8
        - 1 2
            6
```

2. You are left with 6 tenths (0.6). Add a zero to the dividend and divide 60 hundredths (0.60).

```
            4 2.1 5
1 2 ) 5 0 5.8 0
    - 4 8
        2 5
      - 2 4
          1 8
        - 1 2
            6 0
          - 6 0
              0
```

When you get a remainder of zero, the division is complete. When the remainder is zero, it is easy to check the division of a decimal. Multiply the quotient by the divisor to check.

```
      4 2.1 5
    ×   1 2
    8 4 3 0
  4 2 1 5 0
  5 0 5.8 0  ✔
```

Dividing Whole Numbers Without Remainders

Instead of writing a remainder, you can continue to divide whole numbers in the same way. Divide 340 by 16. Remember that 340 = 340.0 = 340.00.

1.
$$16 \overline{)340} = 21$$
$$-32$$
$$20$$
$$-16$$
$$4$$

2. Continue to divide.
340 = 340.0 = 340.00
Divide 40 tenths,
then 80 hundredths.

$$16 \overline{)340.00} = 21.25$$
$$-32$$
$$20$$
$$-16$$
$$40$$
$$-32$$
$$80$$
$$-80$$
$$0$$

3. Check:

$$\begin{array}{r} 21.25 \\ \times\ 16 \\ \hline 12750 \\ 21250 \\ \hline 340.00 \end{array} ✔$$

In fourth-grade mathematics, you would have written the answer to $16 \overline{)340}$ as 21 R4. Or you could have written the quotient as the mixed number 21 $4 \overline{)16}$ = 21 $\frac{1}{4}$. Now you know how to write the quotient in a third way, as a decimal: 340 ÷ 16 = 21.25.

Dividing by 10, 100, 1000

When you divide a number by 10, you simply move its decimal point one place to the left. You make the place value of each digit 10 times smaller.

$$693.8 ÷ 10 = 69.38 \qquad 5.4 ÷ 10 = 0.54$$

When you divide a number by 100, you move its decimal point two places to the left. You make the place value of each digit 100 times smaller.

$$693.8 ÷ 100 = 6.938 \qquad 5.4 ÷ 100 = 0.054$$

When you divide a number by 1000, you move its decimal point three places to the left. You make the place value of each digit 1000 times smaller.

$$693.8 ÷ 1000 = 0.6938 \qquad 5.4 ÷ 1000 = 0.0054$$

Practice multiplying a decimal by 10, 100, 1000, then dividing the same number by 10, 100, 1000, until you can move the decimal point and change the place values easily.

Also practice thinking what the divisor or dividend must have been in problems like these:

$$26.2 \div \underline{\quad} = 2.62$$

$$\underline{\quad} \div 1000 = 0.084$$

$$670 \div \underline{\quad} = 0.67$$

Rounding Decimal Quotients

Even when you continue to add zeros to the dividend, not all divisions finish exactly. In these division problems, you can round the quotient to a certain place. Sometimes you also round the quotient in problems where the division works out exactly. To round a quotient, divide to one place *beyond* the place to which you are rounding.

Find the quotient of 285 divided by 23, to the nearest tenth. Since you are asked for the nearest tenth, divide until you get a quotient with hundredths, and then round.

```
          1 2.3 9
  2 3 ) 2 8 5.0 0
       - 2 3
         5 5
        -4 6
          9 0
         -6 9
          2 1 0
         -2 0 7
              3
```
12.39 rounds to 12.4.
The quotient of 285 ÷ 23 to the nearest tenth is 12.4.

If you'd been asked for a quotient to the nearest hundredth, you would have continued to divide until you had a quotient with thousandths.

```
          1 2.3 9 1
  2 3 ) 2 8 5.0 0 0
       -  2 3
          5 5
        -4 6
          9 0
         -6 9
          2 1 0
         -2 0 7
              3 0
             -2 3
                7
```
12.391 rounds to 12.39. The quotient of 285 ÷ 23 to the nearest hundredth is 12.39.

Often you round quotients because you want to give an answer to the nearest whole unit. Suppose that 4 liters of oil weigh 2850 g. How much does 1 liter of oil weigh, to the nearest gram? Divide to the tenths of grams, then round.

```
          7 1 2.5
   4 ) 2 8 5 0.0
     - 2 8
         0 5
       -   4
         1 0
         - 8
           2 0
         - 2 0
             0
```

712.5 rounds to 713.
To the nearest gram,
1 liter of oil weighs 713 g.

Checking Divisions Which Are Not Exact

Remember that to check a division with a remainder, you multiply the quotient by the divisor and add the remainder. When the quotient is a decimal number, you need to compare the dividend and the remainder carefully to find the place value of the remainder.

To check:

```
             1 2.3
   2 3 ) 2 8 5.0
       - 2 3
           5 5
         - 4 6
             9 0
           - 6 9
             2 1
```

Multiply and add the remainder.

```
           1 2.3
        ×    2 3
           3 6 9
         2 4 6 0
         2 8 2.9
     +       2.1
         2 8 5.0   ✔
```

The remainder is 2.1.

Since you can continue to divide 285 by 23 forever without getting an exact answer, you can divide to as many decimal places as you like. Then you can check by multiplying the quotient by the divisor and adding the remainder. The greater the number of decimal places in the quotient, the smaller the remainder as you can see here:

```
       1 2.3 9           Check:
2 3 ) 2 8 5.0 0          1 2.3 9
    - 2 3                ×   2 3
      5 5                3 7 1 7
    - 4 6              2 4 7 8 0
      9 0              2 8 4.9 7
    - 6 9            +     0.0 3
      2 1 0          2 8 5.0 0  ✔
    - 2 0 7
        3
```
The remainder is 0.03.

```
       1 2.3 9 1           Check:
2 3 ) 2 8 5.0 0 0          1 2.3 9 1
    - 2 3                  ×     2 3
      5 5                  3 7 1 7 3
    - 4 6                2 4 7 8 2 0
      9 0                2 8 4.9 9 3
    - 6 9              +     0.0 0 7
      2 1 0            2 8 5.0 0 0  ✔
    - 2 0 7
        3 0
      - 2 3
          7
```
The remainder is 0.007.

Practice writing, as a multiplication and an addition, answers to division problems that do not divide evenly.

$$285 = (23 \times 12.3) + 2.1$$
$$285 = (23 \times 12.39) + 0.03$$
$$285 = (23 \times 12.391) + 0.007$$

Notice how the answer looks different, depending on how many places you divide to. Remember the more decimal places you find in the quotient, the smaller the remainder will be.

Get a lot of practice dividing decimals and whole numbers by whole numbers. Finish divisions that are exact by continuing to divide. When the division is not exact, divide to a certain place value. Always check each division by multiplying the quotient by the divisor and adding the remainder, if there is one.

Fractions

Greatest Common Factor

The factors of 12 are 1, 2, 3, 4, 6, 12. These whole numbers divide 12 without leaving a remainder. The factors of 16 are 1, 2, 4, 8, 16. The common factors of 12 and 16 are 1, 2, and 4. The *greatest* common factor of 12 and 16 is 4. The term *greatest common factor* is often abbreviated GCF. Notice that the abbreviation is made up of the first letters of the words "greatest common factor."

Equivalent Fractions

Fractions that name the same amount are said to be equivalent. When you multiply or divide both the numerator and the denominator of a fraction by the same number, you make an equivalent fraction. Here are two examples.

$$\frac{1 \times 4}{2 \times 4} = \frac{4}{8} \qquad \frac{1}{2} = \frac{4}{8} \qquad \frac{18 \div 6}{30 \div 6} = \frac{3}{5} \qquad \frac{18}{30} = \frac{3}{5}$$

Practice solving equations like these, so that the fractions are equivalent.

$$\frac{5}{10} = \frac{n}{20} \quad \textbf{Think:} \quad \overset{\times 2}{\frac{5}{10} = \frac{10}{20}}_{\div 2} \quad \text{so} \quad n = 10 \qquad \frac{18}{24} = \frac{6}{n} \quad \textbf{Think:} \quad \overset{\div 3}{\frac{18}{24} = \frac{6}{8}}_{\times 3} \quad \text{so} \quad n = 8$$

Lowest Terms

The numerator and denominator are called the terms of a fraction. A fraction is in lowest terms when its numerator and denominator have no common factor greater than 1. You can write an equivalent fraction in lowest terms by dividing both the numerator and denominator of a fraction by their GCF.

Put $\frac{12}{16}$ in lowest terms. The GCF of 12 and 16 is 4.

$$\frac{12 \div 4}{16 \div 4} = \frac{3}{4} \qquad \frac{3}{4} \text{ is in lowest terms.}$$

Putting a fraction in lowest terms is also called putting it in simplest form. Because you divide to put a fraction in lowest terms, people often say you *reduce* a fraction to its lowest terms.

Least Common Multiple

Remember that 3, 6, 9, 12, 15, . . . are multiples of 3, because you can multiply 3 and a whole number to get them. 2, 4, 6, 8, 10, 12, . . . are multiples of 2. Two common multiples of 2 and 3 are 6 and 12. The least common multiple of 2 and 3 is 6. *Least common multiple* is abbreviated LCM.

Comparing Fractions

You can compare two fractions that have the same denominator by comparing the numerators.

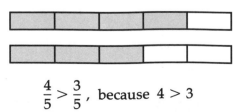

$$\frac{4}{5} > \frac{3}{5}, \text{ because } 4 > 3$$

To compare fractions with different denominators, you first give them a common denominator—you make their denominators the same. Once their denominators are the same, you can compare them easily. To give fractions a common denominator, first find the LCM of the two denominators; then write the fractions as equivalent fractions that have this LCM for a denominator.

For example, to compare $\frac{2}{3}$ and $\frac{3}{5}$, first find the LCM of the denominators 3 and 5. The LCM is 15. Write both $\frac{2}{3}$ and $\frac{3}{5}$ as equivalent fractions with a denominator of 15.

$$\frac{2 \times 5}{3 \times 5} = \frac{10}{15} \qquad \frac{3 \times 3}{5 \times 3} = \frac{9}{15}$$

Now compare the fractions. Since $\frac{10}{15} > \frac{9}{15}$, $\frac{2}{3} > \frac{3}{5}$

You can find many common denominators for fractions. Any common multiple of the denominators can be used as a common denominator for fractions. For example, you can also write $\frac{2}{3}$ and $\frac{3}{5}$ with a common denominator of 30, since 30 is a common multiple of 3 and 5.

When you use the LCM to find a common denominator of fractions, you find their least common denominator. The term *least common denominator* is abbreviated LCD. Learn to compare fractions by writing them with their LCD.

Comparing Fractions on a Number Line

Seeing fractions on a number line can help you to compare them. Here are number lines divided into twelfths, sixths, fourths, thirds, and halves.

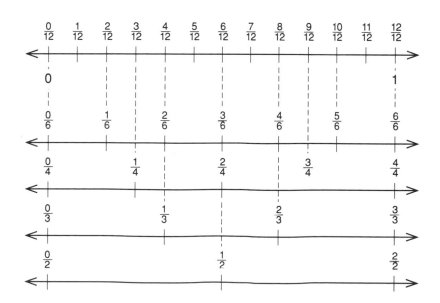

You can see from these number lines that $\frac{2}{3} < \frac{3}{4}$ and that $\frac{3}{6} = \frac{1}{2}$. Practice drawing a number line divided into twelfths in which you also write each fraction in lowest terms.

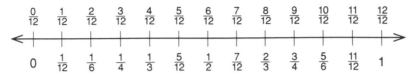

Also practice drawing a number line like this one, divided into eighths or sixteenths. These number lines will help you to get a good sense of which fractions are greater, which are less, and which are equivalent.

Notice that a fraction where the numerator is very small compared to the denominator is close to zero. $\frac{1}{12}$ is close to zero. When the numerator is about half of the denominator, the fraction is about $\frac{1}{2}$. $\frac{5}{12}$ and $\frac{7}{12}$ are both close to $\frac{1}{2}$. When the difference between the numerator and the denominator is small, the fraction is close to 1. $\frac{11}{12}$ is close to 1. Practice estimating whether fractions are close to 0, $\frac{1}{2}$, or 1.

Adding Fractions

You add fractions with the same denominator by adding the numerators. You write each sum in lowest terms.

$$\frac{2}{3} + \frac{2}{3} = \frac{4}{3} = 1\frac{1}{3} \qquad\qquad \frac{3}{16} + \frac{3}{16} = \frac{6}{16} = \frac{3}{8}$$

To add fractions with different denominators, you must first write them with a common denominator. Then you can add. You cannot add fractions when their denominators are different, because you would be adding parts of different sizes.

$$\frac{3}{4} \qquad + \qquad \frac{1}{5} \qquad = \ ?$$

You can't add these fractions because their denominators are different.

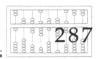
To add, first write $\frac{3}{4}$ and $\frac{1}{5}$ as equivalent fractions with a common denominator. Use the LCM of 4 and 5 to find the LCD. The LCD of $\frac{3}{4}$ and $\frac{1}{5}$ is 20.

$$\frac{3 \times 5}{4 \times 5} = \frac{15}{20} \qquad \frac{1 \times 4}{5 \times 4} = \frac{4}{20}$$

$$\frac{3}{4} + \frac{1}{5} = \qquad \frac{15}{20} \qquad + \qquad \frac{4}{20} \qquad = \qquad \frac{19}{20}$$

Always write a fraction sum as a mixed number or fraction in lowest terms. Sometimes you have to find the LCD of three or more fractions to add them.

The LCD of $\frac{4}{7}$ and $\frac{2}{21}$ is 21.

$$\frac{4}{7} = \frac{12}{21}$$
$$+\frac{2}{21} = +\frac{2}{21}$$
$$\overline{\frac{14}{21}} = \frac{2}{3}$$

The LCD of $\frac{5}{6}$, $\frac{1}{3}$, and $\frac{5}{8}$ is 24.

$$\frac{5}{6} + \frac{1}{3} + \frac{5}{8} = \frac{20}{24} + \frac{8}{24} + \frac{15}{24} = \frac{43}{24} = 1\frac{19}{24}$$

You can write a fraction addition vertically, as on the left, or horizontally, as on the right. Get a lot of practice adding two or more fractions with different denominators.

Subtracting Fractions

You subtract fractions with the same denominator by subtracting the numerators. You write each difference in lowest terms.

$$\frac{7}{8} - \frac{3}{8} = \frac{4}{8} = \frac{1}{2}$$

To subtract fractions with different denominators, you must first write them with a common denominator. You cannot subtract parts that are of a different size. For example, you cannot take $\frac{1}{4}$ from $\frac{3}{5}$, until you make the parts in the two fractions the same size. To find $\frac{3}{5} - \frac{1}{4}$, write $\frac{3}{5}$ and $\frac{1}{4}$ with their LCD, then subtract. The LCD of $\frac{3}{5}$ and $\frac{1}{4}$ is 20.

$$\frac{3}{5} - \frac{1}{4} = \frac{3 \times 4}{5 \times 4} - \frac{1 \times 5}{4 \times 5} = \frac{12}{20} - \frac{5}{20} = \frac{7}{20}$$

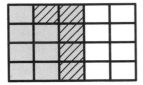

This block is made of 20 boxes. $\frac{3}{5}$ or $\frac{12}{20}$ are orange. If you take away $\frac{1}{4}$ or $\frac{5}{20}$ of these, you have $\frac{7}{20}$ left.

Now try $\frac{5}{6} - \frac{4}{9}$. The LCD of $\frac{5}{6}$ and $\frac{4}{9}$ is 36. (Make sure to write each difference in lowest terms.)

$$\frac{5}{6} = \frac{30}{36}$$

$$-\frac{4}{9} = -\frac{16}{36}$$

$$\frac{14}{36} = \frac{7}{18}$$

You can use any common denominator when you add or subtract fractions with different denominators, but using the LCD as the common denominator will make your work quicker and easier. Get a lot of practice subtracting fractions with different denominators.

Mixed Numbers and Fractions

You can round mixed numbers to the nearest whole number. If the fractional part of a mixed number is less than $\frac{1}{2}$, round the mixed number down. If the fractional part is $\frac{1}{2}$ or greater, round the mixed number up. A fraction equals $\frac{1}{2}$ if its numerator is half its denominator.

Round to the nearest whole number.

$6\frac{2}{7}$ 2 is less than half of 7, so $\frac{2}{7} < \frac{1}{2}$.
$6\frac{2}{7}$ rounds down to 6.

$7\frac{11}{19}$ 11 is more than half of 19, so $\frac{11}{19} > \frac{1}{2}$.
$7\frac{11}{19}$ rounds up to 8.

$5\frac{7}{14}$ 7 is half of 14, so $\frac{7}{14} = \frac{1}{2}$.
$5\frac{7}{14}$ rounds up to 6.

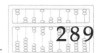
Decimals, Mixed Numbers, and Fractions

You know how to write decimals as fractions or mixed numbers. Here are two examples.

$$0.067 = \frac{67}{1000} \qquad 8.24 = 8\frac{24}{100}$$

You can also write fractions as decimals. There are two ways you can do this. You can write a fraction as an equivalent fraction with a denominator of 10, or 100, or 1000, etc. Then write this equivalent fraction as a decimal. For example, to write $\frac{2}{5}$ as a decimal, write $\frac{2}{5}$ with a denominator of 10.

$$\frac{2}{5} = \frac{2 \times 2}{5 \times 2} = \frac{4}{10} = 0.4 \qquad \text{Another example: } \frac{17}{25} = \frac{68}{100} = 0.68$$

You can use this method only when the denominator is a factor of 10, or 100, or 1000, etc.

You can also remember that the fraction bar is the same as the division sign. To write $\frac{1}{8}$ as a decimal, do the division problem $8\overline{)1}$ until the division finishes.

$$
\begin{array}{r}
0.1\ 2\ 5 \\
8\overline{)1.0\ 0\ 0} \\
-8 \\
\hline
2\ 0 \\
-1\ 6 \\
\hline
4\ 0 \\
-4\ 0 \\
\hline
0
\end{array}
$$

So $\frac{1}{8} = 0.125$

Check:
$$
\begin{array}{r}
0.1\ 2\ 5 \\
\times\ \ 8 \\
\hline
1.0\ 0\ 0 \ \checkmark
\end{array}
$$

For many fractions, this division goes on and on, and the quotient is never exact. These fractions cannot be written as decimals exactly.

Write $\frac{1}{3}$ as a decimal to the nearest hundredth.

$$
\begin{array}{r}
0.3\ 3\ 3 \\
3\overline{)1.0\ 0\ 0} \\
-9 \\
\hline
1\ 0 \\
-9 \\
\hline
1\ 0 \\
-9 \\
\hline
1
\end{array}
$$

Check:
$$
\begin{array}{r}
0.3\ 3\ 3 \\
\times\ \ 3 \\
\hline
0.9\ 9\ 9 \\
+0.0\ 0\ 1 \\
\hline
1.0\ 0\ 0 \ \checkmark
\end{array}
$$

0.333 rounds to 0.33.
$\frac{1}{3}$ to the nearest hundredth is 0.33.

Notice how this division will continue to give a 3 in each decimal place, as long as you divide. When you discover a pattern like this, you can predict the next digit or digits in the quotient without dividing.

To write a mixed number as a decimal, change the fractional part to a decimal. The whole number part remains unchanged.

Write $4\frac{4}{11}$ as a decimal to the nearest thousandth. The whole number 4 remains unchanged. Write $\frac{4}{11}$ as a decimal to the nearest thousandth.

$$
\begin{array}{r}
0.3\ 6\ 3\ 6 \\
11\overline{)4.0\ 0\ 0\ 0} \\
-3\ 3 \\
\hline
7\ 0 \\
-6\ 6 \\
\hline
4\ 0 \\
-3\ 3 \\
\hline
7\ 0 \\
-6\ 6 \\
\hline
4
\end{array}
$$

Notice the pattern. If you were to continue to divide, can you predict what the next two digits of the quotient would be?

0.3636 rounds to 0.364. To the nearest thousandth, $4\frac{4}{11}$ is 4.364.
Practice writing fractions and mixed numbers as decimals.

Adding Mixed Numbers

To add mixed numbers with the same denominators, first add the fractional parts, then add the whole number parts.

Add the fractions.

$$
\begin{array}{r}
12\frac{1}{7} \\
+\ \ 5\frac{3}{7} \\
\hline
\frac{4}{7}
\end{array}
$$

Add the whole numbers.

$$
\begin{array}{r}
12\frac{1}{7} \\
+\ \ 5\frac{3}{7} \\
\hline
17\frac{4}{7}
\end{array}
$$

When the denominators of the fractional parts are different, write the fractions with their LCD, then add. Sometimes you will get an improper fraction in the sum. Always *convert* your answer to a mixed number in lowest terms.

The LCD of $\frac{2}{3}$, $\frac{1}{2}$, and $\frac{1}{6}$ is 6.

$$2 \frac{2}{3} = 2 \frac{4}{6}$$

$$3 \frac{1}{2} = 3 \frac{3}{6}$$

$$+ 6 \frac{1}{6} = + 6 \frac{1}{6}$$

$$11 \frac{8}{6} = 11 + 1 \frac{2}{6} = 12 \frac{2}{6} = 12 \frac{1}{3}$$

Remember that to convert the improper fraction $\frac{8}{6}$ to a mixed number, you do the division:

$$6 \overline{)8} \quad 1 \frac{2}{6} \qquad \text{So} \quad \frac{8}{6} = 1 \frac{2}{6}$$

You can also remember that $\frac{6}{6} = 1$, so $\frac{8}{6} = \frac{6}{6} + \frac{2}{6} = 1 \frac{2}{6}$.

Subtracting Mixed Numbers

To subtract mixed numbers, the fractional parts must have a common denominator. Here are two examples.

1. In this example the denominators are the same. First subtract the fractions. Then subtract the whole numbers.

2. In this example, the denominators are different. Write the fractions with their LCD.

Subtract the fractions, then the whole numbers

$$5 \frac{2}{3}$$
$$- 2 \frac{1}{3}$$
$$\overline{\frac{1}{3}}$$

$$5 \frac{2}{3}$$
$$- 2 \frac{1}{3}$$
$$\overline{3 \frac{1}{3}}$$

$$5 \frac{5}{6} = 5 \frac{10}{12}$$
$$- 2 \frac{3}{4} = - 2 \frac{9}{12}$$
$$\overline{\phantom{-2\frac{9}{12}}\frac{1}{12}}$$

Always remember to write the difference in lowest terms.

Sometimes when you subtract mixed numbers, the fractional part you are subtracting from is too small. Then you need to regroup the number you are subtracting from: you regroup by adding one of the wholes to the fractional part. For example, here is how you subtract a mixed number from a whole number.

You can't take $\frac{3}{16}$ from 0.

$$5$$
$$-\ 2\frac{3}{16}$$

But you can regroup 1 whole as $\frac{16}{16}$, so that there are sixteenths to subtract.

$$5 = 4\frac{16}{16}$$
$$-\ 2\frac{3}{16} = -2\frac{3}{16}$$
$$\overline{2\frac{13}{16}}$$

When the fractions have different denominators, write the fractions with their LCD *first*, before you regroup, if you need to. In the problem $5\frac{3}{16} - 2\frac{11}{12}$, the LCD is 48. Write the fractions with a common denominator.

$$5\frac{3}{16} = 5\frac{9}{48}$$
$$-\ 2\frac{11}{12} = -\ 2\frac{44}{48}$$

To subtract, you need to regroup $5\frac{9}{48}$. Add a whole to the fractional part.

$$5\frac{9}{48} = 4\frac{57}{48}$$
$$-\ 2\frac{44}{48} = -\ 2\frac{44}{48}$$
$$\overline{2\frac{13}{48}}$$

Since you will not always need to regroup, write the fractions with their LCD first.

Multiplying Fractions and Whole Numbers

You can think of multiplying a fraction and a whole number in two ways. Remember that multiplication can be repeated addition. So,

$$6 \times \frac{2}{3} = \frac{2}{3} + \frac{2}{3} + \frac{2}{3} + \frac{2}{3} + \frac{2}{3} + \frac{2}{3} = \frac{12}{3} = 4$$

You can think of $6 \times \frac{2}{3}$ as adding $\frac{2}{3}$ six times. Or you can think of taking part of the whole number.

$$\frac{2}{3} \times 6 = \frac{2}{3} \textbf{ of } 6$$

The word **of** means the same thing here as the multiplication sign.

To find $\frac{2}{3}$ of 6, divide 6 into 3 parts, then take 2 of them.

Divide 6 into 3 parts:

$$6 \div 3 = 2$$

Now take 2 of the 3 parts.

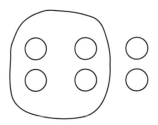

$2 \times 2 = 4$. So $\frac{2}{3}$ of 6 is 4.

Notice that $\frac{2}{3} \times 6 = 4 = 6 \times \frac{2}{3}$. Multiplication is commutative and you will get the same answer whether you think of adding a fraction over and over again or taking part of a whole number.

You can use the following method to multiply a fraction and a whole number. Multiply the whole number and the numerator of the fraction, and write the product over the denominator. Write the product in lowest terms.

$$6 \times \frac{2}{3} = \frac{6 \times 2}{3} = \frac{12}{3} = 4$$

Practice multiplying fractions and whole numbers in this way. Also practice writing a problem like $7 \times \frac{5}{6}$ as repeated addition.

$$7 \times \frac{5}{6} = \frac{5}{6} + \frac{5}{6} + \frac{5}{6} + \frac{5}{6} + \frac{5}{6} + \frac{5}{6} + \frac{5}{6}$$

Practice solving a problem like finding $\frac{3}{7}$ of 56 in two ways. Remember that $\frac{3}{7}$ **of** $56 = \frac{3}{7} \times 56$.

1. Multiply: $\frac{3}{7} \times 56 = \frac{3 \times 56}{7} = \frac{168}{7} = 24$

2. Or to find $\frac{3}{7}$ of 56, divide 56 into 7 equal parts. $56 \div 7 = 8$.

   Now take 3 of the equal parts. $8 \times 3 = 24$.

   $\frac{3}{7}$ of $56 = 24$.

Notice that in the first method, you multiply, then divide. In the second method, you divide, then multiply. You get the same answer either way.

Measurement

Using Metric Units

Here is a table of equivalences among the metric units. Memorize these equivalences if you haven't already.

Length	Mass (and Weight)	Capacity
1 cm (centimeter) = 10 mm (millimeters)	1 cg (centigram) = 10 mg (milligrams)	1 cl (centiliter) = 10 ml 1 dl (deciliter) = 10 cl
1 dm (decimeter) = 10 cm	1 dg (decigram) = 10 cg	1 l = 100 cl
1 m (meter) = 100 cm	1 g = 100 cg	1 l = 10 dl
1 m = 10 dm	1 g = 10 dg	1 l (liter) = 1000 ml (milliliters)
1 km (kilometer) = 1000 m	1 kg (kilogram) = 1000 g (grams)	

Learn this new unit of length, the decimeter. A decimeter is one tenth of a meter. It is also 10 centimeters.

Try to get an approximate sense of the size of each of these metric units. For example, you measure the distance between cities in kilometers—it is about 350 kilometers between New York and Boston. Liquids are sometimes sold in stores by the liter. A large bottle of soda is 2 liters. The weight of items sold in a grocery store is often given in grams. A small bag of potato chips weighs about 40 grams.

Work with and learn about metric measures as much as possible. Metric measures are used more and more often in the United States every year. In other countries, they are almost always used.

Notice that, by definition in the metric system a kilogram is a unit of mass, not a unit of weight. But in practice, we use kilograms to measure weight (how heavy an object is), as well as mass (a measure of how much material an object is made up of).

Changing Units in the Metric System

Because the metric system is based on the decimal system, it is easy to change metric measurements from one unit to another: you only have to change the value of the digits by moving the decimal point.

To change a larger unit to a smaller unit, you multiply: you move the decimal point to the right.

There are 10 mm in 1 cm. To change centimeters to millimeters, multiply by 10:

$$27.6 \text{ cm} = 276 \text{ mm}$$

There are 100 cm in 1 m. To change millimeters to centimeters, multiply by 100:

$$0.023 \text{ m} = 2.3 \text{ cm}$$

There are 1000 m in 1 km. To change kilometers to meters, multiply by 1000:

$$0.153 \text{ km} = 153 \text{ m}$$

To change a smaller unit to a larger unit, you divide: you move the decimal point to the left.

To change millimeters to centimeters, divide by 10:	8.3 mm = 0.83 cm
To change centimeters to meters, divide by 100:	8 cm = 0.08 m
To change meters to kilometers, divide by 1000:	750 m = 0.75 km

In the metric system, measurements are not given in two different units, as they sometimes are in what we call the U.S. customary system—for example, 9 feet 6 inches. If something is 1 meter 14 centimeters long, you give its length as 1.14 meters or 114 centimeters. For this reason metric measurements are very often written as decimals, and it is important to practice working with metric measures in decimal form.

Measuring Length to a Sixteenth of an Inch

In the United States, a ruler is often divided into sixteenths of an inch.

To help you read lengths more quickly, there are longer marks to show where the sixteenths of an inch can be written as a simpler fraction. For example, there is a long mark at $\frac{8}{16}$ of an inch, which equals $\frac{1}{2}$ of an inch; there are slightly shorter marks at $\frac{4}{16}$ and $\frac{12}{16}$ of an inch, which can be written as $\frac{1}{4}$ and $\frac{3}{4}$ of an inch.

Remember that when measuring the length of a real object, you usually estimate to the nearest unit. Look at the nail in the picture.

To the nearest inch, the nail is 2 inches.

To the nearest half inch, the nail is $1\frac{1}{2}$ inches.

To the nearest quarter inch, the nail is $1\frac{3}{4}$ inches.

To the nearest eighth inch, the nail is $1\frac{5}{8}$ inches.

To the nearest sixteenth inch, the nail is $1\frac{11}{16}$ inches.

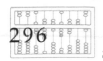

The smaller the unit of measure, the more precise your measurement of the length of the nail will be.

Practice measuring objects to the nearest sixteenth of an inch. You can use the longer marks to find a measurement in sixteenths quickly. Since $\frac{3}{4} = \frac{12}{16}$, the sixteenth mark just past $\frac{3}{4}$ is $\frac{13}{16}$.

Adding and Subtracting with Different Units

When you add or subtract lengths that are in different U.S. customary units, you need to regroup in different ways.

Add the inches first.
Regroup 15 in as
1 ft 3 in.

You can't take 9 in from
4 in. Regroup 21 ft 4 in
as 20 ft 16 in.

$$
\begin{array}{rl}
\mathbf{1} & \\
3 \text{ ft} & 7 \text{ in} \\
+\ 2 \text{ ft} & 8 \text{ in} \\
\hline
& 1\cancel{5} \\
6 \text{ ft} & 3 \text{ in}
\end{array}
\qquad
\begin{array}{rl}
\mathbf{20} \quad\ \mathbf{16} & \\
\mathbf{21} \text{ ft} \quad 4 \text{ in} & \\
-\ 15 \text{ ft} \quad 9 \text{ in} & \\
\hline
5 \text{ ft} \quad 7 \text{ in} &
\end{array}
$$

You can also regroup in the same way to add or subtract feet and yards, or yards and miles.

When you add metric measurements, you write the measurements in the same unit first.

To add 2.68 liters and 27 milliliters, you can write both measurements in either liters or milliliters.

27 ml = 0.027 l
2.68 l = 2680 ml

$$
\begin{array}{r}
2.6\ 8\quad l \\
+\ 0.0\ 2\ 7\ l \\
\hline
2.7\ 0\ 7\ l
\end{array}
\qquad
\begin{array}{r}
2\ 6\ 8\ 0 \text{ ml} \\
+\qquad 2\ 7 \text{ ml} \\
\hline
2\ 7\ 0\ 7 \text{ ml}
\end{array}
$$

Always write metric measurements in a single unit before you add them.

Multiplying and Dividing with Time

Learn how to regroup so that you can multiply and divide amounts of time.

A clerk works 7 hours and 25 minutes a day, Monday through Friday. How many hours does he work in a week?

	hours	minutes
	2	
	7	25
×		5
	35	12̸5
	37	5

$$\begin{array}{r} 2\ \text{R5} \\ 60\overline{)125} \end{array}$$

125 min = 2 h 5 min

Notice how before you multiply the hours, you regroup 125 minutes as 2 hours 5 minutes. The clerk works 37 hours and 5 minutes a week.

A race car makes four circuits around a track in 10 minutes 32 seconds. How long does each circuit take? First you divide the minutes by 4. If there are minutes left over, you write them as seconds, add them to the other seconds, and divide the seconds.

Divide the minutes.

$$\begin{array}{r} 2\ \text{min R2} \\ 4\overline{)10\ \ \text{min}} \\ -8 \\ \hline 2 \end{array}$$

There are 2 min left.

2 min = 120 sec
120 sec + 32 sec = 152 sec

Divide the seconds.

$$\begin{array}{r} 3\ 8\ \ \text{sec} \\ 4\overline{)15\ 2\ \ \text{sec}} \end{array}$$

Each circuit takes 2 min 38 sec.

Plane Figures

Measuring Angles

Remember that an angle is formed by two rays with a common endpoint.

This is ∠EFG or ∠GFE.

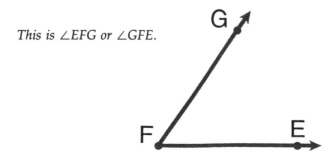

You measure an angle by measuring the size of its opening in degrees. You use a protractor to measure angles. You place the protractor's center on the vertex of the angle and the zero mark along one ray.

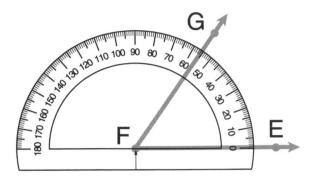

Then you can measure the number of degrees in the angle, where the second ray crosses the protractor. Angle EFG has a measure of 54 degrees. You write m∠EFG = 54°. The symbol ° stands for degrees and "m" is "the measure of."

You can also draw an angle with a certain measure using a protractor. Draw a ray and place the protractor's center on the endpoint and the zero mark along the ray. Then mark a point at the right number of degrees. Draw a second ray from the vertex of the angle through this point.

$m\angle CAB = 45°$

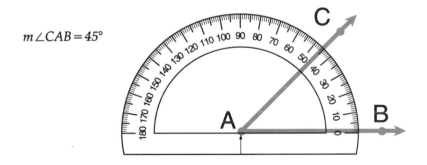

Measuring Kinds of Angles

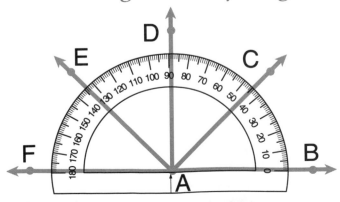

A right angle has a measure of 90°. ∠BAD is a right angle.

An acute angle has a measure of less than 90°. ∠BAC is an acute angle. Remember that acute angles are smaller than right angles.

An obtuse angle has a measure greater than 90°, but less than 180°. ∠BAE is an obtuse angle. Obtuse angles are greater than right angles.

A straight angle is formed when its two rays are part of the same line. A straight angle has a measure of 180°. ∠BAF is a straight angle.

Practice drawing right, acute, or obtuse angles using a protractor. Practice estimating about how large some angles are, using right angles (90°) and straight angles (180°) as a mental guide. For example, a 30° angle would have an opening $\frac{1}{3}$ as wide as a right angle.

Kinds of Triangles

An equilateral triangle has all three sides of the same length.

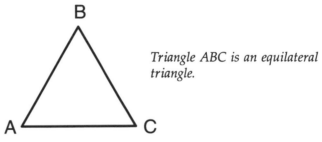

Triangle ABC is an equilateral triangle.

A right triangle has one right angle.

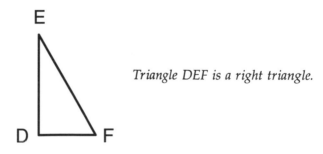

Triangle DEF is a right triangle.

An isosceles triangle has at least two sides of the same length.

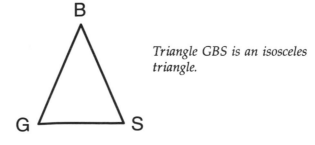

Triangle GBS is an isosceles triangle.

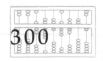
Learn how to construct a triangle with sides of a particular length. To construct a figure means to draw it accurately using certain tools—for example, a ruler and a compass. To construct triangle DGC with sides of 6 inches, $4\frac{1}{2}$ inches, and 3 inches, draw a segment 6 inches long. (You could also start with either of the other two sides.)

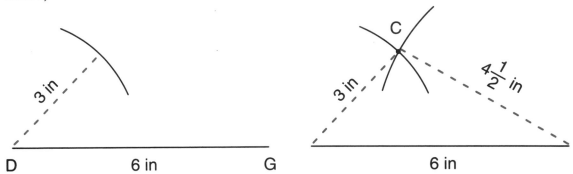

Label the endpoints D and G. Now, using a compass, draw an arc 3 inches from D. An arc is a part of a circle. Drawing an arc 3 inches from D is like drawing part of a circle with radius 3 inches and center D. Now draw an arc $4\frac{1}{2}$ inches from G. Where the two arcs intersect, mark point C. Draw segments DC and GC to complete the triangle.

Now construct two other triangles with sides of 6 inches, $4\frac{1}{2}$ inches and 3 inches, beginning each with one of the other sides. Cut the triangles out and compare them. Notice that all the triangles are congruent. *Triangles that have all three sides of the same length are said to be congruent.*

You can use the method for constructing a triangle to construct equilateral and isosceles triangles. For example, construct an equilateral triangle with sides of 8 centimeters; construct two different isosceles triangles with sides of 5 centimeters and 7 centimeters.

Rhombus

A parallelogram with four sides of the same length is called a rhombus. The diagonals of a rhombus are *perpendicular* to one another, and divide each other in half where they intersect.

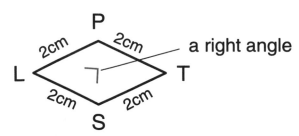

Parallelogram PTSL is a rhombus.
All of its sides have the same length.

Practice constructing a rhombus in this way: draw two perpendicular segments of different lengths that divide each other in half. (These are the diagonals of the rhombus.) Connect their endpoints to form the sides of the rhombus.

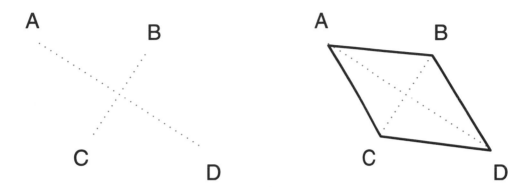

A square is a special kind of rhombus: it has four sides of the same length, *and* four right angles. A square is both a rhombus and a rectangle. A rectangle is a parallelogram with four sides and four right angles.

Other Polygons

Remember that a polygon is a closed figure formed by line segments. A polygon with five sides is called a pentagon.

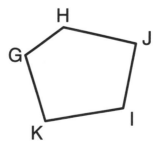

Polygon HJIKG is a pentagon.

A polygon with six sides is called a hexagon.

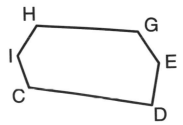

Polygon HGEDCI is a hexagon.

A polygon with eight sides is called an octagon.

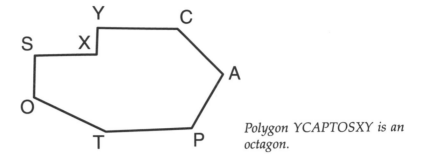

Polygon YCAPTOSXY is an octagon.

A regular polygon has sides of equal length and angles of equal measure.

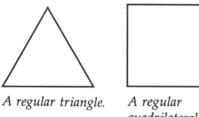

A regular triangle.   *A regular quadrilateral.*   *A regular hexagon.*   *A regular octagon.*

A regular triangle is also called an equilateral triangle and a regular quadrilateral is also called a square. A stop sign has the shape of a regular octagon.

Diagonals

A diagonal is a line segment that is not a side and that joins two vertices of a polygon. A quadrilateral has two diagonals. How many diagonals does a pentagon have?

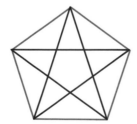
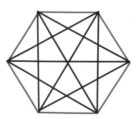

A pentagon has five diagonals. A hexagon has nine diagonals. How many diagonals does an octagon have?

Practice drawing all the diagonals on a pentagon, a hexagon, a seven-sided polygon, and an octagon. See if you can find a pattern.

Perimeters

You can measure the perimeter of any figure by placing a piece of string along the perimeter, then measuring the length of the string that you used.

The perimeter of the figure is 12.5 centimeters.

Circles

A line segment joining two points on a circle is called a chord. Segments DC and TS are chords of the circle with center P.

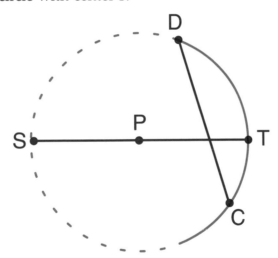

You can define the diameter of a circle as a chord that passes through the center of the circle. $\overline{TS}$ is both a chord and a diameter of the circle. A diameter is the longest possible chord of a circle.

An arc of a circle is a part of the circle. It has two endpoints on the circle.

This is an arc. Because its endpoints are C and D, we can label it arc CD.

The perimeter of a circle is usually called its circumference. You can measure the circumference of a circle with a piece of string. You can also find the circumference of a circle using a formula.

$$\text{Circumference of a circle} = \pi \times \text{diameter}$$
$$C = \pi \times d$$

π is a letter from the Greek alphabet pronounced and spelled out pi. π is a number: it is the number of diameter lengths there are in the circumference of a circle. For example, if you had pieces of string the length of the diameter, it would take you π number of these pieces of string to go all the way around a circle once. You cannot write the number π exactly in decimals. To the nearest hundredth, π is 3.14. It would take you 3 and a fraction pieces of string the length of the diameter to go all the way around any circle once.

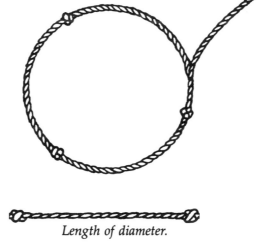

Length of diameter.

Using the value 3.14 for π, practice finding the circumference of a circle. For example, find the circumference of a circle with a diameter of 13 centimeters to the nearest tenth of a centimeter.

$$C = \pi \times d$$
$$\approx 3.14 \times 13 \quad \text{(The symbol} \approx \text{means nearly equal to.)}$$
$$\approx 40.82 \qquad 40.82 \text{ rounds to } 40.8$$

The circumference of a circle with a diameter of 13 centimeters is *about* 40.8 centimeters.

Since the diameter of a circle is twice its radius, you can also write the circumference formula with the radius.

$$C = \pi \times 2 \times r \quad \text{(r stands for radius)}$$

Practice using C = π × 2 × r to calculate the circumference of a circle given its radius. Also make sure to practice using a compass to construct circles that have a certain diameter or a certain radius. For example, construct a circle with a diameter of 8 centimeters and two chords of 3.5 centimeters.

Area

Area Review

Remember that the area of a rectangle is its length times its width. The formula for the area of a rectangle is: A = l × w.

The area of a rectangle with sides 7 yd and 5 yd is 35 yd². (7 × 5 = 35.)

Since the sides of a square all have the same length, you can write the formula for the area of a square like this:

> A = s × s   (s stands for the length of any side)

Metric Units of Area

To change from one metric unit of area to another, you simply change the value of the digits by moving the decimal point. Since there are 10 millimeters in a centimeter, a square centimeter has 10 millimeters for each dimension. There are 10 × 10 or 100 mm² (square millimeters) in a square centimeter (cm²).

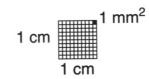

1 cm² = 100 mm²

Learn these equivalences:

> 1 cm² = 100 mm²
> 1 dm² (square decimeter) = 100 cm²
> 1 m² (square meter) = 100 dm²

Practice changing metric units of area. For example, in 1260 cm² there are 12.6 dm² and 0.126 m².

U.S. Customary Units of Area

If you know the equivalences among U.S. customary units of length, you can find the equivalences among U.S. customary units of area.

Since there are 12 inches in a foot, there are 12 × 12 square inches in a square foot.

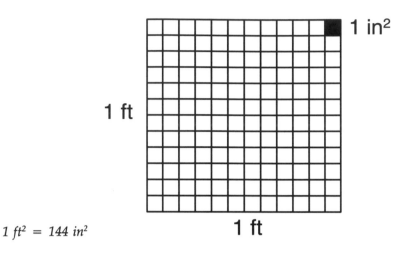

1 ft² = 144 in²

There are also 3 × 3 square feet in a square yard.

$$1 \text{ yd}^2 = 9 \text{ ft}^2$$

Practice changing U.S. customary units of area. For example, Martha is buying squares for a small quilt. The area of the quilt is 13 ft². Each square has a usable area of 9 in² and costs 10¢. How many squares will be needed for the quilt, and how much will they cost?

First change 13 ft² to square inches (in²), to find the area of the quilt in square inches. 1 ft² = 144 in². 13 × 144 = 1872. 13 ft² = 1872 in². The quilt has an area of 1872 in². Now divide by 9 to find how many squares are needed.

$$9)\overline{1872} \quad 208$$

She will need 208 squares. At 10¢ a square, they will cost her $20.80.

$$\begin{array}{r} \$ \, 0.1 \, 0 \\ \times \quad 2 \, 0 \, 8 \\ \hline \$ \, 2 \, 0.8 \, 0 \end{array}$$

Finding the Area of Triangles

To find the area of a triangle, you need to learn to measure the height of a triangle. Start by calling any side of the triangle the base. The height of a triangle is the perpendicular distance from the vertex opposite the base to the line containing the base. Here are examples of heights of triangles.

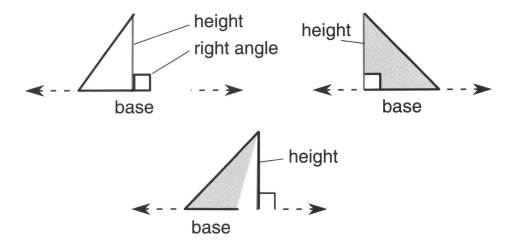

Practice drawing and measuring the heights of different triangles.

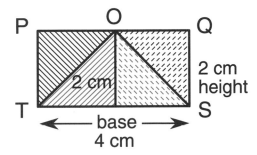

Study the rectangle above. The area of rectangle PQST is 8 cm² (4 × 2 = 8). Triangle OST is half of rectangle PQST: you can see that when you divide triangle OST into two right triangles, there are two matching right triangles left in rectangle PQST. Since triangle OST is half of rectangle PQST, the area of triangle OST must be half of 8 cm². Half of 8 cm² is 4 cm².

You can find the area of triangle OST this way: first multiply its base (4 cm) times its height (2 cm), which gives you the area of a rectangle that is twice its size; then divide by 2.

$$A = (4 \times 2) \div 2$$
$$= 8 \div 2 = 4 \qquad \text{The area of triangle OST is 4 cm².}$$

You can find the area of any triangle by multiplying its base times its height and then dividing by 2.

The formula for the area of a triangle is: A = (b × h) ÷ 2

Practice finding the area of a triangle. For example, construct a triangle with sides of 6 centimeters, 7 centimeters, and 8 centimeters, and draw its three different

heights using each side as a base. (Notice that the heights all intersect each other at the same point.) Measure the heights in millimeters and calculate the area of the triangle in square millimeters all three ways.

Finding the Area of a Parallelogram

You can call any side of a parallelogram its base. The height of a parallelogram is the perpendicular distance from its base to the opposite side. The picture shows you how you can find the area of a parallelogram.

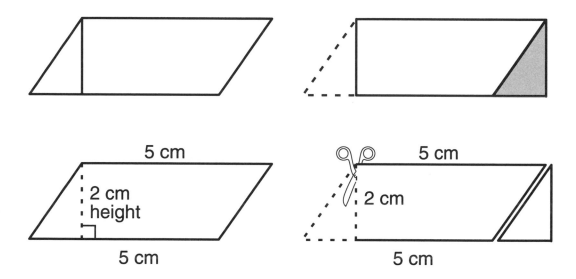

The parallelogram has the same area as a rectangle that has the parallelogram's base and height as its dimensions. $5 \times 2 = 10$. So the area of the parallelogram is 10 cm².

You can always find the area of a parallelogram in the same way, by multiplying its base times its height.

Formula for the area of a parallelogram: $A = b \times h$

Practice using this formula to find the area of parallelograms.

Finding Areas of Other Figures

Sometimes you have to find the area of a figure by dividing it into smaller areas that you know how to find. For example, you can find the area of this trapezoid by dividing it into smaller areas. Here is one way.

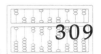
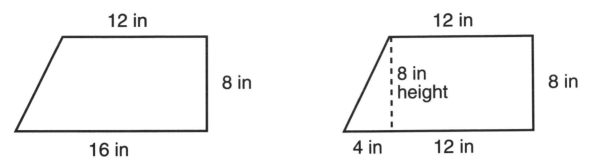

Divide the trapezoid into a rectangle and right triangle. Find the area of each and add to find the total area.

Area of rectangle: $12 \times 8 = 96$
Area of triangle: $(4 \times 8) \div 2 = 16$
Add the two areas. $96 + 16 = 112$
The area of the trapezoid is 112 in^2

See if you can find the area of this trapezoid by dividing it into two triangles.

Ratio, Scale, Percent, Average, Graphs

Ratio

A ratio is a way of comparing the size of two numbers. If a family has three dogs and five cats, the ratio of their dogs to their cats is 3 to 5. You can write that ratio in a number of ways:

$$3 \text{ to } 5 \qquad 3:5 \qquad \frac{3}{5}$$

You read each of these ratios "3 to 5." Notice that a ratio can be written as a fraction. You can write equal ratios the same way you write equivalent fractions, by dividing or multiplying both numbers of the ratio by the same number. Here is how you can write two ratios equal to the ratio $\frac{4}{10}$ (4 to 10).

$$\frac{4 \div 2}{10 \div 2} = \frac{2}{5} \qquad \frac{4}{10} = \frac{2}{5} \qquad \frac{4 \times 2}{10 \times 2} = \frac{8}{20} \qquad \frac{4}{10} = \frac{8}{20}$$

The ratio $\frac{2}{5}$ is in lowest terms. Write ratios that are written as fractions in lowest terms.

Practice writing equal ratios, or checking to see if two ratios are equal.

Solve for a: $\dfrac{8}{21} = \dfrac{24}{a}$

You multiply 8 × 3 to get 24, so
you must multiply 21 × 3 to get a.
a = 21 × 3
a = 63

Does $\dfrac{5}{9} = \dfrac{10}{14}$?

You multiply 5 × 2 to get 10.
You cannot multiply 9 × 2 to get 14.
So $\dfrac{5}{9} \neq \dfrac{10}{14}$.

The sign ≠ means "is not equal to."

Scale

A scale drawing uses a ratio, called its scale, to show the relationship between the size of the things in the drawing and their actual size. For example, on a map of a city with a scale of 1 inch = 2 miles, each inch on the map represents 2 miles of actual distance in the city. A map is one kind of scale drawing; another kind, used by architects, is a floor plan, which indicates the size and arrangement of a building's rooms by showing an outline of its floor.

Meg has made a plan of her room, with the scale 1 inch = 3 feet.

On her plan, the side wall is 5 inches long. How long is it actually? To find out, write the scale as a fraction, and then find a fraction equivalent to it.

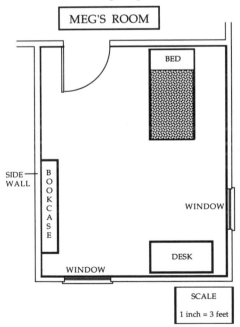

length on the plan — 1 in $\dfrac{1\ \text{in}}{3\ \text{ft}} = \dfrac{5\ \text{in}}{n}$
actual length — 3 ft

You multiply 1 in × 5
to get 5 in, so you must
multiply 3 ft × 5 to get n.
n = 3 ft × 5 = 15 ft

length on the plan — 1 in $\dfrac{1\ \text{in}}{3\ \text{ft}} = \dfrac{5\ \text{in}}{15\ \text{ft}}$
actual length — 3 ft

The side wall is actually 15 ft long.

If her bed is 6 feet long, how long will it appear on the plan? Again find a fraction equivalent to the scale.

$$\times 2$$

length on the plan — $\dfrac{1 \text{ in}}{3 \text{ ft}} = \dfrac{n}{6 \text{ ft}}$ actual length

$\dfrac{1 \text{ in}}{3 \text{ ft}} = \dfrac{2 \text{ in}}{6 \text{ ft}}$

$$\times 2$$

Her bed would be 2 inches long on the plan.

To find a scale, write a ratio of a plan length to the actual length as a fraction in lowest terms. Here is an example.

On a plan, the length of a schoolyard is 2 centimeters. It is actually 50 meters long. What is the scale of the plan?

$$\text{plan length} — \dfrac{2 \text{ cm}}{50 \text{ m}} = \dfrac{1 \text{ cm}}{25 \text{ m}} \quad \text{actual length}$$

The scale of the plan is 1 cm = 25 m.

Percent

The term "percent" means per hundred. Percent is a ratio: a percent compares a number to 100. For example, 40 percent means $\frac{40}{100}$ or 40 out of 100. The symbol % stands for percent. You write 11 out of 100 as 11%.

Often a percent is part of a whole. The whole is 100%. If 45% of a fifth-grade class are boys, then 55% of the class are not boys. They are girls. 100% of the class are either boys or girls.

Boys		Girls		Whole Class
45%	+	55%	=	100%
$\dfrac{45}{100}$	+	$\dfrac{55}{100}$	=	$\dfrac{100}{100}$

Notice that 100% = $\frac{100}{100}$ = 1. When you are talking about a whole, 100% means *all* the parts. For example, if 100% of your friends came to a party, they all came.

Percents and Fractions

Remember that a percent is *always in hundredths*. So to write a percent as a fraction, write the percent over a denominator of 100. Then reduce the fraction to lowest terms.

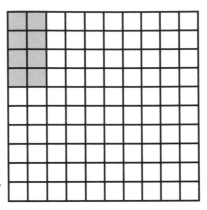

8% or $\frac{2}{25}$ of the square is shaded.

$$35\% = \frac{35}{100} = \frac{7}{20} \qquad 8\% = \frac{8}{100} = \frac{2}{25}$$

To write a fraction as a percent, first write an equivalent fraction that has a denominator of 100. Then you write the percent.

$$\frac{1}{4} = \frac{1 \times 25}{4 \times 25} = \frac{25}{100} = 25\%$$

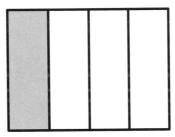

$\frac{1}{4}$ or 25% of the rectangle is shaded.

Percents and Decimals

To write a percent as a decimal, remember that a percent is *always in hundredths*. 35 percent is the same as 35 hundredths, and 8 percent is the same as 8 hundredths.

$$35\% = \frac{35}{100} = 0.35 \qquad\qquad 8\% = \frac{8}{100} = 0.08$$

To write a decimal as a percent, think of the decimal in hundredths. Then you can write it as a percent. 7 tenths (0.7) is the same as 70 hundredths (0.70), is the same as 70%.

$$0.7 = 0.70 = \frac{70}{100} = 70\% \qquad\qquad 0.04 = \frac{4}{100} = 4\%$$

A quick way to write a decimal as a percent is to multiply the decimal by 100. This method works because percents are already in hundredths.

$$0.7 = 70\% \qquad 0.04 = 04\% = 4\%$$ (Move the decimal point two places to the right.)

A quick way to write a percent as a decimal is to divide by 100.

$$35\% = 0.35 \qquad 8\% = 0.08$$ (Move the decimal point two places to the left.)

Writing Fractions, Decimals, or Percents

Fractions, decimals, and percents are often used *interchangeably:* people sometimes use a fraction, sometimes a decimal, or sometimes a percent to mean the same thing.

For example, we might say 25% of Jim's marbles are red, or $\frac{1}{4}$ of Jim's marbles are red, or 0.25 of Jim's marbles are red ($25\% = \frac{1}{4} = 0.25$). Since we are talking about a part of a whole, we could also say that 75% of Jim's marbles are not red, or $\frac{3}{4}$ of Jim's marbles are not red, or 0.75 of Jim's marbles are not red ($75\% = \frac{3}{4} = 0.75$). Given a statement like "40% of the pizza was pepperoni," practice writing six statements like these.

Also learn to complete a table like this one, writing a number as a fraction, a decimal, or a percent.

Fraction	Decimal	Percent	
$\frac{1}{5}$	_____	_____	(0.2, 20%)
_____	0.1	_____	($\frac{1}{10}$, 10%)
_____	_____	65%	($\frac{13}{20}$, 0.65)
_____	0.5	_____	($\frac{1}{2}$, 50%)

You may want to memorize what certain common fractions are as percents: $\frac{1}{4}$ is 25%, $\frac{1}{2}$ is 50%, $\frac{1}{10}$ is 10%.

Finding a Percent of a Number

There are 525 students at the elementary school. 44% of them are in fourth or fifth grade. How many students are in fourth or fifth grade?

To solve this problem, you must find a percent of a number: what is 44% of 525? To find a percent of a number, change the percent to a decimal and multiply.

Remember that 44% = 0.44. To find 0.44 *of* 525 you multiply 0.44 × 525.

$$
\begin{array}{r}
5\ 2\ 5 \\
\times\ 0.4\ 4 \\
\hline
2\ 1\ 0\ 0 \\
2\ 1\ 0\ 0\ 0 \\
\hline
2\ 3\ 1.0\ 0 \\
\end{array}
$$

44% of 525 is 231.

There are 231 fourth and fifth graders at the elementary school.

Finding an Average

To find the average of a set of numbers, you add all the numbers together and then divide by the number of addends. This average can give you an idea of the size of a typical number in the set. For example, Mrs. Tough wants to find the average number of questions out of 20 that Peter has gotten right on his last five quizzes. His scores have been 12, 12, 13, 15, and 17.

She adds his scores:

$$
\begin{array}{r}
12 \\
12 \\
13 \\
15 \\
+17 \\
\hline
69 \\
\end{array}
$$

Then she divides by the number of scores:

$$
\begin{array}{r}
1\ 3.8 \\
5\overline{)6\ 9.0} \\
\end{array}
$$

Peter has averaged 13.8 correct answers on his last five quizzes. Mrs. Tough might round the average and say, "Peter has been getting about 14 questions right out of 20."

Another word for average is the term "mean." Practice finding the average or mean of a set of numbers. For example, to the nearest tenth, the mean of 2.3, 6.8, 9.4 and 8.4 is 6.7.

Graphs

Information, or data, is often given to us in numbers. You can make your own bar graphs, line graphs, or pictographs to show a set of data.

A bar graph is a good way to show the different sizes of amounts. Here is a table of data we will use to make a bar graph.

Rainfall During Charlie's Week in Seattle	
Day	Rainfall in Millimeters
Thursday	24
Friday	9
Saturday	6
Sunday	0
Monday	11
Tuesday	2
Wednesday	9

Along the bottom of the graph we wrote the days of the week. Along the side of the graph we chose a convenient way to show the millimeters of rain: intervals of 2 millimeters made the graph a good size and easy to read. See how we titled the graph, labeled the information along the bottom and the sides, and drew a bar to show each day's rainfall?

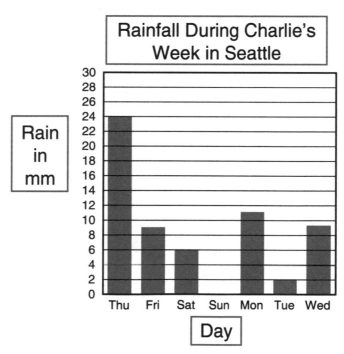

You can see right away from this graph that there was far more rain on Thursday than on any other day.

People often use line graphs to show how amounts or numbers change. At the end of each week for five weeks, Mrs. Sinclair found the average price per share of the stock she owned. Here is her table of data:

Mrs. Sinclair's Stock Prices	
Day	Average Price Per Share of Stock
September 25, 1987	$26.20
October 2, 1987	$27.40
October 9, 1987	$26.40
October 16, 1987	$23.20
October 23, 1987	$16.10

In our line graph we put the dates along the bottom of the graph. Along the side, we chose money amounts in intervals that would make the graph a reasonable size and show the data clearly. And we gave the graph a title and labels along the bottom and side.

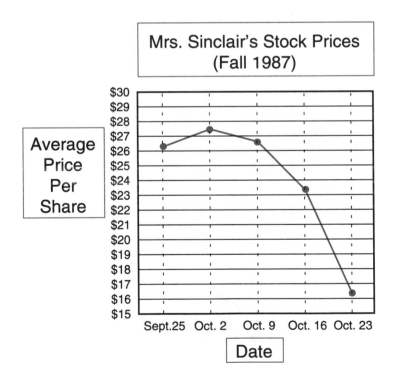

Notice that you have to approximate where a dollars-and-cents amount like $16.10 fits between the dollar amounts of $16 and $17.00.

A pictograph uses a symbol to show amounts. For example, a car dealership made a pictograph of the number of orange, white, or black cars it sold in one month.

Number of Cars Sold at Car City in March	
Color	**Number Sold**
Orange	🚗 🚗 🚗
White	🚗 🚗 🚗 🚗
Black	🚗 🚗 🚗 🚗

🚗 = 10 cars

There are 4 car symbols for white cars, so that means 4 × 10 or 40 white cars were sold. Since a whole car symbol stands for 10 cars, a half car symbol must stand for 5 cars. There were (2 × 10) + 5 orange cars or 25 orange cars sold. Since it is unlikely that the number of cars sold could be shown exactly with the pictograph symbols, the amounts have probably been rounded to the nearest 5.

A Circle Graph

A circle graph is used to show the relationship of different parts to a whole. It is usually divided by fractions or percentages.

The Brown Family Income Last Year (After Taxes)

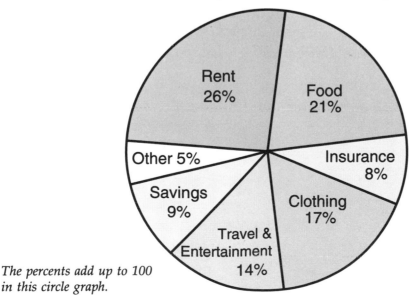

The percents add up to 100 in this circle graph.

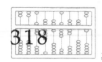

You can see right away from the circle graph where the Browns spent most of their money, and how much of their total income went to each area. If the Brown family had an income after taxes of $21,860 last year, how much did they spend on insurance? You find 8% of $21,860. 8% = 0.08

$$\begin{array}{r} \$2\,1{,}8\,6\,0 \\ \times\ 0.0\,8 \\ \hline \$1\,7\,4\,8.8\,0 \end{array}$$ The Brown family spent $1748.80 on insurance last year.

How much money did they save? You find 9% of $21,860, which is $1967.40.

Practice making your own bar graphs, line graphs, pictographs, and circle graphs from tables of data. Sometimes you may need to round data to show them conveniently on a graph.

A Word Problem

Here is an example of a word problem that uses the math you have learned. This one involves many steps. When you practice doing word problems, some of them should be as complex as this one.

Mr. and Mrs. Sinclair would like to buy a new washer and dryer that together cost $825. The saleswoman offers them a 7% discount if they pay for the washer and dryer now. They can also buy them on an installment plan. On the installment plan, they pay $200 now, and the rest of the cost, increased by 6%, in five equal monthly installments.

a) Find the cost of the washer and dryer if they buy them now.
b) Find the cost of the washer and dryer on the installment plan.
c) Find the amount of each monthly payment.
d) Find how much they would save by paying now.

a) A 7% discount means to take away 7% of the price. So you find 7% of $825, and subtract that amount from $825 to find the price if they pay now.

$$\begin{array}{r} \$\,8\,2\,5 \\ \times\ 0.0\,7 \\ \hline \$5\,7.7\,5 \end{array} \qquad \begin{array}{r} \$\,8\,2\,5.0\,0 \\ -\ \ \ 5\,7.7\,5 \\ \hline \$\,7\,6\,7.2\,5 \end{array}$$

The cost of the washer and dryer if they pay now: $767.25.

b) Installments are payments you make on a schedule: for example, on a certain day of every month. On the installment plan, first the Sinclairs pay $200, then the rest of the cost, increased by 6%. So first subtract $200 from $825. $825 − $200 =

$625. Then increase $625 by 6%: find 6% of $625 and add that amount to $625 to make it 6% bigger.

$$\begin{array}{r} \$\ 6\ 2\ 5 \\ \times\ \ 0.0\ 6 \\ \hline \$3\ 7.5\ 0 \end{array} \qquad \begin{array}{r} \$\ 6\ 2\ 5.0\ 0 \\ +\ \ \ \ 3\ 7.5\ 0 \\ \hline \$\ 6\ 6\ 2.5\ 0 \end{array}$$

The total amount they would pay on the installment plan is $662.50 + $200, or $862.50.

c) The amount they are paying in installments over five months is $662.50. Divide by 5 to find the amount of each equal monthly installment.

$$\begin{array}{r} \$1\ 3\ 2.5\ 0 \\ 5\,)\overline{\$6\ 6\ 2.5\ 0} \end{array}$$ Each monthly installment would be $132.50.

d) On the installment plan, they would pay a total of $862.50. If they pay now, they would pay $767.25.

$$\begin{array}{r} \$\ \ 8\ 6\ 2.5\ 0 \\ -\ \ \ 7\ 6\ 7.2\ 5 \\ \hline \$\ \ \ \ \ 9\ 5.2\ 5 \end{array}$$ They would save $95.25 by paying now, and not buying on credit.

Rectangular Prisms and Cubes

One kind of solid is a rectangular prism.

Opposite faces
are congruent

A rectangular prism.

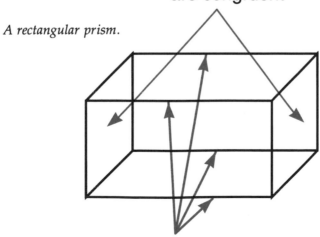

Four edges are parallel
and of equal length

A rectangular prism has six faces that are rectangles, and twelve edges. Each edge is parallel to three other edges, and all four of these edges have the same length. The opposite faces of a rectangular prism are congruent.

A cube is a special rectangular prism: all of its edges have the same length, all of its faces are congruent.

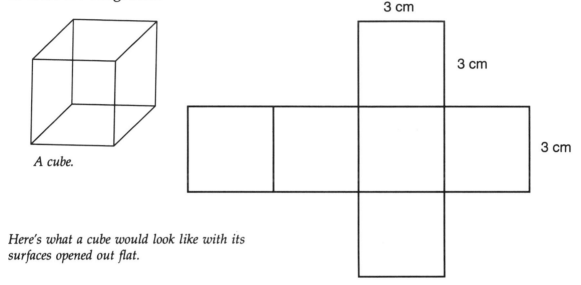

A cube.

Here's what a cube would look like with its surfaces opened out flat.

Constructing Rectangular Prisms and Cubes

Here's what a rectangular prism would look like with its surfaces opened out flat.

You can construct rectangular prisms and cubes by drawing figures like the open ones here on thin cardboard, using the dimensions given. Then cut out the figures and fold them along the line segments. Fasten them with tape to make a rectangular prism and a cube.

Volume

Volume is measured in cubic units, which tell you how much space something occupies. Cubic units have *three* dimensions: usually length, width, and height.

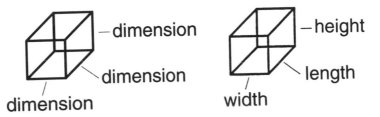

Some common cubic units are a cubic centimeter (cm³), a cubic meter (m³), a cubic inch (in³), and a cubic foot (ft³).

You can count by layers to find the volume of a rectangular prism.

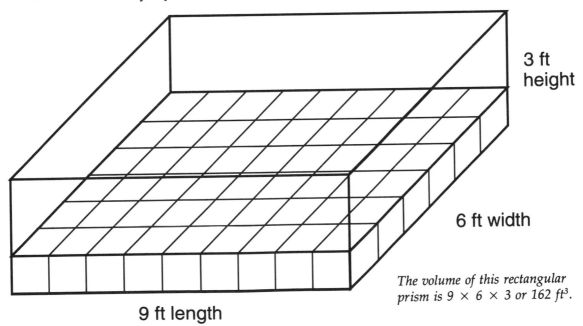

3 ft height

6 ft width

9 ft length

The volume of this rectangular prism is 9 × 6 × 3 or 162 ft³.

On one layer you can fit 9 ft³ (cubic feet) along the length, and 6 ft³ along the width. You can fit 9 × 6 or 54 ft³ on one layer. In a height of 3 ft³ you can fit three layers. Altogether you can fit 54 × 3 or 162 ft³ in the rectangular prism. Its volume is 162 ft³.

Formula for the Volume of a Rectangular Prism

You can always find the volume of a rectangular prism by multiplying its length times its width times its height—even if the length, width, and height are not in whole number units.

Formula for the Volume of a Rectangular Prism:

$$V = l \times w \times h$$

For example, to find the volume of a box with dimensions of 4.3 centimeters, 3.6 centimeters, and 3.9 centimeters, you multiply $4.3 \times 3.6 \times 3.9$.

```
      4.3              1 5.4 8
   ×  3.6            ×    3.9
    2 5 8            1 3 9 3 2
   1 2 9 0           4 6 4 4 0        The volume of the
   1 5.4 8           6 0.3 7 2        box is 60.372 cm³.
```

The dimensions of a rectangular prism are sometimes given in the form of this multiplication: a box 4.3 cm × 3.6 cm × 3.9 cm, which you read as 4.3 cm *by* 3.6 cm *by* 3.9 cm.

Since the length, width, and height of a cube are the same, you can write the formula for the volume of a cube like this:

Volume of a Cube:
$V = e \times e \times e$ (e stands for the length of any edge of the cube)

For example, a cubic container with a length of 8 ft along each edge has a volume of 512 ft³, since $8 \times 8 \times 8 = 512$.

Volume and Surface Area

You can find the *volume* of a rectangular prism and the *area* of its faces. The area of the faces of a solid is called surface area.

Jamie wants to paint his toy-and-sports box with a special bright blue paint. The paint comes in small cans that each hold enough paint to cover 50 ft². If the box has a length of 4 ft, a width of 2 ft, and a height of 3 ft, will one can of paint be enough to cover it completely?

3 ft height

2 ft width

4 ft length

Jamie's box.

Remember that each face of a rectangular prism has an opposite congruent face. The top and the bottom are congruent. The area of each is l × w. The front and back are congruent. The area of each is l × h. The two sides are congruent. The area of each is w × h.

Surface Area of a Rectangular Prism:

$$A = (2 \times l \times w) + (2 \times l \times h) + (2 \times w \times h)$$

top and bottom   front and back   two sides

$$A = (2 \times 4 \times 2) + (2 \times 4 \times 3) + (2 \times 3 \times 2)$$
$$= 16 + 24 + 12$$
$$= 52$$

The surface area of the toy-and-sports box is 52 ft²: Jamie will need more than one can of paint. If he decides not to paint the bottom of the box, will he need more than one can?

Practice finding the volume and surface area of rectangular prisms. Remember that you measure volume in cubic units and surface area in square units. For example, find the volume and surface area of a box with a length of 8 centimeters, a width of 6 centimeters, and a height of 5 centimeters. Then find the volume and surface area of this box if each dimension is doubled. By what number do you multiply (1) the surface area, and (2) the volume of the box, when you double its dimensions?

Changing U.S. Customary Units of Volume

If you know the equivalences among U.S. customary units of length, you can find the equivalences among U.S. customary units of volume.

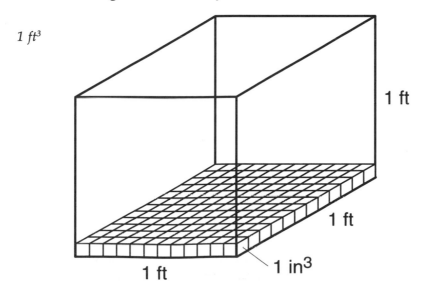

1 ft³

1 ft

1 ft

1 ft

1 in³

There are 12 inches in 1 foot. There are $(12 \times 12 \times 12)$ in³ in 1 ft³.

$$1728 \text{ in}^3 = 1 \text{ ft}^3$$

There are 3 feet in 1 yard. There are $(3 \times 3 \times 3)$ ft³ in 1 yd³.

$$27 \text{ ft}^3 = 1 \text{ yd}^3$$

Practice changing from one U.S. customary unit of volume to another. For example, a small truck has 400 cubic feet of storage space. To the nearest cubic yard, how many cubic yards is that?

$27 \text{ ft}^3 = 1 \text{ yd}^3$. So to find how many cubic yards there are in 400 ft³, divide 400 by 27.

$$
\begin{array}{r}
1\,4.8 \\
27\overline{)4\ 0\ 0.0} \\
-2\,7 \\
\hline
1\,3\,0 \\
-1\,0\,8 \\
\hline
2\,2\,0 \\
-2\,1\,6 \\
\hline
4
\end{array}
$$

14.8 rounds to 15.
400 ft³ is 15 yd³, to the
nearest cubic yard.

Changing Metric Units of Volume

You can change metric units of volume by moving the decimal point.

$$1 \text{ m} = 10 \text{ dm, so } 1 \text{ m}^3 = (10 \times 10 \times 10) \text{ dm}^3$$
$$= 1000 \text{ dm}^3$$
$$1 \text{ dm} = 10 \text{ cm, so } 1 \text{ dm}^3 = (10 \times 10 \times 10) \text{ cm}^3$$
$$= 1000 \text{ cm}^3$$

How many dm³ are in 3.23 m³? $3.23 \text{ m}^3 = 3230 \text{ dm}^3$ (multiply by 1000)

How many dm³ are in 237 cm³? $237 \text{ cm}^3 = 0.237 \text{ dm}^3$ (divide by 1000)

Notice how a decimeter is 10 times as long as a centimeter, but a cubic decimeter is *1000* times as large as a cubic centimeter!

Volume and Capacity

Remember that units of capacity, such as cups and quarts in the U.S. customary system and liters in the metric system, measure how much a container (for example, a bottle) can hold. How much a container can hold and the space inside the container are the same thing: when you measure the capacity of a container, you are measuring the volume of the inside of the container. So units of capacity are also units of volume.

In the U.S. customary system there is no easy equivalence between units of capacity (such as a cup) and units of volume (such as a cubic inch). But in the metric system 1 l (liter) = 1 dm³ (cubic decimeter). Since 1 m³ = 1000 dm³, you also know that 1 m³ = 1000 l.

Practice converting measures that are in cubic centimeters, decimeters, and meters, to liters. For example, 35 dm³ = 35 l; 750 cm³ = 0.75 l; 800 m³ = 800,000 l.

Rates and Speed

A rate is a ratio between two different quantities. Here are some examples of rates: Sally was averaging four hits in each ten at bats; Al was making 10¢ profit on every dollar of apple cider he sold; the car was traveling at 100 kilometers per hour.

One very common rate is speed. Speed is a rate given in distance per unit of time. 100 kilometers per hour is a speed. You can abbreviate it 100 km/h. These are some units of speed: kilometers/hour (km/h); miles/hour (mi/h); miles/minutes (mi/min).

Here is a formula that relates distance, speed, and time.

Distance equals rate times time:

$$D = r \times t$$

Remember that speed is a rate. The formula tells you that you multiply the speed by the time spent traveling at that speed to find the distance traveled. For example, an airplane travels at 550 mi/h for 4 hours. To find how far it has traveled, multiply: D = 550 × 4 = 2200. The plane has traveled 2200 miles in 4 hours.

Sometimes speed is given per minute, or per second. If a train is traveling at 2 km/min, how long will it take to travel 86 km?

Remember D = r × t. The distance is 86 km, the rate is 2 km/min.

$$86 = 2 \times t \qquad \text{(Use opposite operations.)}$$
$$86 \div 2 = \quad t$$
$$43 = t \text{ or } t = 43 \qquad \text{It will take the train 43 min to travel 86 km.}$$

You can change distance per minute to distance per hour by multiplying the distance by 60. 2 km/min = 120 km/h.

You can also change distance per hour to distance per minute by dividing by 60. 90 mi/h = 1.5 mi/min, since 90 ÷ 60 = 1.5.

To find a speed, write the ratio of distance to time per single unit of time. For example, if a train travels 195 miles in 3 hours, what was its speed? The train has traveled 195 mi/3h. Divide by 3 to find the distance traveled in 1 hour.

$$\begin{array}{r} 6\ 5 \\ 3\overline{)1\ 9\ 5} \end{array}$$
The train has traveled at 65 mi/h.

Functions and Equations

Functions; Inverse Operations

add 3	9	13	21
	12	16	24

divide by 2	26	57	16	3
	13	28.5	8	1.5

multiply by 7	6	22	5	11
	42	154	35	77

These tables show functions. A function does the same thing to each number you plug into it. For example, the first function adds 3 to each number.

Opposite operations are also called inverse operations. Functions can help you to see how inverse operations work. For example, the opposite, or inverse, of the function add 3 → is the function subtract 3 →. If you add 3 to 9, then subtract 3, you get back to 9 again. An inverse operation undoes the operation.

add 3	9	13	21	subtract 3
	12	16	24	

Addition and subtraction are inverse operations.

multiply by 2	13	28.5	8	1.5	divide by 2
	26	57	16	3	

Multiplication and division are inverse operations.

Practice filling in function tables like these:

divide by 4	16	27	10	18
	4	6.75	?	?

?	4	7	18	?
	6	?	20	

Graphing Functions

You can make a graph of a function such as <u>add 3</u>.

add (	0	1	2	3	4
3	3	4	5	6	7

Write each pair of numbers as an ordered pair. Then plot the ordered pairs on a grid. (Use graph paper with fairly large squares.) Connect the points, to show that they are on the same line. If the points are not on the same line, you have made a mistake.

Plot the ordered pairs (0,3), (1,4), (2,5), (3,6), (4,7).

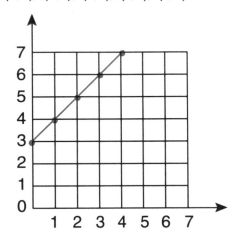

Graph of function <u>add 3</u>.

Now let's graph three more functions for practice. Here are the functions:

multiply (	0	1	2	3	4
by 2	0	2	4	6	8

divide (	0	2	4	6	8
by 2	0	1	2	3	4

subtract (	4	5	6	7	8
4	0	1	2	3	4

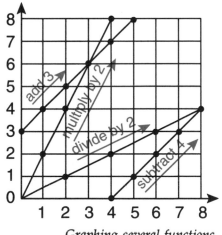

Graphing several functions.

Writing and Solving Equations for Word Problems

You can write an equation for a word problem, using a variable like n or x to stand for an unknown number.

Jennifer buys a mystery book and a romance for $8.90; the mystery costs $0.60 more than the romance. How much does each cost?

Draw a picture with line segments to help you write an equation.

```
                      n amount
cost of romance   |------------------|              ⎫
                                                     ⎬  $8.90 in all
                      n amount      $0.60            ⎭
cost of mystery   |------------------|----------|
```

Write the equation: $n + n + \$0.60 = \$8.90$. Then solve the equation by finding what n is. Use inverse operations.

$$n + n + \$0.60 = \$8.90$$
$$(2 \times n) + \$0.60 = \$8.90 \text{ ------------------ } 2 \times n \text{ is the same as } n + n$$
$$(2 \times n) \qquad\quad = \$8.90 - \$0.60 \text{ ----- Remember, you can write } 4 + 3 = 7 \text{ as}$$
$$4 = 7 - 3$$

$$2 \times n = \$8.30$$
$$n = \$8.30 \div 2 \text{ ----------- You can write } 2 \times 4 = 8 \text{ as } 4 = 8 \div 2$$
$$n = \$4.15$$

The romance costs $4.15, and the mystery costs $0.60 more, or $4.75.

Here is another example. Bill weighs three times as much as his dog Samuel. Together they weigh 128 pounds. How much do they each weigh?

1. Draw line segments to show the variable.

```
                      w lb
Samuel's weight   |-----------|                           ⎫
                                                           ⎬  128 lb in all
                      w lb        w lb        w lb         ⎭
Bill's weight     |-----------|-----------|-----------|
```

2. Write an equation. $w + (3 \times w) = 128$

3. Solve the equation. $4 \times w = 128 \text{ --------- } w + (3 \times w) =$
$$(1 \times w) + (3 \times w) = 4 \times w$$
$$w = 128 \div 4$$
$$w = \ \ 32$$

Samuel weighs 32 pounds. Bill weighs 3×32 pounds or 96 pounds.

Practice writing and solving equations for word problems like these.

V.

NATURAL SCIENCES

Introduction to Life Sciences

FOR PARENTS AND TEACHERS

In Book Four, children learned about ancient forms of life. Building upon this study of life forms, in Book Five children learn how we classify living organisms. They learn about cells, the essential elements of living tissues. They begin to learn in greater detail about life cycles of the different classes of life forms, including plant, animal, and human reproduction. And they begin to learn about the physical changes they may now be experiencing as they enter adolescence.

The topics covered in Book Five lend themselves to learning by direct experience. Children will enjoy activities that heighten their awareness of living organisms. Some of these hands-on learning experiences may include the following:

• Children always enjoy trips to the zoo, but now they can become more aware of the classification systems followed by zoos in laying out visitation areas and in grouping animals. In addition, at the zoo children can directly study the characteristics that link classes and species of animals.

• Children can cultivate and study fungi, or make cuttings from plants.

• During the spring months, children can enjoy collecting, sorting, and classifying leaves or plant seeds.

So important is direct experience in early science teaching that some experts have rejected the very idea of scientific book-learning for young children. But book-learning should not be neglected altogether. It helps bring system and coherence to a young child's developing knowledge of nature, which is often a very disorderly and complex process, and one that is different for each child. A systematic approach to the life sciences provides essential building blocks for deeper understanding at a later time. And we shouldn't forget that some children like book-learning even more than they like experiments and field trips. Both kinds of experiences are needed to ensure that gaps in knowledge will not hinder later understanding.

Some text resources that will enliven a child's understanding of living organisms include the following:

Plant Families by Carol Lerner (Morrow Jr. Books, 1989).
Discovering Trees by Keith Brandt (Troll Associates, 1982).
Bodies by Barbara Brenner (E. P. Dutton, 1973).
What's Happening to My Body: For Boys by Lynda Madaras (New Market Press,1989).
What's Happening to My Body: For Girls by Lynda Madaras (New Market Press, 1987).
How You Were Born by Joanne Cole (Morrow Jr. Books, 1984).

Life Sciences

Classification: Why Classify?

I f someone asked you how to find apples in the grocery store, where would you tell her to look? You'd probably send her to the fruits and vegetables aisle, or tell her to look near the oranges and watermelons. Where would you tell a friend to look if he wanted to borrow a pair of your socks? You'd tell him to look in the particular drawer where you keep your socks.

Grouping things together that are alike makes it easier for us to find them, and easier to add similar new things to the group. Would you find frozen french-fried potatoes in the snack-food aisle? No, although both french-fried potatoes and potato chips have potatoes as ingredients. Frozen french fries, unlike chips, need to be kept in the freezer section. Moreover, french fries are considered a dinner food and chips a snack food. So we put them in different places in the grocery store. We group things together or separate them according to certain similarities or differences. When we group things together because they are alike in certain ways, we are classifying them.

You and your fellow students are probably all grouped in the fifth-grade class. You are placed in that group, or class, because your teachers think you are ready to do fifth-grade work. Within your fifth-grade class, you could think of other classifications. All the boys could be one group, for example, or all the people who have freckles. There are many ways to divide people and things into classes, and it's important to remember that there is never a single right way to divide up and name the things in the world. As Shakespeare said:

> What's in a name? That which we call a rose
> By any other name would smell as sweet.

Still, classes and our names for them are indispensable both for everyday life and for science. We classify and name things for our convenience in talking about them. In fact, we could not talk about most things without using classifications, because the very name we use for a thing is often the word for a whole class of things. Your breakfast table belongs to the class of things called "tables."

Classifying Living Things

We classify natural things for the same reasons we classify fruit and tables—for convenience in finding and talking about them. There are several features that scientists use to help them classify natural things. Do you remember the main differences between plants and animals? Plants usually make their own food from sunlight, water, and air, while animals usually don't. And animals can usually move themselves around, while plants can't. Based on features like these, scientists have classified living things into groups, called *kingdoms.*

People first classified things that were easy to see. So the first two kingdoms that scientists settled on were the plant and animal kingdoms. Within these large kingdoms we can classify things into smaller groups. For instance, we put all flowering plants in one large class, and all nonflowering plants into another. And we put all animals that have hair and give milk into one class, and all animals that have feathers and beaks into another.

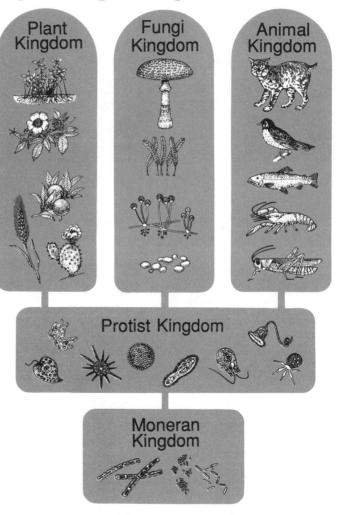

The five kingdoms of our classification system.

Once the microscope was invented—which allowed us to see more creatures— the classifier's job became more difficult. Scientists discovered many new organisms that seemed to be neither plants nor animals, and needed new classifications. Their observations led to the naming of three new kingdoms: the fungi (FUN-jie), protist (PRO-tist), and moneran (muh-NER-uhn) kingdoms. To see why scientists thought these microscopic organisms couldn't be classified as plants or animals, we need to learn about cells.

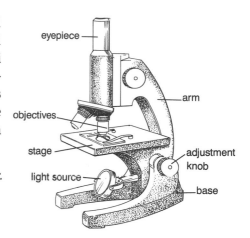

Microscopes use lenses to make objects look larger. Unless you have a specialized need, you would probably use a simple microscope like the one pictured here.

Cells: The Building Blocks of Living Things

Cells, you may remember from Book Two of this series, are the tiny building blocks of living things. Most cells are so small we can see them only with a microscope. Cells were discovered over 300 years ago when an English scientist named Robert Hooke was looking through his micro-scope at thin slices of cork—the material, made from the bark of the cork tree, that is used to seal bottles. When Hooke looked at cork bark under the microscope, he noticed a regular pattern of small, boxlike squares in the cork, which reminded him of little rooms. He named these "cells," after the Latin word for room, *cella.*

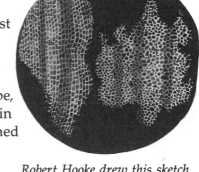

Robert Hooke drew this sketch of the cork cells he saw under his microscope.

Later, when microscopes were further developed, scientists could study the insides of cells and see different structures. Let's look at a picture of a cell and its parts and learn what each part does.

The Parts of a Cell

The cell membrane is a thin covering around the cell that separates it from its sur-roundings. The cell membrane helps give the cell its shape, and controls what goes into it (food, water, and oxygen) and out of it (waste). Inside the cell is the cytoplasm (SY-toe-plaz-um), a jellylike liquid in which all the other cell parts are embedded. Inside the cytoplasm is the nucleus (NOO-klee-us), the cell's control center. The nucleus is surrounded by the nuclear membrane, which controls what goes into and comes out of the nucleus. The nucleus contains all the instructions for running the cell. To reproduce, a cell splits into two cells. But before the cell splits, the nucleus

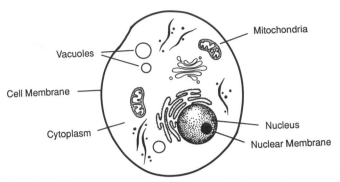

A cell and its parts, seen as magnified under a microscope.

doubles itself and then divides in half so that each new cell has a copy of the cell's instructions.

Also inside the cytoplasm are vacuoles (VAK-you-ohlz), tiny oval structures that store food, water, or wastes, and mitochondria (my-toh-KAHN-dree-uh), small structures shaped like kidney beans. Mitochondria are parts of the cell that help change food into energy the cell can use to do its work. The cells in both plants and animals, though they may differ in shape and size, have the features you've been reading about: the cell membrane, cytoplasm, nucleus, nuclear membrane, vacuoles, and mitochondria. Now you know what your cells have in common with the cells in a blade of grass!

Living versus Nonliving

How do we know whether something is alive? Sometimes it's easy: you know that you are alive and a rock is not. But sometimes it's hard to tell. What about a cloud, a fire, or a tiny virus? Scientists have discovered six activities that all living things do. They: (1) take in nutrients; (2) use energy to do work; (3) reproduce; (4) grow; (5) get rid of wastes; and (6) react to outside changes. Is a cloud alive? What about a fire? Do you think cells inside living organisms are alive? Why, or why not? Can one cell be a living organism?

Not All Cells Are Alike

Not all cells look the same. Cells can be different shapes depending on the jobs they do. Muscle cells are long and thin so they can expand and contract and help the body move. Red blood cells are tiny and rounded so they can squeeze through blood vessels and bring oxygen to other cells of the body. The cells in a tree trunk are long and thin, and form tubes to transport food and water up and down the tree. The cells in a plant's leaves are flattened to catch the maximum amount of the sunlight they use to make food.

While plant cells share parts in common with animal cells, plant cells have two additional parts that animal cells don't have. Let's look at both types of cells. Can you pick out the differences?

Plant cells, unlike animal ones, have cell walls. The cell wall is a sturdy layer around the cell membrane, which helps support and protect the cell. Robert Hooke

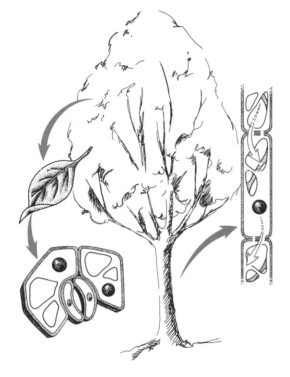

The job a cell does has a lot to do with its shape. Look how differently the cells from a tree's trunk and a tree's leaf are shaped.

was looking at the cell walls of cork cells when he made his discovery. In the cork, the insides of the cells had died and dried up, leaving the pattern of "boxes" he saw.

Another structure that plant cells have that animal cells don't are chloroplasts (KLOR-uh-plasts). Chloroplasts contain chlorophyll (KLOR-uh-fill), the green substance that traps the energy from sunlight and enables plants to make food. The chloroplasts in plant cells, then, have a lot to do with a basic difference between plants and animals: plants usually make their own food, while animals don't. *Think:* why might plant cells need the extra support of cell walls while most animal cells don't?

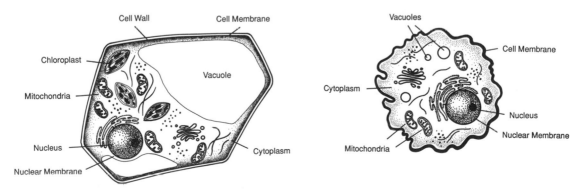

A typical plant cell.

A typical animal cell.

The Other Three Kingdoms

You just learned about some ways scientists look at cells to decide whether to classify a living thing as a plant or an animal. Now we are going to learn about the other three kingdoms—fungi, protists, and monerans—and how scientists decide which organisms are classed in these groups.

Fungi

Fungi (the plural for fungus) were once thought to be part of the plant kingdom because they have cell walls and produce spores. But they were separated into a distinct kingdom because they get their energy from living on dead plants and animals. (Plants, as you'll read later in this section, get energy from sunlight.) The mushrooms that you can buy in the store are created by colonies of fungi that feed on plant material, like decaying trees. From time to time, the colonies of fungi send up mushrooms. When they are ripe, the mushrooms release millions of tiny seedlike eggs called spores from their undersides. The wind blows the spores to distant places where they start new fungus colonies. The yeast that makes bread rise is another type of fungus. So is the green mold that forms on bread. And so is the white, powdery mildew that can appear on houseplants and in moist places.

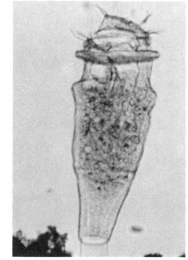

Remarkable Creatures: Protists

Protists (PRO-tists) are so small, you can see them only with a microscope. For many years, scientists were confused about how these organisms should be classified. They saw some that had the features of animals, and others that had the features of plants—and still others that had the features of both! Finally, it was decided that these organisms would make up a kingdom of their own.

Protists that act like animals are called protozoans (proh-toh-ZOH-anz). "Proto" means early in Greek and "zoan" means animal. Protozoans can move around. They can also capture and eat food they find in their environment. Some are found in fresh water, some in salt water. Others live in soil, and still others live inside the bodies of other organisms.

Some protists are plantlike. Most of these are types

This protist is one of the animal-like protozoans.

of algae (AL-jee). You may have seen algae growing as a film on top of a pond or lake. The cells of these organisms contain chlorophyll, which they use to make their own food. Euglena (you-GLEE-nah) are also plantlike protists that have chlorophyll. But when there is no sunlight to help euglena make food, they eat bacteria and other tiny plants and animals.

The Simplest Organisms: Monerans

Monerans are simple single-celled organisms that live in large groups called colonies. The two main groups of monerans are bacteria and blue-green algae. Monerans are similar to protists, and, until high-powered microscopes were developed, scientists had a hard time deciding how to classify them. But once they could see monerans under the microscope, scientists found that they have a very important characteristic that puts them in a class by themselves: monerans have no cell nucleus! The material normally found in a cell nucleus is scattered throughout the cytoplasm of the moneran.

Bacteria: Bacteria are monerans that have a cell wall and a cell membrane, like plant cells, but they do not contain chlorophyll. They are classified according to their shape: some are long, tubelike rods, some are spiral, and some are round. They get their food from other living organisms, or from decaying matter. They are found just about everywhere: in the air, water, and soil, and even inside other organisms, including you!

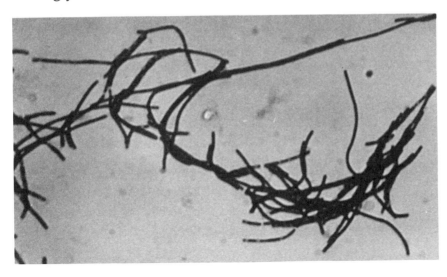

These are rod bacteria.

Some bacteria cause diseases. (Perhaps you've had to take medicine to get rid of a bacterial disease like strep throat or scarlet fever.) Other bacteria are very useful to life on earth. Like fungi, they help break down decaying material in the soil so nutrients can be freed to be used by plants. Certain types of bacteria are necessary for proper digestion in humans. Scientists have even been able to develop bacteria that can "eat" oil and help clean up destructive oil spills in the water.

Blue-green algae: Blue-green algae are monerans that can be found in water or soil. Some have even been found on rocks in Antarctica. They look like some of the protist algae, except that they do not have a nucleus. Nor do they have chloroplasts; instead, their chlorophyll is contained in membranes spread throughout the cell. Many are not even blue-green in color—about half the blue-green algae are other colors, including red!

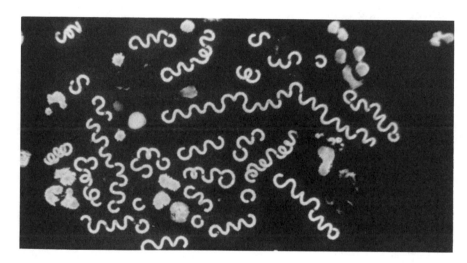

The moneran blue-green algae.

Like protist algae, the blue-green algae are important to life on earth because they form the beginning of the food chain for animals that live in water. As we'll learn in the next section, they also produce oxygen in the water and in the air we breathe.

Photosynthesis:
Energy from the Sun to Food on Your Table

Plants and some types of protists and monerans all have something in common. Do you remember what that is? All these organisms contain chlorophyll, a molecule that makes some or all of their cells appear green. The word "chlorophyll" comes from two Greek words—"chlor," meaning green, and "phyllo," meaning leaf. Chlorophyll can be found in other parts of a plant besides its leaves. And protists and monerans containing chlorophyll have no leaves. But all of these organisms use chlorophyll to trap the energy they need to make food. We call the process they use to make food photosynthesis (fo-toe-SIN-the-sis).

"Photo" means light. (When a camera makes a *photo*graph, it is using light to make a picture.) "Synthesis" means putting together. So photosynthesis means putting together with light. Organisms that contain chlorophyll put together water and carbon dioxide by using the energy from sunlight. The end products of photosynthesis are oxygen and sugars, which the organisms use for food.

How is this done? Where do the water and carbon dioxide come from, and where do the oxygen and sugars go? Let's first trace on a diagram how water and carbon dioxide get to a celery leaf. Then we'll read about how photosynthesis takes place.

Step One: Transporting Water and Nutrients Cars, buses, and subways are all systems of transportation we use to move ourselves from one place to another. Plants transport things too, in order to make and store food.

Look at the drawing of a celery plant. The plant takes in water and nutrients from the soil through tiny hairs on its roots. The water and nutrients are transported through the root hairs to the roots, and then up the stem (or "stalk") of the celery through tubes arranged in bundles.

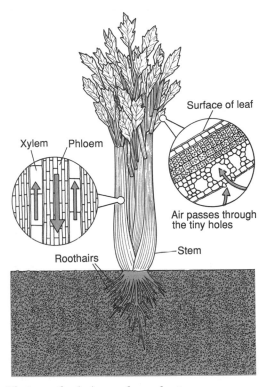

Photosynthesis in a celery plant.

How does the water flow upward through these tubes? Have you ever noticed that the liquid in a straw rises above the level of water in a glass? You can prove this by putting some food-coloring in a small glass of water and putting a straw into the water. Notice as you lift up the straw that the water inside it stays above the water in the glass. The water will rise even further if you put your finger on the opening at the top of the straw before you lift it. The tubes in a plant are like the straw. As water gets used up in the leaves, the water in the tubes rises to replace it.

Water Transportation: See for Yourself

Collect the following materials: a glass large enough to hold a stalk of celery upright, water, blue food coloring, a stalk of celery with leaves, scissors, a magnifying glass or hand lens.

Method: Cut about an inch off the bottom of celery stalk. Place the stalk upright in a glass. Fill the glass half full of water, and add a few drops of food coloring. Let the project sit for about an hour. What do you observe at the end of the hour? Take the stalk out of the water and with scissors cut it above the waterline. Observe the bottom end of the top section of the stalk with the magnifying glass. Draw a picture of what you see.

There are two different types of tubes: xylem (ZYE-lem) and phloem (FLOW-em). Xylem tubes carry water and nutrients *up* the stem to the leaves where photosynthesis occurs. Phloem tubes carry sugars *down* from the leaves to be stored in the lower stem and the roots.

Step Two: Light Energy from the Sun   Look at the cross section of the celery leaf in the illustration. Note the layer of cells just below the top surface of the leaf. These cells contain chloroplasts, where chlorophyll is found. Sunlight shines on the top of the leaf, and the light energy is trapped by the chlorophyll and stored for later use.

Step Three: Carbon Dioxide from the Air   In this step, food is made. Air passes in through tiny holes on the bottom surface of the leaf. Carbon dioxide molecules from the air reach the cells where chlorophyll has trapped energy from sunlight. This energy turns the carbon dioxide into various kinds of sugars.

Step Four: Back to the Transport System   These sugars are transported down the celery plant in phloem tubes, to be stored as sugar or starch in other parts of the plant. The plant's cells later use this stored food to grow and do work.

From Plant Food to Your Table   Think about the taste of an orange. Doesn't it taste sweet? That sweetness comes from the sugars the orange tree has stored in its fruit. Before storing sugar, many plants change it into a substance called starch. Can you think of some starchy parts of plants that you have eaten? Potatoes and corn are two plants that store food as starch.

We eat many plants that provide us with their stored sugar and starch. And just like plants, we convert this stored food into energy for our cells to do work.

Reproduction

All living things are born, grow during their lifetime, and eventually die. Tadpoles are born, grow, change into frogs, and eventually die. Chicks are born, grow to be adult chickens, and eventually die. What would happen if no new chickens were born to replace those that died? There would be no more chickens in the world—they'd be extinct. In order to keep themselves from dying out, all living things reproduce themselves. "Reproduce" means to make again, or to make a copy. Reproduction is the process of making again.

The cells in your body reproduce themselves and increase in number, which is

how you grow. Every day, for example, some of your skin cells reproduce themselves and some of them die. As you get older and bigger, your skin cells reproduce faster than they die, so you can keep fitting into your skin. As you grow taller, your bone cells make more bone cells. When you become an adult, the cells involved in growth reproduce more slowly, and as a result, dead cells are replaced more slowly—so slowly, in fact, that at about age twenty you stop growing. Then the birth and death of cells come into balance. For every new cell that reproduces and lives, another dies, so the number of cells stays about even.

Organisms reproduce in different ways. You already know some of these. Some plants make seeds. Mushrooms make spores. Frogs and chickens lay eggs. Dogs have litters of puppies. But what about protists and monerans? Let's read about two categories of reproduction: asexual and sexual.

Asexual Reproduction

One way that organisms copy themselves is through asexual reproduction. "Asexual" means nonsexual; that is, reproduction without using males and females. The organism simply makes copies of itself through cell division.

Asexual reproduction can be very simple. Monerans (the simplest of all organisms) and many protists reproduce by fission, which means splitting. After duplicating their genetic material, monerans like bacteria simply split their single cell in half. This allows them to grow colonies very quickly. Under the right conditions, bacteria colonies can double their numbers every twenty minutes!

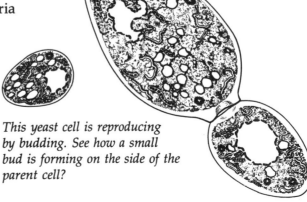

This yeast cell is reproducing by budding. See how a small bud is forming on the side of the parent cell?

Mildews, molds, and mushrooms are fungi that reproduce by forming spores. Spores are single cells often protected by a hard covering. Spores drop off the parent, and become new organisms if there is enough water and food for them to live. Most yeasts, on the other hand, reproduce by budding. A "bud," or enlargement, forms on one side of the cell, and eventually breaks off to form a new yeast cell.

Watching Cells Reproduce

Materials: a dissecting microscope (allows you to place large objects under the lens for observation) and two petri dishes (with lids), agar, and gram-negative and gram-positive stain (to help the organisms show up under the microscope). You can buy agar at many groceries and health food stores, and you can find gram-negative and -positive stain (as well as agar) through a pharmacy or a store that sells supplies to teachers.

Method: Fill each petri dish two-thirds full of agar. Place the petri dishes (without lids) in a warm spot for at least an hour. Put a few drops of gram-negative stain in the middle of one dish, and a few drops of gram-positive stain in the middle of the other. Be sure that the layer of stain is relatively thin in both dishes. If not, tap and swirl each dish to spread out the stain. Put the dishes under the dissecting microscope and observe. Can you pick out any organisms? Draw what you see. Observe at two ten-minute intervals for the next twenty minutes. Cover the petri dishes with lids, and repeat your observations the following day. Note: Wash your hands each day after you complete the experiment, and do not touch the agar at any time. Also, carefully dispose of the agar and wash the petri dishes when you are done with the experiment. Questions: How did the organisms end up on the agar? What shape are they? Did you notice any of the cells in the process of reproducing while you observed? What happened overnight?

Asexual Reproduction in Larger Animals and Plants

Some plants and animals can reproduce themselves asexually in a process called regeneration, meaning to make or generate again. These organisms make new body parts to replace lost ones. In plants, the most familiar example of regeneration is called cloning, in which a piece of the plant—a leaf or stem cutting—is put into some moist material, and a whole new plant forms. Many garden plants like roses are reproduced by cloning, because you can be sure the new plant is exactly like the parent.

A starfish regenerates amputated limbs.

The amount of regeneration that can occur in asexual reproduction depends on the type of organism. You regenerate skin cells when you cut your finger and the wound heals. But for the most part, the human body has little ability to regenerate.

Other animals have a much greater ability to regenerate. A starfish can grow a whole new arm if one is cut off. The lost arm, if it still has a piece of the center of the starfish, can even grow into a new starfish. When certain worms are cut in half, each half grows into a new worm. Salamanders can regenerate a leg if they lose one. The leg can't regenerate a new salamander, though. More complex animals like salamanders and humans have a more limited ability to regenerate.

Sexual Reproduction in Mosses and Ferns

Sexual reproduction requires the joining of special male and female cells before reproduction occurs. These special cells are called gametes. In sexual reproduction, a male and female gamete come together to form a fertilized egg.

Mosses, which you may have seen in shady spots, reproduce by making spores. But, unlike fungi, which form spores without using male and female cells, moss spores are formed by bringing a male and female cell together. Look at the drawing of the moss's life cycle. In the first step, a spore has just landed in a moist, nutrient-rich spot where it grows into a special kind of moss plant. The plant usually looks like a green thread. After a time, something amazing happens. The thread develops buds that grow into small plants, some of which are male and others female. Afterward, the thread usually dies. The male moss plants make male gametes, the female plants make female gametes. When a male and female plant are close enough together, and there is some water present, a male gamete is able to swim to a female gamete and fertilize it. This fertilized egg makes a capsule in which new spores are formed; the mature spores fall on moist ground, and the process starts over again.

The life cycle of a fern is similar to that of a moss, but there are some differences. When the fern spore gets wet it germinates, turning into a tiny, heart-shaped plant that produces both male and female gametes. When these male and female gametes come together, the fertilized egg grows into a totally new and different plant that will become the large fern you can find in the woods. The mature fern produces

The life cycle of a moss.

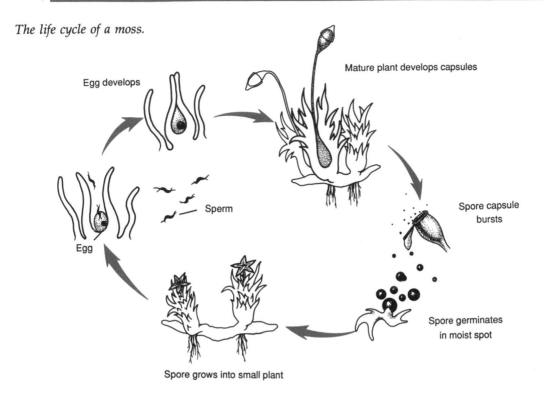

Egg develops

Mature plant develops capsules

Sperm

Spore capsule bursts

Egg

Spore germinates in moist spot

Spore grows into small plant

The life cycle of a fern.

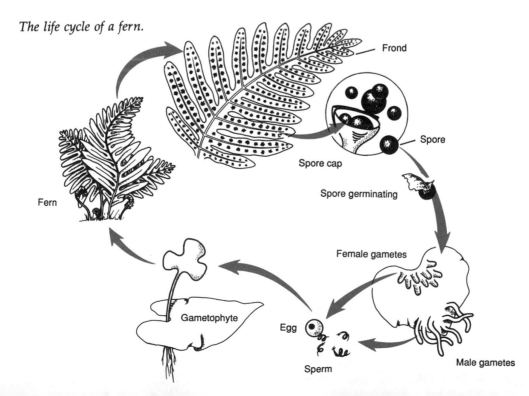

Frond

Spore

Spore cap

Spore germinating

Fern

Female gametes

Gametophyte

Egg

Male gametes

Sperm

spores under its leaves. You can usually see the spore caps if you look under the frond of a mature fern. In time, the spores burst from their caps and start the cycle over again.

Conifer Seeds Are Naked

Most large plants other than mosses and ferns reproduce by sexual reproduction in which a male and female gamete come together to make a seed. Some of the simplest of these seed plants are the conifers, a name that means "cone carriers." You have probably seen a pine cone. Have you wondered what it was for? It is the reproductive part of the pine tree.

If you can find a big pine tree, you may be able to see that there are both big and small cones on it. These two kinds of cones are usually found on the same plant. The small cone carries the male cells. That's because it doesn't take much space to store the millions of tiny grains of pollen that each carry a male gamete.

Pollen from the male pine cone is carried by the wind and sticks to the eggs inside the larger female pine cone. Tubes that grow from the grains of pollen pierce the eggs in the female cone, and a male gamete passes through the egg wall and fertilizes the egg. Each fertilized egg then grows into a seed, which drops to the ground when the cone opens. The seed grows into a new tree if enough food and water are present.

The seed from a conifer is called a naked seed, because it has nothing on except its own skin. So, the conifers belong to the group of plants called gymnosperms, which means "naked seeds."

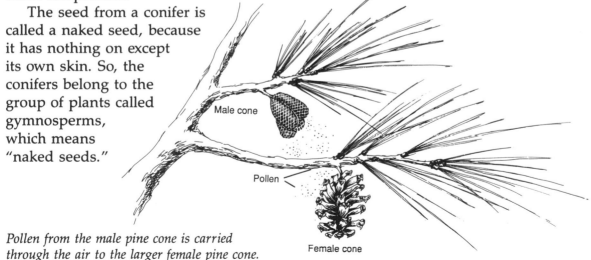

Pollen from the male pine cone is carried through the air to the larger female pine cone.

Seeds of Flowering Plants Have Clothes

Most plants clothe the seeds they make with some sort of covering. The fruit of a cherry is a covering for the seed inside it. Have you ever eaten a peanut from the shell? A peanut is a seed, and the shell is its covering. Tomatoes have seeds inside, and so do oranges. You're probably more interested in the fruit than the seeds, but for the purpose of reproduction, the tomato and the orange are just coverings for seeds.

These plants with covered seeds are called angiosperms, which in Greek means "covered seeds." All these plants have one thing in common: they have flowers. The seed covers, hard or soft, big or small, sweet or sour, have all come from the same place—a flower.

Flowers

Many of the plants you are familiar with, including most trees, shrubs, vines, grasses, and garden plants, produce flowers. They can be as large and showy as sunflowers or as tiny and unnoticeable as the flowers found on a grass plant, but most flowers have essentially the same parts.

Let's look at a diagram of a typical flower to see how seeds are formed. Most flowers form as a series of rings, one inside the other. The outer ring is made up of sepals, which are usually green and look like leaves attached to the stem at the base of a flower. Inside the sepals, the petals make the next ring. The colorful petals attract insects, which are often important for bringing the right sperm (the male gamete) to the egg. Inside the ring of petals in the center of the flower lie the reproductive parts. The stamens are the male reproductive organs. Each stamen has an anther on its tip, where millions of tiny pollen grains, each with a single

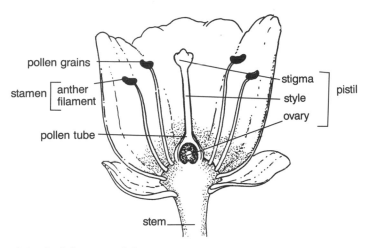

pollen grains

stamen [anther
          filament

pollen tube

stigma
style   } pistil
ovary

stem

A typical flower and its parts.

male gamete, are attached. Nearby is the pistil, a solid tube which leads down to the ovary with its egg.

What is an ovary? In Latin it means "a place for eggs." This place for the egg or eggs is completely closed and protected. Protecting the egg is one of the great advantages of a flower. Sometimes, when there is just one egg, the ovary is called an ovule, which means small ovary. For instance, when there is just one seed inside a berry, you know it came from a single ovule. When there are several eggs, then there will be several ovules inside a larger ovary. And later when that ovary develops into a fruit, there will be several seeds inside, as in a tomato, orange, or apple.

Flower Fertilization

The first step of flower fertilization is pollination, the movement of pollen from the anther to the sticky top of the pistil. But how does the pollen make that trip? Insects or birds are responsible for pollinating many flowers. But wind and rain also assist in pollination. Look at the bee in the picture. When the bee sips nectar from the flower, it also knocks the pollen off the anther and onto the pistil.

In the second step of fertilization, a tube grows out of the pollen grain that is stuck to the pistil. The pistil will not let a pollen tube grow down it unless the pollen comes from the same kind of plant. Inside the pollen tube is the male gamete. The tube grows down, down, down the pistil and into the ovule which is at the bottom of the pistil.

In the last step, the male gamete joins the egg cell in the ovule, and fertilization occurs. The fertilized egg cell begins to divide and form an embryo or young organism. The ovule grows into a covering that protects what is now the seed. As the seed forms in the parent plant, the flower changes. The sepals and petals die and fall off, and the ovule or the ovary grows into a covering—into beans, berries, tomatoes, or the hard shells of nuts. The covering protects the seed or seeds inside it, and also helps scatter the seed. Have you ever seen the fruits of a

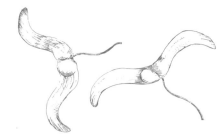

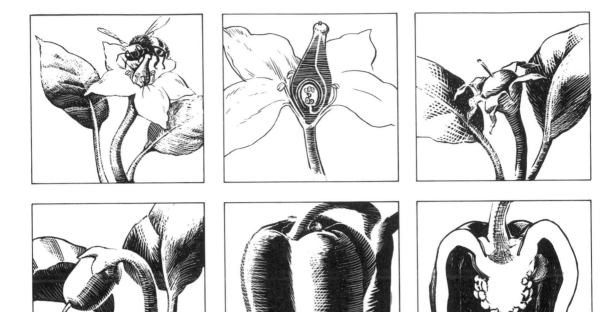

The stages of reproduction in a flowering plant: pollination, fertilization, ovary begins to grow as flower petals die, ovary continues to grow, mature fruit or vegetable houses seeds for next generation.

maple tree flying on the wind? These fruits have tiny "wings" that can carry them for long distances.

When the fruit leaves the parent plant, it starts to decay and fall away from the seed. This allows the seed to reach the soil, where it can grow into a new plant.

Seed Development

Way back in Book One we said that a seed in a fruit is like a little plant in a box with its lunch. Now we're going to learn more about how seeds grow into new plants.

Look at the drawing of a young bean seed. You can clearly see the young plant or embryo inside the seed. Notice the large area where food is stored. This is called the endosperm; it contains food for the young plant—and also for creatures, including humans, who eat seeds. This food keeps the embryo alive until it grows big enough to make its own food. See the seed coat? It protects the seed, and keeps it from drying out.

When a seed falls to the ground, it is sometimes pushed into the soil by heavy rainfall. Certain seeds are buried by animals like squirrels who want to eat them

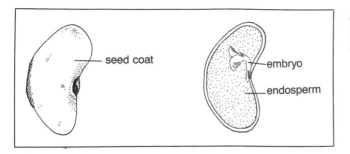

A tough seed coat surrounds and protects the tender embryo and the endosperm of the bean seed.

later. Look at the drawing of the seed in soil. When seeds are planted in moist soil they absorb water. When temperatures become warmer, the cells of the embryo inside the seed begin to divide, and the embryo grows. The tiny embryo continues to use the stored food inside the seed to grow, and eventually it breaks through the seed coat. The embryo sprouts roots, and is now a new plant. This sprouting of the new plant is called germination.

The roots of the new plant take in water and minerals that the plant uses to grow. As the stem grows upward, leaves

Stages of germination in a bean seed. The growing embryo breaks through its seed coat, sprouting roots. The roots grow bigger, pushing the new plant above ground. The plant grows leaves that help it make its own food as an adult.

appear. These leaves help the plant to make its own food, which helps the plant to grow into an adult plant. Later, the adult plant develops flowers, the flowers develop seeds, and the cycle begins again.

Examine a Bean Seed

Materials: *One bean seed, a cup of water, a magnifying glass.*

Method: Soak the bean seed in water overnight. Remove the seed from the water and examine the soaked bean seed. Remove the seed coat, and note its thickness. Carefully separate the two halves of the bean seed with your fingernail. Can you find the embryo inside? Draw a picture of the inside of your seed. Can you find the stored food?

Reproduction in Animals

Although some animals can reproduce asexually, as we read earlier, most animals reproduce sexually. Just as plants produce male and female gametes, so do animals.

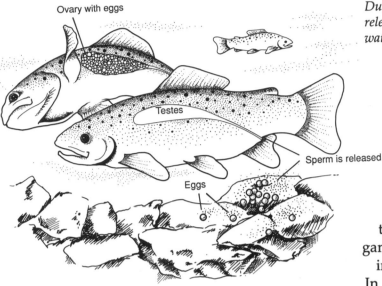

Ovary with eggs

Testes

Sperm is released

Eggs

During spawning season, adult fish release eggs and sperm into the water where fertilization takes place.

In animals, the male gametes or sperm are produced in organs called the testes, while the female gametes or eggs are produced in organs called the ovaries. In some simpler animals, like earthworms, the sperm- and egg-making organs are both in the same creature. But in most animals, male and female gametes are made by separate male and female creatures.

If sperm and egg join *outside* the bodies of the parents, the process is called *external* fertilization. When sperm and egg join *inside* the body of the female, as with humans, it is called *internal* fertilization.

Have you ever seen a film that shows fish spawning? Spawning is a form of external fertilization. During spawning, female fish and male fish come very close together in the water. The female releases her eggs into the water and the male releases his sperm. The sperm swim to the eggs and fertilize them.

Birds and also mammals like horses and humans reproduce by internal fertilization. The female releases an egg from her ovary, and it travels down a tube which leads from the ovary. During mating, the male releases sperm inside the female. The sperm travels to the tube where the egg is, and fertilizes it. If no sperm joins an egg, the egg is unfertilized and leaves the female's body. Other eggs will later travel down the tube leading from the ovary, and one of these may be fertilized.

For birds, fertilization takes place inside the female's body. Whether a bird egg is fertilized or not, it grows larger and gains a shell layer inside the mother's body. Once the mother lays a fertilized egg, she must give it warmth and protection if the chick inside is to develop and eventually hatch.

Egg

Ovary

Have You Ever Seen a Koalaroo?

What makes a species? As we read earlier, scientists use information about reproduction along with other information to classify organisms into smaller and smaller groups. One very important level of grouping is called a species. You are a member of the species homo sapiens *(HO-mo SAY-pee-ens)*. (You might enjoy looking up homo sapiens in the dictionary or encyclopedia to see what the name of our species means.)

For species that reproduce sexually, members usually mate and produce offspring only with other members of the same species. For example, when a female koala bear mates with a male animal and produces a baby koala bear, we know that the male animal must have been a koala bear. Koala bears do not mate with kangaroos and produce young.

Development of the Embryo

Once the egg is fertilized, it is called a zygote (ZYE-goat). The zygote begins to divide and grow, and after several days or weeks—depending on the animal—the zygote becomes an embryo. An embryo, remember, is a developing organism. In most mammals, the embryo develops inside the mother's body in an organ called the uterus (YOO-ter-us). The zygote travels down the tube from the ovary, enters the uterus, and attaches itself to the wall of the uterus. In the uterus the developing embryo gets its food and water from the mother. In the later stages of development, the embryo is called a fetus. When it has developed enough to live on its own, the fetus is born.

Horses take eleven months to develop inside their mothers. Sheep take only five months. Do you know how long it takes a human embryo to develop?

Egg→Zygote→Embryo→Fetus→Newborn

STAGES OF EMBRYO

Care and Growth of Young

Fish do not take care of their young at all. Nor do sea turtles. Female sea turtles lay fifty to one hundred eggs in a hole in the sand and then return to the ocean. Their young hatch, then crawl out of their nest and on to the sea with no protection or help from their mothers. Before reaching the ocean, many are eaten by hungry gulls or crabs. And a good number of those that do reach the water are swallowed up by hungry fish.

But most animals are cared for by one or more parents until they can survive on their own. Usually, birds tend their eggs in a nest until their young are hatched, and then feed the young until they are old enough to fly. Lion cubs stay with their parents for about four years, until the cubs are old enough to defend themselves and to find food.

To reach maturity, this seagoing loggerhead turtle had to survive many hazards.

Growth Stages

As we have learned, the development of an organism from birth through reproduction and death is called the life cycle. Usually there are noticeable stages of development during an organism's life cycle. Look at the drawing of the life cycle of the horse. Reproduction occurs inside the mother when egg and sperm unite, and an embryo develops. The embryo grows into a fetus, which looks like a full-grown horse in miniature. At birth, the mother licks the newborn to stimulate circulation and clean him off. Soon after birth, when he can stand, the young foal drinks milk from his mother's teat. After a year the foal is now a colt. He no longer needs his mother's milk and eats grass beside her. In four years, the colt is a fully mature horse.

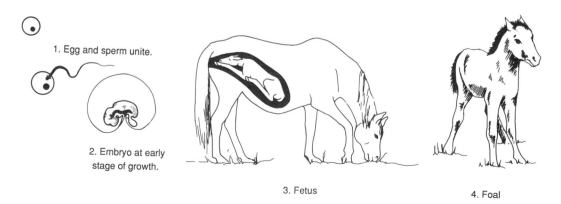

1. Egg and sperm unite.

2. Embryo at early stage of growth.

3. Fetus

4. Foal

Fertilization and much of the development of the young horse takes place within the mother's body.

Human Growth Stages

Humans also show stages in their growth. You developed into an embryo and then a fetus inside your mother's uterus. When you were a newborn baby, also called an infant, you were bottle-fed or you drank breast milk. You grew and developed fairly rapidly, until, when you were about a year old, you learned to walk. Between the ages of eight and seventeen, most of you will experience a period of rapid growth, and your bodies will begin changing as you reach puberty, the age at which you become capable of reproducing. Between the ages of seventeen and twenty-one, you will stop growing. At about forty, your metabolism will begin to slow down, and after you turn sixty-five, you are considered to be in the last stage of life, called old age.

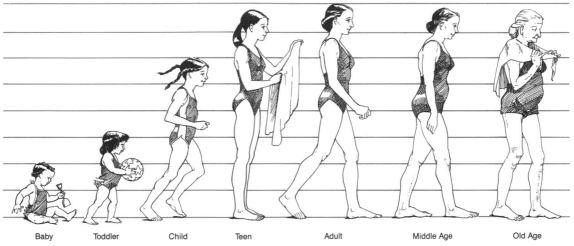

| Baby | Toddler | Child | Teen | Adult | Middle Age | Old Age |

Stages of human growth.

Adolescence and Puberty

The period of rapid growth and changes in the human body that occurs between eight and seventeen is known as adolescence (ad-uhl-ES-ens). During adolescence, changes occur as powerful chemicals called hormones are released into the bloodstream from glands in your body. The process usually begins earlier in girls than it does in boys, and causes physical, mental, and emotional changes in a person's life.

As an adolescent, you may experience an increase in your appetite; you may be hungry all the time. You may become more active during the day, and require more sleep at night. Some people experience a very rapid change in height and weight, sometimes called a "growth spurt." Their muscles and bones get larger, and their favorite clothes don't fit anymore. They may feel awkward, because their hands and feet are growing faster than the other parts of their body.

Girls start to develop breasts, and their hips begin to round out. Boys' shoulders widen, and their voices change, sometimes cracking as they begin to deepen. Both boys and girls develop hair under their arms and around their genitals.

Many other changes occur during adolescence. If you want to know more about this stage of life, you can ask your parents or find books in your local library on the subject. It is important to remember that these changes are normal, and they happen to every human being. Don't think badly of yourself if they start happening to you earlier or later than they do to somebody else. There is a lot of variation in the age at which people begin adolescence. Sooner or later, everybody goes through adolescence—a necessary stage in becoming an adult.

The Human Reproductive System

The changes in a person's body during adolescence are in preparation for puberty, the time when male and female humans undergo physical changes which enable them to produce children. Human reproduction is very similar to reproduction in other mammals. In females, an egg cell is released each month from one of two ovaries. The egg then passes into one of the fallopian (fah-LOW-pee-en) tubes, where it is either fertilized by sperm from a male, or not. If it is not fertilized, it passes into the uterus, and then out of the body along with the lining of the uterus. The uterus lining and egg pass through the vagina (vuh-JY-nuh) on their way out of the body. This monthly process of shedding the unfertilized egg and the lining of the uterus is called menstruation (men-stroo-AY-shun)—from the Latin word *mensis*, meaning month, because it typically occurs about once a month.

How does the sperm reach the egg in the fallopian tube to fertilize it? First we need to learn about the male reproductive organs. Sperm are produced in the testes, oval-shaped glands that are contained in a pouch of skin, the scrotum, which hangs below the penis. The sperm travel through tubes in the testes in a whitish fluid called semen. The semen can exit the male's body through the urethra, a tube in his penis.

During sexual intercourse, the male places his penis inside the female's vagina. The semen shoots out of his penis and into her vagina, and the sperm swim toward her uterus. After reaching the uterus, they swim toward the fallopian tubes, where one sperm cell—and only one—is admitted through the egg's outer covering. When egg and sperm join, fertilization has occurred.

If the egg is fertilized, it develops into a zygote, which travels down the fallopian tube and implants itself in the wall of the

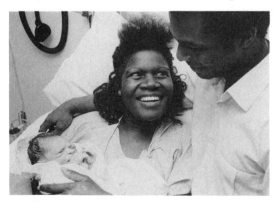

Joyful parents welcome their newborn into their lives.

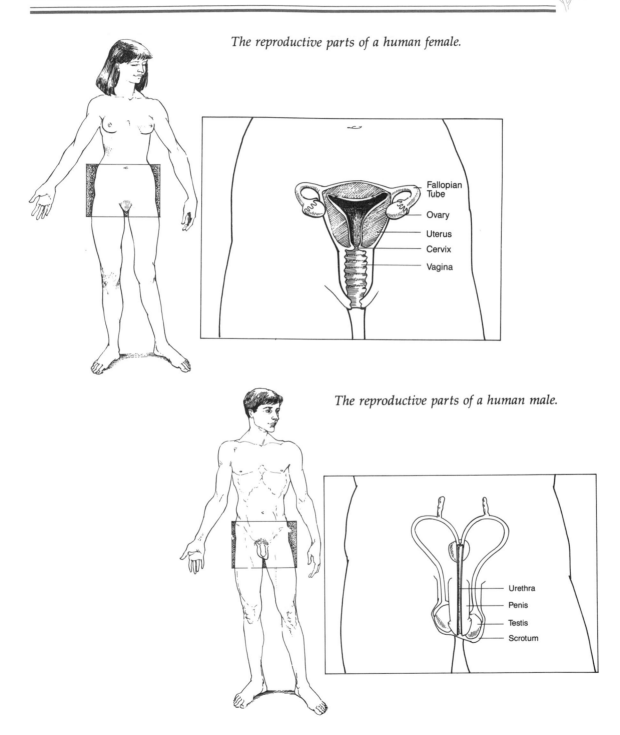

The reproductive parts of a human female.

Fallopian Tube
Ovary
Uterus
Cervix
Vagina

The reproductive parts of a human male.

Urethra
Penis
Testis
Scrotum

uterus. Here it grows into an embryo and further develops into a fetus. The fetus grows inside its mother for nine months, until it is developed enough to live in the outside world. When it is born, a baby needs constant care and attention.

Introduction to Physical Sciences

FOR PARENTS AND TEACHERS

This section continues the study of electricity begun in Book Four and begins a study of such mechanical concepts as mass, speed, force, work, and the ways heat transfers energy. It also introduces engines and technologies of communication.

One feature of this section is that it shows children how to combine ideas from science and math. In today's world, science and math are interrelated, and children who can learn early the very important relationship between these fields will be far better prepared for the future than those who do not. Terms like newton and joule and formulas like $s = d/t$ are part of the new standard of science which our eleven-year-olds, with their flexible, active, and retentive minds, can learn even though we may not have learned them ourselves. Parents and teachers who do not wish to use the mathematical formulas may skip them and follow the nonmathematical explanations and experiments presented, but we urge readers to consider the applications of math as an important challenge.

The following resources may help you in your hands-on exploration of the concepts presented in this section:

Science Book of Electricity by Neil Ardley (Harcourt Brace Jovanovich, 1991).
Electricity by Neil Ardley (Macmillan Children's Group, 1992). From *The Way It Works* Series.
The Science Book of Machines by Neil Ardley (Harcourt Brace Jovanovich, 1992).
Airborne: The Search for the Secret of Flight by Richard Maurer (Simon & Schuster, 1992).
Black Pioneers of Science and Invention by Louis Haber (Harcourt Brace Jovanovich, 1990; paperback, 1992). This book is full of fascinating biographies that are accessible to advanced readers in the fifth grade.

Physical Sciences

MECHANICAL CONCEPTS

Everyday Words in Science

In everyday language, you might hear the words "force," "speed," and "work" used like this:

> We had to *force* the window open.
> *Speed* up. We're late.
> I'm going to *work* now.

In science, these words have special meanings that are slightly different from their everyday meanings. In science, they are used to express ideas that we can measure exactly by using measuring devices like scales, clocks, or rulers. Once we express these measurements in numbers, we can use mathematics to describe how the physical world acts, or predict how it will act. In this section, we are going to show you how to express concepts like speed and force in the form of numbers, exactly as scientists do, and then apply mathematics to figure out some things about the physical world.

To measure things like force, work, and speed, the scientist goes back to the basic characteristics of the world like matter, length, and time. Let's review what we already know about matter, length, and time, and see some ways that scientists measure force, work, speed, and so on.

Matter and Mass

Matter is anything that takes up space. Do you take up space? Of course you do. Can you think of anything that *doesn't* take up space? The nearest we can come to finding something that doesn't take up space is a vacuum. A vacuum is the absence of matter. You can make a vacuum by pumping all the air out of a sealed glass bottle. (Actually, even then you wouldn't quite have a complete vacuum, because there would be a few air molecules left that not even the best pump could remove.)

A scientist is often interested in measuring how much matter there is in a thing. Suppose we take two identical bottles and fill one with air and the other with water. Which bottle has more matter in it? The bottle of water. But why? You can feel that the bottle full of water weighs more than the bottle full of air. A thing that weighs more than another thing has more matter. Weight and matter go together. If we filled another identical bottle with lead marbles, it would weigh still more and contain more matter. You yourself have more matter in you than you did when you were born, because you weigh more now than you did then.

Look at these scales. How do you know which bottle is filled with more matter?

But there is a problem in measuring the amount of matter by how much something weighs. That's because weight changes from place to place. You weigh more at sea level (the midpoint between high tide and low tide levels of the ocean) than you do on top of a mountain, and you weigh more on earth than you would on the moon. But you still have the same amount of matter. Weight depends on how strongly gravity is pulling on something, and the pull of gravity is greater on the earth than on the moon. This means we can't depend on measuring weight alone to tell us exactly how much matter a thing has. We need a measure that is even more constant than weight, something that measures how much matter there is in a thing wherever it is.

The word that scientists use for the amount of matter a thing at rest has, no matter where it is, is "mass." Mass is measured in the same units as weight, because the mass of a thing is the same as its weight when it happens to be resting at sea level on the earth. You can measure mass in pounds, just as checkout clerks measure things in pounds at the grocery store. Always remember, though, that unlike weight, the *mass* of a thing at rest is always the same, even if it is floating in space and doesn't weigh anything at all. In science, the usual units for measuring mass are grams (g) and kilograms (kg). A kilogram is 1000 grams. There are about 2.2 pounds in a kilogram. An average newborn human baby has a mass of about 7.5 pounds, which is around 3400 grams or 3.4 kilograms. That would also be the baby's weight at sea level. As you'll soon see, units of mass like the pound, gram, and kilogram are very important in making all sorts of measurements.

What Are Length and Time?

Two other basic concepts scientists use for measuring force, work, speed, etc., are length and time. Length is the distance between two points. The length of your body is the distance between the soles of your feet and the top of your head. Length isn't always in a straight line. Think of the length of a line around a circle or a curvy road on a map. These could be turned into straight lines if you imagined the line as a string, and then pulled the string into a straight line that you measured with a ruler. Length is measured in inches, feet, miles, centimeters, meters, and kilometers, just to name a few units.

Which unit of length would be appropriate to measure the length of our solar system? Miles or kilometers might do, but inches would be silly. The most convenient unit of length is the light-year, which is the huge distance that light travels in a year. A light-year is almost *six trillion* miles! Astronomers use light-years to measure the distances between stars or galaxies.

Scientists also use time for measuring things.

You know what time is; you know it's going by even as you read these words. You know many units we use to measure time—seconds, minutes, hours, days, years, and centuries.

With these three basic ideas—mass, length, and time—and the units to express them, we can begin to describe things in the world scientifically. That is, we can measure them with numbers and deal with the numbers mathematically. Let's start with the example of measuring speed.

This portion of the constellation Hercules the Hero is more than thirty-three thousand light-years from earth.

Speed

Speed is how far something travels in a unit of time. Have you heard someone say a car is going 60 miles an hour? Since scientists like to define things with mathematics, let's figure out how far that car will go in an hour if its speed is 60 miles an hour. You're right if you said that it would go a distance of 60 miles. Notice that we express speed by using two units, miles and hours. These are units of length and of time.

The speed of anything is the distance or length it travels *per* unit of time. That little word "per" is important and so is the word "unit." "Per" means *for* in Latin, and "unit" means *one*. A good way to think about the "per" is to think of division in arithmetic. The "per" means to divide. If you divide the number of total miles the car goes by the number of hours it goes, you will get its speed expressed in miles *per* hour. So 60 miles divided by 1 hour equals 60 miles per *1* hour.

Dividing distance by time gives us the scientific formula for speed. A scientific formula is an expression with an equals sign (=). Speed equals units of distance divided by (or per) units of time. If we use d to mean distance, and t to mean time, then we can say:

$$\text{speed} = \frac{d}{t}$$

Using this formula, at what speed would someone have to drive in order to travel the distance (d) of 120 miles in the time (t) of 2 hours?

$$\text{speed} = \frac{d}{t}$$

$$\text{speed} = \frac{120 \text{ mi}}{2 \text{ h}}$$

So we divide 120 by 2.

$$\frac{120}{2} = \frac{60}{1}$$

$$\text{speed} = 60 \text{ mi per } 1 \text{ h}$$

You can even figure out the speed of light if you know the distance between the earth and sun and if you also know the time it takes a ray of light to travel that distance. The sun is about 93 million miles away, and its light takes about 500 seconds to travel here. Just divide the distance in miles by the time in seconds and you will get the speed of light in miles per second. If you understand that speed always equals distance divided by time, you know the basic principle of calculating speed. The rest is measurement and arithmetic.

Force

You can think of force as the exertion of a push or a pull. How shoud we measure it? Let's see if we can measure force using only our basic units: mass, distance, and time.

Put a book on top of your open hand. If you lift the book up, you know you are putting force on the book, and you can also feel the book putting force on your hand. If you let the book slowly down, you also feel it putting force on your hand. But if you hold the book steady, is there any force? Yes there is: the book is still pushing down and your hand is still pushing up, and both are exerting equal force. That's why the book is staying in one place. How much force is your hand exerting against the book (and vice versa) when it is *not* moving up or down? That depends on the book's weight. If the book weighs 1 pound,

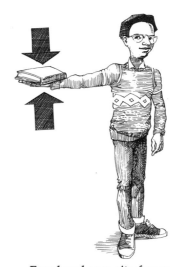

Equal and opposite forces keep the book steady.

you can say your hand is exerting a force of 1 pound on the book and the book is exerting 1 pound of force on your hand. So you can see that force can be expressed in a unit of mass like the pound!

The force of the book on your hand is called gravity. Gravity is a force that pulls bodies toward each other, and it is one of the forces found everywhere in the universe. Other kinds of force are electrical, where two electrons or two protons push each other away, and electrons and protons attract each other. There's also magnetic force, where two north or two south poles repel each other, and north and south poles attract each other. All of these forces could be measured in pounds. But for many reasons scientists often use a special unit, called a newton, to measure forces. A newton is about .225 pounds. How many newtons of force did it take to hold up your 1-pound book?

Here's a problem about force. If you are by the seashore and you pile 2 pounds of sand on your stomach, how much force is the sand putting on your stomach? The answer is 2 pounds of force. But how much force is your stomach putting on the sand? Answer: also 2 pounds. Can you explain why?

Pressure

In the problem above, the total force of sand on your stomach was 2 pounds. The sand also put *pressure* on your stomach, didn't it? The pressure the sand put on your stomach is the average force exerted on the various areas of your stomach. Another way to say that is pressure is force per unit area. Here's the formula:

$$\text{pressure} = \frac{\text{force}}{\text{area}}$$

Let's figure out the pressure of the sand on your stomach. Our unit of force will be the pound and our unit of area will be the square inch. Remember, a square inch is a square with sides of 1 inch, so to get the number of pounds per square inch of pressure we divide the number of pounds of force by the number of square inches of your stomach covered by sand. In our chosen units:

$$\text{pounds per square inch} = \frac{\text{pounds}}{\text{square inches}}$$

We know that the sand had a total of 2 pounds of force. How can we figure out the pressure? We have to know the area. Suppose the 2 pounds of sand were in a box on your stomach, and suppose that the bottom of the box had an area of 16 square inches. We can quickly figure out the pressure per square inch on your stomach.

$$\text{pressure (lbs per in}^2) = \frac{2\,\text{lb}}{16\,\text{in}^2}$$

So the pressure on your stomach would be $\frac{2}{16}$, or $\frac{1}{8}$, of a pound per square inch. From this example, you have learned how to figure out the pressure of *anything*, because pressure is always the number of units of force divided by the number of units of area. The result is expressed as units of force per unit of area.

Here's an example. The weather report often talks about a high pressure or low pressure area moving in. This refers to the pressure of the atmosphere. What makes the atmosphere exert pressure? It's the pull of gravity on the gases in the atmosphere. Atmospheric pressure is the weight of the atmosphere over a particular area on the surface of the earth. It acts like the weight of the sand on your stomach. At sea level on the earth, the atmosphere that lies above 1 square inch of the earth's surface weighs about 14.7 pounds.

$$\text{pressure} = \frac{14.7\,\text{lb}}{1\,\text{sq in}}$$

Therefore, on earth, the atmospheric pressure at sea level is expressed as 14.7 pounds per square inch. The atmosphere on Venus has a pressure of about 1347 pounds per square inch. That is almost 100 times heavier than that of the earth—heavy enough to crush a person!

Work

In everyday language, we might say, it takes a lot of work to learn something. But in physics, work is only being done when something is being moved. If you hold a book in your hand without moving it, the book is pushing down, and you are pushing up, and the two pushes are equal, but no work is being done because nothing is being moved. Only when force moves something is work being done, and the farther it is moved, the more work is done. So in order to find out how much work is being done, we need to measure two things: how *much* force is doing the pushing and how *far* it is being pushed. Just as with speed and pressure, we can define work with a mathematical formula: work is measured by multiplying force times distance.

Because one force is greater than the other, the book moves and work is done.

$$\text{work} = \text{force} \times \text{distance}$$

Let's say we drop a penny from the Empire State Building. How much work is done on the penny as it falls to earth? We first need to know the force of the earth on the penny. The force needed to hold a penny still is the same as its weight, which is about 0.00674 pounds. The distance it drops is the height of the building, which is 1472 feet. So the work done on the penny can be figured out by multiplying units of distance times units of force.

$$work = 1472 \text{ ft} \times 0.00674 \text{ lb}$$

When you multiply 1472 times .00674, you get 9.92. But 9.92 *what?* Well, if work is distance times force, then work can be expressed by *combining* distance and force. In fact, one of the expressions for work is the foot-pound, an expression of distance times force. In the case of the penny, 1472 feet times .00674 pounds is 9.92 foot-pounds.

Now you know how to compute work in terms of foot-pounds. If you know the distance in feet, and if you know the force in pounds, then when you multiply, the result is work expressed in foot-pounds. If you want to use the metric system you could express work as newton-meters, which also measures force times distance.

There are special units scientists use to measure work, like "erg" and "joule." These terms can be translated into foot-pounds or into any other equivalent expression for distance times force. For instance, a joule is about .738 foot-pounds.

Energy

Energy is almost the same as work; after all, it takes energy to do work. Energy is expressed in the same units as work, such as foot-pounds, ergs, and joules. But there's one major difference between energy and work. To have energy, a thing does not have to move. When energy does move things it is the same as work. In that case it is called *kinetic* energy, from the Greek word *kinein,* meaning to move. (That same Greek word is also the basis for "cinema" which means *moving* pictures or movies.) The kind of energy that a thing has before it starts to move is called *potential* energy.

To understand these two kinds of energy, let's think about our penny again. When we hold it at the top of the Empire State Building, it is motionless and so has no kinetic energy. But it has potential energy, because of its position high above the surface of the earth. When we release the penny, it falls to the ground. As it drops, it loses altitude and so loses potential energy. But, because it goes faster and faster as it descends, it gains kinetic energy.

A jack-in-the-box provides another example of the special relationship between potential and kinetic energy. When Jack sits still in his box with the lid shut, he has potential energy only. In this position the spring to which he is attached is tightly compressed. Now open the lid. As the spring expands and Jack pops out, potential energy is converted to kinetic energy.

Since energy and work are expressed in exactly the same units—foot-pounds or joules—doesn't it mean that energy and work are exactly the same? Not quite. Work is a way to transfer energy from one object to another. When you shove Jack into his box, you do work on Jack, because the muscles of your arm exert force to move Jack through a distance. The *work* you do on Jack has *transferred energy* from your body to Jack and the spring.

Power

In talking about force, work, and energy, we have used only two of our three basic ideas: mass and distance. We can also use the third concept, time, in learning about power. Power is a measure of the time in which work can be done. Suppose two young people, each weighing 50 pounds, set out together to run a mile. We know approximately how much work they have to do, since work is force times distance. They each have to move 50 pounds a distance of 1 mile or 5280 feet. The total work they must do is 50 pounds times 5280 feet or 264,000 foot-pounds.

But the faster runner finishes in 10 minutes, while it takes the slower person 20 minutes to complete the same path. Because the runners are the same size and run the same distance, the total amount of work they do is about the same. But because the first runner does the work twice as fast as her slower friend, she has twice as much power. Power equals work per unit of time. The more work per second, the more power. The person who ran the whole distance in 10 minutes did twice as much work in each second, and thus had twice as much power.

Power applies to all work done over time. You may already know that the power of car engines is rated in units called horsepower. A big car engine can have a 100-horsepower rating. Can you guess what 1 horsepower is? It's the amount of work a horse can do in 1 second. Long ago, it was decided that a typical horse is powerful enough to lift 55 pounds a distance of 10 feet in 1 second. If we multiply 10 feet times 55 pounds, we find that 1 horsepower means 550 foot-pounds per second. Here's the general formula:

$$\text{power} = \frac{\text{work}}{\text{time}}$$

$$\text{horsepower} = \frac{\text{foot-pounds}}{\text{seconds}}$$

Have you ever seen a horse-pulling contest at a state or county fair? To see which team of horses is strongest, the horses' power is measured by a dynamometer, the square instrument on top of the wagon.

Let's try to figure out how much horsepower the faster runner had. We already know that the total work done by a 50-pound person to run 1 mile is 264,000 foot-pounds. Now we have to divide that work by the time she took, which was 10 minutes or 600 seconds.

$$\text{runner's power} = \frac{264,000 \text{ foot-pounds}}{600 \text{ seconds}}$$

Since 264,000 divided by 600 equals 440, the power of the runner was 440 foot-pounds per second. So with 440 foot-pounds per second, the first runner did not have quite as much horsepower as a horse does, whose power is 550 foot-pounds per second.

Another way to measure power is in watts, which is the usual unit for electrical power. A watt is measured in joules per second. A joule of work equals about .738 foot-pounds of work, so it obviously would take many watts to equal 1 horsepower. Can you figure out how many? During 1 second 1 horsepower can do 550 foot-pounds of work. By the same token, a watt can do .738 foot-pounds of work in 1 second. How many .738s are there in 550? Answer: There are about 745 watts in 1 horsepower.

Phase Changes: Heat and Matter

The three phases, or states, of matter are solids, liquids, and gases. A solid has a fixed shape and volume: think of a brick. A liquid has a fixed volume, but takes on the shape of its container. Think about how water changes shape when poured from a flower vase to a fishbowl. A gas (vapor) assumes both the shape and volume of its container. For example, if you pop a helium-filled balloon in a large auditorium, the helium atoms will spread over the entire room.

You're familiar with the three different phases of water. As a solid, it's ice. As a liquid, it's liquid water. As a gas, it's steam. All three—ice, liquid water, and steam—are exactly the same kind of matter (H_2O) but in different phases.

Matter can be made to change phases by adding or removing energy. When matter goes through a phase change—for example, when ice turns to water, or water to steam—no new type of matter is produced: only the state (phase) of the matter is altered.

If you put an ice cube in a pan and heat it on a stove, a phase change will happen: the ice will melt to liquid water. Melting is the change from a solid to a liquid state.

The melting point of a solid is the temperature at which it changes into a liquid. You may know the melting point of water, which is 0°C. This same temperature, 0°C, is also the freezing point of water: freezing is the change from a liquid to a solid state.

The melting point and freezing point of a substance are the same temperature. When a substance is at this temperature, what happens to it—whether it melts or freezes—depends on whether we add energy to it or take energy from it.

Let's use water as an example, and begin with it in its solid form, as ice. Imagine we have a block of ice at −30°C. Then we slowly add heat energy, raising the temperature of the ice. As long as the temperature remains below 0°C, the appearance of the ice will not change. But when the ice reaches its melting point, 0°C, then if we continue to add energy in the form of heat, a phase change will occur: the ice will begin to melt into liquid water.

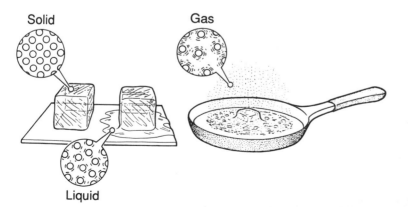

Solid

Gas

Liquid

Energy in the form of heat causes forces of attraction between water molecules in the ice to weaken: the molecules vibrate more rapidly and the ice melts into liquid water. Adding more heat further weakens the molecular attraction: the molecules vibrate even more and the liquid water turns into steam.

Each substance requires a specific amount of energy to make a phase change occur. To turn 1 gram of ice into water at 0°C, we need to add 334 joules of energy. If we keep adding enough energy to our block of ice at 0°C, then it will continue to melt, although the temperature of the ice will remain the same, at 0°C, until all the ice is gone.

What happens if we continue to heat the water that remains? The temperature of the water will rise. If we add enough heat, then the water will begin to boil and turn into water vapor, or steam. Boiling is the change from a liquid to a gas state; the boiling point of a liquid is the temperatue at which it changes to a gas.

The boiling point of water is 100°C. At this temperature, 1 gram of liquid water will change to a gas (steam) if it absorbs 2261 joules of energy. As you can see, it takes more energy to turn water to steam than it does to turn ice to water.

Why are different amounts of energy required for different phase changes? In the case of our example, water, why does it take more energy to turn water to steam than it does to turn ice to water? To answer this, we must understand a bit more about solids, liquids, and gases, using water again as an example.

In solid water (or ice), the molecules are close together and attract one another strongly. This accounts for the fixed shape of an ice cube. In liquid water, the molecules are able to move much more freely, but are still attracted to one another enough to hold a shape. The molecules of steam have very small forces of attraction and are very widely separated. It takes energy (334 joules) to break ice molecules apart from one another to make liquid water. It takes even more energy (2261 joules) to separate liquid water molecules to make steam.

Let's say that we managed to trap a quantity of steam in a balloon. If we place the balloon in a refrigerator, what will happen to the steam? The steam will cool, and then energy, in the form of heat, will be transferred to the refrigerator. Soon the steam will condense to liquid water: condensation is the change of phase from a gas to a liquid state.

Now, let's put the balloon, which has water in it, into the freezer. You know what will eventually happen to the water: it will freeze. Freezing, as mentioned above, is the change from a liquid to a solid state. When the water in the balloon freezes, is energy added to it or released from it?

Expansion and Contraction

Have you ever had trouble opening a jar? One trick you may know is to put the lid-end of the jar under hot water. After you do this, the lid will usually unscrew easily. That is because heat makes the metal in the lid get bigger and become loose. When matter is heated, it usually grows bigger, or expands. When it cools it does the opposite; it grows smaller, or contracts, and fills up less space.

There is a substance—water—that doesn't always get smaller when it cools. At

Distillation

Suppose we have a mixture of two liquids which we want to separate from each other. How can we do this? We can use heat because liquids have different boiling points. First, we gently heat the mixture. Soon the mixture reaches the temperature at which one of its two liquid components boils. Most of this liquid, which is the one with the lower boiling point, escapes from the mixture as vapor. The liquid mixture left behind contains mostly the liquid that is harder to vaporize—the one with the higher boiling point.

The process of separating the components of liquid mixtures based on their separate boiling points is called distillation.

A related process called fractional distillation is used to make gasoline and heating oil from crude oil. Crude oil, a fossil fuel, is a thick dark liquid mixture found beneath the earth's surface. After it is brought to the surface, it is placed in a boiler and heated to a high temperature. The liquids that boil at lower temperatures in the crude oil, like gasoline, can be separated from the ones with higher boiling points, like heating oil.

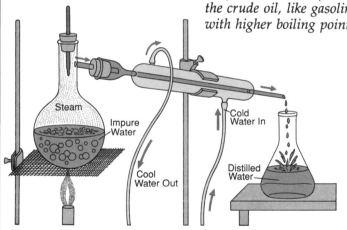

Steam

Impure Water

Cool Water Out

Cold Water In

Distilled Water

Distillation can be used to purify water by separating the water from materials dissolved in it. The impure water is heated until it vaporizes. Then the vapor is passed through the cooling tube so it will condense, and the distilled, or purified, water is collected on the right. (The impurities stay in the bottle on the left.)

first water does contract as it gets cooler, but at 4° Celsius (°C) it begins to expand. As it gets still colder, it expands still more until it reaches its freezing point at 0°C. Therefore 1 cup of solid ice weighs less than 1 cup of cold water. Have you noticed that ice cubes float in a glass of cold water? The ice is lighter than water, so it floats on top. Think about a frozen lake in winter: animals can walk across the icy surface, while plants and fish live below in the cold water.

Heat Isn't the Same as Temperature

Which has more heat, a cup of hot chocolate that is 120°F or a swimming pool that is 70°F? The swimming pool has more heat, even though its temperature is lower. Does that surprise you? Let's see why this is so.

Try this experiment the next time you take a bath. Run your bathwater and get in as usual. Then carefully pour a measuring cup of very hot water into the bathwater and stir it around. What happens? The temperature of the bath feels just about the same as it did before, doesn't it? Here's the reason. It takes only a little heat to raise the temperature of a cup of water, but it takes a lot of heat to raise the temperature of your bath. Adding just a little more heat from the cup of water didn't make much difference to the bath temperature.

To understand the difference between heat and temperature, we have to understand what heat is. Heat is a form of energy. You know that it takes energy to move something. Heat energy also makes things move, only you usually can't see the movement because the particles—atoms and molecules—are too small. The more energy they take in, the more they move and vibrate. This movement of molecules and other particles is what heat is.

Now let's see what temperature is. Think back to the bathtub experiment. The water in the measuring cup was hot and its temperature was high. Its molecules were vibrating very fast. The tub of water was warm, its temperature was lower, and the molecules were vibrating less fast. When the two were mixed together, the temperature of the tub stayed warm. That's because temperature is a measure of the *average* amount of heat or particle movement in a volume of matter. (Volume is the amount of space that a thing fills.) When the small volume of water in the cup and the large volume of water in the bath were mixed, the average heat of the large volume stayed about the same. Remember, temperature measures the average heat of a volume of matter.

Measuring Heat and Temperature

When somebody takes your temperature, it's measured in units called degrees. The average temperature for humans is 98.6° Fahrenheit (°F), or about 37° Celsius (°C). The Celsius scale is easier to measure with because it is based on measurements of water and is divided into 100 units. As we've learned, water freezes at 0°C (32°F), and boils at 100°C (212°F).

Since temperature in degrees measures the average amount of heat in a volume of matter, we can figure out how much total heat is in something by measuring both its temperature and how much of it there is. Let's see how this works. First we have to decide what heat units to use when we are figuring. Heat is a form of energy, so we can use the same terms we used for energy before—joules and foot-pounds. But scientists like to distinguish kinetic energy from heat energy, so to avoid confusion

In this body thermometer, colored alcohol or mercury inside a narrow tube rises or falls to indicate the temperature.

they don't use foot-pounds as units for heat, even though they could. The usual measure for heat is the calorie.

A calorie is defined as the amount of heat that will raise the temperature of 1 gram of water 1° Celsius. To raise a gram of water from 4°C to 7°C, you have to give it 3 calories of heat. The most common use of the word "calorie" is in nutrition. We eat food to get the energy (calories) our bodies need to function properly. When people talk about "counting calories" they really mean watching the number of *kilo-calories* in their diets. What people usually call a calorie is really a kilocalorie, or a thousand calories ("kilo" is Greek for thousand). Do you know a book where you can find out how many calories (really kilocalories) are in an orange? A carrot? A cupcake?

TRANSFERRING HEAT ENERGY

Conduction

If you stir a mug of hot cocoa with a metal spoon, pretty soon the heat will travel up the spoon to your fingers. Heat energy travels up the spoon handle to your fingers by conduction. Conduction is the transfer of heat energy by which moving particles make other particles move. Here's what happens. As heat flows from the cocoa to the immersed part of the spoon, that section of the spoon grows hot. Its atoms begin to vibrate rapidly. The immersed atoms are tightly connected to neighboring atoms along the handle. So these atoms begin vibrating too. Their vibrations cause the molecules of your fingertips to vibrate, creating the feeling of warmth.

Some materials are better conductors than others. For example, if you replace the metal spoon in a mug of hot cocoa with a plastic or wooden spoon, you'll find that the plastic and wooden spoons conduct little heat compared to the metal spoon. (The reasons for this have to do with the behavior of electrons, which you'll learn more about in Book Six of this series.)

Molecules in the immersed section of the spoon vibrate more rapidly because energy has been transferred to them from the hot cocoa. Soon energy will be conducted throughout the spoon.

P ut an index card and a penny in the freezer for several minutes. Now touch each one *with a different fingertip. Which feels colder? Why? Answer: The penny feels colder despite the fact that it and the card are at the same temperature. Metal is a better conductor than paper—the penny is conducting heat away from (removing heat energy from) your fingertips at a greater rate.*

Convection

Convection is transfer of heat that occurs in fluids. A fluid is either a liquid or a gas that can move and flow. Convection is caused by the fact that warm fluids are lighter than cold ones. We often say that a warm, light fluid rises and takes the place of a cooler, heavier one, but it's a little more accurate to say that the cool fluid falls and takes the place of the warm fluid that is below it. Either way you say it, the fluid moves, and heat is transferred by convection.

Here's an example. A pot of water on an electric stove or hot plate gets heated because of both conduction and convection. The pan's metal bottom conducts heat from the burner to the bottom layers of water. As this water expands, it becomes less dense than the cooler water at the top of the pan. The heavier water sinks to the bottom and pushes the lighter water to the top. The hot water is displaced by the cool water through convection. Can you describe what happens now to the cool water at the bottom of the pan? (Answer: It's heated by conduction, and the process keeps going.)

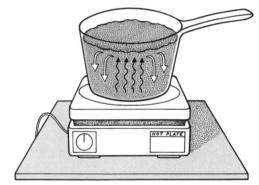

The cooler, heavier water sinks to the bottom of the pan.

P lace one end of a straw in a container of food coloring. Cover the free end with your *fingertip, to pick up a couple of drops. GENTLY transfer the drops to the bottom of a glass beaker filled with water. SLOWLY heat the water on a hot plate or stovetop. What happens to the food coloring? (The food coloring swirls up to the top by convection.)*

Radiation

Radiation is the transfer of heat by means of waves that can go through empty space. A good example would be waves of light such as those that come from the sun. You

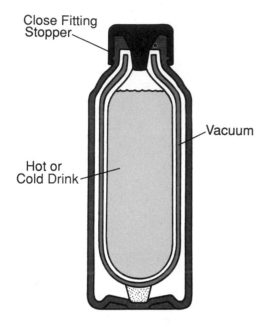

Cross section of a thermos. A silver mirror lines the inside of the thermos and radiates heat back into the liquid inside the thermos cavity. The bottle also has a vacuum between the inner compartment and the outer shell.

can feel the heat being radiated by the sun on a bright day. Radiation is the only way heat can be transferred through a vacuum. Do you remember that most of our solar system is empty space? Energy in the form of electromagnetic waves travels through this vacuum to us from the sun. When this radiation hits you or some other matter, it heats the matter. Very polished surfaces reflect back some of the radiation, just as a mirror reflects light.

It's because of this fact that a thermos uses a mirror to keep liquids hot or cold. A thermos is a bottle designed to reduce heat transfer to or from the liquid stored inside. You may have used a thermos to hold ice-cold lemonade on a hot July day, or steaming cocoa on a snowy day in winter. Here is a diagram of a thermos bottle. What modes of heat transfer are minimized by the empty space between the outer and inner walls of the thermos? Conduction and convection. What mode of heat transfer is reduced by the mirrored surfaces of the inner wall? Radiation.

ELECTRICITY

Remember the Electric Circuit?

In Book Three you read about what an electric circuit is. A circuit is a path through which electrons can be made to flow—usually along a metal wire. This flow of electrons is called an electrical current. Here is an example of a circuit consisting of four parts:

1. a battery
2. an insulated copper wire
3. a light bulb
4. a switch

If the switch is closed, the electrons can travel between the two poles of the battery. The battery pushes electrons from its negative (−) terminal around the loop

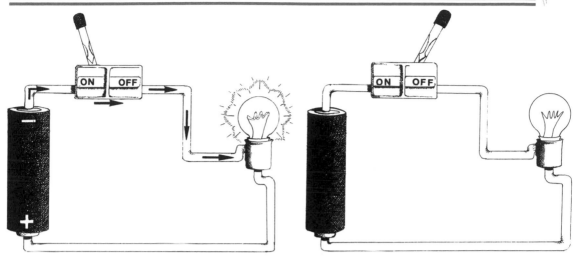

When the switch is "ON" and the circuit is closed, electrons can complete the circuit and the bulb lights. When the switch is "OFF," the circuit is broken. What do you think happens as a result?

of wire to its positive (+) terminal. As the electrons pass through the filament of the light bulb, the bulb lights.

Now suppose the switch is opened. The circuit is broken and electrons cannot move around the loop. In this condition, called an open circuit, the light goes out.

Suppose we unhook the insulated copper wire from the battery and light bulb, and replace it with a loop of string or a piece of rubber. Even if we make all the connections correctly, the bulb will not light. This is because string and rubber are poor conductors of electricity. A good conductor, like our copper wire, allows electrons to flow easily. Insulators, like the rubber in the rubber band, prevent the flow of electrons.

Why Does Electricity Make the Bulb Light?

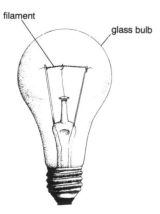

filament

glass bulb

LIGHT BULB

If you look at a clear glass light bulb, you can see a tiny coil of wire being held between two large wires inside the bulb. This tiny coil of thin wire is called the filament. It's the part that glows with light. The metal in the filament of a light bulb is specially made to conduct electricity with some resistance. (Later in this section, we'll see how resistance can be measured.)

When electrons travel through this filament they meet with a greater resistance to flow than they do in the wire.

Have you ever wondered why a light bulb has a glass shield around the filament? The glass shield protects everything around it from the tungsten filament inside, which glows because it reaches white-hot temperatures of up to 4,500°F!

This resistance is similar to friction. You can get an idea of why resistance and friction make heat by rubbing your hands vigorously against one another. Do your hands feel warm? This heat is generated by the friction or resistance to movement between your hands. When you turn on a light switch and send electricity to a light bulb, the filament in the bulb both conducts and resists the flow of electrons. Because of the resistance, heat is produced. The filament gets so hot it glows brightly.

Why Is There Insulation on Electric Wires?

When you plug in a lamp, the cord leading to the lamp probably has two conductors made of copper wire. You don't see the wire, however, because each conductor is separately covered by insulation—a material, like rubber or plastic, that prevents the flow of electricity. The insulation keeps the electric current in the wires and away from you (which is a good thing, because household current can give you a nasty shock or even kill you). The insulation also separates the two conductors from each other, and so prevents a dangerous condition called a short circuit.

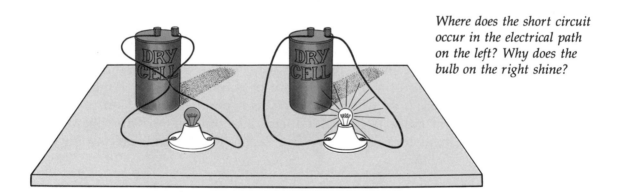

Where does the short circuit occur in the electrical path on the left? Why does the bulb on the right shine?

How does a short circuit happen? Let's take another look at our electric circuit with a light bulb. Imagine that the insulation on our wire is old and cracked, allowing copper wire to touch copper wire. Electrons tend to follow the path of least resistance: where the insulation is cracked, there is very little resistance. What would happen to the light bulb in this case? It would not glow, because the electricity would not get to it: instead, the electrons would follow the shorter path where the main wires touch each other, a path with very low resistance. This is a short circuit, and it can be dangerous. In a house or a factory, the conductors in short circuits can let so many electrons through that they become hot enough to start fires. One of the reasons conductors are insulated is to prevent short circuits.

What Makes Electrons Flow?

When you connect the plus pole (+) and the minus pole (−) of a battery with a conductor, electrons flow, just as water flows when it runs downhill. Let's think about how fast water runs downhill. If the hill is very gentle, almost flat, the water will flow slowly. If the hill is steep, the water will flow fast, with a lot of force. If it is very steep, you get a waterfall, like Niagara Falls.

Something similar happens with electrons. If the difference between the + and the − poles of the battery is small, the electrons will not flow with much force. But if we hook a lot of batteries together, the difference between the + and − becomes great. The electrons will flow with greater force. The force that makes electrons flow is called voltage, and the unit of electrical force or push is called the volt. The more volts, the greater the difference between + and − poles, and the greater the push of the electrons through the conductor. A typical flashlight cell has a voltage of about 1.5 volts. A two-battery flashlight has twice that much: 3 volts. What would be the voltage of a three-battery flashlight?

Alternating Current

Current from a battery moves from the − to the + pole and keeps going in the same direction. It is called direct current, or DC. The electricity that runs refrigerators, television sets, stereos, and washing machines moves back and forth, changing the direction of flow sixty times a second. Because the direction of the flow keeps alternating, it is called alternating current, or AC.

Alternating current is produced in electric power plants by electric generators. The generator in the power plant changes mechanical energy to electrical energy. To lose as little energy as possible as the electricity travels from the power plant to distant places, the electricity is sent by wires at high voltage. At a station near your home, the voltage is reduced from more than 1,000 volts to 110 volts for use in your house or apartment. One reason alternat-

Here you see the three generators in the powerhouse of Fontana Dam, in western North Carolina.

ing current (AC) is used instead of direct current (DC) in your home appliances is that it is much easier to regulate the voltage of AC than of DC.

How Many Electrons?

We have learned about voltage (the push of electrons) and resistance (the opposition to that push). The third thing you need to know for a complete description of a circuit is how many electrons are flowing at a time. That's very important for knowing how much work a circuit can do. The amount of electricity is called amperage, and is measured in a unit called the amp.

Amperage is the capacity of a battery or other source of electricity to produce electrons. You usually can tell whether a battery can produce lots of electrons by looking at its size. The tiny cell that runs a wristwatch produces just as many volts as the bigger cell that you put in a flashlight. But the watch cell couldn't run a flashlight. It couldn't produce enough electrons to make the filament glow. The heavy battery in an automobile has only twelve volts, but it can produce so many electrons that it can help start the heavy engine of a big car. It has lots of amperage.

Measuring Volts, Amps, and Ohms

We have now learned about volts (units of *force* for electron flow), amps (units of *quantity* of electron flow), and ohms (units of *resistance* to electron flow). These three factors determine exactly how electrons will flow in a circuit. In fact, you could make a rule for exactly how the three factors will act together—which is just what Mr. Ohm did when he formulated Ohm's Law. Ohm's Law says that volts equal amps times ohms.

$$\text{volts} = \text{amps} \times \text{ohms}$$

From this law you can see that if you know two of the units, you can always figure out the third. You may already know how to do this, but if you don't you can just remember these other versions of Ohm's Law.

$$\text{amps} = \frac{\text{volts}}{\text{ohms}}$$

$$\text{ohms} = \frac{\text{volts}}{\text{amps}}$$

Let's use Ohm's Law to calculate the amps in the circuit of an electric flashlight. If we know that the two 1.5 volt batteries in the flashlight make a total of 3 volts, and we know that the resistance of the little bulb is 2 ohms, how many amps will there be in the circuit?

$$\frac{\text{volts}}{\text{ohms}} = \text{amps}$$

$$\frac{3 \text{ volts}}{2 \text{ ohms}} = ? \text{ amps}$$

$$\frac{3}{2} = 1.5$$

$$\frac{3 \text{ volts}}{2 \text{ ohms}} = 1.5 \text{ amps}$$

Electric Power

Now that we know that 1.5 amps are moving through a resistance of 2 ohms with a force of 3 volts, there is something else we can say about the flashlight circuit. We can say how much power the flashlight is using. Remember, power is how much work a thing can do in a unit of time. The measurement of electrical power is the watt, which is equal to 1 joule per second. The average home light bulb uses 60 watts. If you look at home appliances, they usually tell you how many watts they use.

You can measure watts by knowing the volts and the amps of a circuit: 1 volt times 1 amp equals 1 watt. To find out how many watts a circuit uses, you just multiply the volts times the amps. Let's see how many watts there were in the flashlight circuit.

$$3 \text{ volts} \times 1.5 \text{ amps} = 4.5 \text{ watts}$$

How many ohms, volts, and amps are there in a circuit that is burning a 60-watt light bulb? First, remember that electricity in an American house is about 110 volts. If we know this, and we know that the light bulb is rated at 60 watts, we can figure out all about the circuit. We know that we can get the amps by dividing the watts by the volts.

$$\frac{60 \text{ watts}}{110 \text{ volts}} = .55 \text{ amps}$$

From this we can find out how much resistance there is because now we can divide the volts by the amps.

$$\frac{110 \text{ volts}}{.55 \text{ amps}} = 200 \text{ ohms}$$

This means that the resistance in a 60-watt bulb has to be about 200 ohms. Can you figure out the volts, ohms, and amps used in the circuit of some other appliance in your house?

Electrified Communications

Think about how many forms of communication today rely on what you've just been reading about: electricity, electric circuits, electromagnets, etc.

The age of mass communication—communication to a vast number of people—began with the invention of the printing press. But it was electricity that made *rapid* mass communications possible.

In the 1830s, Samuel F. B. Morse developed an invention called the telegraph, which could send messages quickly across great distances. The telegraph was a network of electromagnets, each with a beeper. A person in one place could use the telegraph to send electrical impulses over wires to a person far away, where another electromagnet would receive the impulses and sound its beeper. Morse developed a code of long and short beeps, called Morse Code, that people could use to send messages in the relatively short time it took for electrical impulses to travel over wires and be decoded. By 1861, a network of telegraph lines connected the At-

Morse demonstrates how the telegraph works.

lantic and Pacific coasts of the United States. In 1866, the first successful telegraph cable was laid across the Atlantic, which meant that someone in the United States could send a message across the ocean in a matter of seconds instead of days or weeks!

In 1876, Alexander Graham Bell successfully demonstrated the first telephone (see the American Civilization section of this book for more on Bell). Telephones have come a long way since Bell's day, but they still work on the principle of transforming mechanical vibrations into electrical signals. When you speak into the transmitter of

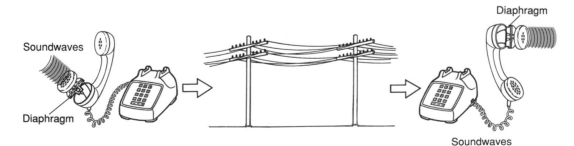

The vibrating diaphragm in the telephone transmitter on the left converts a speaking voice into electronic signals. The vibrating diaphragm in the receiver on the right converts electronic signals into sound waves, which a listener hears as a person's voice.

a telephone, your voice causes the air to vibrate, which causes a metal disk in the phone's mouthpiece, called a diaphragm, to vibrate in response to your different vocal sounds (see diagram). The vibrations of the diaphragm are turned into an electrical current; this current varies according to the sound waves striking the diaphragm. These varying electrical signals travel through a complex array of wires and switches, and eventually reach another telephone, which has a receiver with a diaphragm in the earpiece. In the receiver, the electrical signals cause the diaphragm to vibrate, which produces the sound waves that someone hears as your voice.

By 1915, telephone service was available between New York City and San Francisco. Today, you can pick up a phone and speak to someone across the street or on the other side of the world. Electrified communications almost make it possible, as one telephone company says, for you to "reach out and touch someone."

What are some other ways in which electricity has revolutionized communications? For a start, there's radio, television, communications satellites, computers, and audio and video recordings. For a nicely illustrated explanation of how all these work, check a library or bookstore for a fascinating book by David Macaulay called The Way Things Work *(Houghton Mifflin, 1988).*

Satellites make many kinds of communication devices possible, as well as easier to use. You may already be familiar with one component of satellite transmission—satellite dishes. People who want to get a lot of television channels may install these large dishes in their yards.

MOTION, ENGINES, AND MOTORS

From Steam to Gasoline

An engine is a machine that uses energy to start motion—usually a turning motion. A motor is just a small engine. You see the work of motors and engines everywhere: the motion created by engines and motors may move a car, airplane, or train, or it may do work in a factory to produce goods.

In the eighteenth century, James Watt, a Scottish inventor, developed an efficient steam engine. As you know, steam is created when water is turned into a gas or vapor as it is heated to the boiling point. Steam expands the volume of the water by

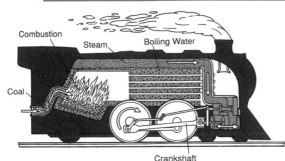

The steam engine that powers a train often uses burning coal to heat water to its boiling point, which creates steam. The steam pushes the pistons that drive the crankshaft, turning the locomotive's wheels.

about 1600 times. The force or pressure caused by this expansion is the basis of all steam engines. The pressure drives a piston back and forth. The piston is attached to a crankshaft, which converts the back-and-forth motion of the piston to a turning motion for driving machinery.

The steam engine played an important role in the Industrial Revolution, when society moved from being centered on farming to being centered on industry. Steam engines helped drain water and raise coal from mines. They powered trains and ships. And they provided power for the factories that produced an ever-growing variety of products.

The Internal Combustion Engine

In a steam engine, the combustion (or burning) of fuel to make steam occurs outside the engine. In an internal combustion engine, the burning of fuel occurs right inside the engine itself. Both types of engines produce hot expanding gases that are the source of the engines' power. It would be hard to find a single modern invention that has changed our lives more than the internal combustion engine. It powers most cars, boats, lawn mowers, tractors, home electrical generators, and many airplanes. It has given us freedom and independence in traveling that people in other ages did not enjoy. It has helped us to produce more food with less back-breaking work.

In the internal combustion engine of an automobile, gasoline and air are mixed in the carburetor and turned to a vapor. As the piston inside one cylinder moves down, the gasoline–air vapor mixture is drawn into the cylinder through a valve. The

In most cars, you find the internal combustion engine under the hood.

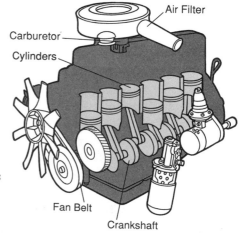

The basic parts of an automobile engine. In addition to the parts you are reading about—the carburetor, pistons, and crankshaft—automobiles also have an air filter that cleans the air drawn into the carburetor, and a fan belt that keeps the engine parts from overheating.

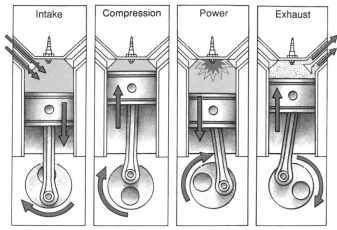

| Intake | Compression | Power | Exhaust |

Cross sections of a piston during the four strokes of the engine's cycle. The spark plug looks like an upside-down cone located on the top of the piston. The crankshaft is the round part below the piston.

valve closes and the piston moves up, squeezing the vapor into a small space at the top of the cylinder, where the spark plug is. When the piston nearly reaches the top of the cylinder, the spark plug lets off an electric spark, which causes the vapor to explode. The explosion forces the piston back down to the bottom of the cylinder. As the piston moves back up the cylinder again, it forces the remaining gases out the exhaust valve. Down, up, down, up; the piston makes four strokes every time it completes the cycle. That's why engines that work this way are called four-stroke engines.

As in the steam engine, the pistons in the internal combustion engine are attached to a crankshaft, which changes their up-and-down motion to a turning motion. Then two parts of the car, the differential and the axle, transfer the mechanical energy of the turning motion to the wheels of the car.

Jet Engines and Rocket Engines

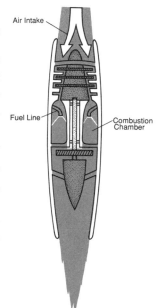

Have you ever let the air out of a balloon and watched the balloon fly off as the air escaped? What happened was that the air went in one direction and pushed the balloon in the opposite direction. Similarly, a jet engine propels a body forward as it shoots a high-speed jet of gas out the rear.

But how is the high-speed jet of gas created? Like the car engine, the jet engine has a combustion chamber where air is mixed with fuel and burned. When the fuel and air burn inside the chamber, the gas that is formed expands greatly. There is a narrow opening at the rear end of the engine through which the gas escapes. This escaping gas causes the force that propels the engine in the opposite direction.

A cross section of a jet engine. The gaseous mixture in the combustion chambers leaves the jet with great force, propelling the engine forward.

Fuel Tank

Liquid Oxygen

Combustion
Chamber

Rockets work much the same way as jet engines, with one important difference. Because rockets must operate out in space where there is little or no oxygen available, they carry their own supply of oxygen-rich material. This material mixes with fuel, and the oxygen-fuel mixture burns in a combustion chamber just as in a jet engine.

Oxygen is needed to burn fuel in this rocket engine, but it has no air intake opening as the jet engine has. Find the tank that stores the rocket's internal supply of oxygen.

Electromagnets

Some motors use electricity to produce mechanical movement that can do work. These motors work on the principle that current flowing through a wire creates a magnetic field. You can see for yourself the presence of this invisible field if you have a compass, a copper wire, and a flashlight battery. First, orient the compass so the needle is pointing to the north (N). Connect one end of the copper wire to the positive terminal of the battery, and the other end to the negative terminal. Place the compass under the copper wire, so the wire is over the needle and parallel to it. What happens? The needle moves away from its north-south orientation. (Do not leave the wire connected to the flashlight cell for more than a few seconds; the battery may overheat.)

The magnetism created by this electric current is even stronger when the wire is coiled around a piece of iron or steel. The piece of metal will act as a magnet when there is current flowing. This special kind of magnet is appropriately called an electromagnet.

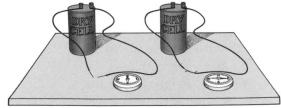

A compass demonstrates that an electric circuit creates a magnetic field. The compass moves away from its east-west orientation when placed under the circuit.

Stories of Scientists

Isaac Newton

Many people think that Sir Isaac Newton was one of the greatest scientists who ever lived. He not only made important discoveries, but also computed the exact laws of nature that made the earth orbit the sun, the moon go round the earth, and the tides ebb and flow. He even discovered what makes the colors of the rainbow.

He was born on Christmas Day, 1642, in a rural English village. Although his family expected him to become a farmer, he was interested in learning, especially in mathematics, and attended Cambridge University. For eighteen months the university was forced to close because of an epidemic, and Isaac had to come home. But even in the country he continued his studies, conducting a series of experiments on light and motion, observing the results and writing down his findings carefully.

When Newton returned to Cambridge, he finished his master's degree and began to develop theories based on his observations of light and motion. He also wrote papers on mathematics. One of these was very highly praised by the mathematics professor at Cambridge who suggested that the young Newton should take over his professorship when he retired. So, at the age of twenty-seven, Isaac Newton assumed the professorship of mathematics that he would hold for the next twenty-seven years.

Newton was also interested in physics and astronomy. He designed a new type of telescope, and in 1672 he sent a description of it to the Royal Society of London, a very distinguished club of scientists. The members of the society were so impressed with his new type of reflecting telescope (one that uses a curved mirror to look at the stars) that they elected him to the society.

He continued to experiment with light, and discovered that a prism breaks up white light into the colors of the rainbow. He also proved that colored light could be recombined to make white light. These theories about light, though true, went against commonly accepted ideas, and stirred up so much controversy that he thought he would stop writing about his findings.

It's fortunate for science that Newton's friends were able to persuade him to persist in writing about his work, for in 1687 he published his most important work, *Mathematical Principles of Natural Philosophy.* This great work used mathematics to explain how gravity causes the laws of motion that govern our universe. Newton's Law of Universal Gravitation helps to explain the orbits of the planets, why the moon does not fall into the earth, and why the tides come and go as they do.

Isaac Newton showing how a prism breaks light into the colors of the rainbow.

His *Principles* were very influential; people began to believe that everything could be explained by science.

Newton became immensely famous during his lifetime. He received the first knighthood ever awarded for scientific achievement, and so was called *Sir* Isaac Newton. He was elected president of the Royal Society for life. He died on March 20, 1727.

Anton van Leeuwenhoek

Not every important scientist is a genius. Some important scientific advances have come from committed people who make new tools for looking at the world, and then report their observations. Such was Anton van Leeuwenhoek (LAY-vun-huk), a Dutch maker of microscopes who lived at the same time as Isaac Newton. As a hobby, van Leeuwenhoek put together over 247 microscopes, some of which were able to magnify objects 270 times! This one man opened up a world that no one had seen before.

The son of a Dutch basket maker, Anton lived in Delft, Holland. Although he never attended a university, never had formal scientific training, and was a largely self-taught amateur scientist, van Leeuwenhoek's explorations resulted in ground-breaking discoveries.

Anton van Leeuwenhoek.

Van Leeuwenhoek set out to study as many things as possible under his homemade microscopes. With his shaving razor he would slice very thin slices of cork, plants, or other specimens. One summer his interest was piqued by reports that nearby Lake Berkel had an unusually greenish, cloudy look to it. So van Leeuwenhoek collected a water sample from the lake and placed it under one of his microscopes. He discovered a whole new world.

> There were very little animalcules . . . some were roundish, while others, a bit bigger, consisted of an oval. Others were somewhat longer than an oval, and they were very slow moving and few in number. These animalcules had diverse colors, some being whitish and transparent; others were green with very glittery little scales; others again were green in the middle, and before and after white, others yet were ashen gray. And the motion of most of these animalcules in the water was so swift, and so various upwards, downwards and roundabout, that it was wonderful to see.

Van Leeuwenhoek made his discoveries known in letters to Europe's outstanding scientific societies. Over the course of fifty years, he wrote more than three hundred such letters, many of which were published. Although his reports were at first received with skepticism, his letters caused the Royal Society of London to send an observer to Delft in 1673. The favorable report that came back caused such a stir that the queen of England and the czar of Russia were soon stopping by to peer through van Leeuwenhoek's microscopes.

Van Leeuwenhoek was the first scientist ever to give a complete description of red blood cells, and the first to see bacteria and the small animals we now call protozoa—thus beginning a voyage of discovery into the very small universe, invisible to the naked eye, that is just as exciting as the very large universe of planets and galaxies.

Ernest Just

Ernest Just.

Some scientists spend their lives doing research that has immediate practical uses. Other scientists conduct experiments just because they want to know why things are the way they are. We call this kind of experimentation "pure" research. Ernest Just was a pure research scientist, and what he wanted to understand was how individual cells function.

Just was born in Charleston, South Carolina, on August 14, 1883. Because schools for African-American children were very poor in South Carolina, Just's mother decided to send her son north to finish his education. So in 1900, Just worked his way to New York City on board a steamship; when he arrived, he had five dollars and two pairs of shoes to his name.

He found a school in New Hampshire called the Kimball School, which accepted African-American boys who couldn't pay tuition. Just did so well there that he went on to Dartmouth College in New Hampshire. At Dartmouth, he was at first disappointed that so many of the students seemed to care only about football. But when he enrolled in his first biology class, he knew he had found what he loved.

From Dartmouth, Just went straight to Howard University in Washington, D.C., to teach. In the summertime, Just worked at the Marine Biological Laboratory in Woods Hole, Massachusetts, probably the most famous marine lab in the world. (A marine lab is a lab that studies life in the sea.) At Woods Hole, Just began his lifelong investigation of how cells work. He used the eggs of marine animals like sea urchins and sandworms to study how cells reproduce and divide. Marine animal eggs were perfect subjects because each egg is a single cell, easily collected and studied under a microscope.

In the Life Sciences section of this book, you've been reading about cells, the basic unit of life. Many cells are made up of a nucleus and cytoplasm, the living substance that surrounds the nucleus. When Just was conducting his research, most scientists focused their attention on the nucleus because they thought it was the only part of the cell that was important in its development and reproduction. As Just studied the eggs he collected, keeping track of how they developed under different conditions, he saw something amazing. He discovered that cell activity depended on the nucleus *and* the cytoplasm, especially the outer part of the cytoplasm, called the ectoplasm. Because the ectoplasm is the part most influenced by the environment outside the cell, Just realized that environment helps determine whether or not the cell develops normally, and whether it will be different from other cells.

Though never fully appreciated in his lifetime, Just's research changed the way scientists thought about cells. For example, his ideas led scientists to think deeply about how the outer layers of the egg influence the process of fertilization. Throughout his life, Just fought for recognition and acceptance from the scientific community; he spent years working in Europe, where he felt his research was taken more seriously. As a professor at Howard University, Just also worked hard to improve the quality of scientific education available to African-Americans, and to make sure that talented students were encouraged to choose science as a career. In recognition of his outstanding work as a researcher and a teacher, the NAACP awarded Just its first Spingarn Medal, given to an African-American for extraordinary achievement.

Illustration and Photo Credits

Text Credits

About the Author

E. D. Hirsch, Jr., a professor at the University of Virginia, is the author or editor of ten books, including *Cultural Literacy, The Dictionary of Cultural Literacy,* and *A First Dictionary of Cultural Literacy.* He and his wife Polly live in Charlottesville, where they raised their three children.

Index

THE CORE KNOWLEDGE SERIES

"The best year of teaching I ever had. This year has been so much fun: fun to learn, fun to teach."

Joanne Anderson, Teacher,
Three Oaks Elementary School
Fort Myers, Florida

COLLECT THE ENTIRE CORE KNOWLEDGE SERIES

ISBN	TITLE	PRICE
41115-4	What Your 1st Grader Needs To Know	$22.50/$28.00Can
41116-2	What Your 2nd Grader Needs To Know	$22.50/$28.00Can
41117-0	What Your 3rd Grader Needs To Know	$22.50/$28.50Can
41118-9	What Your 4th Grader Needs To Know	$22.50/$28.00Can
41119-7	What Your 5th Grader Needs To Know	$22.50/$28.00Can
41120-0	What Your 6th Grader Needs To Know	$22.50/$28.00Can

READERS:

The titles listed above are available in your local bookstore. If you are interested in mail ordering any of the Core Knowledge books listed above, please send a check or money order only to the address below (no C.O.D.s or cash) and indicate the title and ISBN book number with your order. Make check payable to Doubleday Consumer Services (include $2.50 for postage and handling). Allow 4–6 weeks for delivery. Prices and availability subject to change without notice.

Please mail your order and check to:
Doubleday Consumer Services, Dept. CK
2451 South Wolf Road
Des Plaines, IL 60018

EDUCATORS AND LIBRARIANS:

For bulk sales or course adoptions, contact the Bantam Doubleday Dell Education and Library Department. Outside New York State call toll-free 1-800-223-6834 ext. 9238. In New York State call 212-492-9238.

FOR MORE INFORMATION ABOUT CORE KNOWLEDGE:

Call the Core Knowledge Foundation at 1-800-238-3233.

CK-4/94